THE RULING CLASS OF JUDAEA

This book examines why in A.D. 66 a revolt against Rome broke out in Judea. It attempts to explain both the rebellion itself and its temporary success by discussing the role of the Jewish ruling class in the sixty years preceding the war and within the independent state which lasted until the destruction of the Temple in A.D. 70. The author seeks to show that important factors such as economic distress and religious ideology were not a sufficient cause of the outbreak of the revolt, and that a crucial factor previously overlooked was the decision of some factions of the ruling class to cut ties with Rome and seek power for themselves. That decision is itself ascribed to the fact that Jewish rulers of Judaea, having been selected in accordance with non-Jewish status criteria, failed to fulfil the role the Romans expected of them and, losing Roman support for their power during the sixties A.D., appealed to latent anti-gentile prejudices in the rest of the local population in order to preserve their own position.

The importance of the subject lies both in the significance of the history of Judaea in this period for the development of Judaism and early Christianity and in the light shed on Roman methods of provincial administration in general by understanding why Rome was unable to control a society with cultural values so different from its own, both in Judaea and, as the last chapter briefly discusses, in the treatment of druids in Gaul.

Dr Goodman is eminently well qualified to write this book, being as at home with the Jewish texts as he is with the Greek and Latin authors. It is a book for ancient historians studying Roman history and Jewish history and will be of interest to theologians studying the background to the life of Jesus.

THE RULING CLASS OF JUDAEA

THE ORIGINS OF THE JEWISH REVOLT AGAINST ROME A.D. 66–70

MARTIN GOODMAN

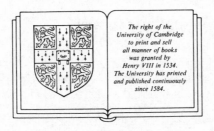

The right of the
University of Cambridge
to print and sell
all manner of books
was granted by
Henry VIII in 1534.
The University has printed
and published continuously
since 1584.

CAMBRIDGE UNIVERSITY PRESS

CAMBRIDGE

NEW YORK   PORT CHESTER

MELBOURNE   SYDNEY

Published by the Press Syndicate of the University of Cambridge
The Pitt Building, Trumpington Street, Cambridge CB2 1RP
35 East 57th Street, New York, NY 10022, USA
10 Stamford Road, Oakleigh, Melbourne 3166, Australia

First published 1987
Reprinted 1988, 1989

Printed in Great Britain at
the University Press, Cambridge

British Library cataloguing in publication data
Goodman, Martin
The ruling class of Judaea: the origins of
the Jewish revolt against Rome A.D. 66–70.
1. Jews—History—Rebellion, 66–73.
I. Title
933'.05   DS122.8

Library of Congress cataloguing in publication data
Goodman, Martin
The ruling class of Judaea.
Bibliography.
Includes index.
1. Jews—History—Rebellion, 66–73—Causes.
2. Jews—Politics and government—To A.D. 70.
3. Political leadership—Palestine—History.
4. Jews—History—168 B.C.–135 A.D.   I. Title.
DS122.8.G66   1987   933'.05   87–6656

ISBN 0 521 33401 2

EA

For C.J.G. and R.G.

CONTENTS

ABBREVIATIONS

A.J.	Josephus, *Antiquitates Judaicae*
b.	Babylonian Talmud
B.J.	Josephus, *Bellum Judaicum*
BMC	*Catalogue of the Greek Coins in the British Museum*, 29 vols., London, 1873–1927
BMCRE	H. Mattingly and R. A. G. Carson, eds., *Coins of the Roman Empire in the British Museum*, 9 vols., 1923–75
c. Ap.	Josephus, *contra Apionem*
CHJ	W. D. Davies and L. Finkelstein, eds., *The Cambridge History of Judaism*, 4 vols., Cambridge 1984–
CIJ	*Corpus Inscriptionum Iudaicarum*
CIL	*Corpus Inscriptionum Latinarum*
CPJ	V. Tcherikover, A. Fuks and M. Stern, *Corpus Papyrorum Judaicarum*, 3 vols., Cambridge, Mass., 1957–64
DJD 2	P. Benoit, J. T. Milik and R. de Vaux, *Les Grottes de Murabba'at* (*Discoveries in the Judaean Desert* II) (Oxford, 1960)
E.T.	English translation
FGrH, Jacoby	F. Jacoby, *Fragmente der griechischen Historiker*, 1923–
Heb.	Hebrew
IGR	R. Cagnat, ed., *Inscriptiones Graecae ad res Romanas pertinentes*, vols. I, III, IV, Paris, 1906–27
ILS	H. Dessau, *Inscriptiones Latinae Selectae*, Berlin, 1892–1916
m.	Mishnah
OGIS	W. Dittenberger, ed., *Orientis Graeci Inscriptiones Selectae*, 2 vols., Leipzig, 1903–5
POxy.	*Oxyrhynchus Papyri*, ed. B. P. Grenfell and A. S. Hunt, 1898–
1QapGen.	*Genesis Apocryphon*, in K. Beyer, *Die aramäischen Texte vom Toten Meer* (Göttingen, 1984), pp. 165–86
4QpPs	*Commentary on Psalms*, in J. M. Allegro, ed., *Qumran Cave 4* (*Discoveries in the Judaean Desert of Jordan* v) (Oxford, 1968), no. 171
1QS	*Community Rule*, in E. Lohse, *Die Texte von Qumran hebräisch und deutsch*, 2nd edn (Darmstadt, 1971), pp. 1–43

Abbreviations

RE	Pauly–Wissowa, *Real-Encyclopädie der classischen Altertums-wissenschaft*
SEG	*Supplementum Epigraphicum Graecum*
t.	Tosefta
TDNT	G. Kittel and G. Friedrich, eds., *Theological Dictionary of the New Testament*, 10 vols., E.T., Grand Rapids, 1964–76
y.	Jerusalem Talmud

Abbreviations of titles of tractates in the Mishnah, Tosefta and Talmuds follow H. Danby, *The Mishnah translated from the Hebrew* (Oxford, 1933), p. 806

JOURNALS

AJAH	*American Journal of Ancient History*
AJP	*American Journal of Philology*
ANRW	*Aufstieg und Niedergang der Römischen Welt*, ed. H. Temporini *et al.*, Berlin 1972–
BASOR	*Bulletin of the American Schools of Oriental Research*
CBQ	*Catholic Biblical Quarterly*
CPh	*Classical Philology*
CQ	*Classical Quarterly*
EI	*Eretz Israel*
GRBS	*Greek, Roman and Byzantine Studies*
HSCP	*Harvard Studies in Classical Philology*
HTR	*Harvard Theological Review*
IEJ	*Israel Exploration Journal*
JAOS	*Journal of the American Oriental Society*
JBL	*Journal of Biblical Literature*
JJS	*Journal of Jewish Studies*
JQR	*Jewish Quarterly Review*
JRS	*Journal of Roman Studies*
JSJ	*Journal for the Study of Judaism*
JSS	*Journal of Semitic Studies*
JTS	*Journal of Theological Studies*
NTS	*New Testament Studies*
PBSR	*Papers of the British School at Rome*
PEQ	*Palestine Exploration Quarterly*
TAPA	*Transactions of the American Philological Association*

PREFACE

This has been a most enjoyable book to write not least because so many people have helped me to write it. Many of the ideas were tried out first on final-year students in Birmingham and then on members of Geza Vermes' seminar at Oxford. An invitation to a conference in Israel by the Universities of Haifa and Tel Aviv and by the Yad ben Zvi opened my eyes to a variety of evidence and theories of which I had previously been culpably ignorant. Dr I. Ben-Shalom kindly sent me a copy of his thesis, which is soon to be published. Fergus Millar, Simon Price, Tessa Rajak and Chris Wickham all made detailed comments of the first draft of the book, Benjamin Isaac on the second. Between them they have radically altered the book's structure and caused me to re-examine more ill-founded assumptions than I care to recall; I know that some of them remain sceptical about my rasher arguments and they should not be held responsible for the misjudgements that remain. My greatest academic debt is to Tessa Rajak, who with great generosity allowed me to see her *Josephus* before publication, criticised my typescript with care and acumen, and encouraged me to press ahead with my own views even when they diverged from hers.

I am grateful to the University of Birmingham and the Wolfson Foundation for grants to defray typing costs and to Marie-Christine Keith, Joan Buckland, Valerie Howard and Sylvia Campbell for doing the typing at different stages; also to Harry Buglass, who drew the maps.

I dedicate this book to my parents not least because it was at the cottage in Tideways in September 1982 that its writing was first conceived.

Oxford Centre for Postgraduate Hebrew Studies
St Cross College, Oxford

April 1987   Martin Goodman

xi

Map I Roman Palestine in A.D. 66

xii

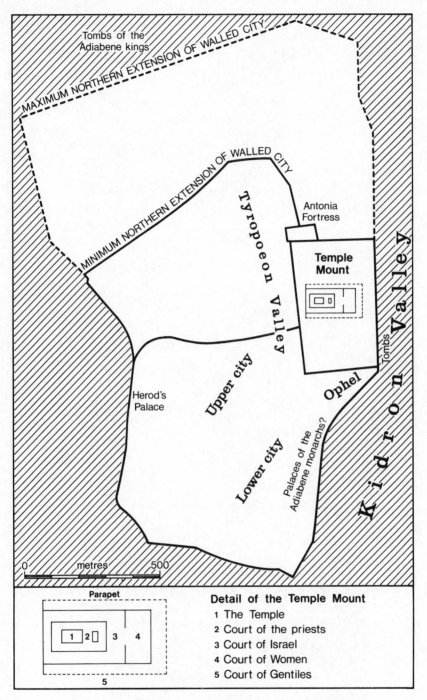

Tombs of the
Adiabene kings

MAXIMUM NORTHERN EXTENSION OF WALLED CITY

MINIMUM NORTHERN EXTENSION OF WALLED CITY

Tyropoeon Valley

Antonia
Fortress

Temple
Mount

Kidron Valley

Tombs

Upper city

Ophel

Herod's
Palace

Lower city

Palaces of the
Adiabene monarchs?

0   metres   500

Parapet

| 1 | 2 | 3 | 4 |

5

Detail of the Temple Mount

1 The Temple
2 Court of the priests
3 Court of Israel
4 Court of Women
5 Court of Gentiles

Map 2   Jerusalem in A.D. 66

xiii

CHAPTER I

INTRODUCTION

i THE PROBLEM

The Roman emperor Augustus created the province of Judaea in A.D. 6 by subjecting to direct Roman rule the central part of the domain once ruled by the Jewish king Herod the Great. Herod's kingdom had proved unruly on his death in 4 B.C. when the widespread resentment he had evoked was able to surface, and a series of revolts then had been suppressed only after intervention by the Roman governor of Syria. Herod's son Archelaus had nonetheless been permitted to inherit control of the area around Jerusalem, although he was granted the title merely of ethnarch. But by A.D. 6 even this appointment no longer seemed satisfactory in the eyes of his Roman patron. Archelaus was sent into exile in Gaul, and Judaea was incorporated into the Roman empire.

The following sixty years witnessed many crises in the relationship of the Jewish population to the Roman government. They ended with the great war of A.D. 66–70 which is the main subject of this book.[1] Hostility to Rome was shown from the foundation of the province. Violent opposition to the imposition of a census was quelled only with difficulty, and in the following years a variety of issues led to frequent riots and demonstrations.

The main grievances voiced were against alleged breaches of Jewish religious susceptibilities. When the Roman procurator Pilate brought the standards revered by the legionary soldiers into the holy city of Jerusalem, there was an outcry; when he abstracted sacred funds from the Jerusalem Temple to build an aqueduct, his sacrilege led to violence; an incident when a Roman soldier exposed himself indecently in the sight of the Temple precincts provoked disorder in

---

[1] For a clear narrative of these events, see E. Schürer, *The History of the Jewish People in the Age of Jesus Christ*, rev. G. Vermes *et al.*, 3 vols. (Edinburgh, 1973–87) I, pp. 336–513; E. M. Smallwood, *The Jews under Roman Rule* (Leiden, 1976), pp. 144–200, 256–330.

which much blood was shed. Most of these riots flared up during the pilgrim festivals, which were celebrated on three occasions in each year. It was then that the city was filled almost to overflowing with a mass of worshippers in a state of religious excitement.

In A.D. 40 such more minor infringements of Jewish religious feelings were put into the shade by a serious assault. The emperor Gaius Caligula, in somewhat megalomaniac mood, determined that his statue should be erected in the Jerusalem Temple as it had been in shrines throughout the rest of his realm. For Jews, this was a direct attack on their monotheistic and aniconic faith; Caligula's statue in the Temple implied Caligula's claim to divinity. Their opposition was absolute. The imperial legate who was governing Syria at the time proved unable to carry out the command. Only Caligula's death prevented the Jews resorting to war, and the anger and suspicion of Rome provoked then was slow to dissipate.

The new emperor Claudius attempted in A.D. 41 to alleviate the hostility of the province by giving control of the Jerusalem cult and Judaea to the Jewish king Agrippa I, a grandson of Herod. This practical policy was evidently successful in restoring peace, however briefly. Claudius was motivated by gratitude as well as good sense, for Agrippa's machinations in Rome had been largely responsible both for his (Claudius') survival after Caligula's assassination and for his rapid elevation to supreme power in its aftermath. It is possible that the imperial favour gained by Agrippa through his aid in the tangled politics of the Roman court did not survive his assumption of the role of a powerful client king: Claudius put a stop to plans to strengthen the fortifications of Jerusalem, and in A.D. 44 a friendly conference between Agrippa and other eastern rulers allied to Rome was abruptly broken up by the governor of Syria. But any serious confrontation between Agrippa and Claudius was preempted by the former's untimely death in the same year. Claudius returned Judaea to direct Roman control under a procurator responsible both to himself and to the governor of Syria.

Within a few years, however, the troubles of the province became palpably worse. Sporadic riots continued and there was also endemic banditry in the countryside.[2] From the early fifties A.D. the atmosphere of violence spread to the capital city, where dagger men, *sicarii*, used the cover of the pilgrim crowds to terrorize the urban populace. Some citizens were sufficiently intimidated by A.D. 64 to

[2] For the argument that revolutionary banditry was not common before *c.* A.D. 50, see D. M. Rhoads, *Israel in Revolution: 6–74 C.E. A political history based on the writings of Josephus* (Philadelphia, 1976), pp. 47–93.

seek safety abroad. It was already apparent to one Jerusalemite, Josephus, that an explosion was imminent (*Vita* 17).

The incident which eventually set the revolt in motion arose from long-standing hostility between the Jews and the local gentiles in the coastal city of Caesarea. Caesarea had been founded by Herod primarily for a non-Jewish population, as he had indicated by building there a great temple to Rome and Augustus, but the Caesarean Jews had nonetheless frequently appealed to Roman authority to be granted greater rights within the city. In A.D. 60 the emperor Nero had given judgement decisively in favour of the gentiles, and when in A.D. 66 some gentile youths, presuming upon this evidence of imperial favour, taunted the local Jews by ostentatiously sacrificing a cock in front of a synagogue on a sabbath, the result was a riot.

The current Roman governor of Judaea, the procurator Florus, suppressed this disorder only after displaying blatant bias against the Jews. Anger was thus already intense at this outrage when he compounded the Jews' hostility by confiscating money from the treasury of the Jerusalem Temple, probably in lieu of tribute. The tumult in Jerusalem which resulted was checked only with much bloodshed. In disgust a few Temple priests decided to suspend those sacrifices which had traditionally been offered up each day in Jerusalem in honour of the Roman emperor. From the Roman point of view such an action constituted rebellion, and the situation was now too serious for Florus to manage. The imperial legate Cestius Gallus marched down from Antioch in Syria with three legions and many auxiliary troops. When he too was met with determined resistance and suffered a disastrous defeat on his retreat from outside Jerusalem, Nero was forced to treat the suppression of the revolt as a major campaign. He sent one of his most experienced generals, the future emperor Vespasian, to fight in Judaea in his name.

The war lasted from A.D. 66 to A.D. 73 or 74, when the last pocket of resistance on Masada was finally overwhelmed. The Roman forces were not always fighting with full intensity: in June A.D. 68 Vespasian called a halt to his campaign on hearing of the death of Nero, in whose name he was commander of his troops, and in July A.D. 69 he again cut short his attack on the Jews, this time in order to concentrate on his own bid for supreme power in Rome. But the main reason for the long duration of the war was the strength of the Jewish resistance. When Vespasian's son Titus, also a future emperor, finally captured the walled city of Jerusalem, it was at the cost of many Roman as well as Jewish lives. Many Jews were enslaved or crucified, and Jerusalem, one of the finest cities of the eastern part of the empire, was devastated. On the 10th Ab (July/ August) A.D 70 the Temple was burnt down. The structure of Jewish religion and society in Judaea was totally destroyed, never to be restored in the same form. It is the aim of this book to explain why the revolt, with its terrible consequences, occurred.

For Roman historians, the problem is worth study partly because the small province of Judaea deserves consideration in its own right, and partly also because an understanding of what went wrong in Judaea may help to illuminate Roman methods of provincial administration employed elsewhere in the empire with greater success. More evidence survives for Roman Palestine in the first century A.D. than for any other province apart from Egypt, and because this evidence emanates from a wide variety of contemporaries who held quite different views on the problems of their time it is possible to build up a uniquely rounded picture of their society. Not all the insights about Judaea presented by such evidence will be directly useful in comprehending other provinces, for some Judaean history was determined by specifically Jewish religious factors, but a full analysis of the Roman government's reaction to this alien society may elucidate the history of unrest and revolt in other areas under Roman control.

For students of Jewish history and society no argument is needed to stress the importance of the war of A.D. 66–70. The failure of the revolt led to the destruction of the last independent Jewish state in Palestine until the establishment of Israel in 1948; only the seizure of power by the military government of a certain Bar Kochba in a final desperate rebellion against Rome under Hadrian testifies to the continued ambitions of the Jewish people for self-rule. The destruction of the Temple in Jerusalem and with it the possibility of expiation for sin through sacrifice led to enormous religious changes. Judaism has developed since A.D. 70 in a variety of ways, but all of them are in some sense a reaction to the fact of exile and the breaking of the link to the divine which had once been provided by the Temple cult.[3]

The events of the first century A.D. have a slightly different but no less important significance for students of early Christianity. The background to the revolt formed also the background to Jesus' teaching and the growth of the early Church in Jerusalem.

[3] Cf. M. E. Stone, 'Reactions to destructions (*sic*) of the Second Temple', *JSJ* 12 (1981) 195–204; J. Neusner, *First-Century Judaism in Crisis: Yohanan ben Zakkai and the Renaissance of Torah* (New York, 1982); G. Alon, *The Jews in their Land in the Talmudic Age*, 2 vols. (Jerusalem, 1980–4).

ii THE CONVENTIONAL EXPLANATIONS

The belief that it is important to discover the causes of the cata-strophe is not new. The first historian known to have attempted to tackle the problem was the contemporary writer Josephus, who him-self took part in the war and provides the fullest account of its course. Many of his serious, reflective comments on the destruction of his own society deserve, and have been accorded, a high value by modern students.[4]

Acceptance of Josephus' analyses is not at first sight unreasonable. His account of events seems essentially truthful, both because it often has the support of other surviving sources and because he apparently made no thorough attempt to iron out internal inconsistencies within his narrative.[5] He was an eye witness of, and a participant in, much of the history he describes. He was trying, as he insists (*B.J.* 1.1–18), to write political history in the style and with the acute interest in causation of Thucydides.

Yet a moment's reflection reveals the dangers in too great a trust. Josephus blames the war on a wide variety of causes. The modern historian needs criteria to judge whether, for instance, the attempt to raise the Levites to equality with the priests in the Temple service really was – as Josephus suggests in claiming that such a sin was bound to make the Jews liable to punishment (*A.J.* 20.218) – no less important a factor in causing the war than others that he stresses. Thus Josephus reckoned that a major reason for the disaster was divine wrath directed against Israel for her wickedness – he evi-dently liked to portray himself as a latterday Jeremiah – but to the modern secular mind such a belief is naturally dismissed as the prod-uct of the contemporary author's primitive intellectual equipment. However, once some elements of Josephus' considered analysis have been rejected, it is not logically justifiable simply to pick and choose from the rest whatever is congenial to the modern historian's preju-dices.

One solution which would have the merit of consistency would be simply to accept the whole of Josephus' view about who was respon-sible for the war, but this would hardly be satisfactory. It was pre-

[4] For Josephus' analysis of the causes of the war, cf. P. Bilde, 'The causes of the Jewish War according to Josephus', *JSJ* 10 (1979) 179–202.
[5] I follow T. Rajak (*Josephus: the historian and his society* (London, 1983), p. 106 n. 3) in finding unduly pessimistic the view of some eminent scholars that Josephus' story must either be reproduced as it stands, with varying degrees of credulity, or dismissed in its entirety. I hope that my approach to the evidence, outlined below, is coherent, but I am aware that it cannot be *proved* correct.

cisely when Josephus stood back from the canvas of his history and pronounced in summary passages such as *B.J.* 7.254–74 his considered view of the factors and people most to be blamed that he may be at his least trustworthy. When in the midst of narrative he exclaimed at the dire consequences of some episode he had just described, it is probable that he gave the reader his honest opinion. But when he tried to pull together his views into an overall ascription of responsibility for the disaster it is all too likely that his instinct for apologetic overcame his conscience as a historian.[6]

For there were many reasons for such apologetic. Eye witnesses may record details accurately, but they are unlikely to gain the deeper understanding which comes from perspective. Josephus in the *B.J.* was trying to describe and to analyse one of the most traumatic events in his nation's history less than ten years after it had occurred. Furthermore, he had himself been too deeply involved in the war to be objective. In A.D. 66 he had been elected as one of the leading generals of the Jewish rebels. In A.D. 67 he had changed sides, becoming first a Roman captive and then an honoured friend of Titus, destroyer of the Temple.

Josephus was proud of his career, and of the social success in Rome after A.D. 70 which set him apart from the rest of the Judaean ruling class from which he had sprung. But his apologetic was intended not so much to justify his own tortuous political progression as to try to show to his gentile readers, particularly those of the *B.J.*, that Jews of the richer class like himself were, despite the revolt, just like other aristocrats in the Greek East of the empire. Above all, he wanted to demonstrate that they should be entrusted again with the Jerusalem Temple and the flourishing Judaean society of which they had lost control in A.D. 70.[7] Clearly, although understanding the causes of the revolt must depend on Josephus' narrative, it is unwise to assume the accuracy of any of his analyses of the events through which he lived.

In practice, though usually with little theoretical justification, modern historians have tended to accept an amalgam of some of the causes proposed by Josephus. But they do so usually only after careful scrutiny of each alleged cause in the light of the ancient author's known bias. Every factor put forward by Josephus is accepted as

---

[6] Cf. Bilde, 'The causes of the Jewish War', for a more detailed analysis. For Josephus' presentation of himself as a Jeremiah figure, see *B.J.* 5.391–3; D. Daube, 'Typology in Josephus', *JJS* 31 (1980) 20.

[7] For a full and excellent account of Josephus' self-representation, see Rajak, *Josephus*, pp. 104–73.

valid except when either his political apologetic or his religious ideology seems to provide the most obvious explanation for his wish to mention it. Conversely, other causes ignored by Josephus are agreed to merit serious consideration only when good grounds for his silence can be postulated.

Such use of Josephus' evidence has come up with five major explanations of why Judaea rebelled.

a. *The incompetence of the Roman governors*

Josephus considered the incompetence and malice of the Roman governors of Judaea to be a prime cause of the revolt. His judgement is significantly echoed from the Roman side by Tacitus (*Hist.* 5.12). The greed, bravado and recklessness of a procurator like Pilate are remarkable not least because he evidently thought he could get away with such behaviour – as, indeed, he did for ten years or more to A.D. 36. Many of Pilate's actions, such as the minting of coins which carry a pagan sacrificial ladle and other religious emblems, seem designed almost deliberately to annoy the Jews.[8] Equally tactless was the action of Felix, procurator probably from A.D. 52 to 60, in, for instance, taking the Herodian princess Drusilla from her husband and marrying her himself without converting to Judaism. Roman recognition of the unsatisfactory nature of the governors can be seen in the way some of them were summarily deposed from office. Most of them, including Pilate, Cumanus and Festus, disappear altogether from the records of the Roman governing hierarchy after their rule over Judaea. Even in Roman eyes, then, these governors were not impressive men. As in other non-senatorial provinces, apart from Egypt, any really difficult task which might require superior military power was handled not by the procurator but by a senatorial governor of a neighbouring region; in the case of Judaea, this was the governor of Syria.[9] Also in favour of taking these governors' incompetence as a serious cause of provincial unrest is the fact that administrative brutality was responsible for revolts elsewhere in the early empire, in Gaul and in Britain.[10] The procurators of Judaea were appointed by the emperor through a patronage system which often took little or no account of merit in selecting for such posts. Appointments could be of any duration. Since the governor's power

[8] Smallwood, *Jews*, p. 167.
[9] On the relationship of the procurator of Judaea to the legate of Syria, see Schürer, *History* I, pp. 360–1.
[10] S. L. Dyson, 'Native revolts in the Roman empire', *Historia* 20 (1971) 239–74.

depended directly and only on imperial support, he often might himself lack prestige as an individual; it is perhaps significant that for some of the early procurators after Coponius (A.D. 6–9) nothing more than the name is known. At least one governor, Felix, was of quite exceptionally low Roman status, for he was an ex-slave;[11] if Josephus is any guide, Jews were as aware as any Roman aristocrat of his servile origins.

The Judaean governors' authority was weakened not only by this low Roman status and by their lack of administrative experience but also by the fact that the governors of Syria had the right to intervene in Judaean affairs and sometimes did so. They thus undermined the procurators' façade of control over Judaea without, because of their prior commitment to their own province, taking over full responsibility themselves. Similarly unsettling for the procurator was the knowledge that an embassy to the emperor could, if successful, at any time remove him from his post and into obscurity. It is hardly surprising that most of the governors felt able to deal with local dissent only by swift suppression or by ignoring the signs of disaffection. What they feared most was not a crisis in the province but the possibility that the emperor might come to hear of such a crisis.[12]

Josephus accused the governors of Judaea not simply of incompetence but also of malevolence towards the Jews, and in this too he may in some cases have been right. Doubtless any such antisemitism may have been simply an irrational dislike of people with idiosyncratic customs, but it may be relevant that most of the procurators were from the Italian gentry and will have known about Jews mostly from the Jewish diaspora in Rome. There a large community had been settled since at least the mid first century B.C., most of them originally brought to Rome as slaves. These freedmen and descendants of freedmen were mostly poor and were, like much of the plebs of the city of Rome, prone to violence. It would not be surprising if most of the governors thus came to Judaea with an unfavourable image of Jews. It was an exceptional thing to learn more about the inhabitants of a province before setting out to govern it (cf. Philo, *Leg.* 245), and no ordinary man could be expected to understand the minutiae of Jewish religious practice without considerable study.

[11] Smallwood, *Jews*, pp. 268–9; only one other freedman governor before A.D. 70 is attested. See in general R. P. Saller, *Personal Patronage under the Early Empire* (Cambridge, 1982), especially pp. 79–111.

[12] Cf. P. A. Brunt, 'Charges of provincial maladministration under the early principate', *Historia* 10 (1961) 189–227, and F. G. B. Millar, *The Emperor in the Roman World (31 B.C.–A.D. 337)* (London, 1977), pp. 375–85, on embassies sent by provincial communities direct to the emperor.

There is no evidence that the governors of Judaea made even a token effort.[13]

b. *The oppressiveness of Roman rule*

But even if the governors were bad, there is much evidence – though it is naturally not stressed by the pro-Roman Josephus – that the roots of their problem lay much further back in long-standing Jewish hostility to Roman rule and many Jews' belief that that rule was in essence oppressive. There were indeed many reasons why a Jew of the first century A.D. might harbour unfriendly feelings towards Rome.

Roman brutality to the inhabitants of Judaea had begun in the mid first century B.C. If there had been a formal treaty of alliance between Rome and the fledgling Jewish state of Judaea which, led by the Maccabees, broke away from the kingdom of the Seleucids in the mid second century B.C., that treaty must have lapsed by 63 B.C. when Pompey's conquest of Syria brought him into direct confrontation with the Hasmonaeans, whose dynasty was descended from the Maccabees.[14] With skilful exploitation of dynastic feuds, Pompey contrived to instal a puppet Hasmonaean monarch on the throne of a diminished state. In the process he conquered Jerusalem and earned himself undying Jewish hatred by wantonly desecrating the Holy of Holies in the Temple, slaughtering many defenders of the capital and enslaving thousands of others; when the Jewish rebels in Egypt desecrated his tomb 178 years later in A.D. 115 they may have done so deliberately in revenge.

The hostility engendered by this first unhappy contact between the Jews and the might of late-republican Rome was to be compounded in the following quarter of a century. Aulus Gabinius in 57 B.C. experimented wilfully with the complete abolition of the Hasmonaean monarchy, leaving only a High Priest shorn of secular power and creating a non-Jewish enclave between Judaea and Gali-

[13] Of the two non-Italian governors, Tiberius Julius Alexander faced special antagonism as a renegade Jew. Gessius Florus, although probably of Italian descent, came from Clazomenae. Appointed because his wife was a friend of the empress Poppaea, he may have been prejudiced against Jews by his experience of the large and powerful Jewish communities in Asia Minor, cf. Smallwood, *Jews*, p. 272.

[14] On the treaty and its lapse, see Smallwood, *Jews*, p. 11; E. R. Gruen, *The Hellenistic World and the Coming of Rome*, 2 vols. (Berkeley and London, 1984) II, pp. 745–51; see also A. N. Sherwin-White, *Roman Foreign Policy in the East: 168 B.C. to A.D. 1* (London, 1984), pp. 70–9, who argues against any formal treaty between Rome and Judaea before the time of Hyrcanus.

lee. Crassus in 55 B.C. robbed gold from the Temple treasury to pay for his Parthian campaign. Perhaps in response to Crassus' disastrous defeat and death, the Jews under a certain Pitholaus rose in revolt against Rome in Galilee; C. Cassius Longinus, Crassus' quaestor and the future liberator of the Roman people from Julius Caesar, suppressed the uprising and sold thousands of Jews into slavery. Jewish support for Caesar against the hated Pompey in the civil war from 49 B.C. was rewarded with somewhat more favourable treatment, recorded in detail, for apologetic purposes, by Josephus (*A.J.* 14.190–222). But Caesar's death brought Cassius again to the East and Roman oppression to something of a peak: the inhabitants of four small towns were sold as slaves to raise cash for the civil war against Mark Antony, Lepidus and Octavian. It was hardly surprising that a Parthian invasion of Palestine in 40 B.C., with the establishment of a Hasmonaean king in Jerusalem under their protection, was greeted with enthusiasm by the Jews; nor that this Hasmonaean's removal in 37 B.C. by the Roman governor of Syria and, after yet another bloody siege of the capital city, the installation as a puppet-king of the half-Jew Herod, were deeply resented. At least on this occasion the Roman general, out of deference to Herod, forbore from desecrating the Temple and called off his troops before all the riches of Jerusalem were plundered. Yet he too carried off thousands to Rome in slavery and celebrated a triumph for his victory.[15]

All these things of course took place over a century before the outbreak of revolt in A.D. 66. But memories were long, as the hatred of Pompey testifies, and more recent cause for grievance could be found for those inclined to look. Taxation was, or felt, excessive under the procurators' rule: it is debated whether taxes were heavier after A.D. 6 than they had been under Herod, but Tacitus records a complaint against the tax burden in A.D. 17 (*Ann.* 2.42). There was, moreover, a general increase in Roman exactions throughout the empire under Nero, and an extraordinary levy of taxes in Judaea under the procurator Albinus in the early sixties A.D.[16] The whole notion of efficient Roman taxation ruthlessly exacted was anyway deeply objectionable: the Jews who caused unrest when the first

[15] For a detailed account of all of this, see Smallwood, *Jews*, pp. 1–59.
[16] For the debate on the weight of Roman compared to Herodian taxation, see Rajak, *Josephus*, p. 122. For the increased pressure on taxpayers under Nero, see *ibid.* pp. 125–6. On Albinus, see R. A. Horsley, 'Ancient Jewish banditry and the revolt against Rome, A.D. 66–70', *CBQ* 43 (1981) 419–20. A sales tax on agricultural produce was also consistently unpopular, cf. *A.J.* 18.90.

Roman census was imposed on the province in A.D. 6 may have been able to cite specifically Jewish reasons for their refusal to cooperate in such an exercise, but for many other provincials too the census had been viewed as a reason for revolt.[17]

Greater anti-Roman sentiment was probably caused, however, not by financial considerations but by the Jews' shock at Caligula's plan to desecrate the Temple with his statue in A.D. 40. That project, though it was never fulfilled, revealed that the impiety of Pompey could all too easily be repeated, and that Roman emperors could no more be trusted than the wicked Seleucid king Antiochus IV Epiphanes, whose plans to destroy Judaism as a religion in 167 B.C. had led to the Maccabees' rebellion and the foundation of the independent Hasmonaean state. The story of the sacrilegious actions of Antiochus remained a potent myth among Jews in the first century A.D. It was not hard for them to see Rome as a similar oppressor, particularly when in the sixties A.D. Nero's mania seemed, to his subjects, dangerously similar to that of Caligula.

c. *Jewish religious susceptibilities*

It is characteristic that the Jews' greatest hostility to Rome was thus directed against attacks on their religious heritage. It is not always clear whether the religious reasons put forward by the Jews for unrest at various times in the first century A.D. should all be accepted as genuine causes of their discontent: in the notorious episode when Pilate's attempt to introduce gilded shields into Jerusalem for display in the Roman garrison was prevented only by fanatical opposition, even the pious Jewish author Philo proved unable to explain clearly how Pilate's intended action would infringe the Jewish law.[18] But there can be no doubt that religious aspirations did sour relations with Rome. Jewish religious literature kept alive the proud past and the promise that eventual divine aid would bring a political triumph over the gentiles. All Jews believed that at the end of days a messiah would come, though they debated what his nature would be

---

[17] For the old Jewish belief that a peace-time census is sinful, cf. 2 Sam. 24.10; 1 Chron. 21.1–8,17. But other rebellions against Rome, in Gaul in 12 B.C. and in Cilicia in A.D. 36, were also sparked off by the introduction of regular tax assessment, cf. Smallwood, *Jews*, p. 152 n. 38.

[18] Philo, *Leg.* 299–305. For suggestions as to what the religious objection may have been, see Smallwood, *Jews*, p. 166; G. Fuks, 'Again on the episode of the gilded Roman shields at Jerusalem', *HTR* 75 (1982) 503–7. P. S. Davies, 'The meaning of Philo's text about the gilded shields', *JTS* n.s. 37 (1986) 109–14, argues that a dedication to the gods was implied by the inscription of the emperor's name on the shields, hence the contravention of the Torah.

and whether he would bring them freedom alone or world domination under his rule. The Jews' sacred texts unequivocally promised them the land of Israel and divine approval of their occupation of it so long as they observed God's law. A hope for their eventual political autonomy in Judaea was thus a religious imperative.[19]

It is possible that for some Jews in Judaea resentment at Rome's denial of these political aspirations inspired by religious tradition was constantly reinforced by the discrepancy between the aspects of their own culture intimately associated with their religious beliefs and the culture favoured by pagan Rome. Opposition to Hellenism had been a professed aim of the Maccabees in their revolt against the Seleucids (cf. 2 Macc. 4.13) and, despite the extensive hellenization of much of first-century Judaean society, the essential cultural divide was still sharply felt by some: the teacher Simon who objected to the games celebrated by Agrippa I in Caesarea collected a great crowd to join his protest even though, as Agrippa rightly pointed out, there was nothing strictly contrary to the law in the enjoyment of such entertainment (*A.J.* 19.332–4). Many Jews retained an instinctive reaction that all things Greek were dangerous to their ancestral religion. The attitude was reinforced by the festival of Hannukah, which celebrated the victory of the Maccabees against Hellenism; despite lack of biblical authority for its observance the festival probably remained popular in the first century A.D.[20]

d. *Class tensions*

Professed opposition to Hellenism sometimes masked expressions of hostility based on class, for it was in general true that the richer Jews were more attracted to, or inclined to indulge in, Greek culture. Herod had introduced athletic festivals, musical contests, wild beast fights and gladiators to Jerusalem (*A.J.* 15.267–75). Not all rich Jews necessarily approved, but they were more likely to speak good Greek and decorate their houses in the latest Roman fashion than their poorer compatriots.[21]

[19] On Jewish theological aspirations for political independence, see, for example, Rhoads, *Israel in Revolution*, pp. 21–2. On messianic beliefs, see Schürer, *History* II, pp. 488–554.

[20] On the limits of the ideological opposition of some Jews to Hellenism, see J. A. Goldstein, 'Jewish acceptance and rejection of Hellenism', in E. P. Sanders *et al.*, eds., *Jewish and Christian Self-Definition* (London, 1981) II, pp. 64–87. On Hannukah, see G. Alon, *Jews, Judaism and the Classical World* (Jerusalem, 1977), pp. 1–17.

[21] For the connection between the class struggle and opposition to cultural Hellenism, see H. Kreissig, 'Die landwirtschaftliche Situation in Palästina vor dem Judäischen Krieg', *Acta Antiqua* 17 (1969) 223–54, especially 231–2.

Whether or not this explains opposition to Hellenism, there is certainly evidence in Josephus for considerable class hatred.[22] In one passage (*B.J.* 7.260–1), the historian explicitly blames the crisis in Judaean society on the oppression of the masses by the powerful and the eagerness of the poor to kill the wealthy and plunder their property. He implies further, though he does not state directly, that this class warfare was somehow responsible for the war.

e. *Quarrels with local gentiles*

Opposition to Hellenism may also have been partly responsible, however indirectly, for the Jewish hostility to Greeks in Caesarea which, as has been seen, provoked the riot that immediately preceded the revolt. Herod had shown that it was possible for a Jewish king to remain on friendly terms with local pagans in the Greek cities around and within Palestine, and his policy was followed by his royal descendants, but such friendship proved impossible for most Jews. The reason lay partly in the common distrust between two communities which retained clearly distinct identities while in close contact (as elsewhere in the diaspora), and partly in past events which had exacerbated this tendency in the cities neighbouring Judaea. Hostilities between the Jews of the Judaean and Galilean hills and the pagan inhabitants of the Greek cities on the coastal plain and in the Decapolis went back to Hasmonaean times. In the late second and early first centuries B.C. the aggressive Hasmonaean state had expanded over surrounding areas and suppressed the freedom of the city states such as Gaza and Ascalon to such an extent that, when Pompey conquered the Jews and restricted their state to the hill country, the cities greeted him as a liberator and began new eras to mark his advent. The Hasmonaeans found their Greek subjects immutably alien: unlike the hill peoples of Galilee and Idumaea, attempts to convert them to Judaism proved ineffective.[23]

Hence the mutual suspicion between Jews and pagans in all the cities bordering Judaea. Hence too the connection with revolt against Rome. The local Greeks consistently backed Roman rule.

---

[22] For Josephus on class conflict, see P. A. Brunt, 'Josephus on social conflicts in Roman Judaea', *Klio* 59 (1977) 149–53.

[23] On the Greek cities in the neighbourhood of Judaea, see Schürer, *History* II, pp. 85–183. On the hostility between Jews and gentiles in these cities, see most recently A. Kasher, 'The connection between the hellenistic cities in Eretz-Israel and Gaius Caligula's rescript to install an idol in the Temple', *Zion* 51 (1986) 135–51 (Heb.).

They provided regular auxiliary troops for the procurator's army[24] and, when war did break out in A.D. 66, a good number of municipal levies, who lacked training but made up for it by their hatred of the Jews, joined the Roman forces (*B.J.* 2.502). In return Rome provided them with consistent support. Roman philhellenism had from the time of Augustus been effective in winning the support of the Greek half of the empire for Roman rule. From the Roman point of view it was just unfortunate that in practice philhellenism in places of mixed population acted to the detriment of the Jews. Josephus claimed that Nero's decision to favour the Greeks against the Jews in Caesarea was a necessary cause of the revolt (*B.J.* 2.284). Certainly the hostility in such places between Jews and Greeks was uncomfortably evident in A.D. 66: the outbreak of war saw appalling massacres in the cities around Judaea, Jews killing gentiles and destroying their property while gentiles killed Jews in a number of cities, most horrifically in Scythopolis (*B.J.* 2.457–98).

iii CIVIL WAR, THE RULING CLASS AND REVOLT

With such a collocation of factors the rebellion against Rome might seem inevitable, and the only task for the historian might seem to be the discovery of precisely when and how the outbreak occurred. Further thought suggests, however, that none of these factors, important though each one was, inevitably led to revolt against Rome.

Thus Josephus' and Tacitus' attack on the good faith of the procurators of Judaea is suspect. Precisely because of their low status in Roman terms and their fall from imperial favour after A.D. 70 they were safe targets for later writers looking for Roman scapegoats for the war: it is striking that one of the few procurators to be praised for his administration before A.D. 66 is also the only procurator known to have progressed to a higher post under imperial patronage after A.D. 70, Tiberius Julius Alexander (*B.J.* 2.220).[25] Albinus, procurator in the key years A.D. 62 to 64 and much disliked by Josephus (*B.J.* 2.272), was not believed by Nero to have bungled the job, for in the late sixties A.D. he is found promoted by Nero to a more senior post in Mauretania.[26] It would be attributing too much to chance to

[24] The argument of Schürer (*History* I, pp. 363–5), that most of the Roman auxiliaries serving in Judaea were recruited locally, still seems to me valid despite the cautionary remarks of M. P. Speidel, 'The Roman army in Judaea under the procurators', *Ancient Society* 13/14 (1982/3) 233–40.

[25] V. A. Burr, *Tiberius Iulius Alexander* (Bonn, 1955).

[26] H.-G. Pflaum, *Les carrières procuratoriennes équestres sous le Haut-Empire romain* (Paris, 1960–1), no. 33.

suppose that the appointment of governors by patronage was responsible for the disaster in Roman Judaea when the same system provided remarkably stable government for most other provinces.

Similar caution is advisable in considering whether Judaean Jews inevitably found Roman rule oppressive. Many of the worst incidents of Roman violence, such as the campaigns of Pompey, had taken place long before the lifetime of those who rebelled in A.D. 66. To counteract the hostile tradition, pro-Roman Jews could point to much evidence of Roman respect for the Jewish cult. Sosius, the governor of Syria who captured Jerusalem for Herod in 37 B.C., gave gold to the Temple before he left; in 15 B.C. Augustus' friend Agrippa sacrificed a hecatomb there to the delight of the populace; Augustus' grandson Gaius was expected to pay a complimentary visit in A.D. 1, though in the event, perhaps for political reasons, he never came (Suet. *Div. Aug.* 93); all the emperors welcomed and perhaps paid for the sacrifices offered on their behalf in Jerusalem.[27] Not all Roman administrative decisions about Judaea were insensitive: for example, Claudius' appointment of Agrippa I as king in A.D. 41 was designed to soothe Jewish feelings after Caligula's enormities. There is no reason to suppose that taxes in Judaea were heavier than elsewhere in the Roman empire: when the Judaeans complained in A.D. 17 at the amount they were required to pay, their distress was apparently shared by the inhabitants of Syria (Tac. *Ann.* 2.42). If Herod had indeed paid tribute to Rome as well as raising his own taxes, as some believe (cf. above, n. 16), direct Roman rule may have even lightened the burden after A.D. 6.

Nor is the religious touchiness of the Jews a sufficient explanation of the war. It has already been seen, from the episode of the shields brought into Jerusalem by Pilate (above, n. 18), that it is sometimes reasonable to suspect a secular explanation for anti-Roman sentiment even when the only motive admitted by the Jews was religious. There was too much variety in first-century Judaism for more than a few clear-cut issues – such as the proposed desecration of the Temple by Caligula – by themselves to unite the nation in opposition. On many religious issues there did not exist even a normative attitude. So, for instance, even the assumption of the Roman authorities that Jews objected to any pictorial representation of living creatures may not have been justified, although most of the procurators apparently took the taboo seriously: most of the buildings of this period exca-

---

[27] For possible political reasons for Gaius' behaviour, see Smallwood, *Jews*, p. 117. For the imperial sacrifice, see Schürer, *History* II, pp. 311–12.

vated in Jerusalem do indeed lack animal motifs in their decoration, but one house has been found with depictions of birds, another house contained an image of a fish on a table top, and a fine Jewish tomb built in Jericho in the mid first century A.D. also had birds painted on the walls.[28]

Nor, although it cannot be doubted that Jewish religious expectations gave a fillip to aspirations for political autonomy, is it clear why this should necessarily have led to revolt in A.D. 66. I shall argue below (Chapter 4) that most Jewish theology of the period was concerned with hope about political independence at some undefined future time and did not consider mandatory any immediate action to achieve such freedom. In their general sense that the nation was effectively protected by national gods the Jews were no different from other ancient peoples. Most ancient religions could be and were put to political account in a similar fashion. The Greeks and Romans expected the gods to fight on their behalf, preserving their national boundaries and aiding them in aggressive wars providing they were just. So far as is known from the limited surviving evidence, most of the peoples subject to Rome had similar traditions.[29] As Agrippa I remarked to Caligula, according to Philo (*Leg.* 277), patriotism and the acceptance of native laws as paramount is only natural. I do not wish to deny that the extent to which political action was thought of and justified in religious terms was probably much greater in Judaea than in some other ancient societies. Just a glance at Josephus' history will suffice to show how religion was infused into almost everything Jews did or thought. But this does not mean that Jewish theology necessarily led to a desire for action to achieve political freedom. Philo, for instance, was able to combine without apparent difficulty a great pride in his people and their customs with a universalist ethic and a practical acceptance of Roman rule. Like many other Jews in voluntary exile he saw no contradiction in the practice of Judaism by Jews living outside Palestine deprived of self-rule.[30]

[28] On the variety to be found in the religious attitudes of Jews in first-century Judaea, see R. A. Kraft, 'The multiform Jewish heritage of early Christianity', in J. Neusner, ed., *Christianity, Judaism and Other Greco-Roman Cults* (Leiden, 1975) III, pp. 174–99; M. E. Stone, *Scriptures, Sects and Visions: a profile of Judaism from Ezra to the Jewish revolt* (Oxford, 1982); cf. below, Chapter 4. On attitudes to images, see M. Broshi in Y. Yadin, ed., *Jerusalem Revealed: archaeology in the holy city 1968–1974* (Jerusalem, 1975), p. 58; N. Avigad, *Discovering Jerusalem* (Oxford, 1984), p. 150. Opinion clearly differed on the permissibility of animal representation.

[29] Cf. S. L. Dyson, 'Native revolt patterns in the Roman Empire', *ANRW* II.3 (1975) 169–70, on the Thracian Bessi in 11 B.C. (but note his cautionary remarks on p. 172).

As for the Jewish opposition to hellenistic culture which was justified in purely religious terms (in, for instance, contemporary apocalyptic texts), it is hard to see how this could have been a cause of revolt since there was no particular reason to expect that Roman rule would encourage any deeper hellenization than had already occurred in Judaea before A.D. 6. By the first century A.D. Jews had already integrated many Greek elements into their cultural life. Art and architecture were being copied from the surrounding culture. Greek was widely spoken, though doubtless more so in cosmopolitan Jerusalem than in the Judaean or Galilean countryside. Hellenization had come about neither through imposition from outside, nor through the spontaneous adoption of Greek culture wholesale, nor through gradual assimilation, but through the deliberate integration of Greek elements to enrich the indigenous culture. Thus Greek ideas informed the argument even of the apocalyptic texts themselves, and Greek architecture adorned the entirely semitic rituals of the Jerusalem cult.[31] Most Jews by this period enjoyed a thoroughly relaxed attitude to the hellenization of their society, even if some of them occasionally made rhetorical attacks upon particular manifestations of this process. This attitude is no more difficult to understand than that of Cato the Censor, whose attacks on Greek culture were notorious even though he was himself one of the more hellenized of the Roman aristocracy in the mid second century B.C.[32]

[30] Much discussion of 'Jewish nationalism' in this period has been written with the problems of the early Church in mind, and has tended towards the view that hope for the restoration of Israel was somehow contradictory to the more universalist view eventually adopted within Christianity. This contradiction, however, is hard to find expressed in Jewish texts. Jews do not seem to have found their (varying) attitudes to gentiles relevant to their own hopes for national restoration in political or other form.

[31] See in general Rajak, *Josephus*, pp. 2–3, 8–9. On apocalyptic, see for example F. Schmidt, 'Hésiode et l'Apocalyptique: acculturation et résistance juive à l'hellénisme', *Quaderni di Storia* 15 (1982) 164–5. On the degree of hellenization in Judaea before 167 B.C., see the cautionary remarks of F. Millar, 'The background to the Maccabean revolution', *JJS* 29 (1978) 1–21. The notion of a clear distinction between 'Palestinian' and 'Hellenistic' Judaism is now obsolete, cf. Schürer, *History* III, pp. 177–8.

[32] Cf. A. E. Astin, *Cato the Censor* (Oxford, 1978), pp. 157–81. Even the Hasmonaean propaganda justifying their seizure of power in terms of a counter-revolution against 'the hellenizers' may be no more than a front to justify their illegal usurpation of the high priesthood. Their revolt had been against Antiochus Epiphanes, not the ruling High Priests, cf. Millar, 'Background to the Maccabean revolution', pp. 12–17, and as late as 162 B.C. the *ḥasidim* were prepared to accept the pro-Greek Alcimus as their High Priest, with only Judas and his followers in opposition (Schürer, *History* I, p. 169). It is curious that later Hasmonaeans probably managed to combine their reputation of having saved the country from Hellenism with the title 'Philhellene', cf. Schürer, *History* I, p. 217.

Similarly, although class tensions were indubitably an unhappy aspect of Judaean society before A.D. 66, it is not obvious how they were connected to the outbreak of rebellion against Roman rule. It is true that some rich Jews sided with the Romans, but many others fought for the rebels until their cause was lost (see below, Chapters 7 and 9). During the four years that the independent Jewish state maintained itself against Roman aggression, no attempt was made at economic reform or at the redistribution of land; Josephus' failure to report any such social programme provides sufficient testimony that none was proposed, for, given his own apologetic interest in presenting the rich as loyal to Rome and the poor as responsible for the revolt, he would not have been slow to attribute such plans to the rebels if he had possessed any evidence for such a charge. According to Josephus – who again would not be tempted to make such a statement falsely – the rebel leaders burned the debt archives in Jerusalem in A.D. 66 not because they were themselves debtors but in order to encourage debtors to rise against Rome; clearly debtors would not recognize that their interests lay in revolt until their sympathy was caught by such a dramatic symbolic act. It is misleading to view the war against Rome as simply the '*Kulminationspunkt des Klassenkampfes*'.[33]

Finally, the constant bickering of Jews and gentiles in the Greek cities around Judaea, including Caesarea, could have continued indefinitely without necessarily ending in a revolt against the suzerain power. Disputes between neighbours and within cities were common throughout the empire. They rarely led to anything more problematic for the provincial authorities than sporadic urban violence. The squabbles of the Jews and the Greeks in Alexandria in Egypt broke out in violent riots in A.D. 66 but were easily suppressed without any serious threat that the Alexandrian Jews might rebel against Rome (*B.J.* 2.487–98). It would have been quite possible for the Caesarean Jews, although they had been worsted by Nero's decision and Florus' bias, to wait for better days when a more favourable verdict on their claims might be expected; this was indeed what, according to Josephus, the Herodian king Agrippa urged them to do (*B.J.* 2.350–4).

The intercommunal violence of A.D. 66 may well have been the consequence rather than the cause of revolt. The Greeks were fearful

[33] The phrase is used by H. Kreissig, *Die sozialen Zusammenhänge des judäischen Krieges: Klassen und Klassenkampf im Palästina des I. Jahrhunderts v.u.Z.* (Berlin, 1970), p. 15, but he does not deny the importance of other factors in the events preceding the revolt.

of the Jews and greedy for their property; the Jews were keen to re-
taliate for similar reasons. Before the war, by contrast, Judaean Jews
cannot have felt entirely hostile towards their gentile neighbours, for
the many Jews who decided to live in these Greek cities presumably
did so voluntarily. It is worth noting that the Jews of Scythopolis
even sided with their gentile neighbours against the rebels in A.D. 66
(*B.J.* 2.466), though this alliance did them little good (467–8) and
may have been under compulsion (*Vita* 26).

It seems probable, then, that the causes of the war proposed by
Josephus and modern historians are not, when taken individually,
sufficient to explain why Judaea went over the brink into rebellion.
A plausible solution to the problem is to posit that an amalgam of all
these causes was responsible: an event like the outbreak of war is not
simple, and the disparate factors suggested may have interreacted in
quite complex ways. Such a hypothesis is very reasonable and cannot be disproved.[34] It would, however, be desirable for those historians who adopt this solution – and most do – to explain precisely how
these factors combined to lead to so disastrous a result. So far as I
know, no such explanation has so far been proposed.

It seems to me that elucidation of one further cause which has
hitherto been ignored may provide, when taken together with the
other factors already discussed, a crucial link in the chain of causation. This further cause, which it is the aim of this book to bring to
prominence, is the power struggle within the Jewish ruling class.

The main evidence for this power struggle comes, as almost always
in investigations of first-century A.D. Judaean history, from
Josephus. It has been noted more than once that one of the causes
most blamed for the Judaean disaster by Josephus in passing comments in the *B.J.* is *stasis*, civil war. The fall of Jerusalem, he claims,
was brought about by Divine Providence because of the absence of
concord (*symphonia*) and harmony (*homonoia*) within the Nation. He
even quotes explicitly a prophecy, whose origin comes perhaps only
from within his own imagination, that the city would be taken only
when Jerusalem was divided against itself (*B.J.* 4.388; 6.109).[35] To
some extent Josephus' castigation of *stasis* might be seen as a reflection of his historiographical model, Thucydides, for this is a frequent
motif in the latter's works, but Josephus insists that harmony and

---

[34] This is the proposal preferred by U. Rappaport, 'Jewish–pagan relations and
the revolt against Rome in 66–70 C.E.', *The Jerusalem Cathedra* 1 (1981) 81 n. 1.

[35] On *stasis* in Josephus, see Bilde, 'The causes of the Jewish War', pp. 190–1, 198;
Rajak, *Josephus*, pp. 91–5.

concord are specifically Jewish virtues through common adherence to the laws of Moses (*c.Ap.* 2.179–81, 294).

The significance of this emphasis by Josephus on the dangers of social division lies precisely in the fact that unity is not one of the Old Testament virtues. Old Testament prophets castigated individual Jews and the nation as a whole for their failings in their relationship to God, but a belief in social disunity as a prime cause of disaster is specifically Greek. Josephus' adoption of it in explaining his own society probably reflects, then, not ideology but the actual state of affairs. Confirmation of the accuracy of his observation can be found in the astonished remark of the Roman historian Tacitus (*Hist.* 5.12.4) that, even as the enemy closed in on Jerusalem in A.D. 70, the Jews were still engaged in civil strife.

But, though clear about the significance of Jewish disunity, Josephus is far less explicit about the nature of these divisions. Since the group of men most often blamed by him for rebellious actions are described as bandits eager for booty and religious fanatics seeking to destroy society, it has seemed to some interpreters most likely that it was class warfare that he had in mind.[36] This is possible, but Josephus does not himself give it as his meaning – except, perhaps, obliquely, at *B.J.* 7.260–1. Other suggestions may be made, particularly since, if Josephus did intend to blame the class struggle, it is strange that he does not always say so outright.

In suggesting that the civil strife which so horrified Josephus was in fact partly a struggle for power within the ruling class, I shall make extensive use of four often neglected passages in Josephus' *Antiquities* (*A.J.* 20.180–1, 197–203, 208–10, 213–14). These passages describe the eruption of violent conflict in the years before the war and state explicitly that the men involved were ex-High Priests and others of the same class. Such men moved in the same social circles as Josephus. With some of them he was himself closely involved politically, whether at the time or later during the revolt. The hypothesis that Josephus believed that it was the quarrels of these men that led to the war thus has some explicit confirmation. It also has the merit that the historian's reticence about the precise participants in the *stasis* he deplores can be fully explained by his apologetic attempt to exculpate his own class from blame for the revolt.

My use of Josephus' own evidence to break through this reticence, and to discover facts which I believe that he well knew but at which he preferred only to hint, will be as far as possible systematic. I shall

---

[36] This central argument is brought out most clearly by Rajak, *Josephus*, pp. 93–4.

rely heavily on Josephus' detailed narrative, attaching special significance to every snippet of information which appears to contra-
dict the main thrust of his apologetic. There are many such items,
and their survival in such numbers confirms their reliability; if
Josephus had been an apologist only and not also a conscientious historian, he could easily have missed them out. In general when his
narrative can be checked against other evidence he emerges as sometimes negligent but often remarkably accurate: his measurements
of Masada are nearly exact – presumably they came from Roman
military records – and his description of Jerusalem has been in
general confirmed by recent archaeology.[37] Even when Josephus
appears at first sight to have given two quite different accounts of his
own command in Galilee (one in the *Vita* and the other in the *B.J.*),
the apparent contradictions can be almost entirely reconciled by
pointing to the different historiographical purposes of the two works;
given his own inglorious involvement, it was anyway far more
tempting for Josephus to lie about this campaign than about the rest
of the war.

Josephus' detailed narrative has therefore been fully exploited in
this book. But his value judgements have been treated as more than
a little suspect. When they cannot be substantiated from his detailed
narrative, they have been taken as representative of the attitude not
of all Judaean Jews but only that of the ruling class to which he
belonged. Nor was he entirely typical even of his own class. His
career in the Roman imperial court may have led him to an enthusiasm about the superiority of Roman power which other wealthy
Judaeans may not have shared, and few other Jews will have sym-
pathized with the way that, in the manner of other contemporary
historians trying to please their patrons, he depicted the emperors
Vespasian and Titus, who had been his benefactors, with excruciat-
ing flattery.

To achieve a better perspective on Josephus' narrative it is therefore necessary to look outside his works and to set the revolt against
the religious, literary, social, economic and cultural background of
Jews in Judaea in so far as it can be culled from other sources. It is
not in fact too difficult to do this. The whole corpus of intertestamental Jewish literature and of Qumran and some writings of the

[37] Cf. B. Mazar, 'Josephus Flavius – the historian of Jerusalem', in U. Rappaport, ed., *Josephus Flavius: historian of Eretz Israel in the Hellenistic–Roman period* (Jerusalem, 1982), pp. 1–5 (Heb.); M. Pucci, 'Jewish–Parthian relations in Josephus',
The Jerusalem Cathedra 3 (1983) 21; M. Broshi, 'The credibility of Josephus', *JJS* 33
(1982) 379–84.

early Church can reasonably be used to show what Jews in Judaea thought about their society.

These religious works are not often considered for this sort of historical purpose. Theological considerations have led scholars to concentrate on those motifs that were to become important in later Christian and Jewish circles, and this has acted to the detriment of the study of the texts both in their own right and to shed light on the society that shaped them. It should be admitted that this latter task is not without its own problems: some notions still widespread in the first-century literature may have had their origin in the quite different circumstances of earlier periods, and it is impossible to say without knowing the tone of voice and intention with which such ideas were repeated whether they still carried conviction in themselves or simply added an aura of religious antiquity to other, more immediately relevant, concepts in the same work. Equally, new ideas might sometimes result from internal development within Jewish thought regardless of social pressures or outside influences. Since pre-rabbinic Palestinian Judaism is not notably characterized by systematic theological thought of any kind, this sort of innovation seems to me unlikely; yet it is at least possible that on occasions religious notions were not formulated in response to social and political conditions, as I (and others) have tended to assume, but rather acted as a major element conditioning social and political behaviour. Influences presumably worked in both directions in ways now impossible to trace with accuracy. On a more basic level, the dating of texts among the pseudepigrapha is often problematic, and, since many texts survive only through later copying by Christians, often in languages other than the original, it is not always possible to know where a particular work was written, for what sort of audience, with what popularity, and with precisely what content.

Two categories of religious text have been the subject of particularly intense study without resolution of basic disagreements on their value as evidence for first-century Palestine. Scepticism about the use of the Gospels and Acts of the Apostles for this purpose remains widespread because the content of these works is so clearly theologically motivated. It is not safe to base statements about Judaean society on dogmatic assertions in these writings, none of which is likely to have been composed in Palestine or with an audience in that country in mind. On the other hand, the reaction of some recent scholars against the extreme uncertainty expressed by many form critics is probably justified: whatever the problems in reconstructing the life and career of Jesus (and they are immense), it is more plausible than otherwise that the general outline of his career as presented in the Gospel biographies is correct, simply because the hypothesis that these accounts were entirely composed, rather than partially altered, to make a theological point is more implausible than the belief that the outlines of Jesus' career are correctly described; among other objections to the former (and commonly held) view are the survival within each Gospel of contradictory views of Jesus and the oddness of biography as a vehicle for theological didacticism. Nonetheless it is clearly desirable to avoid basing major arguments on material which *may* reflect only the views of non-Judaean gentiles in the late first century A.D. and after, when those views were about an alien society that had flourished and perished some years before they wrote.[38]

Equal uncertainty surrounds the value of the rabbinic sources which survive through the Jewish tradition. The redaction of the present texts into more or less their present form took place at the earliest in *c.* A.D. 200, and there is some reason to suppose that they reflect the society of that later time rather than that of the first century A.D. The rabbis of the fourth and fifth centuries A.D. who compiled the Palestinian and Babylonian Talmuds tended to incorporate into these writings legendary stories about the sages of a much earlier period, whom they saw as their own illustrious forerunners. It would, as with the Gospels, be unwise to rely too heavily on these late sources, though the Mishnah (compiled *c.* A.D. 200) and the Tosefta (compiled soon after) may be regarded as more likely to be accurate than the later rabbinic material. On the other hand there is no justification for ignoring those traditions for which no later reason for invention can be surmised.[39]

---

[38] The literature on Gospel criticism is enormous, its primary focus being the reconstruction of the teaching of Jesus and his first followers. For a clear account of recent approaches to the extraction of history from the Gospels, see E. P. Sanders, *Jesus and Judaism* (London, 1985), pp. 23–58.

[39] For intensive and critical use of late rabbinic sources to understand the history of the first century A.D., see, for example, I. Ben-Shalom, 'The Shammai school and its place in the political and social history of Eretz Israel in the first century A.D.' (Ph.D. thesis, Tel Aviv, 1980) (Heb.). See also the justly influential works, published posthumously after his early death, by G. Alon (*Jews, Judaism and the Classical World* and *The Jews in their Land*). Both these writers are ingenious at erecting coherent hypotheses which depend on the assumption that later rabbinic views about the wider political influence of the sages before A.D. 70 are correct, and that therefore behind the entirely legal and religious disputes of these sages recorded in the texts lie also social and political divisions. I am inclined in contrast to suspect later rabbis of exaggerating the political importance of their predecessors, and therefore tend to take the texts at their face value. In support of this decision to take a rather sceptical

The problems in studying these religious ideas in their social context are thus considerable, but the advantages far outweigh the difficulties, and all these problems can with care be minimized. If old ideas were actively chosen by first-century Jews, it is valid to ask why and to suggest possible social or political reasons. Problems in the dating and placing of specific works can be partially overcome by looking for evidence of general trends found in a number of sources, and by giving extra weight to attitudes exemplified by behaviour as reported by Josephus or evidenced in the archaeology rather than simply verbal expression. The danger that the picture of first-century Jewish attitudes will be coloured by the theological beliefs of those who preserved the texts, mostly within the Christian tradition, can be partially circumvented by pointing up those religious attitudes attested in the texts that do not coincide with those of their preservers. Even if the final picture is tentative or imperfect, it will provide a useful corrective to Josephus' assumptions. There are in fact very few ancient societies for which so much evidence survives both of social change and of ideological change over a quite brief period. It will become apparent that Josephus and perhaps the rest of the ruling class espoused some attitudes which were shared by few of their fellow Judaeans.

To the testimony of these religious texts can be added from archaeology much new evidence about social life and attitudes to religious precepts. Archaeologists are producing new material pertinent to first-century society at bewildering speed, particularly in recent excavations in Jerusalem.[40] Useful also are the Jewish coins of the first revolt, now fully studied and valuable in revealing the nature of the Jewish state and the ideology of the rebels.[41]

In sum, it is both possible and desirable to break away from the straitjacket of Josephus' point of view. Once it has been decided thus to ignore his developed explanations of the causes of the revolt, it becomes necessary to produce a new theoretical model into which to place his detailed evidence and that of the other sources just discussed, but this is not difficult. Such models have been sought before to explain the revolt. Some historians have found a pure Marxist

attitude in the use of rabbinic material for political history before A.D. 70, see the cautious discussion by S. J. D. Cohen, *Josephus in Galilee and Rome* (Leiden, 1979), pp. 253–60.

[40] For summary accounts of current knowledge, see Yadin, *Jerusalem Revealed*, and Avigad, *Discovering Jerusalem*.

[41] See L. Kadman, *The Coins of the Jewish War of 66–73 C.E.* (Tel Aviv, 1960); Y. Meshorer, *Ancient Jewish Coinage*, 2 vols. (New York, 1982).

analysis appropriate. Others have looked for parallels in the nationalist revolutions of nineteenth-century Europe or the course of the French Revolution and its aftermath.[42] But it seems to me that models based on other societies and periods of history are so liable to misleading anachronism that, when this is possible, they should only be used to provide a check on results achieved first from the ancient evidence, and that it is not desirable to use them as the basic framework into which the evidence is to be fitted. I have preferred instead, by analysis of provincial administration elsewhere in the empire, to build up a full picture of the way that the Romans are likely to have tried to govern Judaea; from examination of the Jewish sources to estimate the probable Jewish reaction to those methods; and finally to show how one possible reaction might lead to revolt. This purely theoretical model has then been checked against the detailed evidence in Josephus.

I shall be satisfied if this procedure can make plausible the importance of the power struggle within the ruling class as one of the crucial factors which led to the outbreak of the Jewish revolt. I shall begin by showing what sort of men belonged to this class and what function the Romans expected them to fulfil in the province. I shall then examine their relations with the Roman governors and their fellow Jews. Finally, in the second part of the book, I shall discuss the way their faction fighting contributed to the outbreak and course of the war.

[42] An explicit Marxist analysis can be found in Kreissig, *Die sozialen Zusammenhänge*, and an implicit nationalist explanation in Y. Baer, 'Jerusalem in the times of the Great Revolt', *Zion* 36 (1971) 127–90; 37 (1972) 120 (Heb.). Rajak, *Josephus*, pp. 127–8, uses the French Revolution as a model.

PART I

THE RULING CLASS A.D. 6–66

CHAPTER 2

THE NEW RULING CLASS A.D. 6

It was normal Roman practice in the incorporation of a new province into direct rule to build upon existing institutions, and to depose the existing local leaders from power only when it seemed absolutely necessary. It will therefore be helpful in trying to understand the composition of the Judaean ruling class through which Rome ruled from A.D. 6 to 66 to delve back some way into the earlier history of the area.

The independent Jewish state of Judah came to an end in 586 B.C. with the destruction of Jerusalem by the Babylonians. Much of the population was carried off into exile in Mesopotamia. For many, the catastrophe seemed permanent, and they tried to build new lives, and new religious explanations of the world, in a foreign land. Babylon in turn, however, fell in 539 B.C. to Cyrus, the energetic king of Persia, and under his patronage and that of his successor the Jews began to revive their national life in Judah. The temple was gradually rebuilt and the High Priest was eventually recognized by the suzerain as the leader of the nation. This small Persian province was distinctively Jewish. The local representatives of the Persian king are known to have been in some cases Jews who maintained close, if not always friendly, relations with the governor of the neighbouring province of Samaria. Thus by the end of the Persian period Jerusalem was the centre of a small and economically backward but well-established Jewish community, accustomed to considerable autonomy, particularly in religious affairs, and unified around the Temple and the High Priest.[1]

Change was instituted by events far away. Between 334 and 330 B.C. Alexander of Macedon conquered the Persian empire. Palestine fell into his hands in 331 B.C. The area seems to have escaped

---

[1] See W. D. Davies and L. Finkelstein, eds., *The Cambridge History of Judaism* I (1984). Little more can be said about the Persian period with any certainty than the facts given in this paragraph.

unscathed from his campaigns, but it suffered in the wars between his generals which followed his death in 323 B.C., until the battle of Gaza in 312 B.C. gave control of the country to one of them, Ptolemy I Soter, ruler of Egypt. The Ptolemies were to retain Palestine for over a century, exploiting the fertile flat lands with greater intensity than the Persians and creating something of an economic boom. Under them and under the rival Seleucid dynasty based in Syria, which successfully wrested control of Palestine from the Ptolemies in 198 B.C after many ineffective attempts, the rulers of the Jews remained normally the High Priests, as in Persian times. Since this office was in effect hereditary it permitted great continuity, though one exception to continuous high-priestly control is recorded in some detail by Josephus in the history of the Tobiads, local rulers in Transjordan who gained the right to farm the taxes of Palestine on behalf of the Ptolemies by promising a greater return than that provided by the High Priest of the day. Despite the machinations of this family, contemporary Greek sources affirm that Jews were a nation dedicated to religion and ruled by priests. The essence of their nation lay in the Temple in Jerusalem.[2]

It is not then surprising that the attempt in 167 B.C. by the Seleucid king Antiochus IV Epiphanes to abolish the Temple cult met with fierce resistance. It is not necessary here to discuss the reasons for Antiochus' behaviour[3] but only to see the effect of the resistance he provoked on patterns of power in Judaean society. The leaders of the opposition to Antiochus were the family of the Maccabees. They were supported by a volunteer peasant army, fired with religious zeal. They won few military victories but contrived to extort from the Seleucid kings, who were harassed by dynastic pretenders and Roman interference as well as by the break-up of other parts of their extended domain, both religious tolerance and, by 129 B.C., recognition of their political independence.

By that time the normal patterns of Jewish authority had been reasserted. The leaders of the nation were again High Priests. But since 152 B.C. these High Priests were all from the family of the Maccabees. The old family of the Oniads, who had monopolized the

---

[2] Cf. Hecataeus in Diodorus Siculus 40. 3.1–8. On this whole period, see M. Hengel, *Judaism and Hellenism: studies in their encounter in Palestine during the early Hellenistic period*, E.T., 2 vols. (London, 1974). See also V. A. Tcherikover, *Hellenistic Civilization and the Jews*, transl. by S. Applebaum (Philadelphia, 1959).

[3] See the discussion in E. J. Bickerman, *The God of the Maccabees: studies on the meaning and origin of the Maccabean revolt*, E.T. (Leiden, 1979). For a contrasting view, see Millar, 'The background to the Maccabean revolution'.

office since at least the mid third century B.C., were ousted, some of them taking refuge in Egypt and finding employment as mercenaries for the Ptolemies. The Maccabees established a new dynasty, known to Josephus and later historians as the Hasmonaeans.

The opportunities facing the vigorous Hasmonaean rulers were particularly favourable in the late second and the early first centuries B.C. The old hellenistic kingdoms which had been established by the successors of Alexander were gradually breaking up under the pressure of Roman expansion. Like Mithridates to the north and the Nabataean kings to the south, the Hasmonaeans carved out for themselves a great territory, encompassing by the sixties B.C. Galilee, Transjordan, Idumaea and much of the coastal plain of Palestine.

By that stage, however, their rule was no longer based on the peasant religious enthusiasm with which they had begun, nor on the prestige of the high priesthood which they had usurped, but on the trappings of hellenistic kingship. The Hasmonaean Simon had been recognized by the Seleucids as ethnarch in 141 B.C.; either Aristobulus I in 104–103 B.C. or his successor Alexander Jannaeus took the title of king. The presumption that secular authority could be divorced from the office of High Priest was already evident in the terms of the will of John Hyrcanus (135/4–104 B.C.), for he stipulated (unsuccessfully) that secular authority should devolve, astonishingly for Jewish society in which women were usually excluded from political power, upon his wife (*A.J.* 13.302). Similarly Alexander Jannaeus was succeeded by his wife Alexandra, who ruled from 76 to 67 B.C. The power of these kings and queens rested on their mercenary armies, comprised mostly of non-Jews and paid for out of the revenue from their conquests. The title 'Philhellene' adopted by Aristobulus I in 103 B.C. proclaimed the interests of the dynasty in the wider Mediterranean world. It was no accident that the rule of such monarchs was sometimes marred by popular unrest.[4]

This was the Jewish state with which Pompey was faced on his arrival in the East in 66 B.C. On Alexandra's death in 67 B.C. a civil war had broken out between her sons, Aristobulus and Hyrcanus. Hyrcanus, the elder son and legitimate heir both to the high priesthood and to the royal title, was removed from power by Aristobulus after a battle near Jericho. This provided a perfect excuse for Roman intervention: when Pompey conquered Jerusalem in 63 B.C. he was ostensibly restoring Hyrcanus to his rightful position. Roman arms

---

[4] For a more detailed history, see Schürer, *History* i, pp. 137–242.

ensured, however, that Hyrcanus' status was more like that of the Jewish High Priests of old. Deprived of the title of king and of the lands acquired by his forbears, he presided over a city subject to Roman taxation and direction. Once again, as in Persian times, the High Priest was only the mediator between suzerain and people.

Even that position was at the discretion of Rome, as Gabinius showed in 57 B.C. by confining Hyrcanus' power to the care and custody of the Temple and dividing the country into five districts, one of which was Jerusalem, which were to be ruled by aristocratic councils. Hyrcanus himself, a weak man and advised by the ambitious governor of Idumaea, Antipater, who appears to have been shrewdly aware of the advantages to himself of supporting Rome at all times, seems to have accepted this diminution in his power without complaint. His deposed brother Aristobulus, and Aristobulus' son Alexander, were less inclined to allow their dynasty to be confined to a purely religious role. They led uprisings against Rome in 57, 56 and 55 B.C. When they apparently no longer had the energy to struggle, a certain Pitholaus took the same path of revolt in 53 B.C.

It was apparent to the Romans that some of the Hasmonaean dynasty were too ambitious to be trustworthy as client rulers, and that the others, notably Hyrcanus, lacked the support within the Jewish nation that might enable them to control a stable puppet state on Rome's behalf. It was thus without enthusiasm that Roman governors from Pompey to the end of the fifties B.C. supported Hyrcanus. Caesar actually attempted to remove him from power in 49 B.C. by using Aristobulus and Alexander against him as part of a campaign to subvert Pompey's cause in Syria, but when this came to nothing after Aristobulus and Alexander were murdered by Pompey's supporters, Caesar too elected to give all support to Hyrcanus.

But Caesar's backing for the Hasmonaean king was lukewarm. His real trust was put in the Idumaean Antipater, Hyrcanus' closest supporter and adviser. On Antipater's death in 43 B.C. his position as the chief repository of Roman confidence was inherited by his sons Phasael and Herod. Herod's services in collecting taxes for the murderer of Caesar, Cassius, had already won him in 43 B.C. an appointment as *strategos* of Coele-Syria. In 41 B.C. he and Phasael were appointed by Mark Antony as tetrarchs of the Jewish territory under Hyrcanus' nominal rule. It is therefore not entirely surprising that, when Hyrcanus was taken prisoner in 40 B.C. by the Parthians and replaced as both king and High Priest by his nephew Antigonus, Aristobulus' last surviving son, the Roman senate retaliated by declaring Herod king of Judaea and entrusting him with the task of recapturing the territory for himself and for Rome.[5]

Herod's victory was in practice achieved, in 37 B.C., only through the force of the Roman legions. Though married to Mariamme, a granddaughter of Hyrcanus, he could claim no legitimacy as a Jewish king. The high priesthood, the traditional post for the leader of the Jewish nation since Persian times, was also beyond his grasp, for he was not a priest and, indeed, only half a Jew. His power therefore rested entirely on the support first of Mark Antony and then, after Actium, of Octavian, soon to be called the emperor Augustus. He preserved order in the province by instilling fear through his use of mercenary forces and his ability when necessary to conjure up the violence of Roman armies against any who opposed him.

Dynastic intrigue removed, in Herod's lifetime, his two sons by Mariamme who, as descendants of the Hasmonaean line, might have won more popular support among Jews than he could himself command. His appointed successor, Archelaus, proved unable in his ten-year reign (4 B.C. to A.D. 6) to control the hostile population with the ruthless efficiency of his father. Hence his removal, and the beginning of direct Roman rule.[6]

It will be apparent that the problems facing the first Roman governor were not trivial. The procurator was provided by the state with only a small staff to help in the administration of the country, for there was no developed civil service at this period. His aides were chosen by him from among his friends and from within his own household. Since Judaea was a small province and not strategically vital to the eastern frontier, being protected by the Syrian province to the north, the procurator was not even allowed more than a few troops, though he could rely on military intervention from Syria if he found himself in serious difficulties. Stable government was thus possible only with the cooperation of the leaders of the local population.

In other provinces such cooperation by a local elite was an assumed and important element of Roman administration. Local magnates kept order through their prestige among the rest of the population. In their own right they might control a small force of light-armed troops for police work. They used their local knowledge to collect census statistics and were responsible for the gathering of the taxes so crucial for the consumer society in the city of Rome. Above all, they represented Rome to the subject population and the

---

[5] For the history of the last Hasmonaeans, see Schürer, *History* i, pp. 267–86.
[6] On Herod, see A. Schalit, *König Herodes: Der Mann und sein Werk* (Berlin, 1969).

subject population to Rome, going on embassies to governors and emperors with the permission and blessing of the Roman state. This was a crucial function: it was not dangerous for Rome if disaffected peasants in the countryside stayed unrepresented, since they were too disorganized to cause serious trouble, but riots in the cities of the empire threatened the good order of the society as it was perceived by the Romans themselves, and they believed that urban unrest could only be properly controlled through such representation by a trusted elite.

In return for their services the local aristocracies could usually expect to receive benefits from Rome. Prime among these was Roman confirmation and support for their local prestige, but they could also hope to make some profit by creaming off some of the income from tax collection. Eventually they could expect Roman citizenship and would thus merge into the Roman governing class itself, through service in the Roman army or as representatives (procurators) of the emperors.[7]

In many provinces the selection of the elite for this function as a local ruling class was straightforward, for the Romans had a clear understanding of the qualities they required of an aristocracy. These qualities were naturally derived from those accorded high status within their own society. In Rome a clearly defined status group, the senators, monopolized control of military, legal and religious affairs. According to the senators' own self-image, membership of that status group depended primarily on good birth and high morals (*virtus*), but one other criterion was in fact so basic to senatorial status that it did not even need to be stressed. All senators had to be rich. Loss of wealth led to loss of eligibility for office. When a senator in the reign of Tiberius fell below the required census level, it proved impossible to waive the social convention: he remained in the *ordo* only through a personal subvention by the emperor (Tac. *Ann.* 1.75). By contrast, the success of many *novi homines* and of senators described, at least by their enemies, as wicked, shows that the more vociferously pro-

[7] For the small size of a Roman governor's staff, see Millar, *Emperor in the Roman World*, p. 16. On the composition and recruitment of the garrison of Judaea, see Schürer, *History* I, pp. 362–7, but note the arguments of Speidel, 'The Roman army in Judaea', that some auxiliaries were recruited outside the province, at least in A.D. 6. On the administrative functions of local aristocracies, see P. A. Brunt, 'Did imperial Rome disarm her subjects?', *Phoenix* 29 (1975) 264; *idem*, 'The romanization of the local ruling classes in the Roman empire', in D. M. Pippidi, ed., *Assimilation et résistance à la culture greco-romaine dans le monde ancien* (Madrid, 1976), pp. 161–7. For their gradual incorporation into the Roman governing class, see G. W. Bowersock, *Augustus and the Greek World* (Oxford, 1965).

claimed characteristics of the Roman aristocracy were less crucial to high social status.

Rome was in fact a census-based society which, probably because of its early militaristic history, had always given precedence to the rich, who could serve the state more effectively in war because of their superior armour, than to their poorer compatriots. Rome never quite degenerated into a pure plutocracy, as is clear from the refusal of the governing class graciously to accept rich imperial freedmen among their number because of their servile origins despite their great wealth (cf. Pliny, *Epp.* 7.29; 8.6), but the importance of wealth as a status criterion increased rather than diminished with the fall of the Republic and concentration of power in the hands of one man. As some of the private agents (procurators) of the emperors gradually took on more and more public and official roles in provincial administration during the first century A.D., it was (apart from the use of a few trusted imperial freedmen) only to equites, that is, Roman citizens who owned more than four hundred thousand sesterces, that such positions were entrusted.[8]

The Roman governing class applied these criteria with which they were familiar from their own society to select the provincial elites through which their government could control the empire. Romans always tended to see other cultures in their own terms, and this ethnographic illiteracy, in which they were and are not alone, had acted more often than not to their advantage. So, for instance, Rome's disregard for the rules of Greek diplomacy, and her treatment of alliances with Greek states in the Middle Republic in the light of her own notions that her allies were in effect subject to her direction in foreign policy, may have eased the path to her domination of the eastern Mediterranean. The Romans therefore expected to find in each province a clearly defined aristocracy which, like their own, would be in control of war, law, religion and politics, and membership of which would be confined to the landed rich.

Handing over power to such men would also have practical advantages. The desire to preserve their property would keep such

---

[8] On Roman status criteria in this period, see C. Nicolet in F. Millar and E. Segal, eds., *Caesar Augustus: seven aspects* (Oxford, 1984), pp. 89–128. On procurators, see H.-G. Pflaum, *Les carrières procuratoriennes équestres sous le Haut-Empire romain*, 4 vols. (Paris, 1960–1). In the late first century A.D. it began to be possible to earn social prestige through intellectual brilliance (cf. G. W. Bowersock, *Greek Sophists in the Roman Empire* (Oxford, 1969)), but such intellectuals were always suspect in the eyes of traditional aristocrats: sophists were vulnerable to charges of magic, cf. Apuleius (*Apologia sive pro se de magia*) and, in a later period, Libanius (cf. P. R. L. Brown, *Religion and Society in the Age of Saint Augustine* (London, 1972), pp. 127–8).

local leaders in favour of peace and therefore Rome, and their ownership of sufficient wealth would enable them to ensure regular payment of taxes from their own resources even if they came up against difficulties in collecting the required tribute from the rest of the population. Utility thus supported prejudice. During the steady conquest of her empire Rome had always favoured the rich oligarchies of the states with which she came into contact, playing on this fact in, for instance, her relations with Greek cities in the second century B.C., to win greater influence in their internal affairs by partisan support for one element of the population. Once the empire was won, the policy remained. Rome ruled the provinces through the support of the rich provincials.[9]

In many provinces a wealthy aristocracy similar to that in Rome was indeed easily distinguished. In Greece and Asia Minor, for instance, political power had since the age of the tyrants no longer rested on descent but was mainly dependent on the possession of property. The rule of the rich was the standard form of Greek oligarchy. In parts of Syria the local dynasts, such as the priest-kings of Emesa, had adapted their political expectations to hellenistic norms in the same way as the Hasmonaeans in Judaea had done before the Roman conquest, and they too were thus well fitted to play the role of a landed elite. The Romans were happy to leave them in possession of their local prestige; it was to their mutual advantage.[10]

The options facing the Romans when they imposed direct rule on Judaea in A.D. 6 were, however, not so straightforward. Rome had tried to rule through the incumbent elite when she first interfered in the province's affairs: thus Pompey left Hyrcanus in control of Judaea in 63 B.C. But with the demise of the Hasmonaean dynasty in 37 B.C. that course was no longer open. It is probable that some of the leading Jewish supporters of the Hasmonaean kings might have carried the support of the people: Josephus in his narrative of the mid first century B.C. speaks not infrequently of the notables (*dunatoi*) of the Jews as if they were such a natural elite, and claims that such men met Pompey at Damascus in 63 B.C. to ask him to restrict the

[9] On the Roman tendency to favour rich oligarchs, cf. Brunt, 'The romanization of the local ruling classes', and G. E. M. de Ste Croix, *The Class Struggle in the Ancient Greek World* (London, 1981), pp. 518–37, esp. pp. 519, 530.

[10] On Greece, see De Ste Croix, *Class Struggle*, p. 280; on the eastern empire in general, see Bowersock, *Augustus and the Greek World*, pp. 30–61 and *passim*. Wealth-based oligarchies had also been available for Rome to use in gaining control of Italy during the Republic, cf. Brunt, 'The romanization of the local ruling classes', pp. 167–70, but the position may have been more complex in northern provinces (see below, Chapter 10).

power of the Hasmonaean High Priest to a religious and representative role, and to hand over secular authority to them. It can further be assumed that these are the men who Gabinius assumed would be willing to rule the province on Rome's behalf through the regional councils which he set up in 57 B.C.[11] But it is impossible to tell whether these 'notables' in the mid first century B.C. did in fact represent a clearly defined independent group of Jewish aristocratic landowners, or simply the courtiers of one Hasmonaean prince or another (cf., for example, *B.J.* 1.242, about events in 42 B.C.). Nor is it certain whether such men were rich, although wealth was a necessary requirement for a local elite to be recognized by Rome, as has been seen; the striking characteristic of most Jewish leaders before Herod is in fact the origin of their authority not in wealth but in a religious function, usually that of priest.[12] It is of course possible that leading priests had collected much land in Judaea by the end of the Hasmonaean period, but this seems unlikely, especially if, as is often claimed, much of the country was royal property in this period.[13]

---

[11] Cf. Smallwood, *Jews*, pp. 22,32–3. It should be noted that the councils created by Gabinius seem to have paid little regard to local conditions. Their detailed functions and their composition are unknown, but they were either abolished by Caesar without fuss or had already withered away before 49 B.C. Gabinius' prime motive may have been to block the efforts of Roman *publicani*, whom he strongly opposed, to profit by farming the Judaean taxes. D. C. Braund, 'Gabinius, Caesar and the *publicani* of Judaea', *Klio* 65 (1983) 241–4, argues that Gabinius acted against the interests of the *publicani* but did not actually expel them.

[12] See Millar, 'The background to the Maccabean revolution'; both Morton Smith in *CHJ* I, pp. 248–56, and Hengel, *Judaism and Hellenism* I, pp. 26,35,49–50, 267–8, write plausibly about a secular landed lay aristocracy as a constant element of Judaean society from the Persian to the end of the Roman period. This aristocracy is said to have acted as a counter to the priestly elite. But the evidence for a lay aristocracy lies primarily in *a priori* assumptions about the attribution of surviving texts (e.g. *Judith*) to such a group.

[13] Cf. S. Applebaum, 'Economic life in Palestine', in S. Safrai and M. Stern, eds., *The Jewish People in the First Century (Compendia Rerum Iudaicarum ad Novum Testamentum*, Sect. 1), 2 vols. (Assen, 1974–6) II, pp. 635–6. The evidence is in fact tenuous. According to *t.Men.* 9.13, which is an early third-century A.D. text in its present form, portions of the Judaean hills were known colloquially as the 'Mountain of the King'. There is no evidence of Herodian or imperial Roman land in this area, so the name probably derives from an earlier period. The only *explicit* evidence to link royal ownership with the late Hasmonaeans is, however, a quite fantastic tale about King Yannai (Alexander Jannaeus) preserved in a collection of boastful stories about the distant past that is quoted in the fifth-century A.D. Babylonian Talmud (*b.Gitt.* 57a).

Nonetheless it is more likely than not that these traditions have some basis in fact. In the earlier (Davidic) monarchy Jewish kings had probably levied taxes of a tenth of the yield to pay for the state's business (cf. 1 Sam. 8.15,17), but, since the return from exile in the sixth century B.C., such tithes had been expropriated by the

Late Hasmonaean monarchs had no reason to grant great estates to their Jewish supporters, except when they required them as border troops for the expanded kingdom in Idumaea and Galilee, for most of the soldiers in the field armies on which the kings relied were probably non-Jewish mercenaries.[14]

But, even if there were families favoured both by the Hasmonaeans and by the populace, and even if such men were more acceptable to Rome as a local elite than I have suggested was probably the case, they were not available in A.D. 6 for Rome to adopt as a provincial ruling class, since, perhaps in imitation of his Roman masters, Herod had carried out proscriptions of the leading Hasmonaean courtiers once he was firmly established in power in 37 B.C. Forty-five 'notables' of Antigonus' party were killed, and the others disappeared altogether from the historical record (*B.J.* 1.358; cf. *A.J.* 14.175; 15.6). Of all the families influential in Judaea before Herod, only that of Josephus is known to have retained any importance after A.D. 6. Herod was not worried by unruly barons left over from past regimes, for, in the fashion characteristic of hellenistic monarchs, he ensured that all power within his realm stemmed from his patronage alone.[15]

There was thus no natural Judaean elite to which Rome could turn on Herod's death in 4 B.C. or the deposition of Archelaus in A.D. 6, despite the fact that, on both occasions, the Romans much wished that such an elite did exist.

In 4 B.C. the legate of Syria, Varus, faced by a province in turmoil because of the unsatisfactory will left by Herod, seems to have attempted to circumvent the machinations of the surviving

Temple, and a Jewish king and High Priest who tried to use the money for secular purposes would be guilty of sacrilege. Royal ownership of land was thus the safest way to ensure a steady income for the state. Rent could presumably be as high as a third of production; such figures are common elsewhere in the history of the precapitalist economy, cf. T. J. Byres, 'Sharecropping in historical perspective: a general treatment', *Journal of Peasant Studies* 10 (1983) 7–40.

[14] The Herodian family favoured by Rome in 40 B.C. probably owned large estates, but they probably lay in Idumaea rather than Judaea; cf. M. Gichon, 'Idumea and the Herodian limes', *IEJ* 17 (1967) 27–42, on the Idumaean border troops in the Hasmonaean period and the function of Herod's father, Antipater, as their commander. It has also been suggested that the continuous resistance against the Herodian family led by Hezekiah in 47 B.C. and by his son Judas in 4 B.C. was possible because Hezekiah was the commander of Hasmonaean troops in Galilee and his family had been granted land there for military service, cf. S. Freyne, *Galilee from Alexander the Great to Hadrian, 323 B.C.E. to 135 C.E.* (Notre Dame, 1980), p. 63.

[15] On the total disappearance of the Hasmonaean elite, see M. Stern, 'Aspects of Jewish society: the priesthood and other classes', in Safrai and Stern, *The Jewish People* II, p. 570.

Herodian princes by cobbling together a delegation of Jews to request from Augustus the abolition of the monarchy and the transfer of Judaea to his direct control (*A.J.* 17.314). If *epitrepsantos* at *B.J.* 2.80 means 'command' rather than 'permit', Josephus may attribute the whole idea of this delegation to Varus himself, but the wording of the parallel passage at *A.J.* 17.300 makes such an interpretation uncertain. At any rate it is unlikely that the Jews sent to Rome were genuine representatives of the Judaeans.[16]

Similarly, Josephus reports that a delegation of leading Jews went to Rome in A.D. 6 to request the removal of Archelaus from power (*A.J.* 17.342), but the genuineness and voluntary nature of this embassy too is extremely suspect. Despite the general complaints which the ambassadors are said to have brought against Archelaus that he was brutal and tyrannical, Josephus, although neither sympathetic to the man nor inclined to skimp the narrative at this point, cites no examples of such behaviour. Cassius Dio (55.27.6) states that the accusation against Archelaus was in fact brought by his brothers. This is also the most natural meaning of the contemporary but somewhat enigmatic account by Strabo (*Geog.* 16.2.46), and such dynastic intrigue seems to me the most likely explanation of Archelaus' demise.

At any rate, the alacrity of Augustus in responding to the delegation by summoning Archelaus to Rome suggests that he was waiting only for an excuse to remove him.[17] Nor is it hard to explain his desire to impose direct rule on Judaea. Archelaus' property was confiscated to the imperial treasury (*B.J.* 2.111) and, if he had been excused from paying tribute to Rome as is possible, the imposition of direct tax on the province was financially valuable for Rome.[18]

[16] The riots at Pentecost in 4 B.C. were not caused by the failure of this embassy (cf. Smallwood, *Jews*, p. 111 n. 24, on the chronology). One of the problems in discussing the embassies of 4 B.C. is that the content of the speeches of the ambassadors as recorded by Josephus does not accord with the demands ascribed to the speakers by the historian (Smallwood, *Jews*, pp. 108–9 nn. 14 and 19). The speeches are perhaps the more trustworthy since they were taken by Josephus from Nicolaus of Damascus who had himself been present. According to the speech ascribed to Varus' delegation, their main demand was to be put under the control of the legate of Syria (*B.J.* 2.91).

[17] Cf. Smallwood, *Jews*, p. 117. The massive support for direct Roman rule demonstrated by the Jewish community in the city of Rome itself (*B.J.* 2.80) was probably owing to their prejudice against the Herodian family: many Roman Jews in this period will have been descended from the captives of Herod and Sosius sold into slavery in 37 B.C. (Smallwood, *Jews*, p. 131).

[18] For this problem see above, Chapter 1 n. 16. Other reasons for Augustus' decision to remove Archelaus can be surmised. Perhaps Archelaus' loyalty was sus-

Certainly, it is most unlikely that Augustus was in any way pushed into installing a procurator in A.D. 6. It was always possible for him to replace Archelaus with one of his half-brothers. Antipas in particular had some support in Judaea (cf. *B.J.* 2.22) and up to this time he is not known to have shown any faults as a ruler in Galilee.

Finding no natural landed elite in Judaea but needing the co-operation of local rulers of some kind for their administration to work successfully, the Romans elected to entrust power to those Judaean landowners who did exist, regardless of whether such men could command any popular prestige. These men were the creatures of Herod who had been granted land and position within the state since 37 B.C.

The problem with such Jewish landowners from the point of view of the theory of Roman provincial administration was that they were despised by the very populace that they were meant to lead. On Herod's death one of the main demands of the people was the deposition of his favourites from positions of importance such as the high priesthood (*B.J.* 2.7).

Nor was this lack of prestige an accidental fact. Herod's own status as only half-Jew was precarious in the eyes of his subjects, as the number of fortresses he built to ensure their subjection shows he was well aware. He could not afford the rivalry of popular Jewish aristocrats. In so far as he could, therefore, he relied upon the friendship of non-Jews. His closest friend was the Spartan adventurer Eurycles (*B.J.* 1.515). His army commanders were pagan, occasionally indeed probably Roman (cf. *B.J.* 2.52, 74). So were the tutors and eunuchs employed within his court.[19] The Jews he did trust in powerful positions of state were either members of his own family, a remarkable number of whom were given great responsibility at various times, or fellow Idumaeans; in both cases the dis-

pected by Augustus' new successor-designate, Tiberius, since his appointment as ethnarch had been approved by the first imperial council of state at which Tiberius' arch-rival, Gaius, attended (cf. *B.J.* 2.25). Or Archelaus' marriage to Glaphyra, ex-wife of Juba, king of Mauretania, and a favourite of Gaius (cf. the Athenian inscription in her honour, *OGIS* 363), may have earned Tiberius' enmity. On the power struggle between Tiberius and Gaius, see G. W. Bowersock in Millar and Segal, eds., *Caesar Augustus*, pp. 169–88.

[19] Schürer, *History* I, pp. 310–11. Herod also used Samaritans according to Nicolaus of Damascus (Jacoby, *FGrH* 90,F136(8)). Herod's financial minister named Ptolemy may have been Jewish, but he was more probably gentile like Nicolaus of Damascus' brother, who bore the same name. Nothing more is heard of either Ptolemy in Judaean society after A.D. 6.

abilities of Idumaean birth prevented such men being a threat to his power.[20]

For certain public positions, however, these options were not open to him. Prime among these was the high priesthood, for which only priests were eligible. Entrusting the honour to the surviving male members of the Hasmonaean dynasty had proved dangerous already by 35 B.C., when Herod had the young Aristobulus III murdered in Jericho (*B.J.* 1.437). For the rest of his long reign Herod therefore deliberately chose nonentities to fill the post. The High Priests he appointed almost all came from Alexandria and Babylonia, from families which had hitherto had no connection with Judaean politics and which could therefore claim no allegiance from any section of the population. Their only qualification for office came from the purity of their priestly lineage. They were deliberately excluded from secular affairs, and their influence was confined by Herod to the management of the Temple. Lest even this prestige should render them dangerous, their status in the eyes of the Jews was further undermined by Herod's adoption of the hellenistic custom of occasionally transferring the office to a new incumbent on the bases of whim and political calculation. In thirty-three years no fewer than seven High Priests were appointed.

One of these High Priests, a certain Joseph b. Ellem, held the office for one day only (*A.J.* 17.166). It may be no coincidence that he is the only incumbent who may have come from Palestine: according to the Tosefta and the Jerusalem Talmud (*t.Yom.* 1.4; *y. Yom.* 1.38d), he originated in Sepphoris in Galilee. This tradition is not certainly correct, for it was not recorded by Josephus, who described Joseph only as a relative of Matthias b. Theophilus, who was a native of Jerusalem (*A.J.* 17.78). Suspicion about the accuracy of the rabbinic texts is aroused by the facts that Sepphoris was a major centre of Jewish culture when the Tosefta and Talmud were compiled in the third to fifth centuries A.D. and that R. Yose b. Halafta, in whose name the tradition is cited, came from Sepphoris; it is a characteristic of talmudic story-tellers to link tales of the past to the politics and geography of their own society. But if the tradition is correct, the brevity of Joseph's tenure highlights rather than contra-

[20] Of Herod's family, note Phasael, Joseph, Pheroras and Ahiab apart from his own sons; of Idumaeans, note particularly the career of Costobar in Idumaea (*A.J.* 15.253–5). Costobar married into the Herodian family, cf. *B.J.* 1.486. On Idumaean birth as a disability in Judaea, see below, p. 223.

dicts Herod's normal policy in preferring to elevate foreigners to such positions.[21]

Of the four families elevated to the High Priesthood in this way by Herod, one only, that of Simon b. Boethus, the longest serving High Priest of Herod's reign (*c.* 24–5 B.C.), could expect some prominence in court circles. Simon was the father of one of Herod's wives, the second Mariamme; the king presumably hoped to gain some respectability in the eyes of his Jewish subjects by having a High Priest as a father-in-law. It would however be mistaken to believe that this royal connection gave the Boethusian house any more popular prestige in Judaea than the other high-priestly families which were not favoured by Herod in this way. One of the main demands of the rioters who greeted Archelaus after Herod's death was that the Boethusian High Priest Joazar should be deposed from office. In their eyes his piety was dubious precisely because of his close ties to the Idumaean court (*A.J.* 17.207).[22] It can thus be firmly stated that even by A.D. 6 none of the priestly families given land and promoted to high office by Herod had won any prestige in their own right in the eyes of the Judaean populace. In Judaean society they still were, as they had been when plucked from obscurity by Herod, nonentities or worse.

Nonetheless it was to such High Priests that Rome handed over power in A.D. 6 (*A.J.* 20.251). It might seem a little strange that the Romans desired these priests as rulers rather than Herod's Idumaean associates, especially since by the fifties A.D. the relatives both of Herod himself and of Herod's close Idumaean friend Alexas (cf. *A.J.* 19.353 on the prefect Helcias) did indeed become prominent in Judaean politics; it might reasonably be expected that when the province was founded such Idumaeans would already gladly

---

[21] For this policy as deliberate, see Schürer, *History* 1.313. The origins in Sepphoris of Joseph b. Ellem are accepted by S. S. Miller, *Studies in the History and Traditions of Sepphoris* (Leiden, 1984), pp. 63–88.

It is worth noting also that if the formal political authority of Torah scholars, and particularly of Pharisees, was more firmly established under Herod than I have assumed (and see below, pp. 74 and 209 n. 14, for arguments in favour of this view), it may be significant that the Talmud preserves a tradition about the prominence in this period of certain sages called the 'sons of Bathyra' whom it is natural if hazardous to identify with the Babylonian Jews settled by Herod as a garrison in Bathyra in Batanaea (*A.J.* 17.26), cf. Alon, *Jews, Judaism and the Classical World*, pp. 328–34. Note too the suggestion by Ben-Shalom, 'The Shammai school' p. 201, that the Pharisee Hillel owed his prominence to Herod's patronage which was given to him also because of his Babylonian origins (cf. *b.Pes.* 66a), and that he was thus dependent on and loyal to Herod's regime.

[22] On the house of Boethus, see Stern, 'Aspects of Jewish society', pp. 604–6.

have cooperated with Rome and that, although some of them had rebelled against Archelaus in 4 B.C. and been severely punished for their temerity (*B.J.* 2.76–8), the Romans would have trusted them usually to remain loyal. But Josephus does not attest any role at all for such men in the early years of the province and, though it is possible that this silence arises from the historian's comparative ignorance about the period of the first procurators,[23] it is more likely that they remained in political isolation on their estates in the southern part of the province until Agrippa I brought them into prominence in Judaea during his brief but popular reign.[24]

For in fact the prominence of the high-priestly families at the start of Roman rule was quite certainly a deliberate policy by the suzerain. It was normal Roman practice not only to trust existing local leaders but also, and just as importantly, whenever possible to leave established local institutions intact when a province was created (see below, pp. 109–16). In the case of Judaea the obvious institution which might be expected to provide the desired impression of peace and continuity within the country was the Temple and its priesthood. The influence of Herod's Idumaean friends, by contrast, had never been founded in any institutional role; they were merely the king's courtiers. It was just unfortunate, for Rome and for themselves, that the High Priests thus entrusted with power were, because of Herod's deliberate tactics, weak men who lacked the local prestige which might have enabled them to carry the people with them on behalf of Rome.

That these puppet rulers did indeed fail in this task from the very beginning in A.D. 6 can be best demonstrated from the unhappy fate of the high-priestly family already discussed, that of Boethus. Joazar b. Boethus, the High Priest in office in A.D. 6 as in 4 B.C., was entrusted with the function, standard for local rulers acting on behalf of Rome, of helping to organize the census. He was faced by widespread discontent and rioting and a minor rebellion led by a certain Judas the Galilean. The census was pushed through despite

[23] The period A.D. 6 to A.D. 50 falls between the events for which Josephus used the evidence of Nicolaus of Damascus and those of which he had first-hand knowledge. The greater circumstantial detail in *A.J.* compared to *B.J.* may suggest that Josephus had found a new source after completing the *B.J.*, but it is more probably because of the different aim of the later work.

[24] See below, p. 141. On the family of Alexas, cf. Stern, 'Aspects of Jewish society', pp. 612–13; *idem*, 'Social and political realignments in Herodian Judaea', *The Jerusalem Cathedra* 2 (1982) 48. His descendants were prominent in Judaea in the mid-sixties A.D. (see below, p. 141). The influence of the family was boosted by Agrippa I's patronage of Helcias (*A.J.* 19.353).

everything, but Joazar was so widely hated after it that his deposition from the high priesthood was successfully demanded by the people within a few months (*A.J.* 18.26), and the family of Boethus did not produce another High Priest until Agrippa I revived their influence.

Faced by this evidence of the lack of local prestige enjoyed by Herod's creatures, the Roman governor appointed a High Priest from a family probably never previously honoured with the post. Ananus b. Sethi was a figure unknown before Roman rule plucked him from obscurity on the grounds of his priestly birth and, presumably, since he would otherwise have been ineligible in Roman eyes, his wealth (*A.J.* 18.26). His family was to dominate the high priesthood in the next sixty years: he was himself High Priest for nine years, and all five of his sons held the position (*A.J.* 20.198). But in every case their right to lead the Jewish nation rested, as his had done, entirely on the whim of the Romans, or in later cases Herodian princes, who appointed them.[25]

Neither the ciphers trusted by Herod nor the rich new men thrust into positions of importance *faute de mieux* by Roman governors could command the respect and trust of the nation which, according to the Roman view of things, they were expected to lead. This did not prevent the Romans from treating them as if they were such natural leaders. As elsewhere in the empire, the ruling class in Judaea was expected to resist open refusal to collaborate with the census (*A.J.* 18.3), to collect the tribute (*B.J.* 2.405), and to send embassies on behalf of the nation to Rome (e.g. *A.J.* 20.8). When Claudius wrote to the people of Judaea he assumed that they had a natural aristocracy as in a normal Greek city, addressing his letter to the 'rulers, council and people of Jerusalem' (*A.J.* 20.11).

In many ways the men thrust into power by Rome were equally happy to preserve this fiction. Josephus, one of their number, ascribes the tragedy of the years A.D. 6–66 to the undermining of this ruling group by the wild irresponsibility of lower-class fanatics. In doing so, he assumes that in the normal course of events he and his

---

[25] On the career of Joazar, see E. M. Smallwood, 'High priests and politics in Roman Palestine', *JTS* n.s. 13 (1962) 17–21, although her interpretation of events differs from mine (see below, p. 140). On the Boethids after A.D. 40, see Stern, 'Social and political realignments', p. 53. On the house of Ananus, see Stern, 'Aspects of Jewish society', pp. 606–7. Stern suggests that the High Priest Joshua 'son of Σεέ' (or 'the Σεέ') appointed by Archelaus may have been the brother of Ananus, whose father is named Σεθί or Σεθ. But it would be odd of Josephus, who mentions Ananus' father at *A.J.* 18.26, not to mention such a relationship, and the proposed textual emendation is not attractive.

friends could have expected popular support. It naturally suits his polemic thus to portray himself as part of a natural *aristocratia* headed in accordance with the ancient constitution by a High Priest (*A.J.* 20.251). The pretence was indeed necessary to preserve the ruling group in power, since only by claiming local status could its members claim the right to rule on Rome's behalf. Even the terms that Josephus uses to describe the leaders chosen by Rome presume that they were a genuine local elite like that of Greek cities: the rulers are well known (*B.J.* 2.318), eminent (*B.J.* 4.139), the first men of the city (*Vita* 9), the rulers and councillors of Jerusalem (*B.J.* 2.405). This terminology gives the deliberately misleading impression that there could be no doubt who were the natural elite in Judaean society, nor any sympathy for the wicked men who, as Josephus describes it, were partly responsible for provoking the revolt precisely by their opposition to the elite's power.[26]

By the time of Josephus, of course, many years had passed since the establishment of a ruling class in Judaea by Roman governors in A.D. 6. The descendants of the men originally favoured by Rome had gained little prestige among their compatriots in the meantime, for reasons which will be fully argued below (pp. 116–33). Nonetheless it is more reasonable and charitable to assume that Josephus and his friends genuinely deluded themselves that Herodian and Roman favour gave them status in Jewish society than to attribute the picture of the ruling class given in the *B.J.* to a deliberate attempt by Josephus to deceive his readers. When some of the ruling class went on embassies to Roman governors and emperors, they doubtless presented themselves in good faith as representatives of the Judaean populace. It is possible, indeed, that their stock did genuinely rise to some extent on the rare occasions when they succeeded in extorting such concessions from the Roman authorities as the removal of the offensive shields brought by Pilate into Jerusalem (Philo, *Leg.* 299–306) or the agreement of Vitellius not to march with legionary standards through Judaea (*A.J.* 18.121–2).[27]

But their stock will have sunk again on the many occasions when, failing to intervene, they made concessions and exercised forbearance despite the ineptitude and injustice of the procurators. They made such concessions for the good reason that, in the end, it was on

---

[26] For Josephus' picture of the ruling class as a moderate, beleaguered elite, see Rajak, *Josephus*, pp. 65–143.

[27] It is possible but very unlikely that the incident involving the ensigns described by Josephus (*B.J.* 2.169–74) was identical with this episode of the gilded shields mentioned by Philo, cf. Smallwood, *Jews*, p. 166.

the procurator's goodwill that their own power depended. As a result, the Jews demonstrated their lack of confidence in their leaders by relying on mass action on crucial issues such as compelling Pilate to remove from Jerusalem ensigns bearing the emperor's image (*B.J.* 2.169–74), or, more significantly, to protest against Caligula's planned desecration of the Temple (Philo, *Leg.* 225–43; *B.J.* 2.192–201).[28] They did not trust the representations of their would-be leaders. If all the ruling class did indeed manage, as did Josephus, to delude themselves that they were the natural Jewish elite, they were the only section of Jewish society to have this delusion. Other Jews felt no such confidence in the right of the ruling class to rule.

The rulers of Judaea were thus in a sense marginal within their own society. This unhappy position was reinforced by the fact that in most cases their right to rule was also insufficiently strong in Roman terms for them to be able to stand up to the procurators and win for themselves local prestige in that way. Roman governors needed local rulers and so used them constantly in the administration of the province, but they could not bring themselves to see the Jewish ruling class, for all the pretensions they had evolved at least by the time of Josephus, as quite worthy to be treated as an ordinary provincial elite.

Various factors about the rulers of Judaea made them appear anomalous and unimpressive in the eyes of contemporary Romans. They were rich, for that, as has been shown, was a necessary condition for them to be entrusted by Rome with any power at all. But they did not look like the elite of a Greek city: Jerusalem was peculiar as a *polis*, even if technically such at this period, because it was to a large extent administered from the Temple in its midst.[29] Nor did they look like the priest-kings maintained by Rome in other Near Eastern temple states: the Hasmonaeans had been of that status, but

---

[28] It is worth noting that on the one occasion before A.D. 66 when Jewish leaders are recorded as risking Roman wrath on behalf of the people, in the opposition to Caligula's proposed statue in the Temple (Philo, *Leg.* 229), it was the body of elders (*gerousia*) who acted as spokesmen for the massed crowd. No member of any high-priestly family is explicitly named in the delegation, though they were doubtless included in it (cf. Smallwood, 'High priests and politics', p. 23). R. A. Horsley, 'High priests and the politics of Roman Palestine. A contextual analysis of the evidence in Josephus', *JSJ* 17 (1986) 36, notes the significance of the failure of the high priests to lead the opposition to Pilate's plans to introduce ensigns to Jerusalem and to use sacred money to pay for an aqueduct.

[29] On the *polis* status of Jerusalem, see V. A. Tcherikover, 'Was Jerusalem a "polis"?', *IEJ* 14 (1964) 61–78.

the relatives of Herod were not priests and the present High Priests' families had not tasted power until it was granted them by Rome.

Nor did the rulers of Judaea make an effort to present themselves in a guise more familiar to Romans used to other local elites. Greek aristocrats in the first and (more) second centuries A.D. were being welcomed into the Roman governing class itself as they came to the emperors' attention through their rhetorical expertise,[30] but in contrast Jews despised rhetoric as unimportant (*A.J.* 20.264). According to Acts 24.1, the High Priest Ananias even used a rhetor, whose name, Tertullus, suggests that he may have been gentile, to present his case against St Paul before the procurator Felix. Similarly, although Gallic aristocrats in this period were also being afforded, in return for military service on behalf of Rome,[31] a welcome into the Roman equestrian and, eventually, senatorial ranks as warm as that given to the Greeks, most of the Jewish ruling class barred itself from that route to acceptance by Rome by failing to take up posts within the Roman legions or auxiliary units.

This latter failure is slightly surprising. Jews had fought as mercenaries for hellenistic kings and as levied troops for Hasmonaeans and Herod. Indeed Onias, a scion of the high-priestly family which preceded the Maccabees, found favour with the Ptolemies in the mid second century B.C. precisely from his military service in Egypt. Furthermore, the Roman military system could also accommodate Jewish soldiers when necessary, as Tiberius showed in conscripting Jews from the city of Rome to serve in Sardinia (Tac. *Ann.* 2.85). Nonetheless, neither the Hasmonaeans nor the Herods nor the Romans can often be shown to have entrusted their forces to Jewish commanders from Judaea. The rebel Pitholaus who opposed Cassius in 53 B.C. in Galilee was presumably a Jewish commander appointed by the Hasmonaean Aristobulus (*A.J.* 14.120), but Herod's generals seem with few exceptions to have been either Idumaean or gentile, and, apart from Agrippa I's friend Silas, who was promoted out of personal favour rather than for military services (*A.J.* 19.299), later Herodians tended not to use Jewish generals at all. Thus, for instance, Agrippa II appointed at one time a certain Modius Aequus, presumably a Roman, to look after his affairs in the Gaulanitis (*Vita*

---

[30] Cf. Bowersock, *Augustus and the Greek World*, pp. 147–8; *idem, Greek Sophists in the Roman Empire, passim*.

[31] J. F. Drinkwater, 'The rise and fall of the Gallic Iulii', *Latomus* 37 (1978) 817–50. Since the empire's frontiers needed defending and these provincials were prepared to undertake the task, Rome rewarded them for the service, cf. Brunt, 'Did imperial Rome disarm her subjects?', pp. 269–70.

61,180), and such Jewish officers as he did employ were mostly the descendants of the colony of Babylonian Jews settled in Batanaea by Herod to pacify the area (*A.J.* 17.23–31; cf. below, p. 162 n.9).

It seems to me likely that this failure to entrust troops to Jewish commanders was linked to a general lack of enthusiasm among Jews in this period for a professional military career, and that the latter may have been at least partly prompted by the difficulty Jews encountered in fighting with a good conscience on the sabbath. The conflicting statements in Josephus about when the sabbath rest could and could not be infringed during war demonstrates the continuing uncertainty of most Jews about what should be done on the sacred day. When attacked it was obviously necessary to decide a policy on the matter if any sort of self-defence was to be successful, but by avoiding mercenary service most Jews could shelve the problem for their lifetimes.[32]

As a result rich Jews from Judaea, unlike rich Gauls and Greeks and eventually the elites of most other provinces, were never accepted into the ruling echelons of the Roman state. It was rare for the men put in power in A.D. 6 even to have received Roman citizenship by A.D. 66, though by the mid first century this status was becoming quite widespread among favoured individuals in other provinces. The Herods had enjoyed the privilege since Julius Caesar granted it to Antipater in 47 B.C., and Philo's family in Alexandria also held the status. Josephus refers to the crucifixion by Florus in A.D. 66 of Jews of equestrian rank in Jerusalem and explicitly claims that they held that Roman dignity (*B.J.* 2.308), but few of the Judaean ruling class named in his history have Roman names (though it is also possible that Jewish Roman citizens, such as the Herods, did not use

---

[32] S. Applebaum, 'Jews in the Roman army', in *Roman Frontier Studies, 1967: the proceedings of the seventh international congress held at Tel Aviv* (Tel Aviv, 1971), p. 181, suggests that Jews avoided military service out of objections to the ruler cult and other pagan religious acts required of Roman soldiers. Such objections might have been less obviously applicable if Jews had been allowed to serve in their own separate units as in the Hellenistic period, but this privilege was rare in the Roman army, and without such separate units the availability of kosher food would have been a problem, as well as the drinking of wine in the company of gentiles.

Scruples about fighting on the sabbath therefore provides only a part, but I believe a major part, of the explanation for Jews' reluctance to serve Rome as soldiers. According to *B.J.* 2.391–4, *Vita* 161 etc., all fighting on the sabbath is impious; according to *A.J.* 12.277 fighting is permissible only when necessary, presumably for self-defence; in practice the Jewish rebels frequently fought on the holy day during the war against Rome (*B.J.* 2.456,517). These contradictions should not be explained away. Jews were genuinely uncertain what to do. Those who fought will have done so with a bad conscience. Cf. A. J. Holladay and M. D. Goodman, 'Religious scruples in ancient warfare', *CQ* 36 (1986) 165–71.

their full Roman nomenclature in Judaea). Josephus himself only received citizenship after his freedom was granted to him by Vespasian.[33]

If citizenship was rarely achieved, senatorial status was apparently impossible for Jews. Both Agrippa I and Agrippa II were awarded the honorary *ornamenta praetoria* (Philo, *In Flaccum* 40; Cassius Dio, *Epit.* 66.15.4), but this was mere flattery of honoured outsiders parallel to the grant of the same status to Claudius' freedman Pallas (Tac. *Ann.* 12.53). Similarly, though the ex-slave Felix proudly married Drusilla, Agrippa II's sister, it was unthinkable that Titus, a great senator, should marry Berenice, despite her previous marriages to kings (Suet. *Tit.* 7; Cassius Dio 66.15. 4–5). Such prejudices did not relax after the first century A.D. Some of Herod's non-Jewish descendants, who had 'abandoned Jewish customs' (*A.J.* 18.141), achieved consulships in the second century A.D. (cf. *RE* x, 151–2), but no Jewish senator is recorded in the history of the empire and the reason probably does not lie solely in the reluctance of Jews to seek such public office.

Roman governors were consequently reluctant to treat the Jewish ruling class as their social near-equals and natural collaborators, which was how local elites were treated elsewhere in the empire. Thus, for instance, according to Josephus the reaction of the ruling group in Jerusalem to the fighting which broke out during the rule of Cumanus (*c.* A.D. 48–*c.* 52) between the Samaritans and a mob of Galileans and Judaeans was to urge peaceful moderation; furthermore, this intervention was eventually successful (*A.J.* 20.121–3). If Josephus is correct, the behaviour of Quadratus, the legate of Syria, is significant. He sent to Rome in chains the ex-High Priest Ananias with his son Ananus, the Captain of the Temple, and the incumbent High Priest Jonathan (*A.J.* 20.131; *B.J.* 2.243). Sixteen or so years before the revolt the Roman authorities had thus already lost confidence in the ability of the Judaean ruling class to fulfil its function. I have tried to show in this chapter that those Jewish rulers had never deserved such confidence from their first appointment in A.D. 6. They were never a natural elite in Judaean society and were never able to control the population on Rome's behalf.

[33] Note however the Jewish leader named Iulius Capella at Tiberias in Galilee (*Vita* 32). This man was presumably closely connected to Agrippa II, given the names of his pro-Roman and pro-Herodian associates (*Vita* 33). Professor Isaac has pointed out to me that it was not only Jews from this area who failed to enter the Roman hierarchy. Not a single senator, Jewish or gentile, is attested from Judaea or Palestine. The reasons are not clear.

The failure of the ruling class which Josephus so bitterly lamented was thus almost inevitable once the society over which they were meant to preside came under strain. In the following chapters I shall describe the nature and intensity of the social tensions by which the rulers of Judaea found themselves faced in the years before A.D. 66, before showing how their reaction to their failure to deal with them precipitated the nation into war.

CHAPTER 3

PROBLEMS FACING THE RULING CLASS: ECONOMIC AND SOCIAL

The origin of much of the social tension in Judaea lay in the growth and changing nature of the Judaean economy, which fuelled class hostility of increasing intensity. Josephus speaks of a universal sickness in Judaea from A.D. 6, which led the rich to oppress the masses and the masses to plunder the rich (*B.J.* 7.260–1). He sometimes describes the struggle between pro-Roman and revolutionary Jews in terms of a class war;[1] a description which, though probably a misleading picture of the revolt itself when rich and poor were largely united against Rome (see below, pp. 176–201), is a fair reflection of much of the violence in the Judaean countryside both before the war broke out and after. Some of the revolutionaries indulged in banditry, murdering the leading men, looting the houses of the wealthy and setting villages on fire.[2] The causes of such hostility lay in the widening gap between rich and poor as the economy of Judaea was integrated, in a unique fashion, into the wider Mediterranean world.

The centre of the Judaean economy was Jerusalem, which 'dominates all the neighbourhood as the head towers above the body' (*B.J.* 3.54).[3] The countryside was productive: Josephus mentions

---

[1] Brunt, 'Josephus on social conflicts', collects the texts.

[2] Cf. *A.J.* 18.7, re A.D. 6; *B.J.* 2.265, re the procuratorship of Felix. As I have shown in Chapter 2, members of the ruling class were kept in power by Rome and were therefore obvious targets for lower-class rebels, but it is also likely that the rebels used the excuse of nationalism to justify class hostility.

[3] The focus of the revolt, and hence this book, was Judaea, since I believe that the problems of Galilee were rather different. The ruling class described in the last chapter was put in charge of a province in A.D. 6 that excluded Galilee, which was ruled by Antipas for a further thirty-three years and later by Agrippa II. Opposition to Rome after A.D. 6 was always centred in Judaea and its environs (as far west as Caesarea, east as Jericho, and south as Idumaea). It seems to me likely that Josephus' picture in the *B.J.* of Galilee as exceptionally bellicose was invented to bolster his image of himself as a great general, and that in practice Galilee was peripheral to the revolt (cf. Rhoads, *Israel in Revolution*, p. 175 n. 1; Cohen, *Josephus in Galilee and Rome*, pp. 201–3; Freyne, *Galilee*, pp. 208–55), although this may have

grain, wood, fruits and cattle (*B.J.* 3.49–50), to which should be added olives and vines on the terraced hills and sheep and goats for sacrifice in the Temple. But the land is not particularly good, and the distance from the hills to the coast discouraged the growth of any external trade in agricultural surplus.

The stimulus for the change and growth which built Jerusalem into one of the greatest and richest cities of the Near East by the mid first century A.D. thus necessarily came from outside the rural economy, and the two main external sources of income are clear. The Temple attracted constant gifts both from Jewish pilgrims and from gentile visitors from outside Palestine, and Herod and his descendants lavished wealth created in other parts of their kingdom on this, their capital city.

But the Jerusalem economy of the first century A.D. was not entirely parasitic on such munificence from the outside world. The city's inhabitants provided goods and services for the visitors, celebrating the great religious occasions of the year not only for their spiritual significance but also, as in pilgrimage centres today, for the custom that they brought. According to the late second-century A.D. testimony of the Mishnah (*Bikk.* 3.3), the worshippers who brought the first fruits to the Temple each year from all over Palestine were greeted, as they drew close to Jerusalem in a procession led by a gold-horned ox and a flute player, by all the craftsmen of Jerusalem, who used to rise up before them and greet them, saying, 'Brethren, men of such-and-such a place, you are welcome!'

In addition to board and lodging, such pilgrims were offered industrial products of some sophistication. Recent excavations have revealed some of these crafts: the Jerusalem glass workers, whose discovered waste-products have demonstrated their techniques even better than their finished vessels, were producing goods almost on a par with the masterpieces made by their contemporaries in Sidon, and the city was a centre for stone carving of remarkably fine quality.

For non-luxury items the city itself provided a potential market, for public expenditure by the Herods on great building projects such as the Temple and the royal palaces provided employment and spending money for a large number of workmen (cf. *A.J.* 20.219).[4]

---

been as much because Judaea lends itself better to guerrilla fighting as because Galilean Jews may have had different attitudes towards Rome. At any rate, it is in Judaea that the clues to the revolt must lie.

[4] On Jerusalem as a pilgrimage centre, see S. Safrai, *Pilgrimage at the Time of the Second Temple* (Tel Aviv, 1965) (Heb.); J. Jeremias, *Jerusalem in the Time of Jesus,*

Finds of much small-denomination coin scattered in city houses of the Herodian and early Roman periods suggest a fully monetary, thriving market economy. Furthermore, the presence of a large consumer population may have stimulated the production of specialist agricultural goods in the immediate vicinity of the city.

However, this economic infrastructure built up through the stimulus of external investment was never sufficiently strong and sophisticated to survive on its own. The clearest evidence of this came in A.D. 64 when a crisis was caused by the completion of the major employment project in the city, the rebuilding of the Temple (*A.J.* 20.219–22). Alternative jobs for the many labourers left unwaged proved impossible to find in the private sector. A few might find work manufacturing ritual products for the Temple worship, but the secrets of such production were often monopolies jealously preserved by favoured families. Others might seek work in building private houses, but although the expansion of the city and its housing stock had been astonishing between the mid second century B.C. and A.D. 70, and the amount of work available had been much increased by Herod's town planning policy of destroying existing private dwellings to make room for the new city, the rate of erecting new houses was slowing down by the mid first century A.D. There was little else for the unskilled to do.

Even the skilled craftsmen had difficulties. Some luxury goods such as glass and stoneware may have found a ready market, but other luxuries and medium-grade goods such as fineware pottery were often imported from abroad now that the Pax Romana made the long-distance transport of a vast variety of products comparatively easy, and local craftsmen could not compete with the quality of Italian and Greek workshops.

The problem was, in sum, that outsiders tended to spend lavishly in Jerusalem but not to invest in the local economy, and they ignored production in the countryside altogether. Furthermore, some of the locals' wealth lay as unproductive capital in the Temple treasury, awaiting the all too frequent attentions of rapacious Romans such as Crassus. The result was an economy potentially out of balance.[5]

E.T. (London, 1969), pp. 58–84, 134–8. On the glass factory, see Avigad, *Discovering Jerusalem*, p. 186; on the stone workshops, *ibid.* p. 165. But stone vessel workshops are also known north-west and south of the city, cf. S. Gibson, 'The stone vessel industry at Hizma', *IEJ* 33 (1983) 176–88. The remains of the Herodian Temple are the best evidence for the effect of the public building projects, but see also the superb paving stones in the streets of the first-century city (Avigad, pp. 88, 94).

[5] For Temple monopoly crafts, see Jeremias, *Jerusalem*, pp. 25–7. On the rate of house building in Jerusalem after 152 B.C., and especially under Herod, see Avigad,

There is, however, no reason to believe that this imbalance was any more dangerously apparent in A.D. 66 than in the years immediately preceding. The countryside was populated to an extent never before achieved and not to be equalled until the Byzantine period. So too was the city, with the benefit of a better water supply from the high-level aqueduct completed under Agrippa I.[6] Drought had caused famine in the forties and perhaps the early sixties A.D., but the problem was endemic in a country reliant on rainfall for the crops to grow and, in the earlier famine at least, rescue had come from Egypt, through the generosity of Queen Helena of Adiabene, who had the corn transported and distributed (*A.J.* 20.101).[7] The panic apparently aroused in A.D 64 by the prospect of eighteen thousand workmen being left unemployed on the completion of the Temple was at least partially allayed by the plan to pave the city with white stone (*A.J.* 20.222), and by A.D. 66 work was also in hand to underpin the Temple with massive beams brought 'at immense labour and expense' from Mt Lebanon to deal with subsidence in the foundations (*A.J.* 15.391; *B.J.* 5.36).

If this economy, despite the artificial elements within it, showed no signs of collapsing in A.D. 66, the unequal distribution of its benefits was perhaps then at its most blatant. The wealth of the Jerusalem

---

Discovering Jerusalem, p. 74. On the tendency to import medium-grade goods, see in general K. Hopkins, 'Economic growth and towns in classical antiquity', in P. Abrams and E. A. Wrigley, eds., *Towns in Societies: essays in economic history and historical sociology* (Cambridge, 1978), pp. 35–77; for imports of, e.g., Rhodian wine to Jerusalem, see Avigad, *Discovering Jerusalem*, p. 79.

[6] On the new settlements of the early Roman period, and the failure of some of them soon after A.D. 70, see the results of M. Kochavi, ed., *Judaea, Samaria and the Golan: archaeological survey 1967–1968* (Jerusalem, 1972), pp. 84–5. Information from such surface survey can only be tentative, but the cumulative impression of dense village settlements before A.D. 66 is impressive. Professor Isaac informs me that his own discoveries in the region between Lydda and Jerusalem make the depression in the second century A.D. appear an even more marked feature of Judaea. Cf. also S. Gibson, 'Jerusalem (North-East) archaeological survey', *IEJ* 3 (1982) 156–7, on the investigation of numerous farms of the late Hellenistic and early Roman periods. On the economy of Palestine in the Byzantine period, see M. Avi-Yonah, 'The economics of Byzantine Palestine', *IEJ* 8 (1958) 39–51. On the water supply as a criterion for judging the size of the population of Jerusalem, see J. Wilkinson, 'Ancient Jerusalem: its water supply and population', *PEQ* 106 (1974) 33–51, esp. p. 50.

[7] On the famine, see Rajak, *Josephus*, pp. 123–5. S. Applebaum, 'Economic life in Palestine', in Safrai and Stern, *The Jewish People* II, p. 656, suggests that the Jews' loss of political control of the coastal plains to the west of Judaea made it more difficult to buy grain from the farmers there. I am not sure that trade would be affected by political change in this way, but it will in any case have been expensive to carry grain up into the Judaean hills. In normal years, all staple foods must have been grown locally.

rich has become fully apparent only in the last few years as archaeologists have unearthed in Jerusalem private houses of great size and
luxurious appointments. Ordinary members of the Judaean ruling
class could not compete with the magnificence of the Hasmonaean
and Herodian palaces; Herod's homes were particularly impressive
since they were built for protection as well as comfort and used the
same sort of massive masonry blocks as graced the Temple site. But
one private mansion uncovered in the Jewish Quarter covers 600
square metres, and others are not much smaller.[8] No expense was
spared on the decoration of such houses, and Pompeian-style frescoes
and fine mosaics abound. These great town residences were evidently the main dwellings of their owners. Jerusalem was the cultural centre of life and this was the place to spend money; no villas
have yet been found within forty kilometres of Jerusalem in the
Judaean hill country, though some of the ruling class apparently followed the practice of their Herodian mentors by building winter
residences in the warmth of Jericho.[9]

How did these rich Jerusalemites, the men treated by the Romans
as the ruling class of Judaea, become so wealthy? Roman recognition
of their wealth probably implies that their property was in the form
of land, and that would anyway be likely, since land was always the
safest investment for money that had been earned elsewhere: there is
some evidence to suggest a well-developed tenancy system on large
estates in Judaea at this period, though it should be confessed that
the sources are not in themselves compelling.[10] But agriculture will

[8] On Herod's palace, see D. Bahat and M. Broshi in Yadin, *Jerusalem Revealed*,
pp. 55–6. The whole structure was placed upon an artificial platform and surrounded by massive towers, one of which still survives in part. On the palatial mansion, see Avigad, *Discovering Jerusalem*, pp. 97–120; cf. *ibid.* pp. 83–8, 120–39, for
other large houses excavated in the Jewish Quarter in recent years.

[9] For the internal decoration of Jerusalem houses, see Avigad, *Discovering Jerusalem*, pp. 102–3, 144; for Jerusalemites in Jericho, see R. Hachlili, 'A Second Temple
period Jewish necropolis in Jericho', *Biblical Archaeologist* (Fall 1980) 238. Many
Herodian fortresses have been found around Judaea, so the failure to find any trace
of other substantial upper-class dwellings can be taken as significant.

[10] Cf. J. Klausner, 'The economy of Judaea in the Second Temple period', in M.
Avi-Yonah and Z. Baras, eds., *Society and Religion in the Second Temple Period* (The
World History of the Jewish People, I. 8) (London, 1977), p. 190. Josephus writes of
the lands his own family held near Jerusalem (*Vita* 422). According to *m.B.M.* 5.8,
Rabban Gamaliel used both gangs of workers under the control of overseers and
tenants who received seed corn from him; his estates were probably near Jerusalem,
though this cannot be certain. The rest of the first-century evidence comes from
Gospel parables (e.g. Matt. 21.33–41, about serfs as, in effect, tied peasants) which
may not reflect Judaean conditions even when (as is only occasionally the case) the
details about ordinary life assumed in such stories do not seem to have been inserted

not by itself have brought in a great surplus in the countryside around Jerusalem, even if specialist products, such as for instance doves for sacrifice in the Temple, might be worth a good deal and the size of the captive market might ensure a high price for grain. Nor will the provision of services for tourists have made the sort of fortune needed both to impress the Roman governor of a family's right to join the ruling class and for that family to enjoy the standard of life evidently available to the owners of the fine houses described above.

A different route to wealth was clearly needed, and two possible models can be suggested. In both cases it is probable that the route in itself will have added to the hatred felt for the rich by the poor, and hence to the difficulties of the ruling class in dealing with their poor compatriots' grievances.

According to the first model, the rich gained their wealth at the expense of peasants suffering from a bad harvest after one of the periodic droughts already described. On such occasions a fellow-peasant with a slight surplus might be minded to lend to a neighbour whose produce for that year had dropped below the level of viability, but unless the fellow-peasant had a considerably larger farm or many fewer dependants, the drought will have affected him equally. The only people who could afford to lend to the peasant in trouble were therefore either the very rich or those farmers who combined the security of their landholdings with financial interests in ventures which were not affected by the climate, such as the provision of goods to the Temple and services to pilgrims. Thus, although it has been noted that the city economy did not produce massively rich businessmen who could afford to buy up land and dominate agriculture through profits alone, it did more insidiously help to break up old patterns of landholding by giving the Judaeans who creamed off a share of the profits from pilgrimage the opportunity to gain land. Not that the rich often bought land directly, for peasants may well have prevented them from doing so by accepting from relatives prices for family plots lower than the market would pay, but they may have gained no less good title to farms by calling in the security on loans.

That this was a prime route to extending landed property seems

purely to enhance the moral lesson of the tale: as in all New Testament material, the background chosen by the Gospel author to make his story come home to his audience may be that of Christian communities outside Palestine. Nonetheless, it is probable *a priori* that the Jerusalem rich used rents from tenants to ensure a steady income.

probable because there is plentiful evidence for the extent to which cash loans were made in first-century Judaea. The evidence that survives is mostly about the debtors in such transactions. These were the men who, the rebels hoped, might be eager to join the revolt when the debt archive was burnt in Jerusalem in A.D. 66 (*B.J.* 2.427), and I shall say more about them below. But for every borrower there must be a lender, and the expected enthusiasm at the destruction of the archives make it clear that no social ties existed between debtor and creditor. The poor peasant did not always turn for loans to friends and neighbours because, as already suggested, they were unlikely to have sufficient surplus to help out. No lending banks existed. Only the rich, encumbered perhaps with uninvested wealth culled by whatever means from outsiders visiting Jerusalem, could afford to lend.

It is possible that the rich might lend money out of kindness alone, but such cases were perhaps exceptional. They might lend in order to enjoy interest on the loan, for, although the taking of interest was of course forbidden by Jewish law (Lev. 25.36–7), later rabbinic comments about those guilty of usury suggest that it did occur (cf. *m.B.M.* 5.11; *m.Sanh.* 3:3), and the exaction of fines for late repayment, which is a term incorporated within one of the loan agreements of the early second century A.D. found in the Judaean desert (*DJD* II 18), would have much the same effect. However, it was surely unwise to rely on a small farmer being able to pay interest on a loan if he had fallen heavily enough in debt to borrow from an outsider in the first place, and the only logical reason to lend was thus the hope of winning the peasant's land by foreclosing on it when the debt was not paid off as agreed.

The creditor could not lose by such a loan, except marginally in the sense that if the debtor paid off what was owed, the money would from the creditor's point of view have been idle during the period of the loan. On the other hand, he stood to gain much land at well below the market price if he could persuade the borrower to stay on as his tenant rather than paying off the loan from the proceeds raised by selling up the farm.

As evidence that rich creditors really did have this aim in advancing loans in first-century Judaea can be cited their acceptance of the institution of the *prosbul* at some time in the first century. The terms of this legal institution are described in rabbinic texts of the second century A.D. (*m.Shebi.* 10.3–7), but it is almost certain that it was practised by at least some Jews before the time of Nero, for similar terms are contained in the acknowledgement of debt from the

Judaean desert already cited (*DJD* II 18). The prosbul was a public declaration before a court by a man seeking a loan, in which he stated that he would accept his legal duty to repay the money even after the advent of a Sabbatical Year rendered the debt automatically cancelled. Rabbinic texts concentrate on the value of this special declaration to the debtor, given the scarcity of loans otherwise available in the last years of each cycle (*m.Shebi.* 10.3). But the creditors, in agreeing to advance loans on the basis of such a radical change in the law, must have also seen some advantages to themselves. The terms of the prosbul suggest that their motive was not friendship or any other social tie, for it is likely that there was a moral obligation to repay loans after the Sabbatical Year even if no formal statement had been made: according to *m.Shebi.* 10.9, if a man repays a debt in the Seventh Year, 'the sages are well pleased with him'. Friends and family would repay loans at risk of social stigma, while rich traders would rapidly lose all future credit if they once welched on their debt.

Their great motive to lend must thus have been financial. Occasionally the gain from foreclosure may have been the debtor's own person, but the use of debt bondsmen was rather rare given the general availability of cheap gentile slaves and workers who could be hired by the day. The alternative security, land, was a much more worthwhile prize. Thus, on the backs of the indebted peasantry, some of the priests, merchants and artisans of Jerusalem may have converted their profits from the pilgrimage business into real estate and become the natural rulers to whom Rome could turn.[11]

The second route to becoming a major landowner was no more likely to endear the ruling class to the rest of the populace, though it has less to do with the generally peculiar nature of the Judaean economy. It seems to me probable that many of the rich held their land in Judaea simply as gifts from Herod or Archelaus.

The significance of such gifts cannot be proved, but some negative evidence may be adduced. I have noted above (Chapter 2 n. 13) that it is possible that some of the Judaean hill country, though obviously not all, was royal property in late Hasmonaean times. If so, the Herodians may have changed the status of such areas, for no Herodian lands in the hills around Jerusalem are recorded. Furthermore, it was normal Roman practice on incorporating a new province either to leave royal land in the possession of the immediate

[11] For these arguments in more detail, see my article, 'The First Jewish Revolt: social conflict and the problem of debt', *JJS* 33 (1982) 417–27.

relatives of the outgoing dynast, or to confiscate such territory as imperial land – there were thus imperial properties in Judaea after A.D. 6, most notably the balsam plantations in En Gedi and the area of Jamnia, which had been bequeathed by Salome to Augustus' wife Livia and by Livia to Tiberius – but no imperial properties are recorded in the Judaean hills. However, since Josephus states explicitly that Archelaus' property (of unknown extent and nature) was sold off in A.D. 6 (*A.J.*17.355; 18.2), the possibility that this sale included royal land near Jerusalem cannot be ruled out.[12] It may be best to let the argument rest simply on the *a priori* likelihood that Herod rewarded his friends.

In theory it is possible that the Romans' hesitation to take land in Judaea into imperial ownership might have been because some of it was owned by the Temple, as was the case in other Near Eastern states. However, although it was technically possible for the Temple to own land, in practice the Temple authorities seem to have preferred wealth in bullion and to have accepted a cash equivalent for any properties bequeathed or dedicated for its benefit.[13]

In sum, it seems to me probable that the Romans in A.D. 6 left the Judaean hill country in the hands of private landowners because that is how they found it, and that Herod had granted great tracts of land previously in royal ownership, with the incumbent peasants as tenants, to his favourites. There is some explicit evidence for such grants. Admittedly this evidence refers only to the lands given to members of the Herodian family itself and to a certain number of trusted subordinates such as the minister who apparently owned a

---

[12] On Roman attitudes to previously royal land, and for imperial land in Judaea, see D. Crawford in M. I. Finley, ed., *Studies in Roman Property* (Cambridge, 1976), pp. 35–70. The survival of evidence for the transfer of royal land to imperial control in the Jezreel valley (cf. B. Isaac and I. Roll, *Roman Roads in Judaea* (Oxford, 1982), I, pp. 104–8) makes the silence from the Judaean countryside more significant.

[13] For other Temple states owning land under Roman rule, cf. the well-known inscription from Baetocaece (*IGR* III 1020). It is sometimes asserted that the Jerusalem Temple also owned tied peasants (cf. H. Kreissig, 'Die landwirtschaftliche Situation', p. 235), but there is no evidence for this. For dedications of land to the Temple by a formula called *hekdesh*, cf. *m.Arak.* 7.1–5 and *Encylopedia Talmudit* (Jerusalem, 1961) x, pp. 352–442 (Heb.); for the selling of such land and payment of the price received to the Temple, cf. *m.Arak.* 8.1–3. The *hekdesh* formula was apparently sometimes used to forestall others from making use of property on the grounds that it was more daunting for thieves to steal from God than from other men (cf. *t.Men.* 13.20). It is possible that this preference for moveable bullion as the repository of wealth was partly responsible for the Jerusalem Temple being singled out for violation by greedy foreigners more often than other sanctuaries; the fear that Temple funds left unused on deposit were at risk from the Romans in A.D. 64 is stated explicitly by Josephus at *A.J.* 20.220.

village in Samaritis sacked in 4 B.C. by the Nabataeans (*B.J.* 2.69). But it is highly likely that the families brought from Babylonia and Alexandria to provide the nation with a new breed of High Priests were also favoured with estates without which they would find it hard to keep up with the pace of the Herodian court.[14] When Vespasian sold up the conquered land after A.D. 70 he was similarly prepared to benefit his favourites with estates in Judaea, as Josephus, a beneficiary, testifies (*Vita* 425).

The existence of a class of extreme rich is not in itself a sufficient cause of class antagonism. However, in first-century Judaea the same conditions that enabled a few to gain great estates by capitalizing on the effects of bad harvests after drought pushed others into extreme and resentful poverty. Josephus writes about the poor only when they are politically menacing, but that left him plenty to say.

According to Josephus, banditry was endemic in the Judaean countryside from at least the late forties A.D. (cf. *A.J.* 20.124). He has much to say, much of it of dubious authority since he belonged to the class of natural victims of such brigands, about these robbers' motives once embarked on their careers. On one occasion, however, he also lets slip an apparently objective analysis of what pushed poor peasants to leave their land to seek riskier rewards on the hilltops and in the artificial caves frequented by the bandit chieftains and their followers. When the Jewish rulers met Petronius, legate of Syria, to urge him to prevent the installation of Caligula's statue in the Temple, they pointed out that, if the fields were not sown while the people remained on strike in protest at the emperor's plan, the result would be a harvest of banditry through their inability to collect the tribute (*A.J.* 18.274).[15]

This rhetorical statement presupposes two important factors as the origin of banditry. First, some bandits, and perhaps all, come from the class of free independent peasants who in normal times paid

[14] For lands granted within the Herodian family, cf. *B.J.* 1.483; 2.98.

[15] It does not matter for this argument that Josephus was probably rather ignorant about this embassy, cf. Smallwood, *Jews*, p. 117 n. 115, since it in any case reflects Josephus' own view of the origins of banditry. On bandits in general, see the often excellent if sometimes schematic analysis by R. A. Horsley, 'Josephus and the bandits', *JSJ* 10 (1979) 37–63; *idem*, 'Ancient Jewish banditry', pp. 409–32. B. Isaac, 'Bandits in Judaea and Arabia', *HSCP* 88 (1984) 171–203, discusses material down to the late-Roman period. For the many artificial caves dug as hiding-places in Judaea and possibly in use throughout the first century A.D., see A. Kloner, 'Underground hiding complexes from the Bar Kochba war in the Judaean Shephelah', *Biblical Archaeologist* 46.4 (December 1983) 210–21, with the comments of B. Isaac and A. Oppenheimer, 'The revolt of Bar Kochba: ideology and modern scholarship', *JJS* 36 (1985) 43.

regular direct taxes to the Roman government; for tenants of the rich landlords the payment of taxes was probably a problem devolved, except in so far as high taxes would encourage the landowner to demand a high rent. Second, it is the inexorable requirement to pay such taxes that pushes peasants over the brink into outlawry.

This last factor, and indeed banditry, were endemic throughout the Roman world. In Judaea, however, the tax burden was for many peasants the last calamity in an already disastrous situation, and it became the excuse for complaint or banditry only because, unlike the other factors involved, it was fixed and universal in its application.

The position of many peasants was already fraught because an expanding population was trying to support itself from a limited amount of available usable land. The problem was not simply a result of the physical limitations of the land, for it is probable that the total rural population of Judaea in this period was rather smaller than that achieved in the Byzantine period when Jerusalem was by contrast a more modest city. The problem was rather that more and more of the land was being sucked out of its original use as the property of free smallholders to be added to the great estates of the new rich landowners, and that these landowners presumably cut down their use of tenants to the smallest number possible for efficient farming.

The expansion of the population is visible in the mushrooming of new settlements in this period (see above, n. 6). Its causes are primarily ideological. Jews took seriously the injunction in Genesis 9.1, 'Be fruitful and multiply'. Infanticide and abortion, both normal practices in the rest of the contemporary Mediterranean world, were unknown among Jews, as Josephus asserted proudly and Tacitus remarked with amused contempt (*c.Ap.* 2.202; Tac. *Hist.* 5.5.3). Contraception was also avoided. The natural revenge by the climate on such profligacy of progeny was famine when the rains failed, but this was partly forestalled by the demands of religious charity which ensured the saving of life – but little more than that – by the importing of food (cf. *A.J.* 20.51 re the famine of *c.* A.D. 48). The same attitude to charity, unique in the ancient world (see below, p. 65), could preserve the existence of the small children whose survival was precarious for lack of food and whose deaths would otherwise have balanced the population to the available land.

Faced by too many mouths to feed, the impoverished peasant had few opportunities to increase his income. Doubtless all land owned by peasants was used to its maximum potential to ensure full exploitation of the available labour, hence the variety of products grown: the olive harvest in the cold winter months; grain sowing in the late autumn or winter and early spring, and harvest in the late spring or early summer; the fruit picked from the trees in the early autumn, and so on. But it was difficult to find work as a hired hand on the estates of the great landowners even at the busy times of the harvests, for a mass of permanent landless, some of them doubtless normally resident in the city of Jerusalem, competed for the work and the wages. Nor was it easy to supplement income by practising a craft other than those connected with agriculture in spare time, for the city provided manufactured goods of all kinds and only a foolish purchaser would prefer the amateurish efforts of a part-time village artisan.

The spark which set off each family's crisis came probably either from the effects of a bad year and the prospect of immediate starvation or from the death of the farm's owner and the prospect of dividing up the plot between his heirs, usually his sons. Change of ownership made the land no more likely to prove insufficient to feed the same number of people as before, but the future of the inheritors, hoping to start (or continue) to breed children on only a share of an already too small farm, might suddenly look very daunting. The eldest son would have inherited a double portion according to Jewish law, but, if the land as a whole was already not producing a useful surplus, it is unlikely that he could buy out any of his brothers. Short of limiting their children to a certain maximum, which, as has already been seen, was ideologically odious, the heirs of such a farm might seem best served if they sold out to one of the many rich landowners eager to invest their city-won wealth in their property. The alternative was to borrow from the same rich men, but, as described (above, p. 57), the effect would be much the same since their land was then vulnerable security for debts they could not reasonably hope to repay. Doubtless families hung together as long as possible, lending to each other and selling property to relations at prices below that of the market in order to avoid the dead hand of the city investors, but eventually the thought of starvation might press even the most unwilling peasant into their clutches.

Deprived of land such peasants had few options. Some presumably joined one of the great and flourishing communities of the Jewish diaspora, finding a ready welcome and opportunities for income in the cities of the Mediterranean coastline where Jews had settled as ex-slaves or ex-mercenaries since the early Hellenistic period. This solution, however, was not open to all, for some financial backing was needed for an emigrant to set himself up abroad and many of the poor farmers just described lacked such resources, just as they lacked the skill in crafts or trading which could have earned them the necessary capital. It is significant that the only emigrants from Judaea in the years preceding A.D. 66 who may be mentioned by Josephus are those victims of brigandage who may have left their estates in the early sixties A.D. for safer surroundings among the gentiles (*B.J.* 2.279, but since this is part of Josephus' vituperation against Gessius Florus, who 'despoiled whole cities', perhaps it should not be taken literally); these will all have been persons of property since only they had anything to fear from brigands.

Landless peasants could thus choose either to turn to banditry or to seek employment in the cities. The first option was not as drastic as it sounds. Bandits cut themselves off from the normal protection of the Roman state and operated outside the Roman law, but this did not deprive them of their status as members of Jewish society. On the contrary, bandits maintained close links with the peasant villagers from whose ranks they had come, to the extent that many of the common people were punished for complicity with the brigands (*B.J.* 2.253).

Best known of these popular bandits (after the Barabbas released at the time of Jesus' trial) was a certain Eleazar b. Dinai, a robber chieftain who operated in the mountains on the boundary between Judaea and Samaria and gained a reputation as a folk hero like Robin Hood. He was a natural leader for the violent mob when it rampaged northwards from Judaea to punish the Samaritans for the murder of some Galilean pilgrims (*A.J.* 20.121), for he could be trusted to espouse the Jewish cause with a whole heart. Tales of his exploits, suitably romanticized, survived into the rabbinic literature of the second century A.D. (cf. *m.Sot.* 9.9). A similar brigand chief, by name Jesus, who operated in Galilee in A.D. 66 and 67, maintained friendly relations even with the pro-Roman city of Sepphoris (*Vita* 104-5).

Josephus describes these men's acts of brigandage as deeds which are popularly supposed to be for the common welfare but which are actually for private gain (*A.J.* 18.7); he thus testifies that some Judaean villagers at least believed that the bandits were on their side. The finds of numerous artificial caves used as bandit hiding-places in Judaea confirms such local complicity, if they were in use in this period, since the whereabouts of such refuges will have been well known to the inhabitants of nearby villages even if they were invisible to the Roman state's troops. Many of these caves were indeed situated actually within the settlements. This phenomenon of social banditry is well attested from many other peasant societies.[16]

The alternative for the bankrupt peasant was to seek the refuge of the cities. Some Jews must have settled in the gentile cities of the Decapolis and the Mediterranean coast, for large communities there came under threat when the war broke out in A.D. 66 (*B.J.* 2.457–80). They were presumably absorbed in economic terms into the city plebs. Some may have contrived to profit from the transit trade which passed through, for example, Caesarea. For most, however, no economic security was possible, beyond that provided by the institutions of charity set up by the communities in these cities as in those of the further-flung diaspora. Some may have learnt to practise a craft, others taken to petty trading. None will have found it easy to buy or rent land from gentile owners suspicious of Jewish immigrants. The economic instability of the local Jews may have been a major cause of the volatility of Jewish–Greek relations in these cities in the years preceding the revolt.[17]

Other landless peasants, probably the great majority, migrated to Jerusalem and helped to swell the population to the great size already described. The Jerusalem proletariat was unlike that of other cities in Palestine or indeed the rest of the eastern empire, except perhaps for Alexandria. The poor thronged the city in an undifferentiated mass. No system of patronage linked them in normal times to the great menages of the ruling class which relied on domestic slaves for everyday needs. No skills brought them a ready income and identity as craftsmen, for the Jerusalem artisans will have preferred to hand on the secrets of their craft to their sons rather than to destitute countrymen. Only the great building projects of the state and Temple brought employment. Those who worked on the Temple received a guaranteed income while the building lasted, being paid the same for one hour's work as for a whole day (*A.J.* 20.220). Hence the horror in Jerusalem at the social catastrophe of the Temple's completion, and the adoption of another task, the paving of the city, to provide pay for some of the eighteen thousand unemployed (*A.J.* 20.219–22).

This ability in normal times to rely on employment on public works was paralleled nowhere else in the Roman empire. In the towns of Italy, for instance, spending by the state was matched by

[16] See Horsley, 'Josephus and the bandits', *passim; idem,* 'Ancient Jewish banditry', pp. 413–20. On the hiding-places, see n. 15 above.

[17] On the Jewish community in Caesarea, see L. I. Levine, *Caesarea under Roman Rule* (Leiden, 1975), pp. 15–33.

massive public spending by rich aristocrats, competing to win the favour of the populace. This 'evergetism' did not appeal to the Jerusalem rich for reasons to be discussed below (Chapter 5, pp. 126–9). They preferred to spend within the intimate privacy of their luxurious houses, buying in beautiful objects from abroad. Their role in making it possible for the very poor to continue to live in the great city was by the more insidious practice of charity.

Charity in the Jewish and Christian sense was unknown to the pagan world. Pagans did not notice the very poor at all except when they became politically threatening. Assistance was almost always confined to citizens. Slaves and outsiders were ignored when in distress; except in special circumstances, their problems were not the concern of the ordinary man. In Rome the very poor either starved or left the city. Begging was a hazardous occupation; in the eyes of a moralist like Seneca, it was in order but neither necessary nor important to be kind to the poor and the miserable. Free men preferred to surround themselves with their fellow-citizens and to direct their gifts to those whose social and political standing mattered. Both in the city of Rome and in the Egyptian township of Oxyrhynchus free corn was given not to the poverty-stricken but to the privileged among the plebs.[18]

Among Jews, by contrast, it was a religious duty of great moment to care for the destitute. This factor was perhaps one of the main social causes of the cohesion of Jewish diaspora communities, just as it was one of the attractions for converts to Christianity that the early Church inherited this care for its members from its Jewish origins. The incentive to give was not, however, for either Jews or Christians a desire to see poverty eradicated. It might even seem preferable in religious terms that the poor be always with you, for the justification for charity given in ancient texts is in terms of the morality of the donor not the benefit of the recipient.[19] The result in Jerusalem was that the rich kept in their midst a host of shiftless poor sustained just

[18] On pagan attitudes to the poor, see H. Bolkestein, *Wohltätigkeit und Armenpflege im vorchristlichen Altertum* (Utrecht, 1939); P. Veyne, *Le pain et le cirque: sociologie historique d'un pluralisme politique* (Paris, 1976), pp. 45–6, 55, 57; A. R. Hands, *Charities and Social Aid in Greece and Rome* (London, 1968). On the Roman corn dole, see Z. Yavetz, *Plebs and Princeps* (Oxford, 1969); for Oxyrhynchus in the third century A.D., see *POxy.* 2892–2940, with the comments of J. R. Rea in *The Oxyrhynchus Papyri* XL, ed. J. R. Rea (London, 1972), pp. 2–3, 8.

[19] Cf. Veyne, *Le pain et le cirque*, p. 57, on Christian charity. This last argument cannot be pressed too far: many Jewish religious duties, such as marrying the widow of a brother who has died childless, are impossible without prior tragedy which no one would have seen as desirable.

above the breadline by private charity. The rabbinic injunctions compiled in the second century A.D. probably reflect in general the normal Jewish attitude: anyone with enough for two meals was excluded from partaking in the free food given to paupers, and anyone with enough for fourteen meals was forbidden to accept charity from the general funds for the poor (*m.Peah* 8.7), while anyone possessing altogether two hundred zuz, evidently considered quite a low figure, was forbidden to benefit from any of the special provisions for the disadvantaged (*m.Peah* 8.8).

The rabble was thus kept from starvation, but with no prospects and nowhere to turn outside the big city they were a dangerous threat to the very people who helped to keep them alive. They were not likely to ignore the role of these same Jerusalem rich as a class in depriving many of them of their lands, nor were they likely to view the increasing sophistication and luxury of their wealthy lifestyle without envy. This combination of the private luxury of a few with a huge poverty-stricken urban mob was not to be found elsewhere in the Roman empire until the spread of Christianity and Christian notions of charity created the same conditions in the cities of the eastern part of the empire in the fourth to seventh centuries A.D.; in late Roman society, too, the volatile urban masses were a constant source of political and social unrest.[20]

With so much cause for hatred it may seem odd that class hostility was not more explicit and violent than the occasional vandalism of the property of the rich which Josephus records (e.g. *B.J.* 2.264–5). Faint echoes of calls for social justice do indeed percolate through the surviving literature in the angry words of Ben Sira and the Ethiopic Enoch,[21] but there is no record of a demand for a redistribution of land like that achieved by Nehemiah back in the fifth century B.C., although the biblical precedents for such action would have been strong.[22]

The cause of this reticence among the disgruntled poor lies in the general relation of Judaean society to the Judaean economy. In

---

[20] On Jewish ideas of charity, cf. *Encyclopaedia Judaica* v, pp. 338–44, and, more generally, Alon, *The Jews in their Land* ii, pp. 530–6.

On late-Roman cities and the treatment of the poor, see E. Patlagean, *Pauvreté économique et pauvreté sociale à Byzance 4e–7e siècles* (Paris, 1977), esp. pp. 156–235.

[21] *Ecclesiasticus* 34.20–2; I *Enoch* 97.8–10; cf. M. Hengel, *Property and Riches in the Early Church*, E.T. (London, 1974), pp. 16–17.

[22] Nehemiah 5.1–12. It would have been easy to cite the institution of the Jubilee to justify such a redistribution (Lev. 25.10,13), but Josephus simply assumes that the laws of the Jubilee no longer apply in his time, though he describes them quite accurately at the relevant point in the *Antiquities* (*A.J.* 3.284–5).

many traditional societies economic relations were expressed in social terms: to use a phrase of Polanyi's, the economy was 'embedded in society'.[23] But in Judaea this was precisely not the case. There were no social categories to correspond to the function of different groups in economic production. Neither free peasants nor tenant farmers nor craftsmen, nor indeed landowners and rich merchants, used such labels to identify themselves or recognized that as groups they were separate classes with identifiable interests and rights. Important social categories for them were based on religious status: a man felt himself to be an Israelite, a Levite or a priest, a proselyte or a natural-born Jew. He felt no tug of solidarity with others in his economic class. The resentment of the poor at exploitation by the rich remained unfocused.

At the same time, even if there was thus no full-scale class warfare because the poor did not identify with each other, equally the victims of economic change were in no way distracted by social norms from recognizing their personal misfortunes as both regrettable and reversible. When a peasant debtor chose to become the tenant of his creditor landlord rather than sell up the land and move away, their relationship was in every way an economic one. No ties of loyalty, no feudal oath, no sanction of long custom existed to coax the tenant into believing that his payment of rent to his superior was part of the natural order of things; on the contrary, the peasant will have known that the divinely ordained ideal in the Torah required each man to own his own land as a free and equal citizen (cf. Micah 4.4, etc.), for in fact the system of tenancy was probably a late introduction into Judaean society under hellenistic influence and may not have been known until the third century B.C. or later (see above, n. 10).

Similarly, when a poor man received charity from someone with money to spare, no social conventions insisted that he should be grateful. The relationship between patron and client which was fundamental in, for instance, Roman culture was not found among Jews.

Thus resentment based on a combination of economic deprivation and rising expectations bubbled continuously, unchecked by the structures through which authority was customarily channelled in Jewish society. In the process, those structures were themselves weakened: although not blamed for the economic facts which bred

[23] The phrase is quoted by Rajak, *Josephus*, p. 120, to describe first-century Judaea, but without any supporting argument. On Polanyi's analysis of traditional societies and the application of some of his ideas to ancient history, see S. C. Humphreys, *Anthropology and the Greeks* (London, 1978), pp. 31–75.

dissatisfaction, the traditional authorities lost power through their patent inability to do anything to alleviate those economic problems.

On the most basic level, this meant that, although in the theory of the Deuteronomic law code the most pervasive authority of all was that of the autocratic patriarch over his extended family, and although the big communal family tombs of the period of the First Temple (before 586 B.C.) suggest that at that time this theory reflected the actual exercise of power within most and perhaps all of society in Judah, by the first century A.D. such extended families had themselves apparently been split up into their nuclear components and the great influence of the family patriarchs was no more.

The main evidence for this collapse of the extended family as a primary social unit is negative. The emphasis on endogamy which was still dear to the author of *Tobit*, probably in the fourth century B.C., is not echoed in the Roman period except within the Herodian family, who had special political reasons to marry close relatives. Some sects even tried to ban as incestuous such common endogamous links as that of uncle to niece (*Damascus Rule* 5). The widow Babatha, whose private documents written in the late first and early second centuries A.D. were discovered in a cave in the Judaean desert, looked outside the circle of her relatives to find a guardian for her fatherless son. Similarly the rabbinic texts redacted in the late second century A.D. assume that a man will seek economic and social aid from neighbours and his nuclear family rather than any wider group of relatives.[24]

With the dissolution of the extended family as a social group the patriarch's power could no longer be exercised. The main cause of this great social change must be the economic pressures already described. As family plots became too small the nuclear fragments of extended families split off from their origins to seek their fortune in the diaspora or the cities. In the process they lost contact with their more distant relatives. But a second factor may also have had some effect. The extended family had originally acted as a sub-group of the much larger tribe, and that tribal structure had been destroyed by the exile and captivity in Assyria and Babylon. It is rarely that

[24] On the archive of Babatha, see N. Avigad *et al.*, 'The expedition to the Judaean desert, 1961', *IEJ* 12 (1962) 235–62. On tombs of the First Temple period, see R. Hachlili and A. Killebrew, 'Jewish funerary customs during the Second Temple period, in the light of the excavations at the Jericho necropolis', *PEQ* 115 (1983) 126; on the date of *Tobit*, see Schürer, *History* III, pp. 223–4; on Herodian marriages, see, e.g., Schürer, *History* I, 320–2,339,344,351,443,474–5. On the texts of the second century A.D., see M. D. Goodman, *State and Society in Roman Galilee, A.D. 132–212* (Totowa, 1983), p. 36.

the tribe to which figures of the first century A.D. belonged is recorded; the Benjaminite St Paul is an exception (Philippians 3.5). The children of converts, including most Jews from Galilee and Idumaea, were not, so far as is known, assigned to any tribe at all.

In place of the extended family, the nuclear family became the primary social unit. Again, some of the best evidence lies in burial customs. By the late first century B.C., Judaean burials were in small family tomb complexes in which individuals were accorded space in *kokhim*, finger-like narrow loculi with benches to receive the body or ossuary, thus being united with their immediate family in death. Similarly, in describing his family Josephus has much to say about his revered father (*Vita* 7) and takes it as obvious that he would ransom his brother from Roman captivity as soon as possible (*Vita* 419), but he is silent about any marriage connections with other families of the Jerusalem ruling class, though some at least must have been related to him. It is possible that the archaeological evidence over-emphasizes the social ties of richer Judaeans like Josephus, since loculus tombs were expensive and could be sold for a high price, and it may be that poorer Judaeans cared less about their nuclear families and were buried in individual graves, but against this can be set the assumption by Josephus that poorer families too would normally stick together, an assumption which lies behind his horrific description of the communal death of a nuclear family of brigands at Arbel in Galilee in 37 B.C. (*A.J.* 14.429–30; *B.J.* 1.310–15).[25]

Even within the nuclear family, however, the authority of the male head had been severely weakened by the first century A.D. In A.D. 67 Josephus seems to have reckoned that he could identify such a patriarch for each family in Tarichaeae, a town in Galilee, when he summoned to him the 'first men of each household' (*Vita* 163), but it is dubious how much control such men could exercise over their close relatives at times of crisis. Some adult males had begun to assert the importance of the individual even when this acted to the detriment of the family. The individual interments of the sectarians at Qumran and En el-Ghuweir suggest that these men denied their families, and even those young men who remained close to their immediate relatives would not feel it necessary to obey their fathers

---

[25] On burial customs, see Hachlili and Killebrew, 'Jewish funerary customs'. The evidence that the dead in each tomb are related comes from the names inscribed on the ossuary lids. For a sale of a loculus tomb, see Y. Naveh in Yadin, *Jerusalem Revealed*, p. 73. On the 'bandit' family at Arbel, see Freyne, *Galilee*, p. 66; it is unlikely that these martyrs were in fact bandits, but it is significant that Josephus can portray bandits behaving in such a way.

in everything, as they had once taken for granted they should do. It is unlikely that Herod's domination of his grown-up sons' fortunes, which extended to the execution of those who displeased him most severely, was reflected even on a modified scale in the relations between the generations in other families. In one high-priestly family, father and son led opposing factions in A.D. 66 (*B.J.* 2.409,429), a fact interestingly not explicitly brought out to the discredit of the rebellious son by Josephus even though the historian is not inclined to approve of him (see below, p. 154).

At the same time many adult women were probably winning more freedom within the nuclear family. Divorce was evidently common – a fact confirmed rather than denied by moves made by some sectarians to ban divorce altogether, an innovation quite contrary to the plain meaning of the Torah. Polygamy, though legal and practised by Herod, had become very rare, so that a wife was usually sole mistress of her household. Furthermore it is possible that women in some Jewish circles were able to initiate divorce. This had been the case in the community of Jews at Elephantine in the fifth century B.C., and the Herodian princesses Salome and Herodias too got rid of their husbands on their own initiative (*A.J.* 15.259–60; 18.136), though, since Josephus protests against it as unlawful, it is not likely that this practice was widespread.[26]

The authority of the male heads of even nuclear families was thus effectively diminished. When his son, daughter or wife infringed custom or law, there was little a man could do apart from beg them to conform.

The burden was all the greater on the public authorities who tried to keep order in each village. In every community, as from time immemorial, disputes were still decided by local judges, perhaps seven or twenty-three in most places depending on the size of the population; some Gospel parables seem to envisage a single headman as arbiter, but it is not certain that this reflects actual conditions in Judaea.[27] These men became the first line of defence in deflecting

[26] On sectarian divorce, see Jesus' words at Mark 10.2–12 (cf. Sanders, *Jesus and Judaism*, pp. 256–60, on the historicity of this passage), and the possible prohibition of divorce at Qumran (J. A. Fitzmyer, 'Divorce among first-century Palestinian Jews', *EI* 14 (1978) 103*–11*, *contra* G. Vermes, 'Sectarian matrimonial halakhah in the Damascus Rule', *JJS* 25 (1974) 197–202 (*Post-biblical Jewish Studies* (Leiden, 1975), pp. 50–6)). For Elephantine, see B. Porten, *Archives from Elephantine* (Berkeley and Los Angeles, 1968).

[27] On village administration, see Schürer, *History* II, pp. 184–90. The evidence for seven judges comes from Josephus (*B.J.* 2.569–71); that for twenty-three comes from later rabbinic texts (e.g. *m.Sanh.* 1.6). These numbers are not derived from any

any assault on society that might be provoked by economic hardship.

It is possible that the authority of such village leaders in this task was enhanced by their control of the community's synagogue, for a number of texts refer to the 'rulers of the synagogue' as important men (cf. *CIJ* II 991). But it is not necessary to make this identification: as far as is known, the task of the rulers of the synagogue in such villages was simply to choose the reader and interpreter of each week's section of the law set aside for public recitation, and in Judaean communities this could be a purely honorific post, since there is no evidence that the role of the synagogue attested in the diaspora as the place for communal discipline and the resolution of a united front *vis-à-vis* the gentiles was ever known in Palestine, where Jews were the majority of the population. If nonetheless some village judges in the first century A.D. were granted the honour of controlling the administration of the synagogue, any prestige which devolved upon them will have been of some use in facing the considerable problems which dogged them in controlling their communities.[28] In the absence of police or any other instruments of suppression, the traditional basis of the authority of such village leaders had been the consensus of the community in the isolation and punishment of malefactors, but the force of this consensus was being gradually weakened as the communities themselves began to crumble, with bankrupt villagers becoming bandits or migrating to the cities.

Some have argued that social deviants could be subjected to capital punishment without Roman interference by some at least of these local authorities, but continuing lack of certainty on this issue reflects the scarcity of evidence. In normal cases the worst punishment the courts could inflict was excommunication but it is hard to see how this would be effective in communities in such a state of flux. In the diaspora, where Jews lived as a minority among gentiles, exclusion from the synagogue would signify social death unless the victim apostatized altogether, and in Qumran excommunication might

biblical precedents and therefore probably reflect actual practice. For the single judge in the Gospels, see A. N. Sherwin-White, *Roman Society and Roman Law in the New Testament* (Oxford, 1963), p. 133.

[28] On the synagogues and the imposition of community discipline, see Schürer, *History* II, pp. 427–39, where evidence from both Palestine and the diaspora is used. On the comparatively small importance of synagogues in Palestine before A.D. 70, see Goodman, *State and Society*, pp. 85–7. Synagogues in Jerusalem probably served the same function as places of assembly for visiting diaspora Jews as they did for the same Jews in the cities from which they came (cf. Acts 6.9).

mean starvation since the initiates' meals were all rituals eaten in a state of purity within the congregation, but for an ordinary peasant in Judaea the religious world stayed in order so long as the Temple was still standing and the Torah obeyed (see below, p. 76), so there was no rite from which he could be effectively threatened with banishment. Once, then, he learnt to flout the disapproval of his fellow-villagers in the knowledge that in the last resort he could seek a new life elsewhere, there was nothing the village leaders could do to rein in his disobedience.[29]

The rich outsiders who had bought up village land apparently took no action to help preserve order in the countryside settlements. They themselves probably stayed in their city mansions, for no villas have been found in the hills around Jerusalem despite extensive survey work; there is no evidence that they tried to act as a squirearchy. Nor did the state lend its weight to solve local problems, for the Romans preferred to turn a blind eye to local affairs unless public order in the cities or violence to Roman officials was threatened: no trace remained of the close administrative control once favoured by the Ptolemies, apart from the names lingering on as geographical designations.[30] Nor, though some system of reference to a court in Jerusalem to deal with major problems is alleged by the rabbinic sources compiled in the second century A.D., is it likely that such a system would have had much effect in bolstering the general ability of local courts to impose their decisions.

For the problems of the village leaders were compounded further by the fact that they could not hope to control the people simply by natural authority. Even their right to act as judges had for some decades been put into question by those who claimed that the only

---

[29] On capital punishment there is a large literature, cf. P. Winter, *On the Trial of Jesus*, 2nd edn, rev. T. A. Burkill and G. Vermes (London, 1974); see also the discussion in Schürer, *History* II, pp. 221–3, with works cited on pp. 199–200. Alon, *Jews, Judaism and the Classical World*, pp. 103–12, argues that all capital cases were taken to Jerusalem. The Gospel writers (e.g. John 9.22; 12.42) ascribe great importance to excommunication, but they may have seen it in the diaspora context. The rabbis similarly assume the power of such bans, but they take for granted that the victims are fellow rabbis; non-rabbinical Jews would be too far gone to be affected (cf. *m.Taan.* 3.8; *m.Eduy.* 5.6). On the use of the ban at Qumran and elsewhere, see Schürer, *History* II, pp. 431–3, 577. See also W. Horbury, 'Extirpation and excommunication', *Vetus Testamentum* 35.1 (1985) 13–38; Alon, *Jews, Judaism and the Classical World*, pp. 138–45, on possible exclusion from the Temple court (but by whom?).

[30] On the lack of known administrative function for the toparchies, see Goodman, *State and Society*, pp. 135–6. Josephus writes about meridarchs in the second century B.C. and in the reign of Herod, but their areas of control were apparently huge, e.g. Samaria (*A.J.* 12.261; 15.216).

valid authority was that wielded by those who could show expertise in the interpretation of the Torah.

In the traditional local village courts the main qualification for membership was apparently old age. Thus the judges appointed in the villages of Galilee by Josephus were, so he says, all elders noted for their good sense (*B.J.* 2.570). The theory was presumably that old age brought experience and wisdom. Elders had always sat at the city gates (Deut. 19.12, etc.). They had time and patience to ruminate on problems. Many texts of the Roman period still describe Jewish leaders as presbyters (e.g. *A.J.* 13.428).

However, experience and prudence appeared to some Jews no longer to be a sufficient basis on which to judge cases, for self-proclaimed expert interpreters of the Torah pushed themselves forward as preferable arbiters able to discern, through careful perusal of the sacred texts, a divinely inspired pronouncement on each individual problem. When Jesus appeared as a potential trouble-maker in the villages of Galilee, it was, according to the Gospels, the 'scribes and Pharisees' who took it on themselves to check his legitimacy; the references to Pharisees may be suspect in this context because they may reflect the disputes of the late first-century Church, but there is no reason to doubt the historicity of Jesus' encounters with village scribes.[31] The local courts are nowhere to be seen.

In theory the scholars whose legal expertise undermined the authority of ordinary judges could have provided an alternative network of village tribunals. That, after all, is what the rabbinic texts portrayed as the ideal in the late second century A.D. Even then, however, their picture may have been merely the product of wishful thinking,[32] and in the first century this transfer of authority had almost certainly not yet occurred, for good reasons. Scholars were entrusted with legal decisions solely because of the prestige of their learning, for they held no formal position that might grant them such a right. No one, probably not even the elders whose status was diminished in contrast, begrudged such prestige to those who truly possessed wisdom to interpret the divine Torah, but in any individual case it was possible or even likely that even the most learned experts might disagree, not because of the incompetence of one of them but because the methodology by which scriptural law was interpreted differed between schools.

[31] On the reliability of the Gospels on this point, see G. Vermes, *Jesus and the World of Judaism* (London, 1983), p. 31.
[32] Goodman, *State and Society*, pp. 93–118.

Thus a Pharisaic scholar understood Torah in the light of custom sanctified as the 'Oral Law', in effect probably giving a veneer of sanctity to 'commonsense' popular decisions as already reached by using precedents in the established village tribunals (cf. *A.J.* 13.297; 18.17). Sadducees in contrast refused to compromise and to accept anything other than the straightforward meaning of the written law, a self-imposed limitation that presumably left Sadducaic experts at rather a loss when cases came before them that had not been explicitly dealt with in the written sources. Since Josephus describes both Pharisees and Sadducees as small sects (the figure that he gives at *A.J.* 17.42, probably relying on Nicolaus of Damascus, for the Pharisees under Herod is only 'over six thousand'), it is likely enough that yet other scholars operated in Judaea with equal legal expertise but different approaches again to difficult cases. An expert from within the Qumranic tradition, for example, would condemn on good scriptural grounds a man who sought permission to marry his brother's daughter, while a Pharisee operating in the same village would approve.

It is probable that in some cases the standard interpretation was Pharisaic, since that tradition after all incorporated much customary behaviour (e.g. with regard to the distance a man may walk on the sabbath). In favour of this view is the presumption in the rabbinic texts that the rulings of the sages who preceded them were normative in this way, but this presumption is somewhat weakened by the rabbinic tendency to read back the conditions of their own day into the history of the Jews before A.D. 70 to such an extent that even Moses was seen as a rabbinic figure. More significant are the explicit statements by Josephus of the popular support won by the Pharisees (*A.J.* 13.298): Josephus may have exaggerated the importance of the sect because, at least by the nineties A.D., he claimed to be of their number (*Vita* 12), but there is no need to disbelieve his statement that Pharisees were highly influential in controlling behaviour 'in prayer and worship' (*A.J.* 18.15), nor that their interpretation of Torah was much admired (*B.J.* 2.162). It has also been plausibly suggested that the political influence of the Pharisees before and during the revolt was deliberately suppressed in the *B.J.* by Josephus, who wished to exculpate them from responsibility.

But even if the influence of the Pharisees was indeed overwhelming – and it must be emphasized that this is still debated – this does not upset the present argument, for there are good grounds to believe that disputes about legal interpretation between the Pharisees themselves were no less divisive than those between Pharisees and other sects. The disputes between the school of Hillel and that of Shammai had become legendary by the time they were discussed in the surviving rabbinic writings, but the legends are certain to hide a secure foundation of truth about bitter wrangling among the pre-rabbinic sages before A.D. 70, and it is very probable that at least most of these sages were Pharisees (see below, p. 82). Thus Torah scholars diminished by their competition the authority of local courts but replaced it only with confusion.[33]

The problems facing the rulers of Judaea in A.D. 66 were thus deep-seated and serious. Their allotted task was the control of a peasant population which had been thrown into turmoil by economic change, and their ability to do so was seriously undermined by the near collapse of all local forms of authority. It would not be surprising if the countryside was thrown into anarchy, as Josephus indeed says was the case. But the problems were complicated and deepened by the tendency of many Jews to transfer their general resentment and hostility not onto their compatriots but onto the suzerain power Rome. The reasons for that tendency will be discussed in the next chapter.

[33] On the disputes between the House of Hillel and the House of Shammai, see J. Neusner, *The Rabbinic Traditions about the Pharisees before 70* (Leiden, 1971), and, with a very different approach, Ben-Shalom, 'The Shammai school' (Heb.). For arguments in favour of seeing the Pharisees as very influential, see Alon, *Jews, Judaism and the Classical World*, p. 22; D. R. Schwartz, 'Josephus and Nicolaus on the Pharisees', *JSJ* 14 (1983) 157–71; arguments against this view are presented by Sanders, *Jesus and Judaism*, pp. 195–8, citing earlier literature.

CHAPTER 4

PROBLEMS FACING THE RULING CLASS: RELIGIOUS IDEOLOGY

Reasons for blaming the propensity of the Jews to rebel on attitudes derived from their religious ideology have been examined in some detail in Chapter 1 (above, pp. 11–12), as have the limitations in ascribing responsibility for the revolt entirely to such a cause (pp. 15–16). Prime among these limiting factors was the fact that Judaism was too varied for easy generalizations about Jewish beliefs to be made. A few attitudes were standard among all Jews: there was, for instance, universal acceptance that the Torah was in some form the divine law given to Israel in recognition of the Jews' agreement to the covenant with God. But for most of the rest of his explanation of the world each individual Jew felt himself free to drift, as Josephus claims that he did (*Vita* 10–11), from one religious philosophy to another, seeking any one of the many different paths to virtue laid out before him. As a result there were within the Jewish tradition disparate reactions to the social chaos of first-century Judaea.[1]

Of course, the possible reactions to social malaise uncontrolled by accepted authority were logically almost infinite. To some it might seem sensible to withdraw from society altogether, whether alone or in the company of others equally disillusioned. Or it might seem best to accept disasters with resignation, either making a virtue of hopelessness or indulging in speculation about future happiness for individuals or for all society. Others might prefer to influence events by

---

[1] For a general characterization of first-century Judaism, see Stone, *Scriptures, Sects and Visions*, esp. p. 57. For an excellent summary of the religious questions under debate and unresolved in this period, see Kraft, 'Multiform Jewish heritage', esp. 197–8. Few religious statements could be guaranteed universal assent in Judaea.

My objective in this chapter is to examine the extent to which Judaism in this period impelled its adherents towards political rebellion. I do not intend to suggest that religious attitudes can always be explained primarily in terms of reactions to social and political factors, only that they sometimes can and that this fact may help to elucidate the variety in first-century Judaism which I want to stress.

political, military or even religious action, invoking divine aid; yet others might laugh away their troubles or ignore them, or run away, or confront them by the deliberate flouting of conventions, or contrive new theories to explain why the present state of affairs is really all for the best, or seek new unsullied authority to put matters right. There are doubtless other possibilities. Many, if not all, of these reactions appealed to one Jew or another in Judaea in the first century A.D.

Some of the more obvious responses to the problems of society, however, do not seem to have occurred. Thus, no agitation for economic reform is attested – perhaps, as has been suggested above (p. 67), because of the lack of class consciousness among the oppressed peasants despite the clear biblical precedents for redistribution of land. Withdrawal of labour, which proved at least partially effective when carried out by the mass of the population against Caligula's plans to set up his statue in the Temple (*A.J.* 18.272–7), was impossible to organize against more general oppression, again because class solidarity was unknown. Nor did Jews apparently take refuge in the defensive humour so characteristic of later Jewish history: almost no evidence survives for wit in Roman Palestine in contrast to the plentiful information on Greece and Rome, perhaps because no important social attitude not under taboo was sufficiently ambiguous for wit on the subject to be acceptable.[2]

On the other hand, some general reactions were more or less universal within Jewish society. One such well-attested response to near-chaos was a search for a new unambiguous authority to provide certainty in a shifting world.

The best evidence for this attitude lies in the fact that much of the literature produced by Jews in this period is pseudepigraphic. The literary form was not new in the Jewish tradition, but its popularity at this time is best explained by the social function of invented authorities as particularly credible when the actual leaders of society were all discredited for one reason or another. Attribution of a text to a pseudonymous author was not intended to fool or mislead the

---

[2] There is some literary evidence for puns, parody, *reductio ad absurdum*, irony and so on, cf. J. Jónsson, *Humour and Irony in the New Testament* (Reykjavik, 1965). But neither sexual nor religious humour could be indulged in a society where such topics were literally sacrosanct: purity restrictions would make sexual humour seem disgusting rather than amusingly obscene, and other religious observances had felt too much threatened since the persecution by Antiochus Epiphanes for Jews to be able to laugh at their own behaviour.

audience, and the Greek notion that such action is dishonest is wholly alien to Jewish thought, but it did enhance the claims of a text to represent divine inspiration unsullied by the political and social divisions of the day. In Qumran the same effect was sometimes achieved by not ascribing the sect's rules to any single person, but anonymity was not a common feature of Jewish writings of any period. More effective was the citing of names redolent with history. In this sense the ascription of dicta to specific rabbis – which, though first attested only *c.* A.D. 200, is likely to reflect the normal practice of Pharisees before A.D. 70 – filled the same function, for these early sages whose names lend authority to wise sayings are totally lacking in character and personality in the early traditions handed down in their names.[3]

Unambiguous authority was also sought in another figment of the religious imagination, angels. Wherever the origin of this belief is to be sought, it is clear that angelic intermediaries between men and God were firmly established in the religious understanding of most Jews by the first century A.D. Sadducees were the exception in remaining sceptical (*B.J.* 2.165; Acts 23.8).[4]

On a more practical level, recent research has emphasized the role of charismatics in first-century Palestine. The authority of such men as Hanina b. Dosa or Honi the Circle-Drawer depended entirely on their personalities, which suggested to their followers a sort of direct link to the divine evidenced by ostentatious piety and a capacity to work miracles, particularly in time of drought. It is possible that Jesus was such a charismatic, but any attempt to categorize Jesus is of course likely to be tentative, simply because of the special attitude towards him of the Gospel evidence. What the charismatics did with their authority was quite varied; important for the present argument is simply the power ascribed to them precisely because of their lack of institutional authority or social status.[5]

This, however, is one of only few ideological reactions to their sick society which can be predicated of most if not all Jews. For the rest, different Jews explained their predicament in a variety of ways.

[3] On pseudepigraphy, see N. Cohen, 'From *nabi* to *mal'ak* to "ancient figure"', *JJS* 36 (1985) 12–24; F. Schmidt, 'L'écriture falsifiée', *Le temps de la réflexion* 5 (1984) 147–65. On the ascription of teachings to early sages by the rabbis, cf. Rajak, *Josephus*, p. 114.

[4] Angels are assumed in Josephus and the Palestinian targumim as well as at Qumran. For their possible origins, see S. Shaked in *CHJ* 1, pp. 314, 317–18.

[5] Cf. Vermes, *Jesus the Jew*. Note also the ascetic Bannus (*Vita* 11–12; cf. Rajak, *Josephus*, p. 38), and the extent to which John the Baptist 'persuaded the people', making Herod Antipas, probably unjustifiably, afraid of rebellion (*A.J.* 18.117–19).

Only a few could accept the status quo with complacency, but Josephus' description of the Sadducees makes it clear that they at least contrived to make a positive philosophy out of laissez-faire. It is not surprising to find that they all apparently came from the ruling class. The philosophy did not attract the populace but only men of means (*A.J.* 13.298), the kind of public figures of high standing who could expect office, presumably as High Priests (*A.J.* 18.17).

The essence of Sadducaism was a rejection of the oral law beloved of the people and the Pharisees. In the process the Sadducees denied also belief in bodily resurrection and the mediating authority of angels and spirits which, as has already been seen, gave comfort to many who needed it. Sadducaism was adopted by those who did not need such comfort. Against the whole ethos of the Old Testament, whose authority they took as paramount, the Sadducees maintained that God exercised no influence at all on human actions and that a man could choose for himself whether to do good or evil, being entirely responsible for his own fortune or misfortune (*B.J.* 2.164–5). Such ideas in other societies have seemed attractive to political rebels who, rejecting the notion that their poor social position was divinely ordained, used their own efforts to seek change; in Roman Palestine, by contrast, Sadducaism embodied a smug self-congratulation about the status quo that only the rich could accept. It is to their credit that some of the ruling class did not accept such a philosophy; but a few did, although (not surprisingly given their negative conservatism) they apparently accomplished almost nothing in trying to influence the rest of the population (*A.J.* 18.17).[6]

For most Judaeans, however, some theological succour for present ills was imperative. Some found such comfort by elevating withdrawal from society into a positive ideological reaction to social turmoil.

The voluntary asceticism of Bannus and of John the Baptist gave them prestige within society, for many went to John for baptism and forgiveness of sins (*A.J.* 18.117–18; Mark 1.4–5), and Josephus claims that he was himself tempted for three years to retire from his prestigious circles in Jerusalem in order to act as a devoted disciple of Bannus in the desert (*Vita* 11). But equally significant to the status

[6] Against the prevalent view that the Sadducees were, or acted in the interests of, priests, see Jeremias, *Jerusalem*, pp. 228–32. The name is probably derived from that of the priest Zadok, but that in itself proves nothing: the Qumran sect also called themselves 'sons of Zadok' (*1QS* v. 2–3). Some High Priests were Sadducees (*A.J.* 20.199), but not a few influential priests were Pharisees, cf. Schürer, *History* II, p. 405 n. 7. Apart from their appeal to the wealthy, there is no good reason to suppose that Sadducees were more hellenized than other Jews.

they acquired is the fact that these men themselves believed that their behaviour was holy. Both men carefully avoided all manufactured food and clothing, taking only what nature provided. Both men laid great stress on the purificatory power of frequent baths in cold water. The fame of such men suggests that this sort of extreme asceticism was exceptional, in contrast to the plethora of Christian holy men in Syria and Palestine in the late Roman period. It is all the more interesting that Josephus and others accepted the religious value of such behaviour even at a time when involuntary penury pushed other Judaeans into similar destitution without any suggestion of religious worth accruing to them from their poverty. It is evident that ostentatious withdrawal from everything to do with society was regarded by them as a pious act.

The same attitude can also be discerned in the mass withdrawal from society led by a certain Theudas in the mid forties A.D., for his dramatic crossing of the Jordan seems to have been in deliberate imitation of the Exodus, but in reverse (*A.J.* 20.97). Salvation and the cessation of their troubles was sought in the desert by many poor souls in the early sixties A.D. (*A.J.* 20.188). Some of these may have gone to the wilderness to await a messianic leader (see below, p. 92), but the act of ceremoniously casting off society was in itself seen as desirable. There may have been the same rationale behind the request put to the Roman general Titus by the two main leaders of the rebels in A.D. 70, John of Gischala and Simon b. Gioras, that they be permitted in like manner to retire into the desert solitudes (*B.J.* 6.351).

At Qumran and probable sister-settlements such as the recently discovered site of En el-Ghuweir, the process of withdrawal from the ordinary world was institutionalized. The whole myth of the Qumran community was framed in terms of the rejection of ordinary Judaean society. Founded as the 'Pure Israel', it saw its role as opposition to the wicked priests of the Temple and their warped religion symbolized by a calendar out of phase with divinely ordained time. Their physical and mental seclusion from the rest of Palestine was almost complete until the rude interruption of uncomprehending Romans onto the site during the revolt.

The collapse of authority and the pressures of economic and class divisions had no effect on the secluded community, and status outside their number had no meaning at all for them. In place of the old, they produced a new society, self-sufficient in almost all respects, even economic, despite the extreme problems of maintaining a sizeable population in the Judaean desert with limited water supplies and the difficulties in, for example, finding fuel with which to fire the unpolluted pottery that they insisted on baking in their own kilns.

The nature of their society seems to have been conditioned by a desire to reverse the worst elements of Judaea outside. The emphasis was on purity and on hierarchy. The surviving codes are obsessed with the details of authority and its implementation, in quite considerable contrast to the more relaxed approach of the later rabbinic codes. Purity was ensured both by the uncomfortable seclusion of the chosen sites and by strict rules of conduct for the selection and retention of members, as well as by the numerous baths and facilities for the unpolluted preparation and consumption of food.

If, as is much the most likely, the people at Qumran are to be identified with the Essenes described by Josephus, Philo and Pliny, some of the sect will also have been celibate, thereby removing altogether a major source of possible impurity (see *m.Nidd.*, etc.). If this is the case, another conclusion too is possible: of the more than four thousand Essenes (*A.J.* 18.20), most will have entered the community not by birth but through voluntary association after reaching adulthood as described both by the classical sources and by the Dead Sea Scrolls. The existence of the community in the first century A.D., especially after a possible temporary cessation during the reign of Herod, would then in itself be evidence of the popularity of escape from ordinary society into something more pure where authority more obviously derived from the divine. Protected by this ability mentally to exclude the problems of the ordinary world, Essenes were able to submit with passive cheerfulness to the tortures imposed upon them during the revolt by the Romans, despite their generally non-combatant status (*B.J.* 2.152–3).[7]

[7] On the Dead Sea sect, see G. Vermes, *The Dead Sea Scrolls in English* (Harmondsworth, 1975), pp. 16–68. On En el-Ghuweir, see P. Bar-Adon, 'Another settlement of the Judaean desert sect at 'En el-Ghuweir on the shores of the Dead Sea', *BASOR* 277 (1977) 1–22. On the relation of the Essenes to Qumran, see Schürer, *History* II, pp. 583–5. Women were found at both Dead Sea sites, but apparently, according to the siting of their corpses, not as full community members, cf. Vermes, *Dead Sea Scrolls in English*, pp. 30–1; Bar-Adon, 'Another settlement', p. 17. For the temporary cessation in settlement at Qumran, see R. De Vaux, *Archaeology and the Dead Sea Scrolls* (London, 1973), p. 19. For the generally non-combatant status of Essenes, note the name of John 'the Essene' (*B.J.* 2.567); the soubriquet would have been useless if Essenes generally joined the revolt.

On attitudes to purity at Qumran, J. M. Baumgarten, 'The Pharisaic–Sadducean controversies about purity and the Qumran texts', *JJS* 31 (1980) 157–70, observes that the Dead Sea sect followed the Pharisees in extending purity rules to the laity but agreed with the Sadducees when the latter were more strict with regard to immersion after pollution. S. L. Davies, 'John the Baptist and Essene Kashruth',

A similar ascription of sanctity to social withdrawal and separation may have helped to some extent the more widely influential Pharisaic movement. Study of the Pharisees before A.D. 70 is dogged by particularly intractable source problems. Christian writers were deeply prejudiced against them, either because of their hostility to Jesus (if the Gospels are to be believed), or because of the tribulations of the early Church during the protracted break from the fold of Judaism (if this is what the Gospels reflect). Rabbinic sources were also biased since they may have portrayed the early sages in the image of rabbinic teachers of the second century and later. Josephus was hardly objective since he claimed, for respectability's sake perhaps, that he himself was a Pharisee (*Vita* 12). Modern scholarship has not yet reached even a partial consensus on many crucial issues, for all interpretation depends on the stance taken with regard to a number of unresolved matters.

The problem can be stated briefly as follows. The rabbinic texts name a number of sages who lived before A.D. 70 as important contributors towards their traditions. Among these are such figures as Gamaliel and his son Simon, who are described by both Josephus and the New Testament as Pharisees. Most of the rulings specifically ascribed to these proto-rabbinic sages concern the regulation of the purity and tithing of the food eaten in dining clubs (*havuroth*); it seems to be assumed in these texts that some sages are members (*haverim*, 'fellows') of such clubs. It is therefore *possible* that all references by the rabbis to their predecessors before 70 refer to Pharisees and that the main interests of the latter lay in the regulation of food preparation. In favour of this, but of dubious value because of its late date and polemical tone, is the attack in some Gospel texts against Pharisees for allegedly hypocritical concerns about purity and tithing (e.g. Matt. 23.23–6). But it is certainly not *necessary* that the equation between haverim and Pharisees be made. If many of the anonymous rulings in rabbinic texts are to be attributed to Pharisees who taught before 70 (as is possible but cannot be proved), the impression gained from study of rulings assigned in the extant compilations to named sages, i.e. of a concentration on the problems of dining clubs, would be highly misleading, since these anonymous rulings have much wider concerns. It is clear that some proto-rabbinic sages and some Pharisees were haverim, but it is unnecess-

NTS 29 (1983) 569–71, puts forward the interesting observation that John's diet may have been simply that of an Essene living outside any community and that he was not necessarily ascetic: he may have eaten locusts and honey in great quantities. It was the purity of the food that mattered, not its amount.

ary to postulate that all were. It may be significant that Josephus nowhere mentions a concern over the purity of food as a specific trait of Pharisees, despite the fact that he both gives a positive picture of the Pharisees as a whole and considers such behaviour praiseworthy.

Nonetheless it is probable that there was at least a considerable overlap between proto-rabbinic sages, Pharisees and ḥaverim, and in so far as the Pharisees were an identifiable movement with a specific message as Josephus implies (cf. *A.J.* 17.42), it is likely that it was the fellows in their dining clubs who provided their power-base. At any rate, for such 'fellows' the preparation and consumption of correctly tithed foodstuffs in a state of ritual purity became in effect almost a form of worship – a phenomenon that was not, incidentally, in its externals unique in the Greco-Roman world where religious banquets confined to initiates are well attested from the early Hellenistic period. It may well be that, if many of the Pharisees were indeed ḥaverim, the connotations of separation in their name (in Hebrew, *perushim*) referred precisely to this separation from pollution. Such table fellowship could enable them to form a complete alternative society not dissimilar to that in Qumran. Linked by an artificial universe hardly visible to the rest of the population, special boundaries for pollution might fence them into a purified mental world rendered safe and sacred by the vigorous confining of all activity connected with the preparation of meals within clear-cut confines, and the exclusion from meals of all those not prepared voluntarily either to enter into that universe or to obey its rules at least temporarily.

The power of this attitude to life came from its very artificiality and hence its ability to survive even the catastrophe of the destruction of the Temple which saw the end of the Sadducees and of the Qumran community, whose physical presence in the desert was so much a part of their withdrawal; no one would dispute the adoption and elaboration of many of the notions of the ḥaverim by the rabbis after A.D. 70. This mental withdrawal was no less powerful a response to social tensions than the physical withdrawal of other groups, but if, as I have argued is likely, not a few Pharisees were ḥaverim, their mental seclusion clearly did nothing to hinder their continued activity within mainstream society.

On the other hand, the influence of the Pharisees which is so much stressed by Josephus probably derived from factors other than this mental seclusion, for Essenes, who were just as devoted to purification by withdrawal, do not seem to have gained much influence at all. In describing the importance of the Pharisees, Josephus nowhere makes mention of any particular care over purity, beyond a general reference to their avoidance of luxury (*A.J.* 18.12). Pharisaic influence was, therefore, brought about by the other characteristics stressed by Josephus: their ability to combine a belief in fate with belief in free will and other philosophical notions (*A.J.* 18.13–15), their reputation for possessing knowledge of the future perhaps largely through their understanding of the Torah (*A.J.* 17.41–3), and, above all, the fact that by many they were considered the most accurate interpreters of the Law (*B.J.* 2.162, etc.).

Doubtless it was this popularity that enabled the Pharisees to develop harmonious relations with the community even while some or all of them maintained their mental seclusion. Certainly it permitted Josephus to ignore the centrality of this artificial world to the mental universe of those Pharisaic devotees who were ḥaverim, and to portray himself as a Pharisee in so far as he followed their methods in interpreting the Law. But for Pharisees who were ḥaverim it was probably their fellowship that was all-important, binding them together in their common acceptance of purity and tithing.

Both this fellowship and the characteristic Pharisaic methods of interpreting Torah overrode the social distinctions of the rest of Judaean society. Rich Pharisees such as Gamaliel coexisted with poor craftsmen, if the later rabbinic traditions about these early sages are correct, in equal subjugation to the traditions of the fathers. It is not surprising that Pharisees were sometimes identified as a group when they ventured forth into the political arena in the wider world (so, e.g., *B.J.* 2.411 – 'the well-known among the Pharisees'). They entered politics not, necessarily, with any well-defined political programme or even agreement on political cooperation one with another, but with a common self-confidence derived from the firm knowledge of their accuracy in interpreting the divine Law and, for such as were ḥaverim, of their sanctity preserved by the artificial world of purity into which they had withdrawn themselves.[8]

[8] The bibliography on the Pharisees is huge. For a clear discussion of the issues, see Sanders, *Jesus and Judaism*, pp. 187–8, with the review by P. S. Alexander, *JJS* 37 (1986) 104. The full account in Schürer, *History* II, pp. 388–403, equates Pharisees and ḥaverim without argument, following Neusner, *Rabbinic Traditions*. For a quite different approach to the rabbinic evidence, see A. Oppenheimer, *The 'Am Ha-aretz: a study in the social history of the Jewish people in the Hellenistic–Roman period* (Leiden, 1977). Cf. also J. Blenkinsopp, 'Prophecy and priesthood in Josephus', *JJS* 25 (1974) 257, on Pharisees as prophets; Stern, 'Aspects of Jewish society', p. 620, on the social origins of the early sages. On some of the sages before A.D. 70 as poor, see below, p. 124. There is no agreement on the significance of the name of the Pharisees; cf. J. M. Baumgarten, 'The name of the Pharisees', *JBL* 102 (1983) 411–28, for a different suggestion.

Haverim evidently believed that participation in their world of purity could make social misery appear less important. Not everyone accepted the efficacy of their solution. For others, the evils of society were too patently obvious or impinged too closely on their daily lives for them to ignore. Psychologically incapable of withdrawal, whether mental or physical, they had to choose whether to accept with resignation or reject with effort their sad state. Both attitudes are to be found in first-century Judaea, and the justification proposed for both was in terms of religious ideology.

Some Jews demonstrated their piety precisely by their stoic acceptance of suffering. Though the role of fate in human affairs was much debated in this period, as Josephus' description of the Jewish philosophies shows, Essenes were not the only Jews who accepted whatever happened, however bad it appeared, as the will of God (*A.J.* 18.18). The divine will might appear inscrutable at times, but the theme of divine punishment for sins as the cause of human misery and particularly the national misfortunes of Israel is prominent throughout the Old Testament and had not been forgotten. It was hardly flattering, though useful, to Herod that the Pharisee Sameas advocated acceptance of his rule in 37 B.C. on the grounds that his domination was a divine punishment which it would be impious not to bear willingly (*A.J.* 14.176). The theme that God had deserted the Jews during the revolt because of the magnitude of their sins and especially the pollution of the Temple runs through the whole of Josephus' *B.J.* His constant attributions of blame are motivated by theology as well as political apologetics. His perception of the weight of sin on the people and on individuals was clearly shared by those who flocked long before A.D. 70 to John the Baptist to repent in the face of the coming judgement.[9]

It is possible that a few Jews helped to make sense of their acceptance of suffering by shrugging off social problems as unimportant compared to the continuing magnificence of the Divine and the Torah, whose appreciation could thus become a major, though never the only, aim in life. Such speculation by mystical and magical approaches towards the godhead can in fact only be postulated, not proved, in this period. Some contemporary apocalyptic texts de-

---

[9] It is conventional to date the Jewish texts which take this attitude of resigned suffering to the years immediately after the destruction of the Temple, but some of them, e.g. II Baruch, may date before A.D. 70. For dramatic portrayal of national calamity by an author before A.D. 70 seeking to explore theodicies to explain such disasters, the destruction of the first Temple in 587 B.C. would be just as powerful an image before the ruin of the second Temple as after.

scribe visions of the sort later described by exponents of Merkabah mysticism (e.g. 1 *Enoch*. 14.8–25), but it is not possible to be certain when, if ever, the literary descriptions of Ezekiel and others were first translated into mystical practice. On the other hand, the fact that rabbis in the late second century A.D. thought it necessary to restrict study of the Chariot passage in Ezekiel and the early chapters of Genesis suggests that study of these texts was already sometimes esoteric by then, and the likelihood of a Jewish mysticism flourishing in Palestine before A.D. 70 has seemed probable to some scholars. Such mysticism was not 'Gnostic' in the sense appropriated to describe the Christian Gnostic groups of the second century – it implied no rejection of the physical world and the ascent to the divine was undertaken, if the surviving texts are indeed a guide to practice, for instruction in practical Torah rather than salvation at a stroke. The pseudonymous heroes of the apocalypses undertake their journeys to God in order to learn the answer to specific questions, after which they return to normality. If visions like those recorded did indeed occur, their feasibility would make current misfortunes easier to bear.[10]

For most Jews who did not withdraw from or reject their society, however, only hope for the future compensated for the present. An interest in future events is perhaps too obvious to need documentation, but explicit testimony is to be found in the ability to prophesy the future claimed by Josephus himself (*B.J.* 3.405) and attributed by him to, above all, the Essenes (*B.J.* 1.8; 2.113,159; *A.J.* 13.311–13; 15.373–9).

For those sceptical of explicit prophecy much current speculation about the future of both the nation and the individuals within it gave hope of better things to come. The converse of the belief that calamity was the result of Israel's sin was the assurance so often repeated in the prophets that God could intervene in political affairs and bring prosperity and redemption. The whole of Judaism as it had developed was based on the premise that divine favour was efficacious, just as its withdrawal was catastrophic. Identifying the specific sins that had led to divine disapproval was not easy, but it is safe to assert that most unthinking Jews in the first century assumed that, if they kept to the Torah as best they could, then the foreign yoke

[10] On Merkabah mysticism and its possible predecessors in the first century A.D., see, e.g., P. Schäfer, 'New Testament and Hekhalot literature: the journey into heaven in Paul and in Merkavah mysticism', *JJS* 35 (1984) 19–35. On the rabbinic restrictions, see Goodman, *State and Society*, p. 109; P. Schäfer, 'Merkavah mysticism and rabbinic Judaism', *JAOS* 104 (1984) 537–41.

would eventually be lifted and their economic and social troubles resolved.[11]

This general belief in divine intervention in this world was quite distinct from the much more restricted speculation on personal salvation after death and on national salvation in a messianic age. These two latter grounds for hope were evolved quite separately and were never properly welded into a single coherent philosophy.

The spread of belief in life after death in Palestine from the Hellenistic period onwards has been much studied. Josephus (*A.J.* 18.14,16) and Acts (23.6) describe the matter as under dispute between Pharisees and Sadducees, though the Pharisaic view seems certain to have been more popular. Assertions about post-mortem existence were probably fuelled originally by the adoption of hellenistic notions of the immortality of a soul separate from the body, but in Palestine teachings about resurrection in corporeal form are much more common, the assumption being that this resurrection will be pleasant and reserved for those who have earned it by good actions in this life, but that it will be postponed for some time after death. Theories about what happened to a person immediately after decease varied considerably, though it was taken for granted that existence until the great day of resurrection was on a plane quite close to the world, permitting intercession, both kindly and malignant, in human affairs.[12]

It is difficult to estimate the power of such new ideas to affect behaviour in this life. Under the spectre of the Last Judgement and the prospect of eternity, current social problems might logically pale into insignificance. The history of later Christian Europe, where similar theological notions coexisted with great social and political movements, shows that logic does not always control human behaviour in such matters. In Judaea the apparent failure of beliefs in life after death to change burial and funerary customs so as to take account of them suggests that, for many, such speculation was no more than theoretical theology. Josephus records it as exceptional that belief in an afterlife gave Essenes courage to face death without

---

[11] On the popularity of prophecy and the common charge of pseudo-prophecy, see Blenkinsopp, 'Prophecy and priesthood', *passim*; D. E. Aune, 'The use of προφητης in Josephus', *JBL* 101 (1982) 419–21; Rajak, *Josephus*, p. 90. The complication is that inspired prophecy was believed by later rabbis to have ended in the Persian period but that knowledge of the future from studying the Law was still considered by Josephus to be feasible (Blenkinsopp, 'Prophecy and priesthood', p. 258).

[12] For general introductions, see Schürer, *History* II, p. 546; G. W. E. Nickelsburg, *Resurrection, Immortality and Eternal Life in Intertestamental Judaism* (Cambridge, Mass., 1972).

fear (*B.J.* 2.153). In practice, death was treated by all other Jews as unalloyed tragedy.

This attitude emerges most clearly from consideration of mourning customs in this period. Extravagant weeping, professional keening and the playing of flutes were universally observed. Weeping was reckoned essential for a good funeral – Herod was considered by Josephus to be wicked but not irrational to want to ensure tears at his funeral by arranging mass executions in Jericho just before he died, so it did not matter who wept, or why, so long as there were plenty of mourners to join in (*B.J.* 1.659–60). In general, the ceremonial of Jewish funerals was aimed at the social relations of the living rather than the comfort of the dead: the funeral oration, as recorded in rabbinic as opposed to biblical texts, stressed the virtues of the dead man to his surviving relatives rather than his own need for consolation or congratulation on removal to a higher sphere; the burial gave the immediate family the opportunity to display the piety that, even at risk of impoverishing the living, had bought the right to stopping-places for orations on the way to the tomb, as well as the tomb itself and an expensive shroud for the corpse; after the funeral the main religious duty was the comfort of the bereaved, not least in a possibly rather drunken meal of consolation. In particular, the public banquets held to mark the end of mourning were so lavish that they often ruined the pious by the expense (*B.J.* 2.1), suggesting again the centrality of the bereaved rather than the deceased in mourning ritual after death.[13]

More curious is the circumstance that burial customs did change among most of the inhabitants of Judaea in precisely this period, but that the changes brought about seem to have no connection with belief in the afterlife. Near the end of the first century B.C. some Jews in the Jerusalem area took to burying their dead in small stone ossuaries. This required the exhumation of the corpse from its original resting place after sufficient time had elapsed for the flesh to fall away from the bones. The remains were then collected and placed in the loculus-type family tombs which had been in general

---

[13] On mourning in general, see S. Safrai, 'Home and family', in Safrai and Stern, *The Jewish People* II, pp. 773–87. For the funeral oration, see E. Feldman, 'The rabbinic lament', *JQR* 63 (1972–3) 51–75. On the drink consumed at the meal of consolation, note *b.Ket.* 8b and parallels about the need to prevent unseemly inebriation from the drinking of fourteen cups of wine. The implication is that a presumably cheerful state under the influence of ten cups was normal. Note that, at *c.Ap.* 2.195,204, Josephus stresses the sobriety of Jewish ritual in celebrating sacrifices and the birth of children but says nothing about funerals, and that he omits any mention of the funerary feast at *c.Ap.* 2.205, where it would naturally belong.

use for some time (see above, p. 69). The practice may have ended abruptly with the destruction of the Temple.

Some specific impetus must be posited for such a peculiar innovation in burial, and I shall make one suggestion below (p. 104), but it is hard to see how hopes for life after death could have brought such a change. Grave goods were few and unspectacular. No text suggests that secondary burial would aid the resurrection of the whole body; on the contrary, deliberate disturbance of the bones after death might be thought to increase the risk that the bodies of different people would be confused, though careful marking of the ossuaries was presumably intended to prevent this. Nor is it evident how this custom would advantage the resurrection of the soul. In its pure hellenized form, the notion of a re-born soul assumes the unimportance of the body left behind. It would be immaterial how or where the bones were left.[14]

If it is uncertain how much Jews were affected in their attitudes to social turmoil in Judaea by their hopes of individual salvation, it seems likely that many were greatly affected by a general expectation of a total, cataclysmic process of destruction and renewal for the entire world, the messianic age. Messianic ideas owed much to hellenistic, Mesopotamian and Iranian influences already visible in the book of Daniel in the second century B.C., but relevant to present concerns is the wide currency of such notions in Judaea in the first century A.D.

The main evidence for that wide currency lies in the frequent mention of messianic beliefs in the apocrypha and pseudepigrapha preserved by the Christian Church. Given the messianic aspects of early Christianity itself, it might seem circular to accept such testimony. In confirmation of Jewish adherence to such beliefs, however, can be cited the messianic ideas found in the *Psalms of Solomon*, the Dead Sea Scrolls and the messianic oracle, that a ruler would come forth from Judaea, which is mentioned by Suetonius (*Vesp.* 4) and, according to Josephus, was more responsible for the war than any other of the prophecies circulating in the province before and during the revolt (*B.J.* 6.310–15). Even the respectable Alexandrian philosopher and statesman Philo may have awaited the messianic end of days (Philo, *De Praem.* 95,164–5).

The precise nature of the society expected after the coming of the

[14] On ossuary burial as an innovation from *c.* 10 B.C. to *c.* A.D. 70, see Hachlili and Killebrew, 'Jewish funerary customs', but note also the cautionary remarks against over-generalization in L. Y. Rahmani, 'Some remarks on R. Hachlili's and A. Killebrew's "Jewish funerary customs"', *PEQ* 118 (1986) 96–100.

messiah was not clear. Some may have anticipated only a return to kingship by the house of David; others looked forward to the end of days as portrayed in Ezekiel's vision. All agreed that the messiah (whose nature was similarly shrouded in uncertainty, for the word *mashiah* simply means a properly anointed king) would bring the antithesis of present confusion, as is demonstrated by the constant emphasis on the supreme kingship of God in the new order of things (cf., for example, *Psalms of Solomon* 17.1,38,51, and compare the phrase 'kingdom of God' in Mark and Luke, and 'kingdom of heaven' in Matthew (e.g. 3.2)). Various texts ascribe untroubled joy and gladness, the cessation of strife, wealth, prosperity and so on to the messianic age, but they all assume that these blessings depended on the restoration of pure divine authority.

Quite when in the future that new age would come about was an unknown mystery. Some Jews in the first century A.D. might reasonably have expected that it would be soon, for there was a general assumption that it was to be preceded by a period of special distress and affliction, and it did not take much to interpret the state of Judaea in that light. Such immediate expectation was perhaps explicitly enunciated once the revolt had broken out, but in the preceding period current tribulations were for most too long-term to be seen by many in this dramatic light. Thus the prophecies of doom by a peasant called Jesus b. Ananias, uttered in Jerusalem from autumn A.D. 62 for seven years and five months, were taken by most Jews simply as ill-omened speech (*B.J.* 6.300–9); no one seems to have rejoiced at the imminent coming of the messiah that his words might seem to imply.

What all this suggests is that belief in future messianic upheaval sometimes encouraged not unrest but acceptance of the political and social situation. There was nothing to be done to hasten the messiah apart from righteousness in influencing the divine timetable. Political intervention, violent or otherwise, was meanwhile irrelevant or even wicked in its presumption to preempt God. Fervent millenarian expectation could coexist with complete loyalty to the political order: as in Christian circles in the second century A.D., so in first-century Judaea, such hopes might provoke only political quietism. It is admittedly now difficult to tell how much this was the case in first-century Judaea, for neither Josephus nor the New Testament was likely to give an honest description of contemporary messianic fervour if it tended commonly to impel Jews towards irrational hostility to Rome. Nonetheless it is striking that even when the siege of Jerusalem was at its height in A.D. 70, the belief that God was about to deliver to the Jews the signs of their salvation led a crowd of six thousand, including women and children, to await their deliverance by just standing passively in the Temple court at the urging of a 'false prophet' (*B.J.* 6.283–5). They were all burnt to death.[15]

Resigned acceptance of social turmoil or withdrawal from it by mental or physical means were thus perfectly possible reactions of first-century Judaeans to the collapse of authority and increase in economic pressures. Josephus' account of the Jewish war naturally highlighted, as do many modern accounts, a third sort of reaction which consisted in attempts to change the status quo, but it should be apparent that hindsight in this case may be a curse rather than a blessing. The impulse to throw off the shackles of Rome cannot have been an inevitable reaction to universally accepted religious tenets because many, probably most, Jews before A.D. 6 espoused with a good conscience the more peaceful, passive reactions already described. I do not want to deny an increasing tendency to excuse anti-Roman violence in religious terms, but only to emphasize that religious ideology in this case seems to have been used to justify political action felt to be desirable on other grounds rather than itself being the prime motivation for revolution.

Furthermore, even those who wanted to bring changes to society did not necessarily have to use force. The obvious way to challenge the political and social status quo under Roman rule was by diplomacy. There was nothing at all un-Jewish or irreligious in such negotiations with a foreign power. Nehemiah had been the representative of the Persian king, the Tobiad folk-heroes had won their influence from the Ptolemies, and the Maccabees had opened diplomatic relations with the Seleucid dynasty very soon after their first successful rebellion. Much could often be achieved by applying pressure on the Roman state through embassies, but it must be recognized that the achievement of change by such methods was usually only available to those richer men whose approaches were acceptable to the Romans. As has been seen (above, Chapter 2), other Judaeans could only influence Roman rule by mass protest, and, in the absence of leaders, such protest was rare and confined to specific issues of overwhelming importance.

If most Judaeans wanted to do something to alter their situation it would have to be by much more violent action, and some Jews on some occasions seem to have believed that such violence was divinely ordained.

[15] On messianic beliefs and the evidence for them in general, see J. Klausner, *The Messianic Idea in Israel* (London, 1956); Schürer, *History* II, pp. 488–554.

The most compelling motive for any Jew to join in violent struggle was a belief that the messianic age was not just a future hope, for which people could only patiently wait (see above, p. 90), but a present actuality. Once the messiah had arrived and the last battles, so graphically imagined in the Qumran War Scroll, were ready to commence, those truly convinced of such a turn of events had no choice but to participate. In the final messianic struggle it was hardly possible to stand on one side to await the outcome.

It is probable that at least a few Jews in first-century Judaea did believe, at least for brief periods, that the messiah had arrived. There is only scant evidence of radicals who subscribed to this conviction, but the survival of any hints at all is instructive given the tendency of Josephus and early Christian writers to play down all religious justi-fication given in their day for anti-Roman actions. Josephus men-tions popular support for a number of 'pseudo-prophets' who 'disturbed the people'. Their prophecies may well have been of mes-sianic content and may well have encouraged political revolt. It should however be noted that neither Josephus, nor the other main source for their activities, Acts 21.38, makes this clear, for Roman opposition to popular movements of all kinds could be guaranteed whatever their intent, and Festus would have sent a force to destroy the poor souls who sought salvation in the Judaean wilderness even if they were of no danger to him or the rest of Judaean society (*A.J.* 20.188). Of those popular leaders who claimed either kingship, such as the shepherd Athronges in 4 B.C. (*A.J.* 17.278–84; *B.J.* 2.60–5), or the right to be a 'tyrant of the people', such as the Egyptian 'false prophet' who appeared during Felix's governorship (*B.J.* 2.262), some or all may have claimed religious justification for their claims, though not every leader who wished to be styled a king or a prophet was necessarily a messianic pretender.[16]

Perhaps the Egyptian who led his followers out of the desert to

---

[16] This point is well made by Rajak, *Josephus*, pp. 140–2, who rightly takes to task those who with little evidence exaggerate the significance of messianic beliefs in the political history of first-century Judaea; on the other hand, undue reliance on Josephus may have led her too far in the opposite direction. For a less sceptical approach, see R. A. Horsley, 'Popular messianic movements around the time of Jesus', *CBQ* 46 (1984) 471–95. On Roman suppression of popular religious move-ments regardless of their teaching, see Rhoads, *Israel in Revolution*, p. 84. On the 'pseudo-prophets' as foretelling and perhaps trying to activate eschatological salva-tion by conjuring up before crowds the symbols of the Exodus, see P. W. Barnett, 'The Jewish sign prophets – A.D. 40–70. Their intentions and origin', *NTS* 27 (1980–1) 679–97. Horsley, 'Popular prophetic movements', denies that these prophets ever tried to force the divine timetable and claims that they believed them-selves to be participating in a salvation not of the future but of the present.

march on Jerusalem and trusted divine aid sufficiently to face the Roman heavy infantry with them alone is the most plausible candidate for a would-be messiah (*B.J.* 2.261–3). According to *A.J.* 20.171, he expected the walls of Jerusalem to collapse at his command. If so, his fate is instructive, for it is unlikely that there was any mass movement to join him. His followers according to *B.J.* 2.261 numbered thirty thousand, but in *A.J.* 20.171 the number killed and taken prisoner (according to *B.J.* 2.263, most of them) is put at only four hundred dead and two hundred prisoners, so a lower figure is likely.[17] At any rate, according to the (admittedly dubious) testimony of Josephus, the people of Jerusalem supported the procurator in his suppression of the uprising (*B.J.* 2.263). Few were prepared to accept that the days of the messiah had really arrived.

Without the excuse of messianic fervour, and so long as the Temple service was still being carried out, it was difficult for Jews to claim divine favour for armed revolt without importing new notions into the theology of Judaism. According to Josephus, whose account is of course particularly tendentious in this instance, that was exactly what some of them, under the leadership of a certain teacher called Judas of Galilee, did in the creation of the so-called Fourth Philosophy. The main tenet of this theology was that Jews should prefer death to submission to any mortal master instead of God. This was, so Josephus says, an impious innovation bound to provoke divine wrath, because it changed ancient tradition (*A.J.* 18.9).

What Judas is said to have proposed was not just that subjection to Rome was evil but that acceptance of *any* human master was wrong since Jews should be ruled by God alone (*A.J.* 18.23). The immediate impetus to this teaching was apparently the imposition of the first Roman census in A.D. 6, with its clear implication that the land now belonged to Rome (*A.J.* 18.4), but the philosophy, as reported, was at least potentially equally aimed against Jewish leaders of all kinds. A Herodian prince was just as much to be opposed as a Roman procurator. The whole burden of the teaching is that no one, gentile or Jew, should be ruler over Judaea. (It is true that Menahem, the descendant of Judas, seems to have believed in kingship since he dressed up in royal robes at the start of the revolt in A.D. 66 (*B.J.* 2.444), but, though he was probably a teacher of *some* ideology since he is described as a sophist at *B.J.* 2.445, he did not necessarily subscribe to the same views as his ancestor.) Josephus' in-

---

[17] Acts 21.38 refers to the same incident and assigns the Egyptian four thousand sicarii. Despite the confused state of the passage as a whole, this testimony is accepted in preference to Josephus' by Smallwood, p. 276 n. 67.

sistence that Judaea was a theocracy under the guidance of the High
Priest even after A.D. 6 (*c.Ap* 2.165,185) may be a characteristic use
of reverse polemic against the adherents of this philosophy, who
claimed that only God should govern.[18]

The effect of this ideology carried to its logical conclusion was
anarchy and political revolution. There should be no secular government: presumably it was assumed that God's decisions could be well
enough mediated through the Torah scholars who interpret the
divine will and the problems caused by the existence of conflicting
legal traditions (see above, p. 74) were conveniently ignored. For a
man to rule over Jews was, it was claimed, simply sacrilege.

Some of these ideas, despite Josephus' protestations, were not
entirely new in Judaism. In the days of Samuel, divine objection to
the appointment of a king over Israel was only finally overruled with
the elevation of Saul to the monarchy (I Sam. 10.17–25). According
to Josephus, the only source of evidence for the Fourth Philosophy,
no such appeal to earlier Jewish ideology was made, but since
Josephus wished to discredit such ideas by claiming their novelty he
may have left out this more respectable, if distant, background on
purpose.

It is more difficult to judge what else Josephus is likely to have
omitted since everything he writes about the philosophy is conditioned by two essentially contradictory aims. At times he wants to
state that this philosophy had a massive influence in provoking the
war, while at other times he strives to push it to the margins of Jewish
beliefs; his aim throughout was to free the majority of Jews (and
Judaism) from responsibility for a rebellion in which so many were
eventually involved. The resulting picture is frankly confused.

Thus on occasions Josephus explicitly blames the Fourth Philosophy for the war: at *A.J.* 18.6–10 he states that Judas and his
accomplices sowed the seeds in A.D. 6 which were to grow into rebellion sixty years later, and in describing the defence of Masada in A.D.
73 or 74 he explicitly links the sicarii or dagger-men of that siege
with those who followed Judas, ascribing to both groups a virulent
hatred of those who consented to submit to Rome (*B.J.* 7.253–5).
Elsewhere by contrast Josephus presents a view of first-century
Judaea in which Judas' ideas play only a minor role: they receive no
mention at all in his general accounts in *A.J.* and *B.J.* of the years
between A.D. 6 and the end of the revolt. Thus it is striking that in his

---

[18] On Josephus' use of reverse polemic, see Rhoads, *Israel in Revolution*, pp. 166–
73.

introduction of the sicarii to his history at *B.J.* 2.254–5 he states that they were a new sort of brigand first seen in Judaea only under the procurator Felix and that their name derived from their *modus operandi* (the commission of murders with short daggers) rather than their ideology; although he heartily disliked both these bandits and Judas' philosophy, he passed over the opportunity to make clear any link between them.

Two methods of resolving the conflict within Josephus' account are possible. One is to claim that Josephus invented the Fourth Philosophy as a device to push to the margins what was in fact a much more widespread tendency among first-century Jews, thereby attributing the revolt to a few mavericks rather than to the nation as a whole. In favour of this approach are both the fact that such an apologetic is central to Josephus' historical work on the period and the discrepancy between *B.J.* 2.118, where Josephus states that the Fourth Philosophy had nothing in common with the other sects, and *A.J.* 18.23, where he states that its adherents agreed with the Pharisees in all respects except their love for liberty. This last statement has suggested to some that the divisions among the pre-A.D. 70 sages recorded in later rabbinic literature as the conflict between the houses of Shammai and Hillel (see above, p. 75) will have made the adherence of some of them to revolutionary concepts a much more important factor in the preliminaries to the revolt than the marginal role ascribed by Josephus to the Fourth Philosophy.[19]

Such a reconstruction is certainly possible, but certain factors make it seem to me less attractive than the main alternative. The prime objection to the view just outlined is that if Josephus was embarrassed by this anarchist philosophy he did not need to mention it at all. It was quite open to him to explain the outbreak of the war in terms of the wickedness of the rebels without ascribing to any of them a religious motivation of any kind: the public slogans of the rebels as advertised on their coins evoked the Temple cult and might have needed explaining away to his gentile audience, but they did

---

[19] For a thorough exposition of this view, see Ben-Shalom, 'The Shammai school'. His argument that an anti-gentile trend was to be found in Judaism long before A.D. 6 seems to me entirely persuasive, and I shall present a similar view below, p. 108. Ben-Shalom is in distinguished company in conflating the anarchist Fourth Philosophy with the anti-Roman Zealot movement, but there are good grounds to distinguish the Zealots as a separate group first found only in A.D. 67, as M. Smith, 'Zealots and sicarii: their origins and relations', *HTR* 64 (1971) 1–19, has shown. For general discussion, see L. I. Levine in A. Kasher, ed., *The Great Jewish Revolt: factors and circumstances leading to its outbreak* (Jerusalem, 1983), pp. 367–76 (Heb.).

not in any way imply the tenets of the Fourth Philosophy. Furthermore, the anti-gentile rulings ascribed by the rabbis to the house of
Shammai are concerned not with political matters but with questions such as the avoidance of gentile foodstuffs; if these are clarion
calls to rebellion, they are carefully coded. Finally, Josephus' specific
attack on the *novelty* of the philosophy (*A.J.* 18.9) seems very peculiar
if in fact this was an established tendency among the Pharisees;
again, it was always possible for him to remain silent.

Thus an alternative explanation of Josephus' peculiar statements
seems to me preferable. I suggest that this call to anarchy was indeed
novel in A.D. 6 and that Josephus' only attempt to mislead is in the
claim that the philosophy was of great importance in fostering the
dissension which led to the revolt. Two things are in favour of this
view. One is that Josephus tends, when he wishes to mislead, to mislead in this way, with lies not about the facts but about their interpretation. Secondly, the value to Josephus' apologetic of mentioning
and enhancing the political effect of the Fourth Philosophy is in this
case obvious.

On this hypothesis Josephus failed to mention the philosophy in
the detailed narrative of events after A.D. 6 not because he suppressed its vital role but because it was in practice of marginal importance. Not even the factions who controlled Jerusalem from
A.D. 67–70 and evoked so much of Josephus' contempt (below, pp.
198–9) were linked by him to Judas' philosophy; even the so-called
Zealots are treated as a separate phenomenon (below, p. 219). It is
worth pointing out that in any case Josephus' general attack on
Judas at *A.J.* 18.6–10 may be accusing him not so much for his influence in leading the people astray as for bringing down divine
wrath by his interference with ancient tradition (*A.J.* 18.9); this type
of explanation of the war is perhaps to be taken no more seriously
than the accusation against Agrippa II that his innovation in the
Temple worship was bound to lead to the punishment of the nation
(*A.J.* 20.218).

In sum, it seems to me most likely that Judas did indeed teach
some novel ideas in A.D. 6, or at least revive some long-buried
ancient notions, but that he founded no sect and that his philosophy
was of marginal effect in the increasingly violent confrontations in
Judaea.[20]

[20] For this view, see also Rhoads, *Israel in Revolution*, pp. 52–5. Rhoads takes the
philosophy to be opposed to human authority which is not submitted to God's even
though he himself notes that what Josephus appears to imply is a rejection of all
human authority regardless of its nature (pp. 49–50).

What emerges from all this is that the only religious ideology which turned political opposition to Rome into a compulsory act for the pious was subscribed to by only a small fraction of the population at all times except, perhaps, in A.D. 6.

And yet Jews were generally considered in the ancient world to be hostile, prickly people, quick to take offence and unfriendly to aliens, and it is hard not to believe that this view may be partially justified and that these characteristics somehow made them more inclined to protest at Roman rule than other subject peoples. It seems to me that Jews tended naturally towards revolt, not because of any explicit ideology but as an unstated consequence of their whole religious outlook.

Jews were never in any doubt about the religious significance of their national identity. The boundaries of the community had been firmly fixed by the clear legal forms laid down by Ezra in the fifth century B.C., and they were still intact five centuries later. Jews were marked out by the basic religious rites of the sabbath, the eating of kosher food and the practice of circumcision. So distinctive were such practices that adoption of them could bring converts of other races within the Jewish fold. Jews stuck together, in normal circumstances helping one another as a matter of course.

With their awareness of the close bands within their community went an instinctive, though of course neither logically necessary nor universal, tendency to be suspicious of those excluded from it. Samaritans, who claimed sometimes to be Jews but in Jewish eyes were beyond the pale (*A.J.* 11.340–4), were despised and hated. Gentiles, according to some views, could positively pollute any Jew with whom they came into contact. Their touch was thus to be avoided if at all possible. It is not surprising that the Jewish communities in the pagan cities around Judaea were so easily identifiable as such in A.D. 66. Whereas the Germans in Cologne hesitated three years later to kill the Romans who lived among them on the grounds that they had married into German families and were now their relatives (Tac. *Hist.* 4.64–5), the gentiles of the Decapolis were constrained against barbarity in their actions against the Jews by no such social contacts.[21]

---

[21] Note that the hesitation at Damascus was not because of social contact but because the local Greeks' wives were attracted by Jewish religion (*B.J.* 2.559–61); hence the Damascus Jews were in fact killed. On Jewish self-identity in the diaspora, see J. J. Collins, *Between Athens and Jerusalem: Jewish identity in the hellenistic diaspora* (New York, 1983), and my review in *JJS* 35 (1984) 214–17. On conversion, note the conversion of the Galileans and Idumaeans by the Hasmonaeans (Schürer,

From the point of view of non-Jews this standoffishness was equally noticeable. It was also considered reprehensible. Tacitus (*Hist.* 5.5.1) remarks that Jews are extremely loyal towards one another, and always ready to show compassion, but toward every other people they feel only hate and enmity. Gentile authors since Hecataeus (in Diodorus 40.3.4) in the fourth century B.C. had stressed Jewish separateness.

It might be argued that defensive antagonistic attitudes of the sort described, perhaps caricatured, by these gentile writers were more likely to be found in beleaguered diaspora communities than in Judaea, where Jews were in the majority. It is of course true that the non-Jewish traditions about Jews were formed from knowledge primarily of Jews in exile from their homeland, in Egypt, Asia Minor and Rome, and it might seem natural for such small immigrant groups to be viewed with suspicion by their neighbours. In fact, however, some of the diaspora communities seem to have contrived to be even more welcoming to converts than Jews in Judaea and even more prone to view their religion as relevant to all mankind as well as to Jews.[22]

The fact is that, whether social relations with neighbours were friendly or not, particularism was unavoidable for Jews wherever they were. Jews such as Philo might also show an interest in the welfare of the rest of the world but they could not avoid their primary social and religious identity being within the Jewish community. The Jewish notion that religious conversion could bring an outsider within the Jewish social fold with rights almost equal to those of existing members is unique in the annals of ancient history, but what this demonstrates is not that some forms of Judaism were exceptionally open to outside influences but, on the contrary, that adoption of

History I, pp. 207,218) and Josephus' account of the Adiabene royal family (*A.J.* 20.17–96); note that all three convert groups fought with the Jews against Rome in the revolt.

On gentile pollution as applicable even outside the Temple precincts, see Alon, *Jews, Judaism and the Classical World*, pp. 146–9; Schürer, *History* II, pp. 83–4.

Proselytes seem to have been less common in Judaea than in the diaspora, but perhaps only because there were fewer gentiles around.

[22] For a rather rosy picture of Jewish life in the diaspora, see A. T. Kraabel, 'The Roman diaspora: six questionable assumptions', *JJS* 33 (1982) 445–64. The problem is that generalizations about Jewish life outside Palestine are bound to be misleading. So, for instance, the fine Sardis synagogue *may* be evidence for the cheerful coexistence of Jews and Greeks in that city, but it might also be a monument to a brashly assertive Jewish lobby like that in Alexandria, where a famous synagogue also stood, as a symbol of the prosperity and power of that community in its constant struggle *against* the Greek population.

Jewish religious practices by non-Jews meant that the new worshipper, once accepted within the Jewish fold, became equally alien to
the rest of civilized society.[23]

This suspicious attitude towards outsiders, which is so easy to
document from the behaviour of Jews in this period, is actually
rather difficult to justify in terms of particular laws of the Torah. So,
for instance, although intermarriage with gentiles had of course been
clearly forbidden by Ezra (Ezra 10.1–44), it was quite possible to
marry partners who had been converted, as the behaviour of some of
Herod's family shows (cf. *A.J.* 20.145), and yet little conversion for
marriage, apart from that within the royal house, is recorded from
Judaea simply because most Jews normally just did not meet gentiles
in social situations.

It seems that separation from gentiles and trust in their own tight-
knit community were so much part of the mentality of Jews that they
could no longer recall precisely the reasons for it. It may be indeed
that they treated their prejudices as having the force of religious injunctions precisely because they would otherwise be at a loss to justify to themselves this instinctive desire for separateness (below, p.
103). I hope to show that such prejudices were reinforced by the
everyday behaviour of Palestinian Jews, and that they may bear
some responsibility for the enthusiasm with which, faced with the
prospect of possible war against Rome, they were prepared to try to
solve internal social problems by rebellion against the external
power.

The belief that an individual's everyday behaviour, and in particular his attitude towards his own body, may indicate something
about his attitudes towards society comes from the findings of recent
anthropology. Mary Douglas has pointed to empirical evidence that
a view of society as untroubled and united within itself but in need of
protection against outside pressures is likely to coincide with a similar attitude towards the body.

It seems to me that such a congruence of the two views is also to be
found among Judaean Jews. The general suspicion shown by Jews
towards outsiders coincided with the development of a coherent sys-

---

[23] Other Jews might doubt the status of a self-proclaimed convert (cf. Goodman,
State and Society, p. 53), but the individual himself would not be uncertain whether or
not to consider himself a Jew.

The notion of a universalist Hellenistic Judaism to be contrasted with a particu-
larist Palestinian Judaism is now generally discredited, cf. Schürer, *History* III, pp.
177–8. There was rarely if ever any perceived incompatibility between the exclu-
sivist, restrictive elements of Judaism and an interest in the wider moral issues of
universal salvation.

tem for understanding illness in their bodies and ill luck in their lives in terms of pollution and the illicit crossing of firm boundaries. It will therefore have seemed to most Jews psychologically satisfying to try to set right social problems, like physical ones, by the protection of boundaries and the expulsion of the polluting invader. It will have seemed less obvious to concentrate on readjusting the internal balance of social forces. It was thus all too easy, for instance, not to pay sufficient attention to the growing pressures created by economic injustice. In brief, it seems to me that the central importance of purity notions in the attitude of Palestinian Jews to their bodies will have made them tend to see their society in a structurally similar fashion.[24]

Comparison with contemporary Greeks may help to illustrate the exceptional structure of Jewish thought with regard to their bodies (and hence, I am suggesting, to their society). Greeks would not deny the power of magic and demons or the ability of the gods to punish whom they will, but they believed such external interference in human affairs to be the exception rather than the rule. It was rare for the gods to intervene directly with mankind by inflicting ill-health on the guilty. Pollution, *miasma*, could disqualify a worshipper from a particular sacred rite, but did not in general threaten health. In so far as medical notions of the wider populace can be judged from theoretical constructions made by doctors such as Galen and from the evidence for practical cures applied to the sick, it is fair to assert that Greeks believed that the crucial conditions for health lay in the balance of forces within the body rather than the exclusion of forces pressing in from outside or the expulsion of destructive elements from within. Thus healing was attempted through the application of drugs or water-treatments intended to alter the sufferer's internal state; even when the god Asclepius intervened directly, the general method he used was the same as that of human doctors, except that the drugs prescribed were often more bizarre.

It seems to be no accident that this Greek tendency to see illness in terms of internal stresses appears to reflect the stresses of Greek urban life in the early empire, in the way postulated by Mary Douglas. In the societies where these Greek doctors taught and practised, small aristocracies flourished despite a constant danger of social collapse when quarrels and rivalries threatened their unity in the face of the Roman state. The many appeals to concord in the extant speeches of

[24] See the analysis of body symbolism in M. Douglas, *Natural Symbols: explorations in cosmology* (London, 1970). It is no accident that the early Church combined the decision to widen the social net of its membership with the dropping of Jewish food laws; the connection was as much symbolic as practical (cf. Acts 11.1–18).

members of the Second Sophistic such as Dio Chrysostom and Aelius Aristides suggest that such concord was constantly under threat.

This congruence can perhaps be demonstrated most clearly in the teachings of Galen, who studied and wrote in the mid to late second century A.D. Galen reintroduced to Greek thought the Hippocratic doctrine of health as consisting in the competition of four humours, all of which needed to be powerful but no one more powerful than the other, and his theories proved overwhelmingly popular among his fellow Greeks during his own lifetime. The enthusiasm with which his ideas were greeted can hardly be because of their empirical truth, for they describe human physiology no better than other ancient theories, but the explanations of physical illness that he cites are structurally identical to current diagnoses of the problems of Greek cities. The health of urban society in the eastern empire of his time depended on the eagerness of members of the city elite to win prestige by acts of generosity in both public service and the provision of finance for public facilities, a procedure described by modern writers as 'evergetism' (see below, p. 125), but this rivalry for honours was reckoned to be only possible so long as no single aristocrat became so powerful that he tyrannically crushed the rest. In sum, Galen's notions of the way a body worked were closely correlated to his understanding of his own society, and in both cases health was seen to lie in the balance of internal forces above all.[25]

The contrast with the attitudes of Jews to physical and social sickness should be clear. Jews' understanding of their bodies was based on totally different premises backed by a host of taboos and customs kept with a fierce tenacity.

Thus when Jews provided sustenance for their physical wellbeing, their prime concern was not with the dietetics reckoned crucial by Greeks but with the dietary laws laid down in Leviticus 11. The point of the story about Daniel in Dan. 1.8–16 is to show that a ten-day diet of kosher vegetables makes a man 'better in appearance

---

[25] An explicit correlation of social analysis with physiology goes back to Plato's *Republic*. Aristotle believed his doctrine of the Mean applied as much to man as to society, cf. T. J. Tracy, *Physiological Theory and the Doctrine of the Mean in Plato and Aristotle* (The Hague, 1969). On non-interference by the gods, see A. Wardman, *Religion and Statecraft among the Romans* (London, 1982), pp. 9–10; on pollution, see R. C. T. Parker, *Miasma: pollution and purification in early Greek religion* (Oxford, 1983); on healing, see J. Scarborough, *Roman Medicine* (London, 1969); on Asclepius' cures, see C. A. Behr, *Aelius Aristides and the Sacred Tales* (Amsterdam, 1968); on urban aristocratic competitiveness, see P. Brown, *The Making of Late Antiquity* (Cambridge, Mass., 1978); C. P. Jones, *The Roman World of Dio Chrysostom* (Cambridge, Mass., 1978); on Galen's revival of Hippocratic notions, see O. Temkin, *Galenism: rise and decline of a medical philosophy* (Ithaca, 1973).

and fatter in flesh' than the rich food and wine of the royal table. For many gentile writers food taboos were a prime mark of the Jews, whether they found them silly and superstitious (e.g. Strabo, *Geog.* 16.2.37) or insulting (e.g. Tac. *Hist.* 5.5.2). The extent to which these regulations mattered to Jews can be seen from the behaviour of the early Christian Cephas (Simon Peter): as a Jew he naturally felt it necessary in the presence of other Jews to eat separately from his gentile brothers in Christ (Galatians 2.12). No Jew could deny the significance of the food laws.[26]

Precisely what the rules required was naturally a matter for dispute at the margins. On the extreme view, anything touched by gentiles could become polluted if it was made from a material subject to impurity. Gentile oil, bread, wine, preserves and stews were thus reckoned by some to be forbidden, and *Jubilees* 22.16 reinforces the injunction observed by Cephas that it is better not to eat with gentiles at all. Some Jews even lived off figs and nuts alone when unable to control the preparation of their food (*Vita* 14).

Much could be and was done to prevent the transference of such impurity to food. The Jews who lived in the fine houses of Jerusalem dined off stoneware, which was not reckoned susceptible to impurity. Similar vessels were in use in Cana in Galilee for the 'Jewish rites of purification' according to John 2.6. Stone tables minimized the risk of pollution still further, as did the use of glass, which was also declared incapable of absorbing impurities. Bronze bowls were used because they could be scoured out. Everything possible was done to avoid preparation and consumption of food in contaminated vessels. Occasional use of wood and pottery, both highly susceptible to impurity, was unavoidable, but it was kept to a minimum: expensive pottery was rarely imported, though a few *terra sigillata* pots have been excavated, and cooking pots, once defiled, were regularly

---

[26] The assertion to the contrary by J. Riches, *Jesus and the Transformation of Judaism* (London, 1980), that Jesus' great message was precisely the abrogation of such rules, seems to me most implausible, not least because the dispute about their significance in the early Church would have been impossible if Jesus had taken such an uncompromising stand on the issue. See the excellent discussion in Sanders, *Jesus and Judaism*, p. 246 and *passim*.

Philo, *De Migr. Abrahami* 87–91, mentions one small group of Jews who believed that the practice of the injunctions of the Torah was less important than their spiritual and moral meaning. Philo attacks such an attitude and makes clear that very few subscribe to it. Jews would not readily understand the notion in Matt. 22.25–8 that food taboos were irrelevant because they were only an outward sign; the injunctions of the prophets (e.g. Isaiah 58.3–7) taught them that outward rituals were indeed useless on their own, but that this in no way prevented them being both desirable and necessary when combined with the right attitude of worship.

thrown away into cisterns or deliberately pierced to render them unfit for use.[27]

Such care over food preparation seems to have been universal among Jews. More disputed was the permissibility of products not actually mentioned in the Torah as forbidden.

So, for example, not everyone accepted that wine made by gentiles was forbidden to Jews, as finds in the Jerusalem excavations of many amphorae from Rhodes and Italy show. It should also be noted that, according to a late Talmudic source, even the incense prepared for the Temple used Cyprus wine (*b.Ker.* 6a), although presumably this might have been manufactured by Cypriot Jews. Nor was this leniency unreasonable. Restrictions on gentile wine had no biblical base and were unknown before the Hellenistic period, and they were only justified *post hoc* by the rabbis of the late second century A.D. with an argument – that gentiles might just possibly have consecrated such wine to a pagan deity – that is singularly unconvincing (*m.A.Zar.* 4.9–5.10). As for the ban on gentile oil, no rationale was ever even proposed, and the ban was lifted by the rabbinic patriarch Judah around A.D. 200 (*m.A.Zar.* 2.6).

But these bans on wine and oil were in keeping with the general spirit of Jewish food laws by this period. Laws originally designed to define the holy within Judaism now had a separate function of separating the whole community from the outside world. For the haverim and the Dead Sea sect the very act of eating in a state of purity became a religious statement of great moment. Their worship centred around meals from which all pollution had been excluded with the greatest care. Careful eating made their bodies separate from the defiled secular world and made their dinner tables as sacred as the Temple sanctuary. In effect they were symbolically making separation from the gentile world into an act of worship.[28]

[27] For the extension of pollution taboos by most Jews to all Jews and not just priests, see Alon, *Jews, Judaism and the Classical World*, pp. 190–234; cf. p. 181 for gentile impurity as the only plausible explanation for the products considered defiling. On the materials used in Jerusalem for eating vessels, see Avigad, *Discovering Jerusalem*, pp. 125,127 (stone tables and vessels); p. 107 (glass); p. 117 (bronze). Cf. Avigad's remark (*ibid.* p. 127) that scant pottery was found in the Burnt House and (p. 119) that 35 intact pots in the palatial mansion were deliberately pierced to render them unusable.

[28] For Rhodian and Italian wine, see Avigad, *Discovering Jerusalem*, pp. 79, 87. Such wine could in theory have been grown and marketed by Jews, but it is hard to imagine Italian Jews in the first century A.D. owning vineyards large enough to export. On gentile oil, see Goodman, *State and Society*, pp. 179–80, 276–7. On the haverim as primarily a society for table-fellowship, see Neusner, *Rabbinic Traditions* III, p. 318; on the Dead Sea sect, see Schürer, *History* II, pp. 579,582.

But pollution inevitably broke in, for the world was full of dangerous impurity, and with great zeal all Jews thus regularly sought to cleanse their bodies of contamination. Pollution could be suffered from outside, impersonal forces, such as the pollution of a corpse or the touch of a menstruating woman. Or it could be caused by imperfections in the body's exterior, from the cutting off of an ear which rendered priests unfit to officiate in the Temple (cf. *A.J.* 14.366) to the oozing secretions of skin infections or the loss of semen during sex (cf. *c.Ap.* 2.198). For women, such imperfections occurred monthly and, with particular force, in childbirth. Such notions of purity were only loosely connected to cleanliness, for only Essenes seem to have been worried that excrement and urine could pollute (*B.J.* 2.149), and no special facilities for lavatorial functions have been excavated around the town houses in Jerusalem. Pollutions, like germs, were invisible forces which attacked the physical and spiritual well-being of men.

That all Jews took pollution seriously is clear from the standard techniques used to remove its effects. All Jews washed frequently, before prayer according to *Ps.Aristeas* 305–6, after funerals, childbirth and sexual relations according to Josephus (*c.Ap.* 2.198,205). The big mansions of Jerusalem housed 'virtually a cult of immersion', with numerous ritual baths of a variety of designs intended to cleanse the body of all impurity and prevent further contamination either from the water itself or from the ground previously trodden in pollution. The size of the baths in a region where water was not abundant is significant evidence of the seriousness with which the ritual was treated. Similar baths have been excavated at Jericho and in other first-century Jewish sites. The fact that most of the baths excavated in Jerusalem do not conform to the strict rules for immersion pools as known to the rabbis by the time of the Mishnah, while others do, suggests that ritual cleansing was not confined to the rabbis' forerunners alone.

Some Jews tried to avoid pollution as much as possible by avoiding graveyards (cf. *A.J.* 18.38) and espousing celibacy, but complete purity was impossible until after death. It has been plausibly suggested that the custom of deliberately stripping the bones of corpses in order to rebury them in ossuaries, a new practice known in Jerusalem and Jericho only in the last years of Herod's rule and in the first century A.D. (see above, p. 89), was intended to leave them in the state of greatest purity.[29]

[29] Cf. Hachlili and Killebrew, 'Jewish funerary customs', esp. p. 119. Stripping

In contrast to Greek concern for concord, pollution thus became the most common Jewish explanation of illness and metaphor for sin. Baptizing groups offered rebirth to the sinner washed free of moral and physical pollution in one repentant plunge into the water (cf. Mark 1.4–5 and note the insistence of *A.J.* 18.117 that the soul must be purged by just behaviour for the water to be efficacious). So long as the body's surface was clean and the mind pure, health was guaranteed.

So when illness struck it was usually viewed as the work of outside forces. Jewish writers, dwelling with gruesome detail on the internal rotting of Antiochus Epiphanes, Herod the Great, Agrippa I and Catullus, the governor of Libya, ascribe their sickness to external, divine punishment for their sins. According to the Gospel authors, who are most unlikely to have invented the fact for theological or polemical reasons, the sick healed by Jesus suffered mostly from the attack of malevolent invading spirits (e.g. Mark 1.23–6; cf. *Jubilees* 10.10–14), and cures could be achieved only by their expulsion.

Medicine thus consisted in the application of magical formulas to root out the evil from within the sufferer. The wisdom of Solomon was thought to have resided in his magical ability to combat devils (cf. Ps. Philo, *Biblical Antiquities* 60.2; *Wisdom of Solomon* 7.20; *A.J.* 8.45). Jewish healers were famous throughout the Greek world for their magical medicine (cf. Acts 13.6–8; 19.13–20), which promised simple cures rather than the delicate restoration of internal balance demanded by Greek medical theory. Jewish healing required no dietetics or complex drugs. A word or a touch sufficed. References to exorcism are frequently found in the literature (e.g. *Tobit* 6.7,17–18; 8.1–3; *1 Qap Gen.* 20.16–31), and Josephus describes one such cure which he saw performed by a certain Eleazar in front of Vespasian

the flesh from the bones must have been done deliberately in the dry climate of Jericho, where natural rotting would be too slow. The significance of this change in burial practice would repay a full investigation. Secondary burial of the cleansed bones of the dead in communal tombs fulfilled an important social function in other societies, cf. R. Hertz, 'The collective representation of death', in *Death and the Right Hand*, transl. by R. and C. Needham (London, 1960), pp. 27–86.

On celibacy, see Kraft, 'Multiform Jewish heritage', p. 198. See in general Alon, *Jews, Judaism and the Classical World*, pp. 190–234, for discussion of the literary evidence on Jewish attitudes to purity.

For the excavated baths and ritual immersion, see Avigad, *Jerusalem Revealed*, pp. 105, 139–42; E. Netzer, 'Ancient ritual baths (Miqvaot) in Jericho', *The Jerusalem Cathedra* 2 (1982) 106–19; B. G. Wood, 'To dip or sprinkle? The Qumran cisterns in perspective', *BASOR* 256 (1984) 45–60.

The baptism of repentance is not to be confused with the baptism of proselytes, cf., among others, Alon, *Jews, Judaism and the Classical World*, pp. 172–3.

and his officers (*A.J.* 8.45–8). Illness, like pollution, was an external evil which, given the right means, could be extracted at a stroke, leaving the patient healthy and pure.[30]

It is worth noting briefly that this Jewish preoccupation with the fixing of boundaries between the pure and the impure, the good and the bad, is reflected also in their attitude to religious space and time. For the majority of Jews who treated the Jerusalem Temple as the centre of their devotions, holiness was seen as spreading out from the Holy of Holies in a series of concentric circles. Most sacred was the inner sanctum, next came the Court of the Priests, the Court of the Israelites, the Court of the Women, the Court of the Gentiles, the holy city of Jerusalem, the land of Israel and finally the secular world outside. Only with this mental image of their spatial universe did the strong feelings of the Jews make sense when they demonstrated, firstly, against legionary standards being brought into the country (*A.J.* 18.121) (remaining unworried when they were kept in Akko); secondly, against such standards being brought into Jerusalem (*A.J.* 18.55–9) (remaining happy when they were elsewhere in Judaea); and thirdly, against gentiles entering into the inner Temple (Acts 21.28–9; cf. *CIJ* II 1400), being unconcerned when they remained in the rest of Jerusalem. Spatial boundaries on the land needed protection as much as those of the body.[31]

It is also striking that, just as the boundaries of the pure body and sacred space were marked out with a zeal not paralleled in other ancient societies, so too Jews imposed a religious structure on time with a unique unbending clarity. Devotion to the sabbath was, with their food laws, the most obvious characteristic of Jewish society when viewed by pagans (cf. Tac. *Hist.* 5.4.3). All ancient peoples had religious calendars but the scrupulousness with which they kept them varied considerably. Apart from the Spartans, Jews alone are recorded as consistently risking disaster for the sake of the divine timetable in the sole circumstances when such zeal really mattered in

[30] On the deaths of Antiochus Epiphanes and the others, see Rajak, *Josephus*, p. 98. For Jewish ideas on healing, see now Schürer, *History* III, p. 342; H. C. Kee, *Medicine, Miracle and Magic in New Testament Times* (Cambridge, 1986); J. Wilkinson, *Health and Healing: studies in New Testament principles and practice* (Edinburgh, 1980), especially pp. 3–16; G. Vermes, *Jesus and the World of Judaism* (London, 1983), pp. 6–10.

[31] Note that Josephus imagines the divinity as dwelling in the Temple (*B.J.* 6.299–300).
Greek and Roman temples also had around the sanctuary a sacred area marked off from the secular world but less taboo than the altar. But the Jewish notion of degrees of sanctity dividing up the entire world does not seem to have parallels.

practice – that is, in time of war. The details of the extent to which self-defence was permissible on the sabbath were much debated in the first century A.D. and never properly resolved (see above, p. 48). What is significant is that the debate had to happen. The religious calendar was not just a convenience to ensure that all the required sacrifices were performed at some time during the year, as, for example, at Argos in the classical period of Greece. It embodied a rigid division of time enforced by God as part of the divine plan for separating the sacred from the profane.[32]

To return to Jews' understanding of their own bodies and society. Both physical and social sickness came from pollution and could be cured by purification and exorcism. It was all too apparent to the people of Judaea that their society in the years before A.D. 66 was sick, for Josephus uses the image on a number of occasions (*B.J.* 2.264; 7.260). When he does so it is with reference to the internal conflicts between Jews, the civil strife he so much laments, and I have argued above (p. 20) that he was impelled to this analysis, which is essentially not typical for a Jewish writer, by the facts: Judaea *was* rent by internal dissension in this period. It is probable that some other Judaeans could also see the true nature of their troubles. But in general Jews who reacted instinctively and unthinkingly to social upheaval will have done so in accordance with their normal prescription for social disease. When Josephus wrote of Jerusalem's internal pollution which needed to be purged (*B.J.* 5.19), they will instinctively have understood and approved.

When called to restore Judaea to purity by the expulsion of alien gentiles from the city of the sanctuary, they thus felt this to be an obvious solution to their troubles. The exclusion of everything gentile from what they considered sacred was, after all, an attitude reinforced by almost every aspect of their daily lives.

It is at this level that the disputes within the circles of the pre-rabbinic sages before A.D. 70 over attitudes towards gentiles may usefully be understood. The stringent demands recorded of the house of Shammai, particularly in the eighteen rulings reportedly imposed on all the sages at the beginning of the war (cf. *m.Shab.* 1.4), over the use of gentile foods and other such matters were probably not, as has

---

[32] On the sabbath and warfare, and Greek and Roman parallels, see Holladay and Goodman, 'Religious scruples'. The calendar was of sufficient significance to be a possible cause, or at least justification, of the secession of the Dead Sea sect from the rest of Jewish society, since they used a different time-reckoning (cf. Schürer, *History* II, p. 581). Cf. also Goodman, *State and Society*, p. 108, on rabbinic controls over the calendar after A.D. 70.

been suggested, covert calls to revolution, but nor were they simply the result of the uncompromising, idealistic attitude towards legal interpretation generally taken by this group of sages in matters quite unconnected to politics. It seems to me that they reflect rather the intensification of a general tendency to dislike gentile rule *qua* gentile. There was no separate anti-Roman movement in first-century Judaism; rather, anti-gentile attitudes which originated long before A.D. 6, perhaps in Maccabean times, inspired many different groups, permeating the whole Jewish population and varying only in their intensity.[33]

For most Jews before A.D. 66, including the house of Shammai, such attitudes naturally found only a symbolic expression in the form of purity and pollution taboos. But when trouble loomed and once the revolt was under way it was this aspect of Judaism that instilled religious fervour into the masses who rose against Rome.

---

[33] Despite our quite different approaches to the subject I am here largely in agreement with Ben-Shalom, 'The Shammai school'. I differ from his analysis primarily in my belief that anti-Roman sentiment was implicit rather than explicit in most first-century Judaism. In practice the distinction may not have mattered very much. For a more sceptical view than Ben-Shalom's of the relation of the internal disputes of the pre-70 sages to external politics, see Schürer, *History* II, pp. 365–6.

CHAPTER 5

WHY THE RULING CLASS FAILED

The problems faced by the government of Judaea before A.D. 66 were, as has been seen, considerable. A disintegrating society had been thrown into turmoil by growing economic disparities, while native ideology encouraged Jews to blame the Roman aliens for their plight. It was imperative that Jewish leaders should guide their people safely into calm cooperation with Rome if catastrophe was to be avoided. But in fact, as has been shown (above, pp. 40–6), the Jewish ruling class lacked the confidence of the Jewish nation which might have enabled them to carry out such a task. The reasons for this lack of trust and natural authority will be the subject of this chapter. It has already been noted that the men treated as rulers by Rome after A.D. 6 did not in the first place come to power with any status in Jewish eyes inherited from their role in previous regimes (above, pp. 38–40), but the Romans may have expected that occupancy of the leading positions within national institutions by such men, and their ownership of great landed estates, would in time give them the local prestige they so lacked at the beginning. Precisely such a transformation had, after all, taken place within the Roman ruling class itself under Augustus. There were special Jewish reasons why this Roman expectation was to be dashed in Judaea.

Thus, although it was normal Roman practice on taking a province under direct rule to leave local institutions intact in so far as this could be achieved without prejudice to the privileged position of the ruling class responsible for tax collection and public order, in Judaea the Romans could not follow this procedure, and as a result the institutions which they hoped would channel Jewish aspirations into peaceful paths proved incapable of fulfilling this function.

The problem can be summarized as follows. Judaea had been ruled for nearly a century and a half by monarchs in the hellenistic mould. When the institutions of monarchy naturally disappeared with the deposition of Archelaus, the Romans looked for alternative native institutions to replace them. They were drawn to promote the

109

high priesthood to the leadership of the nation only because that
position was clearly both ancient and venerated by the Jews. When
they realized that the High Priest's function did not in itself fit him
for secular government, the Romans were forced to invent an 'aristocracy' to act under his supervision (*A.J.* 20.251).

The artificial nature of this 'aristocracy' was responsible for much
that went wrong in the province, and it will need to be demonstrated
in rather more detail than was possible in Chapter 2. I have already
suggested there that the men pushed into prominence in A.D. 6 were
far from being an existing elite but, on the contrary, were elected by
the Romans from some of Herod and Archelaus' least influential
Jewish courtiers (above, p. 40). Rather more contentious will be the
further arguments to be proposed below (p. 113) that no independent aristocratic political *institutions* existed before A.D. 6 to enable the
granting of influence to such men to be cloaked by an illusion of continuity with the past.

What is not contentious, however, is that by choosing to grant
power to such an oligarchy led by the High Priest, the Romans deliberately excluded from influence the one institution whose support
could in Jewish eyes have underpinned the secular authority of a
national leader. That institution was the popular assembly. For
Jews, no important constitutional decision was binding unless it had
been confirmed by such an assembly. The Hasmonaean Simon had
recognized this fact in 140 B.C. by seeking ratification from a mass
meeting for his family's usurpation of the high priesthood (I Macc.
14.25–49). Similarly Herod convened an assembly in 12 B.C. to
recognize his heirs (*B.J.* 1.457–66). The theological justification for
the assembly's importance was clear. The whole nation had coven-
anted with God on Mt Sinai in just such a mass meeting (cf. Exod.
19.8), and the popular voice was thus in constitutional terms particularly effective at the pilgrim festivals to which every adult male
Jew was in theory bound to go (Exod. 23.14–17). Hence the danger
for Herod of the support expressed at such a feast for the last
Hasmonaean High Priest, Aristobulus (*B.J.* 1.437).

Such popular assemblies were anathema to Rome. When the
assemblies of Greek cities continued to meet under Roman rule, as
some did down to the late third century A.D., it was as powerless
institutions providing only approval of decisions reached by small
oligarchic councils. The assembly of the Jews was not accorded even
this right in A.D. 6, perhaps because it had never convened for political decisions on regular occasions but only when a particular issue
was deemed worth discussion by the country's rulers. Nonetheless

the Jews did not forget the right, in their eyes, of the crowd at pilgrim festivals to have its say, and it is no accident that this was the form in which many of the decisions most hostile to Rome were apparently reached. Nor was it surprising that attempts by the Rome-appointed oligarchy to countermand such decisions met with no success (cf. *B.J.* 2.234).[1]

The sole traditional institution which the Romans permitted to continue in Judaea after A.D. 6 was thus the high priesthood. The High Priest, in Josephus' phrase, was the representative, *prostates*, of the nation (*A.J.* 20.251), to the Roman government in the same way as to God.

To some extent promotion of the high priesthood to such prominence was justified by its ancient role in Judaea. It is significant that the Hasmonaeans had seen the position as sufficiently crucial to usurp it for their own benefit. Josephus even claims that according to Moses' constitution kings were powerless in all matters without the High Priest's consent, though this is clearly nonsense in the case of the Herods (*A.J.* 4.224), and Philo asserts that the position of High Priest is as much superior to that of a king as the divine is to the human (*Leg.* 278). By virtue of his role the High Priest was in theory blessed with prophetic powers (cf. *Testament of Levi* 8.2,15), even if in practice such powers were not always available to him, and the glory of the man who bore the sins of the nation and won forgiveness for them each year on the Day of Atonement (Lev. 16; cf. *m.Yom.* 1.1–7) was sufficient to give him prestige among Jews whatever the origins of his family, as Paul recognized when he apologized for insulting the High Priest Ananias (Acts 23.4–5).

However, if the Romans hoped that any priest they chose could win paramount authority in Judaea simply by acting as High Priest, they were much mistaken. The prestige of the High Priest's office had been drastically diminished after 37 B.C., and no Jewish sources from the years after A.D. 70 regret the complete disappearance of these 'leaders of the nation'.

The problem was not just that the High Priests appointed by Herod were his puppets (above, p. 41) but that they were *blatantly* his puppets, just as the incumbents after A.D. 6 were blatantly the political choices of Roman procurators (from A.D. 6 to 41), or Herodian princes (from A.D. 41 to 66). As has just been noted, for the mass of Jews a High Priest was only legitimate if he had been confirmed in

[1] For Roman opposition to democracy, see De Ste Croix, *Class Struggle*, pp. 518–37. For pilgrim festivals as times of political disturbance, see Smallwood, p. 146; C. Roth, 'The constitution of the Jewish republic of 66–70', *JSS* 9 (1964) 304.

post by the nation as a whole – hence not only the mass meeting to confirm the Hasmonaean Simon as High Priest in 140 B.C., but further assemblies at which a new incumbent was either demanded, in 4 B.C. (*B.J.* 2.7), or, as in A.D. 67, elected by lot (*B.J.* 4.155). In contrast, the dependence of High Priests from A.D. 6 to 66 on Herodian or Roman patronage was made embarrassingly obvious by Herod's practice, continued by his successors, of deposing High Priests so frequently that the confused author of the Gospel of John writes as if the post was changed annually (John 11.49; 18.13), and at least six High Priests were deposed by Agrippa II in the turbulent ten years before the revolt. This dependency was further emphasized when the secular authorities insisted, to the fury of priests and people (*A.J.* 20.6–9), on holding onto the High Priest's garments without which he could not carry out the full glory of his role in the Temple. If, as is possible, one of the sources of the High Priest's prestige had been his use of the oracular Urim and Thummim, which may have constituted part of this ceremonial dress, the causes of this resentment would be even more clear, but Josephus states that these magical stones no longer shone by his day (*A.J.* 3.214–18).

Even if the incumbents had come from more prestigious families than in fact they did, the post was thus too much emasculated to look like the high priesthood of old. From *m. Yom.* 1.3,6 it appears that the High Priest was considered at times incapable of carrying out the most elementary duties at the Day of Atonement without careful instruction. Since new High Priests took over no more than the prestige of the position, gaining control neither of land, which the Jerusalem Temple unlike others in the Near East seems not to have possessed (see above, p. 59), nor of the Temple's funds, which were specifically kept under the close supervision first of the procurator and later of Herod of Chalcis and Agrippa II (cf. *A.J.* 20.222), they had no opportunity to gain overriding authority.[2]

This was all the more unfortunate because, I believe, no other institution with comparable links with ancient tradition and poten-

---

[2] D. R. Schwartz, 'Josephus on the Jewish constitutions and community', *Scripta Classica Israelica* 7 (1983/4) 30–52, suggests that even the theoretical preeminence of the high priesthood was partly the figment of Josephus' apologetic after A.D. 70, when he wanted to portray the Jews as a non-political religious community. On the deterioration of the image of the High Priests in this period, see Alon, *Jews, Judaism and the Classical World*, pp. 57–75. Note, however, that the prestige of the High Priest Hyrcanus was sufficient for it to be worthwhile for Antigonus and the Parthians to cut off his ear to disqualify him from office (*B.J.* 1.270), although deposed High Priests of the procuratorial period were by contrast left free to meddle in Judaean politics, see below, p. 141.

tial authority to control the populace survived into the first century A.D. Since the Sanhedrin has sometimes been accorded this crucial role as the main bearer of constitutional continuity independent of the High Priests from Hasmonaean times to the great revolt, I shall argue in some detail why this view seems to me untenable.

All assertions about the function and composition of the Sanhedrin are fraught with problems because of a radical conflict between the evidence of the rabbinic sources of the second century A.D. and later and that of the New Testament and Acts. The rabbis almost always claimed that the members of the Sanhedrin were all Torah scholars in the rabbinic tradition, a statement directly contradicted by the partly Sadducee membership of the council as described in the Gospels and Acts (e.g. Acts 23.6). The rabbis asserted that the president of the Sanhedrin was a leading rabbinic sage of the day; the New Testament and Josephus claim that the High Priest presided (Acts 5.21; *A.J.* 20.200). It would not be safe to treat as secure the confused and biased New Testament evidence, much of which concerns the trial of Jesus, but it is probably reasonable to assign rather greater weight to these sources than to the rabbinic since many rabbinic tales about the Sanhedrin before A.D. 70 may be a fiction intended to enhance the prestige of the rabbinic courts of the late second century by suggesting a spurious link with the authority of the Temple a century and a half earlier.[3]

It is certain that Jerusalem had some sort of non-democratic council (*gerousia*) recognized by the Seleucid kings in the early second century B.C. (*A.J.* 12.138), but this is only known to have been for the purpose of tax-collection, and there is no good reason to suppose that it ever acted independently of the High Priest, who remained firmly in control of the country down to the end of the Hasmonaean period. There is no evidence for a powerful independent political and judicial council in Jerusalem in the years immediately before the

---

[3] No one denies the discrepancies between the rabbinic and the other evidence for the Sanhedrin before A.D. 70. Some have tried to resolve the conflict by positing more than one separate Sanhedrin (cf. for example, H. Mantel, *Studies in the History of the Sanhedrin* (Cambridge, Mass., 1961), pp. 61–101, following A. Büchler, *Das Synedrion in Jerusalem* (Vienna, 1902)), but this solution has no ancient authority. Others rely basically on the New Testament and Josephus, using the rabbinic evidence when it can be conflated with them without overdue violence but ignoring it when it appears directly contradictory (cf., with large bibliography, Schürer, *History* II, pp. 199–226, esp. pp. 211,215,217,225–6), but it is not clear how this latter approach can be justified. The rabbinic evidence is accorded greater prominence without recourse to Büchler's theory in a particularly judicious chapter by Alon, *The Jews in their Land* I, pp. 185–205.

arrival of the Romans.[4] Hence, I suggest, the extraordinary vagueness of the sources which refer to this council from the time of Pompey onwards. The title Sanhedrin or (in Greek) *synedrion* is only one of many. The New Testament uses also *presbyterion* (e.g. Luke 22.66) and *gerousia* (e.g. Acts 5.21); both the Gospels and Josephus use *boule* (cf. *B.J.* 2.331; Mark 15.43). For thorough confusion, note that Acts 5.21 uses two of these terms as if they meant different things. If this was the real governing institution of Judaea after the deposition of the Herods, why did people not know its name, function, composition, competence and procedures?[5]

I suggest that one possible explanation may be that the Sanhedrin was not a regular political council at all, that it met only at the request of the High Priest as his advisory body, and that its influence was only as great as that of the sum total of its members.

Thus, when in 57 B.C. Gabinius deprived the High Priest Hyrcanus of secular power, he presumably did not find any obvious political council to use for tax-collection in the environs of Jerusalem since he appointed three different councils within Judaea, and Josephus' terminological vagueness about these councils – he calls them *synodoi* at *B.J.* 1.170 but *synedria* at *A.J.* 14.91 – suggests that the one which was based on Jerusalem was not an already established body converted to a new use. By contrast, on Caesar's reappointment of the High Priest Hyrcanus as ethnarch in 47 B.C., the Jerusalem council became more politically significant and was entrusted as a court of law with the trial of the young Herod for his illegal actions in Galilee (*A.J.* 14.165–79). It is clear from the parallel account at *B.J.* 1.208–11 that the council on this occasion was no more than the body of the High Priest's advisers. Josephus explicitly states that the members of the Sanhedrin executed by Herod after his accession in 37 B.C. (*A.J.* 14.175) were in fact 'the forty-five chief men of the party of Antigonus', the Hasmonaean High Priest (*A.J.* 15.6) who had just been deposed.

Once Herod came to power the Sanhedrin therefore lost all political significance because that was the fate of the High Priests themselves. It thus matters little whether the *synedrion* before which the

---

[4] In a number of passages, e.g. I Macc. 7.33, the 'elders of the people' are described as a clearly separate institution but there is no reason to suppose these to be equivalent to the council of the Seleucid period. These are the village elders who still held natural authority in the countryside of Judaea (see above, p. 73). Cf. *TDNT* VII 862–3 on the *gerousia*.

[5] The significance of the murkiness of the evidence is noted also by Sanders, *Jesus and Judaism*, pp. 312–17.

elderly Hyrcanus was charged was the advisory council of Herod, as some believe, or of his stooge High Priest, the Babylonian Ananel (*A.J.* 15.173); for it can be asserted with certainty that no Sanhedrin would ever oppose Herod. The activities of the Sanhedrin in Herod's time, apart from this occasion, thus went unrecorded, so that it has even been doubted whether it continued to exist during his reign.[6]

There is no reason to suppose that with these origins an independent Sanhedrin emerged after A.D. 6. Josephus and the Gospels usually refer to *the* Sanhedrin, but on one occasion Josephus describes the High Priest as convening *a* Sanhedrin (*A.J.* 20.202). It was clearly still up to the High Priest to decide when to call together his advisers. Among the diverse meanings of the Greek term *synedrion*, one used by Josephus is that of a Roman senator's advisory council of friends; he used the word in this sense to describe Augustus' *consilium* (*B.J.* 2.25). Like a Roman senator, the High Priest called his associates to his house to decide on matters of moment, as Caiaphas is said to have done when faced with the problem of Jesus (Matt. 26.57; Mark 14.53). It is noticeable that High Priests do not seem to have asked relatives of the Herods to attend such Sanhedrin meetings, though non-priests were certainly present; only their friends and equals were invited. Thus the important political decisions described by Josephus are just as often ascribed to other small groups of the ruling class as to meetings and decision of the high-priestly Sanhedrin.[7]

If the Sanhedrin was thus only an extension of the High Priest, why was such a council needed at all after A.D. 6? Two reasons can be suggested.

Rome like the Seleucids needed a defined institutional body to which the responsibility for collecting taxes in Judaea could be delegated. The emperor Claudius assumed such an institution, which he terms a 'council' (*boule*), when he wrote to the Jews of Jerusalem (*A.J.* 20.11), and it was the *bouleutai* who went to the villages to collect the tribute in A.D. 66 (*B.J.* 2.405). To fulfil its duties to Rome the *boule* had an appointed secretary (*B.J.* 5.532) and could point to its ten leading men (*dekaprotoi*) for sending on embassies (*A.J.* 20.194). Since no ancient source refers to the existence of more than

---

[6] Schürer, *History* I, p. 313. For the view that Hyrcanus was charged before the Sanhedrin, see Schürer, *History* II, p. 206; for the view that Herod used his own 'privy council', see among others Smallwood, *Jews*, p. 68.

[7] Rajak, *Josephus*, p. 42. I owe this interpretation of the Sanhedrin as the High Priest's *consilium* to a suggestion by Fergus Millar. Note that Agrippa II called his own *synedrion* to discuss the robes to be worn by Levites in the Temple (*A.J.* 20.216).

one council in Jerusalem (cf. above, n. 3), it is likely that this tax-collecting body was the High Priest's Sanhedrin in another guise, though this cannot be certain.

The second reason springs from the internal needs of Judaean society. It was the task of the procurator to deal with violent political crime, but, for want of staff and time, he necessarily left less danger-ous criminals to the disposition of local tribunals.[8] Jerusalem there-fore needed a court, just as the villages did (see above, p. 73), and that was the function of the Sanhedrin on most of the occasions when it was convened by the High Priest, as the narrative of the trials of, for instance, Paul and James makes clear (Acts 22.30–23.10; *A.J.* 20.200).

There was nothing odd about a High Priest's advisory body having such a judicial function, for Josephus often speaks of the High Priest as the supreme judge (cf. *c.Ap.* 2.194). Much of the implemen-tation of Roman law in this period was done by a magistrate with the help of friends. The 'council of judges' (cf. the phrase in *A.J.* 20.200) called by the High Priest could include whomever he thought fit (cf. *c.Ap.* 2.187,194), hence the silence of the sources about the methods and criteria for appointments to the Sanhedrin. The judges might naturally include members of the High Priest's family, known colloquially as 'the high priests' (see below, p. 120), and, since difficult legal problems might well crop up, they might also include expert interpreters of the law, like the Pharisee Gamaliel (Acts 5.34). The only restriction on the High Priest's choice would thus stem from the Sanhedrin's other function as a tax-collecting body: to satisfy Roman tastes, the High Priest's advisers had to be rich; and this characteristic, wealth, was not, as I shall try to show below (pp. 126–32), calculated to give either the High Priest or his Sanhedrin the status in the eyes of Jews which their office could not otherwise be guaranteed to bring.

Not only were such local institutions as were left intact by Rome in A.D. 6 not likely in themselves to command much respect among the people of Judaea; and not only did the men installed in those offices when the province was created lack support and sympathy among

[8] I am not sure that the later rabbinic comments about the Sanhedrin as a *civil* court should be believed (cf. *m.Sanh.* 11.2). The suggestion implicit in Schürer, *History* II, p. 218, that contemporary conditions are reflected by Josephus in *A.J.* 4.218, which states that Moses ordained that all cases which could not be decided locally should be taken to the High Priest, the Prophet or the Council (*gerousia*), does not seem to me convincing: there is no candidate in first-century Judaea for the role of Prophet. But strong arguments for a different view can be found in Alon, *The Jews in their Land*, pp. 196–205.

those same Judaeans because their families had risen to prominence only through the patronage of the hated Herods; but, just as disastrously, precisely because the prime criterion used by Rome to establish who should belong to the ruling class was the possession of property, even in later generations few members of that class could point to sufficient personal qualities, innate or acquired, which they could use to justify to their compatriots the power that continued to be given to them by Rome.

Between A.D. 6 and 66 Judaea's rulers naturally did their best to win the prestige that they lacked at the start. Their attempt failed not for lack of effort but because they could not claim a monopoly of any of the crucial marks of distinction generally accepted as worthy of respect by their fellow Jews.

Thus the claim most often made by some of them was that they deserved prestige because of the superiority of their birth, but the origins they boasted either appeared less impressive than they might wish to the rest of the population or, when their excellence of lineage was generally recognized, that ancestry was shared by them with many other Jews who were excluded from power by Rome solely because of poverty.

The significance of descent was generally recognized by all Jews. Thus Josephus began his own defensive autobiography with his claim to be of good birth (*Vita* 1–7), and he often points out the fine ancestry (*eugeneia*) of characters in his history (e.g. *B.J.* 4.416; 6.201). Family origins mattered so much that descent on the mother's side could be recalled to good effect no less than that on the father's (cf. *B.J.* 1.435).[9] Herod, who had nothing to boast about in this line, either invented a better ancestry for himself or was presented with one by Nicolaus of Damascus (*A.J.* 14.9). The very fact that Idumaeans like Herod were sometimes considered half-Jews by Judaeans like Josephus (*A.J.* 14.403), even though conversion had in terms of Jewish law brought them entirely within the Jewish fold, is evidence of the importance of ancestry in defining a man's position in Jewish society.

Men thus understood their social roles primarily in relation to

---

[9] On citizenship passed down through the female line, see L. M. Epstein, *Marriage Laws in the Bible and the Talmud* (Cambridge, Mass., 1942), pp. 195–6; note however the remark by S. J. D. Cohen, 'Was Timothy Jewish (Acts 16.1–3)? Patristic exegesis, rabbinic law, and matrilineal descent', *JBL* 105 (1986) 251–68, that there is no explicit evidence for this matrilineal principle before the second century A.D. Rajak, *Josephus*, p. 13, points out that the family smear against Josephus is a convention of Greek invective, but there is much other evidence for the importance of birth in Jewish society.

their fathers. The general coherence of the nuclear family as the main social unit will have aided this process (see above, p. 69). Within particular groups and sects leadership was often in practice passed down from father to son. Among the Pharisees who were seen by the second-century rabbis as their predecessors, the family of Hillel became a dynasty in this way. Inherited status was of course assumed in the transfer of power within the royal families of the Hasmonaeans and Herodians. For all Jews it was normal practice for a man to be known as the son of his father (or, very occasionally, his mother): in Josephus' writings, the omission of a patronymic generally indicates or implies that the person concerned is of low social status. The practice of naming boys after their grandfathers was also common, although having the same name as the father was a practice apparently confined to priests.[10]

Josephus' summary of his own family tree (*Vita* 1–6) suggests that the ancestral origins of which the ruling class found it most useful to boast, when they could validly do so, were those from either priests or kings.

The value of priestly origins was generally recognized by Judaean Jews. Not everyone went as far as Josephus, himself of course a priest, who palpably exaggerated the priests' role in his paraphrase of the biblical narrative in *A.J.* and made the demonstrably untrue claim that they were responsible as a class in his time for the interpretation of scripture. But, though they might jib at the suggestion, attributed to the opponents of the Hasmonaeans in 63 B.C., that the ideal Jewish state should be governed by priests (*A.J.* 14.41),[11] all Jews except perhaps the schismatics of the Dead Sea sect, who considered the

---

[10] The importance for Jews of inherited status, which is not so marked in other societies, is well made by Stern, 'Aspects of Jewish society', pp. 572–4.

For a matronymic, see R. Hachlili, 'Names and nicknames of Jews in Second Temple times', *EI* 17 (1984) 202 (Heb.); for the absence of a patronymic as possibly an indication, or implication by Josephus, of low status, see *B.J.* 1.544; 2.60,118; 5.317,474; 6.169. The criterion is not absolute, cf. *B.J.* 4.18,140–1,358; 6.390; in these cases Josephus perhaps just did not know the names of the fathers of the men concerned. The use of patronymics was standard among Nabataeans, cf. B. Isaac, *IEJ* 34 (1984) 280. On naming children after grandfathers and fathers, see Hachlili, 'Names and nicknames', p. 192.

[11] See Rajak, *Josephus*, p. 20; H. W. Attridge, *The Interpretation of Biblical History in the Antiquitates Judaicae of Flavius Josephus* (Missoula, 1976); Stern, 'Aspects of Jewish society', p. 589. Sanders, *Jesus and Judaism*, p. 316, takes at face value Josephus' statement at *c.Ap.* 2.187 that the priests controlled the strict observance of the law, but this picture is idealized for his gentile audience and ignores the role of non-priestly interpreters including the Pharisees, whose importance Josephus elsewhere lauds.

functionaries in the Jerusalem Temple as sinners but significantly accorded great honour to their own priests, accepted that priestly status did bring a social cachet quite separate from the priests' functions in the Temple. Tithes could be brought to priests wherever they might be in the land of Israel (cf. *Vita* 63, about Galilee), and even when the Temple's destruction made the performance of their functions impossible some Jews may have continued to bring them their dues (cf. *m.Shek.* 8.8; *Sifre to Numbers* (ed. Horovitz), p. 133). The prestige bestowed upon priests as mediators between God and man was not challenged by other Jews, who sought at the most to interfere with the procedures of the Temple service.

Priestly status depended entirely on descent, and their special aura was therefore carefully preserved by jealous control of the genetic purity of priestly families. Priests usually found their wives from among the daughters of other priests. They avoided marriage to widows and divorcees in case the offspring's parentage be dubious. They kept the records of their lineage in special archives. Their scrupulousness must have been effective, for it was apparently not challenged.

Those members of the ruling class who were priests – and they were a sizeable proportion and possibly even the majority – thus emphasized their priestly origins as much as they could. They will have won respect by the claim, but not enough to justify their rule. For there were thousands of other priests whose birth was just as impressive as theirs but who were excluded from power because they were poor. Those poor priests had just as much status in Jewish terms as their richer brethren, and they much resented attempts by the wealthy priests to seize the tithes at their expense (cf. *A.J.* 20.181).[12]

Some of the ruling class could, however, claim other distinctions of birth which were not shared by anyone outside their number, and the question arises why these distinctions failed to win them the clear authority they sought.

Thus, only members of the ruling class could point with pride to their descent from High Priests, and there is no doubt that, despite the obscure origins of the first members of their families honoured with the post (see above, p. 41), relatives of the High Priests retained a cachet unique to them. The evidence is simple: it was as 'high

---

[12] See in general Stern, 'Aspects of Jewish society', p. 583. On tithes still being paid after A.D. 70, see Goodman, *State and Society*, p. 98. On the number of priests, see Schürer, *History* II, pp. 238–56.

priests', referring to status rather than function, that their families were known, whether or not more than one individual member of the family had held, or was holding, the post.

But this prestige was much diminished by the limitations on those who held the office itself after 37 B.C., and even this limited prestige was diluted by the large number of Jews who could claim it by the mid first century A.D. By A.D. 15, there were at least five families 'from which the High Priests had in succession been drawn' (*B.J.* 4.148), and the name 'high priest' was accorded to so many such relatives (cf. *B.J.* 6.114) that some modern historians have even claimed that it was used with the more general meaning of 'leading priests'. This is not, I think, plausible, but it is right to note that the number of Jews who claimed such status of birth by the time of the revolt does seem to have been large.[13]

Almost as widespread within the ruling class were claims to prestige on the grounds of descent from kings. Just like boasts of high-priestly birth, such claims were recognized by all Jews as in principle valid but in practice vitiated by the disputed right of the incumbents of the office itself, in this case the monarchy, to hold that position.

Thus, anyone who could have claimed descent from the last Jewish kings with a clear moral right to rule, the line of David, would have won the highest possible prestige, but none of the ruling class in the first century A.D. could make such a claim. It is probable that some of the leaders in Judah after the return from exile had been of David's descent, but quite soon in the Persian period the line seems to have died out, for it is from this period that a belief in the more than human authority of rulers from the Davidic house begins to be found in Jewish literature. As a result Davidic origins tended to be ascribed by their followers in the first century A.D. to leaders such as Jesus whose authority was already established from other criteria (cf. Matt. 1.6), but no case is recorded of a figure coming to prominence *because* of Davidic descent. The Church historian Eusebius preserves a tradition from Hegesippus that members of the family of David were hunted down in Palestine during Domitian's rule (*Ecc. Hist.* 3.19–20), but, since according to him the people arrested, including

---

[13] For the argument that the word *archiereis* in Josephus and the Gospels must refer to the families of the High Priests and not just the incumbents of the office, see Schürer, *History* II, pp. 232–5. The only slightly less influential view of Jeremias, *Jerusalem*, pp. 175–81, that *archiereis* means 'leading priests' seems to me less plausible since the term most naturally indicates some connection to *the archiereis*, i.e. the High Priests in office. On the high-priestly families, see Stern, 'Aspects of Jewish society', pp. 600–12.

some of Jesus' family in Galilee, were set free when discovered not to be dangerous to Roman power, this police operation may reflect no more than natural Roman concern at rumours about messianic movements attached to the early Church.[14]

Similarly powerful would have been claims to status on the grounds of relationship to the Hasmonaean kings but, again, few within the ruling class could make such a claim without a rather forced interpretation of the family tree like that which enabled Josephus to claim royal origins merely on the grounds of the birth of one grandfather of his great-grandparents, out of the sixteen he must have had (*Vita* 2–4).

Josephus' appeal to this distant link shows that popular affection for the Hasmonaeans continued despite the behaviour of the last kings and ethnarchs of their house, which had led to much unrest and to widespread revolt in the reign of Alexander Jannaeus (*B.J.* 1.88–98). Thus, when Herod ousted the last Hasmonaean ruler in 37 B.C., the Jews in Babylonia showed their continuing affection for the old dynasty by honouring Hyrcanus as king and High Priest (*A.J.* 15.15), although with his ears cut off he was technically disbarred from the latter role (*B.J.* 1.270); the Jews of Jerusalem demonstrated in favour of the young Hasmonaean High Priest Aristobulus in 36 B.C. with such vehemence that Herod had him murdered (*A.J.* 15.50–6); and when Herod's erstwhile supporter in Idumaea, Costobar, plotted rebellion, he harboured more distant relations of the Hasmonaean house to use as pretenders to the throne (*A.J.* 15.259–66). The festival of Hannukah kept alive memories of the miracle which had accompanied Hasmonaean seizure of power and the heroic piety with which they had fought for the purification of the defiled Temple. It is no accident that the most popular personal names of this period were adopted in Judaea in imitation of the royal Hasmonaean house.[15]

But the direct line of this royal family had been broken with the death of Hyrcanus in 30 B.C., and the Hasmonaean princesses married off to various relatives of Herod do not seem to have pro-

[14] On the house of David after the exile, see J. Liver, *The House of David from the Fall of the Kingdom of Judah to after the Destruction of the Second Temple* (Jerusalem, 1959), pp. 68–104 (Heb.). On the persecutions after A.D. 70, see Smallwood, *Jews*, pp. 351–2.

[15] On popular support for the Hasmonaean house in the late first century B.C., see Alon, *Jews, Judaism and the Classical World*, pp. 1–15; W. R. Farmer, *Maccabees, Zealots and Josephus: an inquiry into Jewish nationalism in the Greco-Roman period* (New York, 1956). On names, see Hachlili, 'Names and nicknames', p. 192.

duced children. Some of Agrippa I's popularity with the Jews probably stemmed from respect for his Hasmonaean grandmother,
Mariamme, but Josephus is the only other person known to have
claimed prestige in the first century A.D. because his family had
married into that of the Hasmonaeans. This is a little surprising, for
presumably just as one Hasmonaean king, probably Alexander
Jannaeus, apparently married his daughter to Josephus' ancestor
(*Vita* 4), others also must have disposed their offspring among leading Jerusalem families. If so, however, these families seem not to
have survived in the forefront of Judaean politics into the Roman
period. Either they were too poor to be granted any recognition by
Rome or they had all been eliminated in Herod's purges (see above,
p. 38).

The royal descent most often boasted by upper-class Judaean politicians in the first century A.D. was thus perforce derived from Herod
(cf. for instance, *B.J.* 2.418; 4.140–1). Most of those who claimed
such regal origins will have been direct descendants of Herod
(though fewer of these survived by A.D. 66 than one might expect, cf.
A.J. 18.128) or of one of his many siblings, for Herod rarely allowed
his relatives to marry Judaean Jews in case they won dangerous
prominence by the connection with the royal court. The Jerusalem
public was impressed by those junior members of the Herodian
house who chose to interest themselves in their affairs (cf. *A.J.*
20.214).

But they were never sufficiently impressed to believe that these
Herodians had a natural right to rule over them, for the rule of
Herod himself had been achieved only through the force of Roman
arms, and his reign was resented both in his lifetime and after his
death. The Romans assumed throughout the first century A.D. that
Herodian birth somehow made young princes of this royal house
eligible for power, so that Herodian monarchs were installed in territories as far away from Judaea as Asia Minor (cf. *A.J.* 20.158). But
Jews were never so impressed by the dynasty's claims. Ordinary Jews
never adopted the names favoured by Herod's family as they had
imitated the Hasmonaeans, and Agrippa I, the only ruler descended
from Herod who achieved real popularity in Judaea, tried to ignore
his Herodian origins altogether on his official coins and inscriptions,
preferring to portray himself as a legitimate Hasmonaean king.[16]

---

[16] Cf. Smallwood, *Jews*, p. 193. Note in contrast to Jewish practice the regular
finds of the name Agrippa on inscriptions in North Arabia and Southern Syria
where Agrippa II ruled, cf. M. Sartre in J.-M. Dentzer, ed., *Hauran I* (Paris, 1985) I,

By A.D 66 the careers of Agrippa I and Agrippa II must have done a little to enhance the status of the Herodian house in the eyes of the Jews, both because theirs was the only surviving Jewish royal family and, more particularly, by their zealous defence of Jewish interests in Rome. But Agrippa II, who was keen enough in this regard before he was granted a kingdom in A.D. 52 (cf. *A.J.* 20.10–14,134–6), seems to have forfeited this role once in power and to have sided consistently with the Roman procurator on all occasions when conflict seemed likely, even though his sister Berenice was capable of a tougher stance (*B.J.* 2.310–14). Not even his guardianship of the Temple finances was calculated to please the people, for he irritated some of them needlessly by building a tower to overlook the Temple site (*A.J.* 20.189–95) and by changing the traditional role of the Levites in the ritual of the service (*A.J.* 20.216–18).

It was thus useful for members of the Judaean ruling class to emphasize such Herodian or high-priestly connections as they could boast, but in no case could they expect to win unthinking obedience from the populace just because of their birth. Their prestige was in neither case reckoned by other Jews to have been a divine gift, and anyway, much though ancestry mattered in Jewish society, it was only one factor among others in the allotment of status: power was never based on caste.[17]

Some of the ruling class thus tried to bolster their popular support by claiming excellence in the main source of prestige in Judaean society other than ancestry, namely wisdom. Traditionally, it had been believed that this was the preserve of old age (see above, p. 73 on elders), but this belief seems to have diminished as the commonsense of experience was increasingly challenged by expert interpretation of the Torah (above, p. 73). Moreover, Jews do not seem to have reacted with hostility to precocious youths: whereas the Romans imposed minimum age-limits on holders of magistracies, the Jews did not apparently disqualify young men from the high priesthood; neither Josephus nor the Gospels seem abashed in reporting the juvenile genius of their heroes; and it is striking that inscriptions on Judaean ossuaries do not include the age of the de-

p. 200 n.29, p. 201 fig. 2. On Herodian intermarriage with other Jews, see Stern, 'Aspects of Jewish society', pp. 604–5.

[17] Jeremias, *Jerusalem*, p. 270, states that 'the entire population . . . was classified according to purity of descent . . . This division of the people into *social* classes was entirely ruled by the principle of maintaining racial purity' (my italics). But this is to confuse inherited religious privilege with social position: there were many poor and powerless priests.

ceased even when he is elderly, in contrast to common practice elsewhere.[18]

It was thus not on the grounds of their age but by claiming wisdom through understanding the Law that some of the ruling class sought to win the confidence of the public (cf. *A.J.* 20.263). Just as Josephus boasted about his intellectual brilliance in interpreting the Torah (*Vita* 9; *A.J.* 20.263), other Jews in positions of prominence might stress their status as Pharisees for the same purpose (see below, p. 219). When these rich Jews put great effort into learning traditional law they did so partly from a pious love of learning for its own sake, and partly because they believed that their expertise would bring them popularity and acknowledged authority among their compatriots, rather than to impress the Romans.

And to a considerable extent their confidence was justified; thus a man like the leading Pharisee Gamaliel was influential among the people because of his learning (cf. Acts 5.34; *B.J.* 2.162). But, as with priestly status, status through learning in the Torah was not sufficient to win the ruling class all the prestige they needed, for it was just as available to the poor as to the rich. As Josephus stressed (*c.Ap.* 2.175), expert knowledge of the law was possible for all Jews if intelligence and memory were put to good use when the Torah was read and commented on at the regular public meetings. Rabbis of the third and fourth centuries A.D. indeed believed that the experts in legal interpretation who had taught in the first century A.D. were poor artisans, and their belief is not likely to be entirely the product of late romances about the early sages since by the late-Roman period rabbis themselves were not infrequently rich. Neither low birth nor poverty was a bar to membership of the Jewish intelligentsia.[19]

Thus the Judaean ruling class was quite unable to point to any qualifications that in Jewish terms might justify their tenure of power. They had a monopoly of high-priestly and Herodian birth, but other Jews were not much impressed either by the High Priests, whom they saw as the creatures of Roman favour, or by the Idumaean dynasty of the Herods. When the ruling class chose to

[18] On the lack of a minimum age for the high priesthood, see Smallwood, *Jews*, p. 64; on Josephus and Jesus as young geniuses, see Rajak, *Josephus*, p. 28; on the ossuaries, see Hachlili and Killebrew, 'Jewish funerary customs', p. 122. Note, however, that Josephus still believes young people to be particularly likely to be rash and foolish (*B.J.* 4.128).

[19] Cf. Rajak, *Josephus*, p. 26. On Torah scholars, often called somewhat misleadingly 'scribes', see Schürer, *History* II, pp. 322–36. On the rabbinic evidence, see Hengel, *Property and Riches*, pp. 19–22; cf. p. 22 on later rabbinic attitudes.

stress their priestly origins and Torah scholarship, their compatriots were more inclined to accept their claims to high authority, but both these criteria for status could and did cut across class lines, and any prestige the ruling class claimed on such grounds would have to be shared with them by many poor Judaeans who were excluded from power by Rome.

It is probable that the Romans were not even aware that the local rulers faced a problem of this kind. They certainly did not realize its magnitude, for they simply assumed that in time the landed wealth of the ruling class would bring them authority.

This mistaken Roman assumption was caused by their tendency, which has already been noted (above, p. 35), to analyse all other societies in terms of their own. Thus in Rome property was by far the most important determinant of social status. The census marked out those who deserved honours (Ovid, *Amores* 3.8.55) because nothing in human affairs shows up a man's virtues more clearly than wealth (Seneca, *Controv.* 2.1.17).

This was not the view just of a few Roman writers who might reflect only the view of the upper class. Latin vocabulary contained an inextricable mixture of socio-economic and moral terminology. Above all, the social value of being rich was indicated by the institution of evergetism, through which the wealthy paid out vast sums to their fellow-citizens in order to increase their prestige. These gifts were not intended simply to show off the donors' means (though that was also common), nor particularly to benefit the recipients (since the rich gave most handsomely to friends of their own class and ignored the very poor), but to demonstrate the natural superiority of those with money and their subjective right to command. The notion that property could be evil was almost impossible to conceive: it was entertained only by philosophers moralizing about the long-past Golden Age and the transitoriness of material things (e.g. Seneca, *Epistulae Morales* 90.3.38). Thus, for most Romans the term *bonus* referred simultaneously to the rich and to the good (cf. Cic. *Ad Att.* 8.1.3).[20]

In Roman society it would thus not take long after a *coup* for the victors, whatever their origins, to establish their right to rule simply by being ensconced on their great estates. The idea that social prestige derived from wealth was not unique to Rome: by the first cen-

---

[20] See in general De Ste Croix, *Class Struggle*, pp. 425–6; cf. Hengel, *Property and Riches*, pp. 3–10, where attempts at egalitarian societies in Greece and Asia Minor in the second century B.C. are ascribed to the influence of oriental ideas. On evergetism, see Veyne, *Le pain et le cirque*, esp. pp. 9,15,25,488.

tury A.D. it was, for instance, shared by most Greeks and by Nabataean Arabs (Strabo, *Geog.* 16.4.26). But it was not a notion that won wide acceptance in Judaea.[21]

It should not of course be inferred that Jews were actually ashamed of wealth. Every man, they affirmed, should have his own vine and fig tree, and traditional wisdom texts praised honest riches earned in justice without abuse of power (e.g. *Ecclesiasticus* 10.27; 13.24). Nor did they believe that riches should prevent a man winning prestige on other grounds, such as good birth or skill in interpreting the Law: Gamaliel (Acts 5.34) and, according to John 3.1, Nicodemus were just such rich and learned Pharisees. But the idea that ownership of much property was a reason in itself to grant status and power did not make sense to Jewish society.

The Torah envisages a society devoted to the egalitarian ideals of the Mosaic covenant. A chapter of Leviticus (Lev. 25.8–17) discusses the institution of the Jubilee when, every fifty years, the land was to be redistributed to end the conglomeration of property by the rich and restore peasants to their farms. Every seventh year the ground was to be left to rest unworked because it belongs to the Lord and to no human owner (Lev. 25.1–7), and this practice was still being observed in the first century B.C. at least since the Romans permitted the waiving of land taxes to take account of it (*A.J.* 14.202). Also according to the Law, those of the ruling class who claimed status on the grounds of their priestly origins should not have been owning land at all (Deut. 10.9), and Philo still cites this prohibition (*De Spec. Leg.* 1.131), even though by his day it had been flouted by some priests for years (cf. I Kings 2.26). Josephus states explicitly (*c.Ap.* 2.186) that the wealth of the candidate was not a factor in appointing to the most prestigious position in Judaean society, the high priesthood.

In recognition of the unimportance of wealth as a status criterion, evergetism in the form common to both Greek and Roman society was never practised by the Judaean ruling class. It is not that Jews could not understand how to spend lavishly in the hope of winning prestige: Herod, who learnt from his Roman patrons, was one of the greatest evergetes, lavishing bountiful gifts on Greek cities both near

---

[21] On the Greek view, see De Ste Croix, *Class Struggle*, pp. 425–6; on the Nabataeans, see G. W. Bowersock, *Roman Arabia* (Cambridge, Mass., and London, 1983), p. 16. On all the following arguments, see my forthcoming paper, 'The origins of the Great Revolt: a conflict of status criteria', in the proceedings of the conference on *Greece and Rome in Eretz Israel* (Haifa and Tel Aviv, March 1985). See in contrast the assertion by Rajak, *Josephus*, p. 25: 'ownership of land. . . . was in itself also a source of status in Jerusalem society'.

Judaea and further away, as well as spending massively on the Jewish Temple and other public projects such as, probably, the Patriarchs' Tombs at Hebron, where the rectangular enclosure belongs to this period. But Herod won gratitude from the Greeks alone, for the Jews continued to hate him however much they admired the edifices he erected, and rulers of the following century did not often waste their money seeking Jewish popularity or esteem by such means.

Thus, if the histories of Josephus did not survive, the Judaean ruling class would be almost unknown, for, unlike contemporary rich men all over the Roman empire, they did not pick up the epigraphic habit and did not subscribe to public buildings. Donations to the building of the Temple were made by none of the Judaean rich apart from Herod himself. The gift of gold and silver plate for the gates of the Temple court made by the Alexandrian Alexander (*B.J.* 5.205), and the pavement given by a Rhodian Jew according to an inscription recently unearthed near the Temple site, make this reticence of the Judaean ruling class the more remarkable. Not even the building of synagogues seems to have been considered a worthwhile act by rich Judaeans in this period: according to Luke 7.5, a centurion in Capernaum was respected by the elders of the Jews because 'he loves our nation and built us our synagogue', but, even assuming that the story is true rather than a gloss on the simpler story in the other Gospels, with the gentile author reflecting conditions outside Palestine, it is significant that the man was gentile and that his action therefore won approval not in itself but because it demonstrated his pro-Jewish sympathies; a synagogue was built by a certain Theodotus in first-century Jerusalem (*CIJ* 1404), but it was intended more for the benefit of pilgrims than the local population, for the inscription recording this act of evergetism lay directly adjacent to the Temple mount, and Theodotus himself was more probably a Roman freedman's son or grandson than a local rich Jew. Similarly, the classic act of a Greek or Roman evergete was the provision of food in a famine, whereas in Judaea this act of generosity was performed not by the local ruling class but by the converted royal family of Adiabene (*A.J.* 20.101). The Jerusalem rich had plenty of money, as their fine houses show (see above, p. 55), but they evidently did not believe that spending it on their fellow-citizens through public projects would bring them prestige.[22]

[22] For the Rhodian Jew's inscription, see B. Isaac, 'A donation for Herod's Temple in Jerusalem', *IEJ* 33 (1983) 86–92. The ex-High Priest Ananias is said by Josephus at *A.J.* 20.205 to have advanced daily in the goodwill and esteem of the

The failure of wealth to bring social esteem among Jews was only partly caused by the egalitarian ideals of the Torah. It has already been noted that in Judaea economic relations did not promote social ties, so that rich landowners could expect no particular loyalty from their tenants (above, p. 67). Neither Hebrew nor Aramaic had a term like the Latin *bonus*, which equated high social standing and morality with riches. The prestige gained by many rich Greeks and Romans by paying for their city's religious cults was undermined by the uniquely Jewish and deliberately egalitarian tradition that every adult male Jew should pay a half-shekel towards the upkeep of the sacrifices, the rich being positively prohibited from contributing more (Exod. 30.15). Other forms of evergetism were weakened by the Jewish tradition of charity as a duty incumbent on everyone not himself destitute and aimed not at fellow-citizens who might repay the donor with social prestige but at the very poor. Furthermore, the custom of regular taxes for the redistribution of wealth to the poverty-stricken – the corner of the field left unharvested, the second tithe donated in some years to the destitute, and so on – destroyed the element of spontaneous voluntary gift-giving which was the essence of the achievement of prestige by evergetism.[23]

It may validly be objected that in denying that Jews recognized wealth as a mark of social status I have generalized too far, for it is certainly likely that some inhabitants of Judaea had adopted Greco-Roman values in this matter as in others by the first century A.D. Any Judaean who thought primarily in Greek rather than in a

citizens: ἦν γὰρ χρημάτων ποριστικός · καθ' ἡμέραν γοῦν τὸν Ἀλβῖνον καὶ τὸν ἀρχιερέα δώροις ἐθεράπευεν. Feldman in the Loeb edition translates this to mean that Ananias' popularity stemmed from his provision of money *to the people*, in which case he would be a classic evergete, but it is better to understand from 'γοῦν' that Ananias' daily provision of money was to the procurator Albinus and to the High Priest (cf. *B.J.* 2.274 on bribery of Albinus by such faction leaders).

On the status and origins of Theodotus, see S. Safrai, 'The synagogue', in Safrai and Stern, *The Jewish People* II, p. 910, *pace* Rajak, *Josephus*, p. 56 n. 28; Roman citizenship was not common among Jews in Judaea (see above, p. 48).

[23] Alon, *Jews, Judaism and the Classical World*, pp. 344–53, especially p. 347 n. 12, points to the words *ge'im* and *gedolim* as Hebrew terms which imply both wealth and power, but the sources cited are all tannaitic (i.e. redacted *c.* A.D. 200) or later and reflect the actual power of the rich in contemporary Jewish society rather than a belief that wealth should bring social status.

The contrast between charity and evergetism is best shown by Veyne in his discussion of the changes in pagan evergetism with the adoption throughout the empire after Constantine of Christian (originally Jewish) notions of charity (*Le pain et le cirque*, pp. 44–5,52,66).

For the second tithe and other taxes for the relief of the poor, see Jeremias, *Jerusalem*, pp. 131–4.

semitic language, as some of the upper class itself may well have done, would be lulled by a Greek term like *dunatos* into assuming, as Romans did, that political power implied wealth. Josephus thus writes occasionally as if he has adopted this Greek notion: a certain Dolesus in Gadara, described as 'by birth and reputation the first citizen', is assumed by the author to represent the rich of that city (*B.J.* 4.414,416).

But the kind of Jews likely to pick up such Greek ideas were of course precisely, like Josephus, the ruling class whose status was in question (see above, p. 12). They might impress one another by their magnificent houses, some of which were sufficiently noticeable to act as landmarks (cf. *B.J.* 4.567), and by the fine family tombs which preserved the memory of their ancestors (cf. *B.J.* 5.468,506), but the rest of the Judaean populace was more likely to react to such displays of wealth with envy than with admiration; indeed, Josephus states that the erection of conspicuous funerary monuments was not considered pious by Jews (*c.Ap.* 2.205).

In practice, therefore, much of the ostentatious expenditure of the rich was directed towards the interiors of their earthly and eternal dwellings, where only family and friends could admire the evidence of wealth. There was just no point in showing off to the poorer citizens. When rich Jews did use their money for the public's welfare, they did so not to win public esteem but because of the requirements of piety: Josephus records that all Jews in his time used to provide a funeral banquet for the people at the completion of seven days' mourning for the deceased, and that this act reduced many to penury (*B.J.* 2.1), but he also writes that this banquet was provided 'not without compulsion' because failure to do so would be impious, and his implication is that *every* Jew put on a public meal, not just the rich.[24]

A few Jews were not only unimpressed by wealth but even went so

---

[24] On the houses, see Avigad, *Discovering Jerusalem*, pp. 95-131; Rajak, *Josephus*, p. 24. On the tombs, see L. Y. Rahmani, 'Ancient Jerusalem's funerary customs and tombs: part three', *Biblical Archaeologist* 45.1 (Winter 1982) 43-53; N. Avigad in Yadin, *Jerusalem Revealed*, pp. 17-20; Hachlili and Killebrew, 'Jewish funerary customs'; on the tomb interiors, see Rahmani, 'Ancient Jerusalem's funerary customs', p. 44 (burial goods); Avigad in Yadin, *Jerusalem Revealed*, pp. 19 (Jason's tomb), 66 (Nazirite's tomb); R. Hachlili, 'A Jewish funerary wall-painting of the first century A.D.', *PEQ* 117 (1985) 112-27, cf. p. 125: 'The fact that only one decorated tomb has been found to date may be a matter of chance or due to favourable conditions of preservation.'

The depiction of God as a rich landowner in Gospel parables (e.g. Matt. 21.33-41) is likely to reflect (if it reflects anything at all in existing society) the *actual* disposition of power in first-century Judaea, not what ought to be the case.

far as to contest that riches were a positive hindrance to moral behaviour and that true authority was to be sought among the poor,
notions quite incredible to contemporary Romans or Greeks. The
impetus to such ideas in the Jewish tradition lay far back in the writings of prophets such as Isaiah, who associated the poor with meek-
ness and humility and then praised humility before God as a
supreme virtue. Praise of poverty is picked up by some Jewish writers
of the first century A.D.: the poor man is described as the righteous at
Qumran (cf. *4QpPs* 37, col. II, 9–10) and Jesus is said to have echoed
the same theme (Luke 6.20; 16.22). Conversely, such texts suggest
that ownership of wealth makes virtue hard to achieve: it is harder
for the rich man to enter the Kingdom of Heaven than for a camel to
pass through the eye of a needle (Matt. 19.23), and perfection can
only be achieved when all goods are sold and given to the poor
(Mark 10.17–22). Impossible though it is to prove that such views
were rightly attributed to Jesus himself rather than the early
Church, they are much more likely to have arisen in Jewish Palestine
than in any other of the milieux which shaped the Gospels. The
homily in the Christian Ps. Clementines (*Hom.* 3.25) which explains
the origin of Cain's sin as his possession of property is similarly likely
to go back to Jewish teaching since it involves a play on the Hebrew
root *qana*, to possess.

For some Jews such praise of poverty was not mere rhetoric. The
popularity of asceticism and general recognition that denial of
material possessions could be pious rather than stupid (see above,
p. 79) show the wide distribution of such ideas. Few rich young
Romans or Greeks would have seen any point in a spell of self-denial
in the Judaean desert like that enjoyed by Josephus in his late teens
(*Vita* 11–12). The Essenes consciously prevented the accumulation of
property by holding all their goods in common (*B.J.* 2.127).[25]

Such opposition to the ownership of property was not, however,
common: Jesus' disciples were, according to the Gospel authors
themselves, surprised at his revelation that the rich will find salvation hard to achieve (Mark 10.23–4; Matt. 19.23–5), and the fact
that Pliny (*Nat. Hist.* 5.73) remarked on the way that the Essenes did
not use money suggests that this extreme attitude was rare. Most
Jews believed simply that wealth was irrelevant to the achievement
of social status.

But even this milder attitude was sufficient to account for the

---

[25] The contrast between Greco-Roman and Jewish evaluations of poverty is
noted by De Ste Croix, *Class Struggle*, pp. 431–2; Hengel, *Property and Riches*, pp. 12–
19. Cf. also Kreissig, pp. 93–4.

denigration by Jews of those whose only claim to power in Judaea rested on the fact that they had been singled out by Rome or the Herodian dynasty for special attention entirely because of their wealth. Such men were the tax-collectors, known in the Gospels as publicans.

Publicans had to be rich to carry out their duties, for when the right to collect taxes was farmed out by auction the successful bidder guaranteed payment of a minimum amount in the expectation that he would earn more than his original bid through conscientious collection. Thus Zacchaeus, who farmed taxes in Jericho, was described as well-to-do (Luke 19.1–2), as was John of Caesarea, who tried in vain to bribe the procurator Florus in A.D. 66 (*B.J.* 2.287). As far as the Romans were concerned, these tax collectors were respectable members of the ruling class – hence John's inclusion on the deputation by Caesarean Jews to Florus. But among Jews, publicans were despised.

For the Gospel writers, publicans are aligned alongside sinners and there is no reason to suggest that such a view was derived from Christian milieux outside Palestine. In rabbinic texts also, tax collectors (*mokhsin*) are abused (cf. *t.B.M.* 8.26). It is not easy to find reasons. The taxes they farmed were indirect tolls on the passage and sale of goods, and the fact that Archelaus in 4 B.C. and Vitellius in A.D. 37 agreed to lighten some such taxes (*A.J.* 17.205; 18.90) shows that these tolls were disliked, but that is hardly sufficient to account for the disdain for publicans expressed in the sources. Nor can the complaint against these men be their collaboration with the oppressive power of Rome, for the more lucrative direct taxes were collected by the High Priest and his 'council' in Jerusalem (cf. *B.J.* 2.405) without this apparently being counted to their discredit, and many of the publicans abused in the Gospels will, like Matthew, presumably have been employed by the Herodian Antipas rather than by Rome to farm taxes in Galilee (cf. Matt. 9.9–13). According to Luke (19.8), the charge against Zacchaeus was that he cheated tax payers to his own benefit, and it was this sin that John the Baptist singled out for censure in the tax collectors who came to him to be baptized (Luke 3.12–13), but Jewish sources do not contain general attacks on, for instance, shopkeepers and merchants, who presumably fell into similar temptation at times, and Luke's comment may reflect an attempt by a non-Palestinian and non-Jew to make sense of the puzzling antagonism towards publicans which he found in his sources on Jesus.

For in other provinces of the Roman empire, the rich men who farmed the state taxes were among the most respected members of society. Coming to the attention of Roman governors through such services, they were just the sort of men who became procurators of the emperor and whose descendants progressed in time into the Roman ruling class.

In Judaea by contrast the Jewish attitude towards publicans embodied the conflict of Roman status criteria against those of the local population which this chapter has discussed. Tax collectors achieved power through Roman patronage alone, without any of the criteria for status generally accepted by Jews, such as good birth or wisdom through knowledge of Torah. Their power was thus bitterly resented because in Jewish eyes it was undeserved, and, since their position in society was in effect defined by their wealth, they bore the brunt of class resentment as the gap between rich and poor widened during the first century A.D.[26]

Unlike the publicans, most members of the Judaean ruling class were not despised by their fellow Jews. Most of them, after all, could shelter behind a recognized status, derived from birth or learning, to try to justify to Jews their tenure of power. But, if not despised, nor did the ruling class enjoy much authority. Rich priests could not justify claiming more power than poor priests. High-priestly status was prejudiced by the proliferation of High Priests and the weakened role of the incumbent of the post. Links with the Herodian royal family could not be guaranteed to win a man popular affection. Expertise in the interpretation of the Law could always be challenged by experts working in a different tradition, be it Pharisee, Sadducee, Essene or other.

---

[26] Schürer, *History* I, p. 376, describes Zacchaeus as 'well-to-do and respectable'. So he would have been considered in any other part of the Roman empire. On the rabbinic evidence, see Goodman, *State and Society*, pp. 131–2; cf., for complaints against shopkeepers, especially butchers, *ibid.* p. 211 n. 8. See also M. Hadas-Lebel, 'La fiscalité romaine dans la littérature rabbinique jusqu'à la fin du IIIe siècle', *Revue des études juives* 143 (1984) 23–6.

It is often assumed that the Matthew (or Levi) depicted in the Gospels was not a publican himself but only an employee of a rich tax-farmer, cf. E. Badian, *Publicans and Sinners: private enterprise in the service of the Roman Republic* (Oxford, 1972), p. 11. This may be correct (cf. Matt. 9.9, where he is described as sitting to receive taxes in person), but according to Luke 5.29 he was at least rich enough to afford a great feast in his house to which other publicans were invited.

The common assertion that publicans were considered to be wicked simply because they were collaborating with Rome (so, for example, Sanders, *Jesus and Judaism*, p. 178) is not based on any explicit evidence, so far as I know. J. Donahue, 'Tax collectors and sinners', *CBQ* 33 (1971) 39–61, sees that this fact creates a problem for interpreters of the Gospels.

In sum, the ruling class of Judaea looked no more like the natural elite of Judaean society in A.D. 66 than they had when installed by Rome in A.D. 6. They were not capable of controlling the increasing expressions of social discontent, fuelled by economic disparities, that afflicted the population over which they tried to rule.

FACTION STRUGGLE WITHIN THE RULING CLASS

CHAPTER 6

REACTIONS TO FAILURE: THE RULING CLASS A.D. 6–66

How was the ruling class to react as their inability to win authority over Judaea became gradually more apparent? They could hardly opt out of the invidious position into which they had been placed by Rome, except perhaps by the last resort of emigration, which was indeed quite probably the eventual fate of some of them (cf. *B.J.* 2.279). Rome needed local rulers and insisted that the rich took on that role. They had little choice.

Some of the ruling class presumably accepted their lot and soldiered on with blind disregard of the disorder in the countryside and among their poorer compatriots. Disorder and brigandage will have affected them directly only rarely. In the luxury of their homes they could ignore the problems of the peasants. Josephus even writes once, astonishingly, that four years before the revolt the city of Jerusalem was enjoying exceptional peace and prosperity (*B.J.* 6.300).

The rich themselves were not threatened by the social disorder. No class leaders had come forward to demand social justice on behalf of the oppressed (see above, p. 67). There were occasional charismatic figures who challenged their right to rule, but they won few supporters and were easily dealt with by the Roman governor (see above, p. 92). There were many priests and experts in Torah interpretation who, despite being excluded from the ruling class, could command much prestige among the population, but they made no attempt to seize power on their own behalf because, like the poor in general, they lacked the institutions through which such an attack on the established order could be made. The dangers to society lay not in revolution but, more insidiously, in anarchy.

For the ruling class there was thus no incentive to bind together for self-protection because they did not feel themselves to be under attack. On the other hand simple competition for office and titles of local significance, although doubtless always intrinsically desirable to some, must have seemed of less value when the Jewish population tended to accord only slight honour to those who won such positions and when the Roman hierarchy made no concessions to allow more than a few Jews to enter their ranks. Miserable resignation to their lot might seem the obvious alternative.

But by the fifties A.D. some of the ruling class seem to have realized that the prevailing anarchy was not so much a hindrance as an opportunity for greater power. With the benefit of money and institutional position, they began to use the complaints of the dispossessed and disaffected to win control and influence exceeding that of their fellow-rulers. Their aim, so far as is known, was power for its own sake, although opportunities to hive off some of the wealth which came to Jerusalem in connection with the Temple were also much enhanced for those with influence (cf. *A.J.* 20.206 on the forcible extraction of priestly tithes). The result was faction struggle of increasing vehemence and bitterness, the civil dissension (*stasis*) which Josephus so often deplored.[1]

Josephus' explicit evidence about this struggle commences with the emergence of faction fighting from probable earlier clandestine skulduggery into open clashes on the streets of Jerusalem.

Thus, in the time of the High Priest Ishmael b. Phiabi, appointed in the late forties or the fifties A.D., some of the ruling class tried to overcome their political rivals by using gangs to hurl insults and stones and to seize the tithes due to poorer priests (*A.J.* 20.179–81).[2]

In A.D. 62 the violence became worse, both during the interregnum after the procurator Festus died and after the arrival of Albinus. In *B.J.* 2.274–6 Josephus describes how at this time the 'revolutionary party', the *poneroi*, acted like brigand-chiefs and tyrants, each with his own band of followers acting like a bodyguard to help in the plunder of 'moderate', *metrion*, men. It is already clear from this account that these 'revolutionaries' were not actually brigands, for Josephus only says of them that they imitated brigand behaviour, but the more detailed narrative in *A.J.* 20.206–14 makes

[1] Rajak, *Josephus*, pp. 91–4, gives an excellent account of Josephus' preoccupation with *stasis*. See now in general Horsley, 'High priests', especially 44–8, with a useful analysis similar in method and conclusions to, but independent of, Rajak.

[2] Josephus claims (*A.J.* 20.181) that some of the poorer priests starved to death as a result, and it is therefore often claimed that this was 'something like a class struggle', cf. Brunt, 'Josephus on social conflicts', p. 151. But Josephus states explicitly that the struggle was partly between men of high-priestly status and the first men (*protoi*) of the Jerusalem populace (*A.J.* 20.180). By the term *protoi* Josephus usually means members of the ruling class. Furthermore, the phrase '*tois archiereusi echthra tis eis allelous*' (*ibid.*) most naturally means that a hatred arose between one group of high priests and another, in which case this is mistranslated in the Loeb edition.

it plain who in fact they were. The chief culprit was the ex-High Priest Ananias, whose household servants acted as bully-boys in establishing his power (*A.J.* 20.206). And the other gang leaders were equally distinguished members of the ruling class. Two other ex-High Priests, Jesus b. Damnaeus and Jesus b. Gamalas, carried out a feud, with their respective gangs throwing stones and insults at each other (*A.J.* 20.213), and two relatives of the Herodian dynasty, Costobar and Saul, collected gangs of villains to plunder the property of others (*A.J.* 20.214).

Earlier, in the governorship of Felix, some priests had been sent to Rome in chains for an unrecorded misdemeanour, for Josephus says that he travelled there to plead on their behalf (*Vita* 13–16). They too must have been rich enough to deserve a trial at Rome rather than in the provinces. Josephus calls them gentlemen (*kalous kagathous*) and describes the charge against them as small and, significantly, 'ordinary': the arrest of members of the ruling class was evidently common by this time. Josephus does not even bother to record the incident in his general histories. Violent faction struggle within the ruling class was apparently endemic.[3]

It is likely that peaceful competition for power had been normal long before the violence which Josephus records broke out. So, for instance, the tortuous career of Joazar, High Priest in A.D. 6, already discussed above (pp. 43–4), most probably to some extent reflects manoeuvrings within the ruling class.

Joazar had been High Priest on Herod's death in 4 B.C. As a son of Boethus he was a brother-in-law of Herod and a politician well integrated into the Herodian court. He may have had his own ideas about the succession to the dead king, for Archelaus, once safely installed as ethnarch, accused him of having supported some of the rebels in the uprisings that had preceded his return from Rome (*A.J.* 17.339). It is not necessary to assume that this charge was trumped up just to please the people who hated Joazar for his impiety (see above, p. 44), for even some of Herod's soldiers joined the rebels (probably in opposition not so much to Archelaus himself as to

---

[3] The provision of more detail in *A.J.* than in *B.J.* can be explained both by Josephus' different intentions in the two works and by his apologetic interest in the *B.J.* in absolving the ruling class from responsibility for the revolt. Cohen, *Josephus in Galilee and Rome*, pp. 150–1, suggests that in *A.J.* the historian wrote with disapproval about high priests because by this time he was a Pharisee and 'Pharisees never did like high priests'. I am not sure that this last generalization can be justified, but it is anyway simpler to assume that the details about the misdemeanours of the ruling class were included in *A.J.* primarily because they were true, and that they were omitted in *B.J.* only because they were embarrassing.

Sabinus, the Roman procurator who had looted four hundred talents from the Temple (*A.J.* 17.250–68)), and in Idumaea two thousand of Herod's veterans, with perhaps up to eight thousand armed supporters, held out against his cousin Achiab in an attempt to bring to power other relatives of the king not named by Josephus (*B.J.* 2.55, 76–8; see below, p. 173 n. 25). But anyway, whether or not Joazar was involved in these revolts – and his opposition at least to Sabinus' sacrilege would be expected in a High Priest – he was deposed by Archelaus in 4 B.C. or soon after.

Joazar's political machinations were, however, evidently forgivable in Archelaus' eyes, for within ten years he had been reinstated and in A.D. 6 was again the incumbent High Priest (*A.J.* 18.3). In that post he worked as hard and competently for the governor of the new province as Rome could hope for a leading member of the new ruling class to do, trying hard to persuade the reluctant people to submit to the census. And yet within months he had been deposed by Quirinius, the legate of Syria (*A.J.* 18.26), and none of his family was to resurface as a leader in Judaea until Agrippa I appointed Simon Cantheras as High Priest in A.D. 41 (*A.J.* 19.297).

Josephus explains Joazar's reversal of fortunes by alleging that he has been 'overpowered by the populace'. Popular discontent is indeed likely enough (see above, p. 44), but it is most implausible that dissatisfaction expressed by the people would lead Quirinius to so drastic a step as the removal of a High Priest so early in the life of the province. The sacrifice of a loyal and effective member of the ruling class is comprehensible only if Joazar had been attacked by other members of the same class whose status in Roman eyes was as impressive as his.[4]

Unfortunately, the details of the struggle for power in this and in other cases between A.D. 6 and A.D. 50 are impossible to retrieve. Josephus provides only skimpy indications, both because he probably did not know much about those events which had occurred before his own lifetime, and because this factional strife was not an important subject for him in the composition of the *A.J.*, where he had most opportunity to dwell on this period.

From A.D. 50 onwards, however, the main lines of the power struggle can be delineated. Many of the ruling group involved were the descendants of the men favoured by Rome in A.D. 6, the 'high

---

[4] For a full discussion of Joazar's career, see Smallwood, 'High priests and politics', pp. 17–21; *eadem, Jews*, pp. 114–16. I do not however follow all of her interpretation here. In particular, the assumption that the charge of 4 B.C. was trumped-up seems to me unwarranted.

priests', as the families from which the post was customarily filled were called (see above, p. 120), but members of Herod's family had also been prominent since at least A.D. 40, when some of them were part of the delegation which went to the governor of Syria to complain against Caligula's plan to desecrate the Temple (*A.J.* 18.273), and some Idumaean associates of Herod had been sucked back into Judaean affairs by Agrippa I – most noticeably Helcias, a son of Herod the Great's friend Alexas and himself commander-in-chief of Agrippa's army and father of a certain Julius Archelaus; this latter married Agrippa's daughter, Mariamme (*A.J.* 20.140) and was friendly enough with Josephus after the revolt to buy a copy of his book (*c.Ap.* 1.51).

There were quite certainly others within the ruling group who cannot be put into any of these categories but, perhaps precisely because they lacked such claims to local status, they are not recorded as taking part in factional politics. When an embassy was sent to Claudius to ask for custody of the high-priestly robes, the procurator Fadus took the matter sufficiently seriously to take hostage the children of the Jerusalem authorities until it was resolved (*A.J.* 20.8). Josephus preserves the text of Claudius' letter to the people of Jerusalem in which he gave his decision in their favour, and in this letter Claudius cites the names of the four ambassadors sent to Rome by the ruling class on this important business. They are called Cornelius b. Ceron, Tryphon b. Theudion, Dorotheus b. Nathanael and John b. John (*A.J.* 20.14). Nothing is heard of any of these men in any other context, and little more can be surmised about them than that they must have been rich to be acceptable as ambassadors to Claudius, that they were not from high-priestly families despite the object of their mission, and that Cornelius, given his name, may have been a Roman citizen. The ruling class may have contained many such rich men who, like the publicans, crop up rarely in the sources because of their lack of local prestige.

The leading figures in the factional fray were thus certain incumbent and retired High Priests and junior members of the Herodian house. By no means every High Priest continued to seek influence after losing office, for nothing is known of any political role after retirement for twenty or so of the twenty-seven High Priests deposed between 37 B.C. and A.D. 66. Nonetheless the factions which flourished in the late fifties and early sixties A.D. were led by just such men, the sons of Ananus (High Priest in A.D. 6) and of Ananias b. Nedebaeus (High Priest from A.D. 47 to at least A.D. 49 and perhaps to A.D. 59), as well as by the current High Priest Ishmael b. Phiabi

(High Priest from A.D. 49 at the earliest to A.D. 61 at latest) and by the Herodians Saul and Costobar.[5]

The supporters and opponents of one of the most powerful factions when political violence of this kind first sullied the streets of Jerusalem, that of the reigning High Priest Ishmael b. Phiabi, are hard to trace. The main public issue over which Ishmael fell out with one at least of his fellow Jewish leaders was the building of a tower by Agrippa II to enable him to see into the Temple and watch the priests performing the sacrifices (*A.J.* 20.189–96), but the complaint by Ishmael was probably only an excuse for a quarrel. Many of the houses in the upper city probably could, as they still can, see down into the Temple site and it is hard to see why this should be religiously objectionable.[6] Certainly Ishmael's refusal to pull down the wall he built to block Agrippa's view was on laughable grounds: he claimed that the wall was now part of the Temple structure and it would be sacrilege to destroy it (*A.J.* 20.193), a principle which, if consistently followed, would have prevented all alterations at any time to the Temple buildings.

Ishmael was, then, deliberately and provocatively opposed to Agrippa, whose status in Jerusalem, as a young man only recently appointed ruler of Galilee and its environs, was not much higher than that of other scions of the Herodian house; his only constitutional advantage lay in his right to appoint High Priests. Ishmael must have had powerful backers since Agrippa's response to his op-

[5] Uncertainty over the dates of Ananias' and Ishmael's tenures of the high priesthood derives from three apparently irreconcilable statements in the sources. In *A.J.* (20.179) Ishmael's appointment to replace Ananias is put late in Felix's procuratorship; the late rabbinic tradition in *b.Yom.* 9a asserts that Ishmael was High Priest for ten years; at *A.J.* 3.320 Josephus states that Ishmael was High Priest during a great famine, which would most naturally refer to that which occurred in the forties A.D. during the rule of Claudius. Various solutions have been proposed. If the rabbinic story is disregarded as unreliably late and the famine assumed to be a different one to that in Claudius' time, Ishmael could have been High Priest *c.* A.D. 59–61 (cf. Schürer, *History* II, p. 231). Alternatively, if the ten-year incumbency to which the rabbinic tradition refers is taken seriously, it can be suggested that Ishmael was appointed between late A.D. 49 and A.D. 52 when Ananias was sent in chains to Rome by Cumanus following the fighting against the Samaritans (*A.J.* 20.131; cf. D. R. Schwartz, 'Ishmael ben Phiabi and the chronology of Provincia Judaea', *Tarbiz* 52 (1983) 177–200 (Heb.)). In favour of Schwartz's detailed hypothesis, note that Ananias in *c.* A.D. 54 was no longer obviously the High Priest in the eyes of an uninformed observer, since St Paul had to be told about his status according to Acts 23.2.
[6] Note, however, the evidence adduced by D. R. Schwartz, 'Viewing the holy utensils (*POxy.* v, 840)', *NTS* 32 (1986) 153–9, to show that a belief that it was impious for some people to see the Temple utensils was found among some Jews in this period but not others.

position was not, as it might have been, simply to depose him from office and appoint a more amenable man. Josephus writes as if the whole ruling class united with Ishmael on this issue (*A.J.* 20.191). The keeper of the treasury, a certain Helcias, clearly supported him against Agrippa, for he was sent with Ishmael on the embassy to Rome (*A.J.* 20.194). Helcias' name suggests a close relationship to his homonym who had been a powerful friend of Agrippa I (see above, p. 141); since the elder Helcias was surnamed 'the Great' (*A.J.* 18.273), this Helcias was perhaps his son. A reason for the estrangement between the two families may be surmised, for another son of the elder Helcias, Julius Archelaus, was abandoned early in their marriage by his wife, Agrippa II's sister Mariamme (*A.J.* 20.147); but it is not certain that the divorce had taken place before the incident involving the wall. Of those apart from Agrippa who opposed Ishmael, few can be named. It can be plausibly surmised that one of them was the man who was appointed as High Priest by Agrippa when Ishmael, at Agrippa's request, was detained by the empress Poppaea at Rome (*A.J.* 20.195–6), but nothing is known about this new incumbent, Joseph Cabi b. Simon (*A.J.* 20.196), who did not last long in the post.

But, even if the details of their alignments are hazy, it is clear that the faction fighting that was to blossom in the sixties A.D. had already begun before the end of Cumanus' procuratorship in A.D. 52 (cf. *A.J.* 20.180) and it is highly likely that Ishmael was already opposed by the factions which came to the fore then, for the ambitious ex-High Priests who led them may well have been irked by the influence of a reigning High Priest as powerful as Ishmael.

The first of those factions clustered around the sons of Ananus, who had been High Priest in A.D. 6 and was the father of five incumbents of the office (*A.J.* 18.26; 20.198). Three of those sons seem to have sunk into obscurity after their tenure, but two, Jonathan b. Ananus, High Priest in A.D. 36–7, and Ananus b. Ananus, High Priest in A.D. 62, did not. It is clear that the five brothers were politically united: Matthias only became High Priest at all because Jonathan, when offered a second period of tenure by Agrippa I in *c.* A.D. 42 and declining it, explicitly recommended him as more pious than himself (*A.J.* 19.315–16). It can also be surmised that the long-serving High Priest Caiaphas (*c.* A.D. 18–36), who was brother-in-law to the five of them according to John 18.13, was a political ally; the portrayal in Acts 4.6 of his association with the elder Ananus at the trial of Peter makes this especially plausible.

In that case Elionaeus b. Cithaerus or Cantheras, who replaced

Matthias b. Ananus as High Priest under Agrippa I after a short period of office (*A.J.* 19.342), may have been another adherent, since he may be named at *m.Par.* 3.5 as 'Elihoenai son of ha-Kayyaph' and thus may have been Caiaphas' son. It has been further conjectured that the last High Priest to hold office before the revolt was connected to Ananus' dynasty, but this view is based only on the fact that his names, Matthias and Theophilus, are attested as the names of two of Ananus' sons, and these names are too common for the hypothesis to be firmly accepted.[7]

The prolific family of Ananus was thus in itself a powerful faction, but they also attracted allies from outside. One of these, a certain Doras, was Jonathan's most trusted friend, suborned, according to *A.J.* 20.163, by the procurator Felix to turn traitor and have him assassinated. More significantly, Ananus' sons may, by the sixties A.D., have maintained close links with the dynasty of Boethus despite any initial antagonism between the two families caused by the replacement of Joazar b. Boethus by Ananus in A.D. 6.

The (slim) evidence for such a rapprochement lies in the friendship with Ananus b. Ananus of Jesus b. Gamalas, who was High Priest in *c.* A.D. 63 and, according to a probably trustworthy rabbinic source (*m.Yeb.* 6.4), was married to a certain Martha from the family of Boethus. Not only were these two men closely associated after the outbreak of revolt (see below, p. 165), but they probably had an alliance in the immediately preceding years based on considerations of their mutual interest. When in *c.* A.D. 63 a violent feud broke out between Jesus b. Gamalas and his predecessor as High Priest, Jesus b. Damnaeus (cf. *A.J.* 20.213), Ananus will naturally have taken the side of Jesus b. Gamalas, for Jesus b. Damnaeus had probably been among the enemies who brought his own tenure of office to a premature end in A.D. 62: Jesus b. Damnaeus had profited by his deposition to obtain the high priesthood for himself (*A.J.* 20.203), and Ananus will have hated him for that just as Jesus b. Damnaeus loathed his successor, the other Jesus.

It is not certain when, if it genuinely existed, this new rapprochement between the two families began. In *c.* A.D. 41 the last Boethid High Priest before the sixties A.D., Simon Cantheras, had been, like Joazar, deposed in favour of the house of Ananus. It is unlikely, however, that this was caused by rivalry between the families. The original intention of Agrippa I in deposing Simon was to replace him

---

[7] For a clear presentation of these conjectures see Stern, 'Aspects of Jewish society', pp. 600–12, esp. 607–8.

with Jonathan b. Ananus, considering him 'more worthy of the honour', but Jonathan was evidently unaware of the king's plan since he refused the post when it was offered to him (*A.J.* 19.313).

Of the probable opponents of the sons of Ananus, Jesus b. Damnaeus has already been mentioned. There were other enemies too, some of them, like James the brother of Jesus, killed by Ananus b. Ananus in the procurator's absence in A.D. 62 (*A.J.* 20.200).[8] It is possible that the murder of Jonathan b. Ananus, which Josephus paints in vivid colours, was also part of the faction struggle, though precisely which of his enemies arranged the killing was evidently unknown to Josephus, who blames the procurator Felix at *A.J.* 20.162–4 but not at *B.J.* 2.256; the whole point of the assassination methods used by the sicarii who killed Jonathan was that the murderers were not detected (*B.J.* 2.255; see below, p. 214).

A plausible culprit would be Ananias b. Nedebaeus, who was the leading politician in Judaea apart from Jonathan in the late forties and early fifties and was the incumbent High Priest for much if not all of that period (see above, n. 5). His prominence in Judaea is clear from the reaction of Quadratus, legate of Syria, to the fighting between Jews and Samaritans after the incident when a Galilean pilgrim was killed on the way to Jerusalem. Quadratus held the Judaean authorities at least partly responsible and therefore sent the leading Jews in chains to Rome. These prisoners included Ananias b. Nedebaeus with one of his sons, and Jonathan b. Ananus (*B.J.* 2.243). In Rome, however, Jonathan may have achieved something of a political coup, for, by arranging that the next procurator should be the ex-slave Felix, he seems to have ensured that he (Jonathan) should be guaranteed a special place in his counsels (cf. *A.J.* 20.162 on his frequent advice to Felix). It would not be surprising if Ananias in retaliation and jealousy contrived to have Jonathan put out of the way by murder, particularly if he had also lost the high priesthood on Felix's arrival as governor (above, n. 5).

Certainly by A.D. 62 Ananias was in firm opposition to Jonathan's

---

[8] The authenticity of this account of Ananus in *A.J.* has been challenged by, among others, Rajak, *Josephus*, p. 131, n. 73, who claims it is a Christian interpolation. However, the vocabulary here is standard for Josephus, unlike that in the Testimonium Flavianum about Jesus (*A.J.* 18.63–4). The contrast between Josephus' condemnation of Ananus here and his praise for him at *B.J.* 4.319–25 can be explained by Josephus' apologetic aims in the *B.J.*: there he needed to portray Ananus as a statesman because he had himself been in political alliance with the man early in the revolt and praise of him made easier the denigration of his murderers, the Zealots and the followers of John of Gischala. See below, p. 156. I owe the analysis of the vocabulary to Professor J. N. Birdsall.

brother Ananus b. Ananus. When Ananus was deposed as High Priest in A.D. 62 at the request of the new procurator Albinus and to the benefit of the new High Priest Jesus b. Damnaeus, Ananias took good care to be on friendly terms with both the procurator and Jesus, deploying his great wealth to good effect and reaching a peak of influence with Ananus b. Ananus' temporary decline (*A.J.* 20.205). In A.D. 66 Ananias' vehement opposition to revolt is in marked contrast to Ananus's eventual leadership of the rebels (see below, p. 163).

Ananias b. Nedebaeus too could usually rely on support from powerful relatives. He was the first of his family to be High Priest, but his sons reached positions of prominence. Two of them became captain (*strategos*) of the Temple and used the post to meddle in politics: Ananus b. Ananias was treated with his father as a prime suspect in the fighting against the Samaritans in *c.* A.D. 52 (*A.J.* 20.131; *B.J.* 2.243), and ten years later Eleazar b. Ananias was a sufficiently prominent member of Ananias' faction for the latter's enemies to blackmail him by kidnapping Eleazar's secretary (*A.J.* 20.208–9).[9] In A.D. 66 Eleazar was to swap sides, leading the revolt against Rome even as his father protested the loyalty of the ruling class to the empire (*B.J.* 2.409), but even in A.D. 66 Ananias was still probably supported by another son, Simon b. Ananias (*B.J.* 2.418), and by his brother Ezechias (*B.J.* 2.429).

Outside the family Ananias increased his influence by judicious use of bribes. Jesus b. Damnaeus when High Priest was won to his support by such means (*A.J.* 20.205), and on Jesus' deposition Ananias succeeded in maintaining his own influence by giving money to others not named by Josephus (*A.J.* 20.213). If, as is plausible, Ananias was no longer High Priest in A.D. 54 when Paul was accused by the Jerusalem authorities of agitation (above, n. 5), his preeminence in the council of rulers which is reported to have decided Paul's fate and attacked him before the governor is striking (Acts 23.2; 24.1).

Quite separate from the factions led by the sons of Ananus and by Ananias was that which followed Costobar and Saul. Josephus is explicit that their gangs were not connected with the other authors of disturbances (*A.J.* 20.214). Costobar and Saul were themselves brothers (*B.J.* 2.556) but their other supporters can only be surmised. In October A.D. 66 Josephus says that they left Jerusalem with (*syn*) Philip b. Jacimus, prefect of Agrippa's army (*B.J.* 2.556),

[9] It is clearly necessary to read 'Avaνίου at *A.J.* 20.208 in place of 'Avάνου, cf. Schürer, *History* I, p. 469 n. 53.

and earlier in that year they went on a deputation to Agrippa with a certain Antipas who, like them, was related to the Herodian house (*B.J.* 2.418). Since they particularly emphasized their royal lineage in seeking influence (*A.J.* 20.214), it is possible that their supporters included those other members of Agrippa's extended family or entourage who wished to meddle in the politics of Jerusalem. In that case the family of Helcias, who had been active in support of Ishmael b. Phiabi a few years previously (see above, p. 143), may have been among their adherents now that Ishmael was *hors de combat* in Rome (*A.J.* 20.195).

Much of the detail of this faction struggle can, as is evident, be suggested only very hypothetically, though even the few indications that can be derived from Josephus will prove useful in understanding the alignments of various members of the ruling class immediately before and during the revolt (see below, pp. 154–97). The existence of a genuine power struggle does emerge clearly, however. These politicians did not act in isolation. Nor apparently did they group according to parties or policies or religious beliefs (see below, pp. 198–212). They grouped around individual leaders, looking for influence and power: Josephus describes such groups as 'those around Ananias' (*A.J.* 20.131), 'those around Eleazar b. Ananias' (*B.J.* 2.443,445,453) or 'those around Ananus b. Jonathan' (*B.J.* 2.534), using the same phrase as that employed to describe the brigand followers of Eleazar b. Dinai (*B.J.* 2.236) and the sicarii who looked to Menahem b. Judas for leadership (*B.J.* 2.446); at *B.J.* 2.274–6, indeed, this is just the image used by Josephus when he describes the influential men (*dunatoi*) in Albinus' procuratorship as acting just like such brigand-chiefs or tyrants, towering above their supporters as they used their bodyguards to plunder their opponents.

This use of violence is evidence that these factions took their quarrels seriously, but hurling stones and insults (*A.J.* 20.213) was unlikely to be effective in winning much power for one side or the other. Real influence could be gained only by acquiring the support of the Roman administrators, particularly the procurator, or by appealing by popular measures to the mass support of the people.

The effectiveness of the procurator's support for one faction against another became abundantly clear when Albinus forced Ananus' removal from the high priesthood on the strength of a report by his opponents that he had taken illegal advantage of the interregnum after Festus' death to have some of his enemies put out of the way (*A.J.* 20.203).

Such play on the procurator's *amour propre* required finesse.

Members of the Herodian house sometimes had an advantage in influencing some procurators because of their family relationships: Agrippa II's sister Berenice had been briefly married to M. Julius Alexander, the brother of Tiberius Julius Alexander, procurator *c.* A.D. 46–8 (*A.J.* 19.277), and his other sister, Drusilla, married Felix, though Agrippa himself seems to have viewed this latter connection with distaste and avoided meeting his brother-in-law as far as possible.[10] At other times, however, Herodians were reduced as much as other members of the Judaean ruling class to flattery, as is clear from the great pomp with which Agrippa and Berenice came to Caesarea to greet Festus when he arrived in Palestine as the new governor in about A.D. 60 (Acts 25.13,23). Agrippa's flattery of Festus was perhaps successful, for the procurator enthusiastically supported the king in his tussle with Ishmael b. Phiabi over the tower built to overlook the Temple (*A.J.* 20.193).

Even lesser members of the ruling class might reasonably expect to influence procurators by this sort of patronage, so familiar in the Roman context, if they could establish contacts with the court at Rome. Agrippa I's glittering rise from penury to greatness was made entirely through such personal contacts in Italy. On a less ambitious scale the friendship of the ex-High Priest Jonathan b. Ananus with Claudius' freedman Pallas may have encouraged Jonathan to press for the appointment of Pallas' brother Felix in the hope that the new procurator could be manipulated by him (*A.J.* 20.162; cf. *B.J.* 2.247 for the relationship to Pallas).[11] Even the young Josephus cultivated friends in Rome, securing an introduction to Nero's wife Poppaea through an actor called Aliturus and thereby securing the release of his friends who had been imprisoned, probably for factional violence, by Felix (*Vita* 13–16).

Only by travelling to Rome was it possible to build up influence of this kind with the procurator. Within the province, however, members of the local ruling class could, if they so wished, provide useful services to the governor in bids to win his favour. The position of Temple treasurer might be a powerful one in helping or preventing procurators using money for public projects: the outrage felt at

[10] Cf. Smallwood, *Jews*, pp. 273–4, mainly using evidence from Acts. Cf. also M. Stern, 'The status of Provincia Judaea and its governors in the Roman Empire under the Julio-Claudian dynasty', *EI* 10 (1971) 274–82 (Heb.), on the social connections of governors in the province.

[11] Cf. Smallwood, *Jews*, p. 268. Pallas' support for Jonathan is deduced from the favour shown to the Jewish cause by Agrippina (*A.J.* 20.135), over whom in turn Pallas had great influence at this time, cf. S. I. Oost, 'The career of M. Antonius Pallas', *AJP* 79 (1958) 113–39.

Pilate's use of sacred moneys to build an aqueduct (*B.J.* 2.175–7) or Florus' exaction of seventeen talents for the emperor's use (*B.J.* 2.293) will have been much increased if, like Sabinus in 4 B.C., they seized the treasury by force (*B.J.* 2.50). Hence a man like Antipas, the Herodian relative charged in A.D. 67 with the public treasury according to *B.J.* 4.140, could win the governor's gratitude in normal times by opening the coffers to him, and another treasurer, Helcias, was prominent in the time of Festus (*A.J.* 20.194). The potential influence of such men will have been increased if, as is likely, they were appointed independently of the procurator or their fellow Judaeans by Herod of Chalcis or Agrippa II (cf. *A.J.* 20.15–16,222).

Some Judaean politicians lacking such control of public funds sought to influence the procurators by bribes from their private property. Tacitus (*Ann.* 12.54) claims that as early as *c.* A.D. 48–52 Cumanus cheerfully took money from the Jews in their battles against the Samaritans and, though this passage of Tacitus is very confused, it is worth noting that the politician most plausibly involved in such bribery (since he was sent in chains to Rome for the incident) was the High Priest Ananias (see above, p. 145), and that this man's wealth and penchant for giving bribes were notorious hardly more than ten years later (*A.J.* 20.205).[12]

But it was from the time of the procurator Albinus, in *c.* A.D. 62, that such gifts of money became more and more frequent. According to *A.J.* 20.205, Ananias paid court to Albinus with gifts, but this general statement is elucidated by *B.J.* 2.274, where members of the ruling class (the *dunatoi*) are said to have paid money to secure from Albinus immunity for their civil dissension (*stasiazein*).

Similarly, when riots broke out in Caesarea in A.D. 66 over the building of workshops by a Greek in front of a synagogue, the Jewish leader John the tax-collector assumed that the natural way of winning the new procurator Florus to favour the Jewish case was to bribe him with eight talents of silver (*B.J.* 2.287), and he was shocked and bewildered rather than angry when Florus, although pocketing the money, decided not to side with the Jews (*B.J.* 2.292). But by then, as will be shown in the next chapter (pp. 152–3), attempting to gain influence by good relations with the procurator was something of a lost cause.

---

[12] Smallwood, *Jews*, p. 266 n. 30, does not believe the charge against Cumanus on the grounds that Josephus does not mention it and that he (Josephus) had no known reasons to whitewash the procurator. But Josephus did have good reasons to disguise the record of wayward members of the Jewish ruling class, such as Ananias.

The other source of power before A.D. 66 was the people. It has already been seen that none of the ruling class could assume much popular support just because of their status. It has also been noted that the people were not granted any formal power within the constitution favoured by Rome. Nonetheless popularity mattered. The whim of the Jerusalem crowd, particularly at festival times, was in practice the most powerful mouthpiece of the nation's will and, regardless of the disapproval of the Roman governor, its will was on occasions triumphant. Thus mass opposition to Pilate's plan to introduce effigies into Jerusalem succeeded (*B.J.* 2.174), as did the mass demand for Cumanus to punish a soldier who had destroyed a copy of the Law (*B.J.* 2.230–1). The crowd which dashed off to Samaria to avenge a Galilean murdered on the way to Jerusalem (*B.J.* 2.234) was tamed by the procurator only with great difficulty. Any Judaean politician who could win the full confidence of the Jerusalem crowd would be a force to be reckoned with. At the least he could be guaranteed the respect of the governor because it was in the governor's interest to have such a leader on his side so as to help maintain order; and with the governor's confidence came real power.

But, as has been seen repeatedly (above, pp. 109–33), it was not easy for any of the ruling class to achieve such popularity. Naturally they emphasized as much as possible such status in Jewish terms as they did possess. Costobar and Saul found some favour because of their royal lineage (*A.J.* 20.214). Pharisees like Gamaliel and his son Simon (cf. *Vita* 190–4) will have played on the respect they were accorded for their expertise in the interpretation of the Law.

But for most of the ruling class real popular recognition could only be achieved by putting themselves forward, sometimes at some personal risk, as spokesmen for the people to Rome. It is striking how often members of the Herodian house are found in this role, as in the complaint to Tiberius against Pilate's plan to set up shields in Jerusalem (*Leg.* 300). They won popular support by it primarily because they were successful. In other words, the power to influence Rome brought prestige from the Jews, just as the power to influence the Jews brought recognition from the procurator. The two sources of power fed on each other. Hence the remarkable statement by Josephus that Ananias advanced daily in the goodwill and esteem of the citizens in *c.* A.D. 62 (*A.J.* 20.205) even as his servants with a gang of reckless thugs and other men of high-priestly status stole by force from the threshing floors the tithes which rightfully belonged to their poorer priestly colleagues (*A.J.* 20.206–7).

One further route to public popularity was also in theory open to the ruling class, but it was fraught with danger. Given widespread suspicion of the procurators, any Judaean politician who ostentatiously opposed one of them could expect popular sympathy. In normal circumstances that sympathy would be of little use in promoting such a politician's power. He would simply, like Ananus b. Ananus in A.D. 62 after he flouted Albinus' authority, be removed from the political scene (*A.J.* 20.203). But it may be no accident that it was Ananus who was chosen by a popular assembly four years later as one of the two main directors of the Jewish nation as it proclaimed its freedom and independence from Rome (*B.J.* 2.562–3).[13]

[13] The point is made by Smallwood, 'High priests and politics', pp. 25–6, 30. As Horsley, 'High priests', pp. 23–55, argues cogently against Smallwood, this need not imply that Ananus in A.D. 62, or any other high priest before A.D. 66, was ideologically opposed to Rome rather than intent on 'short-sighted self-aggrandisement' (p. 45).

CHAPTER 7

THE OUTBREAK OF REVOLT

In A.D. 66 the ability of any of the ruling class to win power through the procurator's favour rapidly declined as the country moved towards revolt. The slide into war was rapid and dramatic.

Intercommunal tensions led to fighting between Jews and Greeks in the city of Caesarea early in the year. The procurator Florus favoured the Greek cause, as Nero had done six years earlier, and, ignoring Jewish grievances in that city, compounded his unpopularity with the Jews by taking seventeen talents from the Temple in Jerusalem 'for Caesar's use' (*B.J.* 2.293).

It is likely that the money was needed for arrears of tribute (cf. *B.J.* 2.405), but if so this justification for Florus' behaviour was ignored by his subjects and his action was greeted by widespread rioting in Jerusalem. Incensed by this display of opposition, and in particular by the ridicule poured on his greed by a few wits, Florus marched to the city and ransacked a good part of it. But when he attempted to achieve a public display of Jewish submissiveness by forcing the population to greet with humility two further cohorts sent from Caesarea, and to accept without demur the insulting silence with which their greetings were received by the troops (*B.J.* 2.318–19), his plan misfired and the mob's anger proved so violent that he was forced to withdraw to Caesarea himself, leaving only one cohort behind (*B.J.* 2.332).

In the absence of the Roman governor, Agrippa II attempted to restore order (*B.J.* 2.344–406), but, although some of the Jews did begin to rebuild some of the structures destroyed in the rioting and to collect the tax arrears, he too was eventually driven from the city (*B.J.* 2.406–7).

Thus in May/June some of the priests in the Temple took the decisive act which Rome regarded as constituting rebellion. They decided to suspend the daily sacrifice traditionally offered on behalf of the emperor and stood firm in this decision despite the best efforts of some of their compatriots over two or three months to restore loyalty

The outbreak of revolt

to Rome (*B.J.* 2.408–24). Jerusalem was in turmoil as the citizens disputed the desirability of revolt, and in the chaos a group of sicarii under the leadership of a certain Menahem b. Judas tried unsuccessfully to seize power and booty for themselves (*B.J.* 2.433–48).

The disorder was now clearly too great for Florus' limited military forces to control. Cestius Gallus, legate of Syria, marched from Antioch with a large army, arriving in Palestine by September/ October and outside Jerusalem by October/November. But he too suffered defeat, first when approaching the city and then when, perhaps troubled by lack of supplies, he withdrew back to the coast in incompetent haste (*B.J.* 2.499–555). For the rest of the year Judaea was in effect an independent Jewish state.[1]

From the beginning of these events it had become evident that it was no longer worthwhile for any Judaean leader to try to seek influence through the governor, for Florus made it entirely clear that he had no confidence in the ability of any of the ruling class to control the population. Nor was his scepticism unjustified: both in Caesarea and in Jerusalem the pleas of the Jewish leaders to the rioters proved useless. Florus could not rely on them to keep order and decided not to try. He even demonstrated his lack of regard for the ruling class by including the chief priests and magistrates among those to be humiliated by being forced to greet the unresponsive cohorts as they arrived in Jerusalem (*B.J.* 2.318–20). Only when all was lost and the city in such disarray that his troops could not cut their way through from one side to the other did he again entrust the restoration of order to the Jewish leaders (*B.J.* 2.332). But by that time it was not much of a favour to be granted such a role, and the double fact that Florus sent a report to Cestius Gallus accusing the Jews of revolt and that the rulers of Jerusalem responded with a counter-accusation suggests that Florus was still even then by no means convinced of the loyalty of the Judaean rulers (333).

Deprived of access to power through the procurator, some Judaean politicians thus began to find the alternative route to influence, through popular support, increasingly attractive. Feelings against Florus were running high in the city. The money taken from the Temple had probably been part of the sum intended to provide employment through the repairs to the Temple and the paving of the city (see above, p. 54). In the aftermath of the riots protesting at the theft many had been killed (*B.J.* 2.305–7,327). The power of the

[1] On the reasons for Cestius Gallus' withdrawal from Jerusalem, see B. Bar-Kochva, 'Seron and Cestius at Beith Horon', *PEQ* 108 (1976) 18; M. Gichon, 'Cestius Gallus' campaign in Judaea', *PEQ* 113 (1981) 56; see below, p. 181.

mob to frustrate even armed troops through massed resistance in the narrow alleys and with missiles thrown from rooftops had been demonstrated when Florus' attempt to cut from the north of the city through to the Temple was successfully thwarted (*B.J.* 2.329).

It was thus not altogether surprising that some of the ruling class, rendered frustrated and powerless by the procurator, were attracted to harness the latent power of the people's resentment to their own ends. The first faction to do so was led by Eleazar b. Ananias, the captain of the Temple. By a single symbolic act, the decision to stop the loyal sacrifices, he and his friends proclaimed themselves the popular leaders of an independent nation (*B.J.* 2.409).

The claim was naturally immediately challenged by the rest of the ruling class. Eleazar's faction had the advantage that it was protected from physical attack by the walls of the Temple (cf. *B.J.* 2.422–4), and on the propaganda front he and his friends remained on the offensive, trying to harness the grievances of the impoverished to their cause by the burning of the debt archives (*B.J.* 2.427). This act was probably, like the cessation of the sacrifices, only symbolic, for creditors usually kept a second copy of debts owed and would not be more than inconvenienced by the loss of the archive records, but the appeal to the poor might be no less effective for that, especially since Eleazar's main opponents within the ruling class, especially his father Ananias, had been responsible for some of the most blatant oppression of the lower class (cf. *A.J.* 20.206). The urban plebs will have watched the dramatic destruction of Ananias' house by his son's companions with particular satisfaction, and this act of vandalism was perhaps deliberately calculated to appeal to their feelings of resentment (*B.J.* 2.426).[2]

The opposition of his fellow-rulers to Eleazar's action was only partly caused by disagreement over the desirability and feasibility of revolt against Rome.[3] Eleazar, though a leading politician since at least A.D. 62 (see above, p. 146), had never before claimed such over-

[2] This last point is made by R. A. Horsley, 'The sicarii: ancient Jewish "terrorists"', *Journal of Religion* 52 (1979) 459. On the burning of the debt archives as symbolic rather than practical because creditors kept second copies, see Goodman, 'The First Jewish Revolt', p. 418 n. 12.

[3] In most discussions (e.g. Rajak, *Josephus*, pp. 128–9), this is seen as the *only* issue, but after the faction struggles before A.D. 66 that is implausible. With hindsight the cessation of the loyal sacrifices seems to have been a decisive act, but at the time the move towards revolt still seemed reversible, as the behaviour of Eleazar b. Ananias' opponents shows. There is a good analysis of the outbreak of the revolt in Cohen, *Josephus in Galilee and Rome*, pp. 181–206. The account given here differs only in details and emphasis.

whelming power. His father, Ananias, had by contrast been pre-eminent in Judaea for some years (*A.J.* 20.213; see above, p. 145), and he did not take lightly his son's attempt to supplant him. But neither for Ananias nor for the other faction leaders was it easy to depose Eleazar from his position as people's champion. Their natural status in Jewish eyes was no greater than his and there was nothing they could offer more likely to appeal to the mob, though they did try to destroy his support by claiming that his refusal to accept sacrifices for the emperor was an impious innovation in the Temple worship (*B.J.* 2.414).

Without popular support Eleazar's rivals were thus powerless unless they could win the governor to their side. Their only choice was to send a deputation to Florus to request his armed intervention (*B.J.* 2.418–19), while, in a dramatic escalation of the level of urban violence previously used in political infighting, they themselves borrowed two thousand cavalry from King Agrippa to try to gain control of the city (*B.J.* 2.421–2). It is not to be supposed that these politicians had changed their minds about the wickedness of Florus. They appealed to him only because otherwise all their power was gone.

But the intervention by Florus and Agrippa failed, and Judaea was soon at war with Rome. Once this was inevitable, the choice for the ruling class was even more stark. For the time being, if they wished to influence events at all (and for the sake of their property if nothing else they needed to), it could only be with the support of the people. Nonetheless these politicians were not likely to forget the alternative route to power through Rome's patronage whenever the opportunity presented itself in the coming years. So, for instance, when Cestius Gallus arrived outside Jerusalem, a certain Ananus b. Jonathan, with others (unnamed) of the ruling class, sought Roman gratitude and certain preeminence in the future affairs of the province by trying to betray the city to him (*B.J.* 2.533). The attempt failed, but all rich Judaean politicians for the rest of the war were justifiably suspected by those who were not wealthy of being willing to help the Romans in return for power (cf. *B.J.* 4.218, etc.). Their treachery was thwarted by practicalities, not by anti-Roman ideology. Josephus was thus right to emphasize the 'moderation' of those like himself who led the rebellion but longed for a return to a Roman rule in which power was delegated to people like themselves, but implausible in his insistence that this demonstrated good sense; what it really showed was their intense desire for power in Judaea.[4]

[4] Rajak, *Josephus*, p. 129, rightly emphasizes that Josephus' portrayal of such 'moderates' is likely to be, within limits, accurate.

Faction struggle of the kind experienced in Judaea for the past ten years or so thus continued, with higher stakes, in A.D. 66. Under this increased pressure alliances shifted and some ambitious politicians retired from the field, but the links to pre-war power struggles are clear, as I hope to show.

The demonstration will not, however, be straightforward, for reconstruction of the internal politics of Jerusalem in the year A.D. 66 is faced by a particular problem. The sole extant source is the narrative of Josephus, and he was an interested party in the events he describes. By the end of October A.D. 66 Josephus had himself been appointed by the people as commander of the rebel forces in Galilee (*B.J.* 2.568). He describes that command in detail in the *B.J.* and in the *Vita*; it was the turning point in his life. It was in his clear apologetic interest to display the government of which he was a part as the only legitimate leadership of the Jews during the war, and he attempted this primarily by heaping lavish praise upon the colleagues alongside whom he fought from October 66 to summer 67: his commander-in-chief, Ananus b. Ananus, thus comes in for a particularly effusive encomium (*B.J.* 4.319–21), although in an earlier context (*A.J.* 20.199) he had been described in rather more cynical fashion.

Such specific value judgements by Josephus can be balanced without much difficulty, but more of a problem is a second effect of Josephus' need for self-defence. Throughout his narrative he tries to disassociate his own actions and that of his colleagues appointed in October/November 66 from those of the rash revolutionaries who preceded them and the wicked brigands and tyrants who replaced them in command of the Jewish forces. By doing so Josephus hoped to avoid blame both for the outbreak of the war and for its terrible conclusion; that aim indeed is the main theme of his apologetic *Vita*. But there are good grounds for supposing, from the detailed evidence provided by Josephus himself, that the break in the nature of the Jewish leadership was not as drastic as he suggests either at the beginning or at the end of his tenure of office.

Thus it is very likely that Judaea was under firm and efficient rebel government long before Josephus himself came to power in October/November. The best evidence for strong leadership once Florus had left Jerusalem for good and the Roman garrison had been massacred by Eleazar b. Ananias and his supporters (*B.J.* 2.449–56) lies in the conduct of the campaign of the Jews against Cestius Gallus when he arrived in Judaea two months later, in October. Josephus says nothing explicit about the composition of this Jewish leadership during those two months, so the reader is presumably expected to assume that Eleazar remained supreme in Jerusalem; attention is distracted from the city in the *B.J.* by a long digression on the intercommunal strife of Jews against gentiles in the cities neighbouring Judaea (*B.J.* 2.457–98).

However, despite Josephus' reticence, it is impossible to imagine the Jerusalem ruling class taking no steps to protect their interests. Gallus approached the city with at least twenty-five thousand troops (*B.J.* 2.499–502). He made it clear, by a deliberate policy of slaughter and destruction, that he meant to be vicious to the inhabitants of Jerusalem if they continued to rebel. Chabulon was set on fire (503), eight thousand four hundred undefended civilians in Joppa were killed (509), the toparchy of Narbatene was ravaged (509) and Narbata itself was probably at this point subjected to an intensive siege. Discovering Lydda deserted he had fifty people found in the place put to the sword and the town burnt down (516). It is inconceivable that the Jews did not react to this campaign of terror by taking some preparations for the defence of Jerusalem.[5]

And there is in fact positive evidence that steps were indeed taken. With 'great confidence in their numbers' (517) the Jews met Gallus six miles from Jerusalem and won a fine victory (518–19). For such a frontal assault the Jews must have had swords and spears, which they did not usually possess to any noticeable degree (cf. *B.J.* 2.361), so weapons must have been made very rapidly. The attack on Gallus' line seems to have involved a coordinated assault on the van and the rear as the troops marched up the Bethhoron road, for one leading general, Simon b. Gioras, was able to cut up the Roman rear-guard and carry off many of the baggage mules (521).[6]

[5] For Cestius' campaign, see Gichon, 'Cestius Gallus' campaign', with timetable on p. 62. Gichon describes the expeditions to Chabulon, Gabara, etc., as sidetracks caused by Gallus' inexperience and the urgings of local gentile allies. Such an explanation is plausible, but Josephus does not suggest it though he could have done, and a policy based on terror accords well with later Roman tactics, see below, p. 182. For the siege of Narbata, see the siege works reported by A. Zertal, 'The Roman siege system at Khirbet el-Hammam (Narbata) in Samaria', *Qadmoniot* 14 (1981) 112–18 (Heb.). No coins of the revolt have so far been found on the site, which suggests that the place fell in A.D. 66 to Gallus rather than later to Vespasian; but the siege wall is huge and its construction will have tied down much of Gallus' force for a longer period than, according to Josephus, he spent before marching on Jerusalem. Perhaps he split his forces.

[6] For the significance of the Jews' possession of weapons, see Brunt, 'Did imperial Rome disarm her subjects?', p. 267; for the attack on Gallus as coordinated, see Bar-Kochva, 'Seron and Cestius', p. 18, who bases his argument on the approximate length of a Roman marching line composed of the number of troops Gallus is said to have had.

Other indications confirm the rebels' organization, for an established government was probably already minting coins of the free Jewish state.[7] When, therefore, Josephus deliberately avoided describing the appointment of this government, about which as an active politician he must have known, his silence must be interpreted as political in intention: he wanted to deny validity to all appointments that preceded his own. It is characteristic of his writing that, despite this apologetic intention, he let slip (at *B.J.* 2.562) that the assembly by which he himself was eventually to be appointed was convened not to provide leadership for a directionless mob but to elect *additional* generals, thereby tacitly admitting that *some* generals were already leading the rebels before the meeting which brought Josephus and his friends to prominence.

Who, then, were these generals, and what political infighting had gone on in Jerusalem over the long summer months while Gallus' arrival was awaited? In the absence of hard evidence, only surmise is possible, but it seems most improbable that the faction fighting within the ruling class came suddenly to a halt with the expulsion of Roman forces by Eleazar. On the contrary, the removal of Rome's restraining hand will, as in A.D. 62 (see above, p. 145), have given longer rein to the ambitions of the faction leaders, and the setting up of an independent state will have given them more for which to compete.

Investigation of the composition of the factions involved in A.D. 66 suggests that the groups which had fought for power in A.D. 62 were still well represented in this more fervid political climate. Of these, Ananias' faction had of course split in two, one led by himself, the other by one of his sons, Eleazar.

Eleazar's main supporters in his dramatic bid for popularity by stopping the loyal sacrifices were as much members of the ruling class as he was himself. Not only did the priests in the Temple at the time give him their support (*B.J.* 2.410) but so did named individuals of some clout, including a certain Gorion b. Nicomedes, Ananias b. Sadok (a Pharisee later sent by the Jerusalem authorities to recall Josephus from Galilee (628)), and his companion on the same embassy to Josephus called (probably) Judas b. Jonathan (see below, p. 185 n. 7). These men were the envoys sent by Eleazar to

[7] For the rebel coinage as beginning in May/June A.D. 66, see C. Roth, 'The historical implications of the Jewish coinage of the First Revolt', *IEJ* 12 (1962) 37–8. This date for the renewal of the coinage each year would, I think, best explain the very small number of surviving coins of the fifth year, but for alternative explanations and dates, see below, p. 178 n. 1.

the commander of the Roman garrison to negotiate the withdrawal of his troops (*B.J.* 2.451) and were evidently the kind of rich Jews the Romans were accustomed to find cooperating with them in peaceful times: the Roman commander accepted their word that the lives of his soldiers would be spared and, when Eleazar's faction ('those around Eleazar') broke their oath and murdered them, they could do nothing but appeal with loud cries to the agreement they thought they had made (*B.J.* 2.453).

Furthermore, Eleazar's achievement of extraordinary popular acclaim seems to have attracted other members of the ruling class not previously allied to him to throw in their lot, at least temporarily, with his faction. One such may have been the historian Josephus, for at *Vita* 20–1 he claims that, in his desire to avoid being suspected of siding with Rome, he took refuge in the inner court of the Temple at the moment when the Antonia had been captured but Menahem and his sicarii had not yet been killed. This short period is described at *B.J.* 2.431–48; throughout it, the inner court of the Temple remained firmly in the hands of Eleazar's supporters (cf. 422), and opponents of Eleazar were excluded (425).

The rest of Ananias' original faction, which he had headed with such success in *c.* A.D. 63, included, beside Ananias himself, his son Simon b. Ananias (*B.J.* 2.418) and his brother Ezechias (441). How much further support within the ruling class there was for the man who had so recently dominated Jerusalem politics is not clear, for his ability to oppose his son's followers was largely derived from the efforts of Agrippa's soldiers on his behalf (423, 429).

He seems to have made temporary common cause with Saul and Costobar, his opponents of previous years (see above, p. 146), for they were in the party around Ananias which took refuge from Eleazar in Herod's palace in the upper city (429, cf. 418). But these two Herodians seem to have been able to swap sides with surprising ease. When the palace proved impossible to defend they were probably among those who received permission from Eleazar to retire into obscurity, perhaps under the protection of the Babylonian Jewish soldiers of their kinsman Agrippa (437) who were commanded by a certain Philip b. Jacimus (421). They and this Philip were still at liberty in Jerusalem in November A.D. 66 when, on the defeat of Cestius Gallus, all three finally decided to quit the city (556). Philip at least had apparently succeeded in getting away from the palace grounds when it was besieged by Eleazar, for, when it became clear that, whatever the attitude of Eleazar himself, his wild brigand supporters led by Menahem b. Judas were thirsty for Philip's blood, he was able to hide with some of his Babylonian kinsmen (probably fellow-soldiers) and escape from the city in disguise (*Vita* 46–7).

Ananias and his brother Ezechias, by contrast, seem to have received no such guarantee of safe conduct from Eleazar. Perhaps he wanted his father and uncle safely captured and neutralized. At any rate, the two men were trapped in the palace grounds, where they hid by a canal, only to be found there the following day and butchered by Menahem's brigands (*B.J.* 2.441).

After the bloodshed in late August/early September A.D. 66, the faction of Eleazar b. Ananias temporarily reigned supreme. Eleazar's popularity was proved by the cooperation of the people in helping him to crush the same brigands under Menahem b. Judas (445), for this act was totally unconnected to the revolt against Rome and was apparently motivated entirely by Eleazar's horror that the faction struggle had led to the death of his father and uncle, who had been killed by Menahem but in his (Eleazar's) name (442–3). Through such popularity Eleazar was, for the time being, commander-in-chief.

This preeminence could not last, if only because his popular style of leadership did not obviously make Eleazar a good general, and with the rapid approach of Cestius Gallus military preparations were urgently needed. On the other hand few others in the Judaean ruling class had military experience.

From this point of view the sensible leaders for the Jews to choose were those Jewish officers of Agrippa's cavalry detachment who had come over to the side of the rebels when Herod's palace proved impossible to defend. Some of these soldiers, if not all their officers, seem to have cooperated with Eleazar's faction with enthusiasm once Menahem b. Judas was dead and his brigands dispersed, probably helping to besiege the Roman garrison which remained in the palace from which they had themselves only just escaped (compare 450 with 437). Some of them, like the man mentioned at *Vita* 220, became firmly committed to the rebel cause.

Thus, when the Jews marched against Cestius Gallus in October/November, one of those who distinguished themselves was a certain Silas the Babylonian, who is explicitly described by Josephus as a deserter from Agrippa's forces (*B.J.* 2.520). It is likely that this Silas was one of a number of similar men: another hero against Gallus was a man called Niger the Peraean (520) who had apparently been given command over Idumaea at this time since, when the commands were reorganized after Gallus' defeat, Niger, 'who was then governor', was ordered to relinquish overall control of that area to two rivals (566). Niger's friendship with Silas can be deduced from the latter's support for him when Niger marched later in the year against Ascalon; Silas was to die in that campaign (*B.J.* 3.11,19).[8]

The role of Agrippa's general who had brought the Babylonian troops to Jerusalem, Philip b. Jacimus, is more difficult to ascertain. Josephus makes it clear that Philip was later suspected of having led some Jewish rebels at some point (*Vita* 50,182–3). If the accounts of his career in *B.J.* and *Vita* are conflated, as with some ingenuity I believe that they can be, it becomes clear that Philip cannot have commanded any rebels before the moment when he escaped from Jerusalem in fear of Menahem b. Judas (*Vita* 46–7): the worst charge that pro-Romans could bring against him at this point was his betrayal and desertion of the Roman soldiers in Herod's palace who were eventually killed by Eleazar (cf. *Vita* 407).

Furthermore, after complicated negotiations in and around Gamala with Agrippa's two lieutenants – first a certain Varus or Noarus, whose anti-Jewish actions on behalf of the gentile population of Caesarea Philippi appear nearly (but not quite) to have pushed Philip into leading the Jewish rebels in Gamala against him (Varus) and therefore against Rome and Agrippa (*Vita* 48–53, 59–61), and then a Roman called Aequus Modius – Philip was finally sent to Beirut in, probably, September/October A.D. 66 and apparently without difficulty persuaded Agrippa of his loyalty to him and to Rome (*Vita* 180–4). As evidence of his confidence in Philip, Agrippa sent him with cavalry back to the area round Gamala, with a brief to evacuate those of his close acquaintances who had taken refuge there (*Vita* 184).

However, when that operation had been completed – not totally successfully, since a few months later some of Philip's relations were still in Gamala and were killed there in his absence (*Vita* 177,186) – Philip seems to have returned to Jerusalem, for he was in the city when Cestius Gallus arrived outside the walls (*B.J.* 2.556). Was he hoping to lead the rebels? It is possible, but it was hardly likely that after his activities in the preceding months the Jews will have trusted him with a command against the Romans. Perhaps his intention was to recover the loyalty to him and to Agrippa of the troops such as Silas who had joined the rebels.[9]

[8] It does not seem to me likely that Niger or any other Jew was ever appointed by the Romans to command military forces in Idumaea as is implied by Gichon, 'Idumea and the Herodian limes', p. 34.

[9] Josephus' account of Philip b. Jacimus is notoriously lacunose. For a useful discussion of the problems, see Cohen, *Josephus in Galilee and Rome*, pp. 160–9. I do not

Men like Silas and Niger who came to the fore in Judaea in summer A.D. 66 only because of their military experience do not seem to have taken any part in the earlier internal politics of the ruling class. The same is probably true of the two members of the royal family of Adiabene who were also prominent in the battle against Gallus (*B.J.* 2.520). But two other leaders who played important parts in that battle were ambitious politicians who were to gain great power later in the revolt, and it is probable that both of them had been involved in the faction struggle for some years.

The first of these is Eleazar b. Simon, the future leader of the so-called Zealot faction (see below, p. 185). Josephus admits in describing the selection of generals after Gallus' defeat that Eleazar would have been a natural choice then because he had played an important part in the earlier battle (*B.J.* 2.564–5). He had taken possession of the Roman spoils and of the money seized from Gallus. This he could have achieved simply by determined looting in the wake of the Roman retreat (cf. 544), but more significantly he held much of the contents of the local public treasuries (564), which gave him great potential influence (565). Now, Josephus disliked Eleazar intensely (cf. *B.J.* 5.5–6) and would not hesitate to accuse him of stealing such communal wealth if the charge would stick. On the other hand, Eleazar was probably not formally in control of the public treasury since that role was – certainly later and probably also at this time – performed by a certain Antipas, a relative of Agrippa and friend of Saul and Costobar (*B.J.* 4.140). The best explanation of Eleazar's possession of such public money may be, then, that he was given funds to help run the campaign against Gallus. Someone had to organize the minting of coins, pay for new weapons to be made, and so on.

think that *B.J.* 2.558 implies that Philip was sent to Nero by Cestius Gallus (*pace* Cohen, pp. 161–2). I believe that is possible to construct a chronology which accepts as true all of Josephus' explicit evidence about Philip while assuming that the historian omitted much to protect Philip's reputation, and I hope to present detailed arguments for this elsewhere.

If Alon, *Jews, Judaism and the Classical World*, pp. 328–34, is right to follow Graetz in identifying the Sons of Bathyra who are mentioned in the Babylonian Talmud (as sages in dispute with Yohanan b. Zakkai after A.D. 70) with the Babylonians settled by Herod in Bathyra (see above, p. 42 n. 21), Philip will have been of this family and therefore may have been powerful in Judaea after the destruction of the Temple. But Alon himself points (p. 329) to powerful arguments which have been brought against the identification, and I am not sure that much can be deduced from it.

The other ambitious Jewish commander against Gallus was Simon b. Gioras, who was to emerge by A.D. 69 as commander in all Jerusalem. As Gallus was advancing towards Jerusalem, Simon fell upon his rearguard, carried off many of the baggage mules and brought them to the city (*B.J.* 2.521). The attack was probably timed to coincide with the frontal check to Gallus by the mass of the Jewish troops (518–20; see above, n. 6). To attack the Roman rear, Simon must have been stationed with a fair supply of troops either to north or south of the Bethhoron defile. It seems likely from Josephus' account that he was in fact commander to the north of Bethhoron, in the toparchy of Acrabatene, for in the following year it was from that region 'which he had once commanded' that he was expelled by the new government in Jerusalem (*B.J.* 4.504).[10] By mid A.D. 67 Simon was being portrayed by his enemies as little more than a bandit, but in October A.D. 66 he was probably a leading and successful general with the rebel forces; hence his decision to take the spoils he won to the city of Jerusalem and not to any hypothetical robber's nest (*B.J.* 2.521; see below, p. 202).

However, as soon as Gallus had retreated and Jerusalem was temporarily no longer under threat, faction rivalry broke out again. Not all the participants in the pre-war struggle for influence were still in a position to compete. Politicians such as Costobar and Saul had no further chance of winning public popularity and left the city (*B.J.* 2.556): they had found favour three years earlier as relatives of Agrippa (*A.J.* 20.214), but now that Agrippa had sided firmly with the Romans (cf. *B.J.* 2.502) their position was hopeless. The rest of their faction ('those around Saul') followed them into exile (*B.J.* 2.558), and among the other 'distinguished Jews' (556) who, having compromised all chance of winning any influence with the populace, went over to Rome, should probably be numbered Ananus b. Jonathan, who had tried to open the gates of Jerusalem to Gallus and had been caught in the act (533–4).

But the rest of the ruling class remained in the city (see below, p. 168) and their factional struggles continued. Most of the generals who had been appointed against Gallus, including Eleazar b. Simon and Simon b. Gioras, were rudely ousted from their positions, and Ananus b. Ananus, the High Priest of A.D. 62, emerged by October/ November A.D. 66 as supreme leader with the support of a jumble of

---

[10] The best reading here is that suggested by Dindorf with the support of one manuscript, which reads ἧς ἦρχε rather than ἧς εἶχε. ἦρχε is surely preferable with the genitive, though, if ἧς has been attracted into the genitive by ἐξ, εἶχε would technically be possible.

factions, which, though not always united, had temporarily combined to serve their common interests (*B.J.* 2.563,566–8).[11]

Ananus' success can be quite easily explained. The most serious competition to supremacy had been removed, for Ananias was dead and Saul and Costobar had left the city, and his other main rivals were won over to his side.

Thus Ananus brought into his alliance the splinter group from Ananias' faction which was led by Eleazar b. Ananias and had been responsible for stopping the loyal sacrifices. Eleazar himself was probably given a joint command over Idumaea, pushing Niger the Peraean, hero of the recent battle, into a subordinate position (566).[12] A man called John b. Ananias was given control over Acrabetta and Gophna (568), ousting Simon b. Gioras if my argument above (p. 163) is correct, and this John may have been Eleazar's brother, though Josephus does not say so. Two of Eleazar's closest supporters, Ananias b. Sadok and Judas b. Jonathan (451), were certainly allied to Ananus since they were sent out in A.D. 67 by his party[13] to investigate Josephus' behaviour in Galilee (628). The deep involvement of Simon b. Gamaliel, the leading Pharisee, in the same plot against Josephus (*Vita* 190–6), and the close ties of John of Gischala and his brother Simon b. Levi with Simon b. Gamaliel (*Vita* 192,195), may suggest that these three were also allied to Eleazar b. Ananias by that time, even if they had taken no part in the original instigation of the war.[14] This cannot be proved, but it is worth noting that they too worked in close cooperation with Ananus (see below, p. 183).

Eleazar b. Ananias' faction, however, by no means ruled supreme within Ananus' party, for of equal and growing power was the fac-

---

[11] Ananus was undoubtedly the leader, although nominally he shared the command with a certain Joseph b. Gorion. This Joseph may have retained some authority through his family until February A.D. 68 (*B.J.* 4.159,358), if the 'Gorion b. Joseph' and 'Gurion' in these later passages refer to his son, as seems likely. But Joseph seems to have played only a minor role in the internal political strife within Judaea. It is tempting to speculate that, despite the references at *B.J.* 4.358 to his (or rather his son's) high birth, he was primarily retained as a general because of his military expertise, like Silas the Babylonian. Ananus would certainly have known little about the task allotted to him and Joseph jointly, the improvement of the city's defences.

[12] Reading, as proposed by Hudson and accepted by most later editors, Ἀνανίου rather than Νέου.

[13] The term used at *Vita* 192 is 'stasis'.

[14] At *Vita* 192, Simon b. Gamaliel is described as an 'old and habitual friend' of John of Gischala.

tion led by Jesus b. Gamalas, who had been High Priest in A.D. 63–4. His faction had taken to the streets then, in a three-cornered struggle involving the deposed Jesus b. Damnaeus and the now defunct veteran Ananias (*A.J.* 20.213; see above, p. 139), and it is probable that he had already been allied to Ananus at that time (see above, p. 144). At any rate, Jesus b. Gamalas emerged by the middle of A.D. 67 as a leading figure in Ananus' party (*Vita* 193; *B.J.* 4.160) even though, perhaps in recognition of his military incompetence, he received no commission in the original division of responsibilities. His faction was, however, represented in that division – by the historian Josephus. Josephus' close relationship to Jesus b. Gamalas kept him in command in Galilee despite the efforts of Eleazar b. Ananias' supporters, for Jesus, being his close friend (*philos on kai sunethes*), sent through his (Josephus') father news of the plot to remove him (*Vita* 204). This political allegiance explains the eulogy delivered by Josephus on Jesus b. Gamalas' death (*B.J.* 4.322) and the lack of specific criticism of him by the historian in the passage in *A.J.* 20.213 that describes his use of gang warfare, in contrast to the vituperation against Costobar and Saul (*A.J.* 20.214) and, notoriously, Ananus (*A.J.* 20.199).

The coalition under Ananus was, then, made up of a number of different factions, and the internal dissensions that this fact caused in A.D. 67 will be examined in the next chapter (below, pp. 183–90). It will be useful to note here, however, which groups were excluded from power by Ananus' coup and how they reacted.

The most disgruntled opponents of Ananus were the ousted generals who had led the people against Gallus. Not all of them were deprived of office. Niger the Peraean was granted a post in Idumaea, though at a lower level than previously since he now had to report to two seniors (*B.J.* 2.566). It may be that John the Essene, given a command by Ananus over northern Judaea (567), was an associate of Niger from earlier in the revolt: he rather surprisingly fought with Niger against Ascalon (*B.J.* 3.11) despite the fact that his responsibilities would normally have kept him at the other end of the country; but his death in that expedition precludes further speculation about his political ties (3.19).[15]

---

[15] Three generals appointed with Ananus in November cannot be identified or allotted to any faction with confidence. These are Jesus b. Sapphas, Manasseh, and Joseph b. Simon. It is not likely that the last of these was identical with Joseph Kabi b. Simon, High Priest in A.D. 62, *pace* L. H. Feldman in the Loeb edition, *ad A.J.* 20.196. It is Josephus' normal practice to be explicit about high-priestly origins when introducing a new figure to the narrative.

But two of the most powerful leaders against Gallus did lose power and they did not accept their ousting passively. The ambitious Eleazar b. Simon surrounded himself with devoted supporters who acted like a bodyguard (*B.J.* 2.564–5). Though deprived of office now, he had a bloody revenge on his opponents just over a year later when he had Ananus and Jesus b. Gamalas killed by his Idumaean allies (*B.J.* 4.316). Equally unforgiving was Simon b. Gioras who, spurned when Ananus handed over his former command to John b. Ananias (above, p. 164), declined to relinquish the area to its new general until compelled to do so by an army sent by his opponent (*B.J.* 2.652–3). He withdrew with his men to Masada and refused to cooperate with the Jerusalem authorities until Ananus and his other enemies were dead (653; *B.J.* 4.504).

These frustrated politicians were only part of the external danger which threatened the stability of Ananus' government as the war progressed. Other leaders from Galilee and Idumaea, hitherto uninterested in seeking power in Jerusalem, were drawn into the Judaean power struggle as the Romans pushed the whole country into revolt by choosing to demonstrate in outlying areas the terror tactics which might eventually force the capital city into submission (see below, p. 182). Thus, for the time being the leaders of the Idumaeans were quiescent as Ananus seized power, even cooperating with him in his opposition to Simon b. Gioras when the latter installed himself in Masada (*B.J.* 2.654). But their exclusion from all power, even in their own area, was potentially dangerous for the faction controlling Jerusalem, for their military expertise may have been much greater than that of Ananus' supporters; Josephus claims that they were always spoiling for a fight (*B.J.* 4.231). It may perhaps have been to pacify their incipient demands for power, finally voiced only when they joined the faction struggle in early 68 (*B.J.* 4.233–5), that after Gallus' retreat Niger the Peraean was left by Ananus in partial command of their country and permitted to mount an immediate attack on Ascalon. He at least was undoubtedly competent as a general unlike his official superiors, Jesus b. Sapphas and Eleazar b. Ananias, who are not reported as having taken part in any campaigns at all.

At the end of A.D. 66 such threats both from other Judaean factions and from the Idumaeans still lay some time in the future. In the meantime Ananus was in firm control of the city and the rebel forces. But in the process of winning this supremacy in the internal political struggle Ananus had committed himself irrevocably to revolt. He could never again hope that a Roman governor would entrust him with power. His only political future lay within an independent Jewish state.

Josephus does not explain why Ananus and many others of the ruling class, among whom should be included most of Ananus' opponents who have just been described, burnt their boats in this way. When the loyal sacrifices were stopped and the Roman garrison in the Antonia was murdered, only the men responsible, Eleazar b. Ananias and his associates, were thereby committed to the break with Rome. All the other rich inhabitants of Jerusalem could have chosen to disown such actions and remain loyal to the emperor, as indeed some, such as Costobar and Saul, eventually did. The worst they might expect to suffer would be temporary exile until Roman forces triumphantly returned them to their homes. But in fact most of the Judaean ruling class preferred to follow Eleazar into revolt, and the reasons for their strange and, as it turned out, disastrous choice need some investigation.

Josephus was of course at pains in his history precisely to deny this participation in the revolt by his own class. He portrays his friends as moderate leaders who tried to provide a stable government for Jerusalem while negotiating for an agreement with Rome. He constantly emphasizes that they were impelled to stay in the rebellious city only out of indecision, hope, a sentimental affinity with fellow-Jews killed elsewhere in and near Palestine, and the pious wish to preserve the Temple from destruction either by extremist Jews or by Rome. According to Josephus the ruling class were throughout the innocent victims of the war, moderate good men either killed by the Jewish fanatics or forced by them into the exile of the Roman camp.[16]

Now, in the earlier chapters of this book it has been shown that Josephus' picture was plausible enough. The ruling class *might* have chosen to behave in this way. Mediation between the people and Rome was indeed its natural function. Even the *attitude* of moderation ascribed to it by Josephus was probably often real.[17] Nonetheless I believe that the historian's apologetic must be rejected in its entirety, for the revolutionary *actions* taken by many members of the ruling class are too well documented to deny.

Indeed the central role of the upper class in the war is all the more evident from the fact that it can be reconstructed despite Josephus' reluctance to admit its existence. When Josephus writes that it was Florus' wickedness that pushed *us* collectively into war against Rome

[16] Josephus' account is well elucidated by Rajak, *Josephus*, pp. 108, 128–32, with parallels from the French revolution.
[17] Cf. Rajak, *Josephus*, p. 129; Cohen, *Josephus in Galilee and Rome*, esp. pp. 183–4.

(*A.J.* 20.257), he implies that the revolt involved the whole Jewish nation, and not just the poorer section of it. Thus, it had been possible to escape from Jerusalem after June A.D. 66, as Agrippa did, but many of the ruling class were still there when Cestius Gallus was defeated (*B.J.* 2.556), and they must have stayed voluntarily. Even more damning was the decision of many of the ruling class to remain in Jerusalem *after* Gallus' defeat: Josephus claims that they joined the revolt because they succumbed 'partly to force and partly to persuasion' (*B.J.* 2.562), but just the act of staying in the city when others had left and war was inevitable showed that these men were committed to fight on behalf of the independent Jewish state.

Nor were these rulers who stayed with their people simply passive observers of the revolution. All of the leaders of the main factions came from the wealthy class which had been entrusted with local power by Rome. Eleazar b. Ananias was the son of a High Priest and held the command of the armed Temple guard. Of the leading fighters against Cestius Gallus the two kinsmen of the king of Adiabene were natural allies of Rome (*B.J.* 2.520); even Simon b. Gioras may well have derived from the ruling class (see below, p. 206). It is not surprising that Gallus did not distinguish the upper class from the rebels and would not trust Ananus b. Jonathan when he offered to betray the city to him (*B.J.* 2.534).

As for the generals appointed after Gallus' defeat, Josephus did not even try to deny their upper-class origins since he was himself one of their number. Ananus, who presided, was a descendant of the first High Priest appointed by a Roman governor in A.D. 6; the credentials of his allies were equally impressive.

Nor, despite Josephus' attempts to claim the contrary, can there be any doubt that these generals tried their best to prosecute the war against Rome, as they had been elected to do. Josephus in the *Vita* tries to minimize his own operations against Roman forces in Galilee, but he must have taken *some* action on behalf of the rebels to deserve both his capture and his later prominence among the Romans. His lack of success as a general was probably caused not by his own doubts about the war but by the failure of the people of Galilee to rise in his support.[18]

In contrast to this involvement by the ruling class, lower-class leaders are noticeable by their absence or irrelevance at the outbreak of revolt. The bandit chiefs who had overrun much of the country-

---

[18] On Galilee as not revolutionary, see Freyne, *Galilee*, pp. 208–55; above, p. 51 n. 3.

side and plundered the estates of the rich in the years before A.D. 66 did not become the instigators or leaders of the rebels. One group of sicarii led by Menahem b. Judas, a relation of the Judas who had instigated unrest against the Roman census in A.D. 6, took advantage of the unrest in June A.D. 66 to break into the Roman armoury at Masada, gaining both a stronghold for their banditry and weapons, but they did not cause any mass uprising by such actions. Coming well-armed to Jerusalem they infiltrated by stealth into the Temple and joined Eleazar b. Ananias' faction in its opposition to those still keen on loyalty to Rome. But their aims were different from his, though Eleazar was prepared to use their military skills for his own ends. The sicarii appear to have sought booty and a general attack on the rich rather than political independence, and Menahem soon showed that he wished to further this plan by winning control of Jerusalem (*B.J.* 2.442). Eleazar's supporters were shocked by such presumption by a man of inferior class (443: *tapeinoteron*), particularly, as has been noted, after the sicarii had murdered Eleazar's father Ananias, and Menahem was killed and his surviving followers dispersed to Masada. The revolt went on, but neither the sicarii nor any other bandit group was to take a leading part again after this brief and ineffectual attempt to influence the politics of the capital city.[19]

The revolt was thus led from the start by the ruling class in a desperate attempt to keep their prominence in Jewish society after the Roman backing, on which they had previously relied, was withdrawn. The sorry story of the gradual alienation of the procurator from the local rulers after May A.D. 66 has already been sketched. But it is possible to go further and suggest the precise point when the old order of collaboration became in effect impossible. That break occurred some time before the cessation of the loyal sacrifices, which,

---

[19] *B.J.* 2.408,433–49. For a fuller discussion of the irrelevance of the sicarii to the outbreak of the revolt, see Rhoads, *Israel in Revolution*, pp. 111–12, and, especially, Horsley, 'Ancient Jewish banditry', p. 410; *idem*, 'Menahem in Jerusalem. A brief messianic episode among the sicarii – not "Zealot Messianism"', *Novum Testamentum* 27 (1985) 334–48. The account in Josephus is admittedly confused: the attack on Masada is recounted in two places (*B.J.* 2.408,433), and at *B.J.* 2.434 Josephus writes of Menahem *returning* to Jerusalem, which has suggested to some that Menahem might have been involved in the revolt before Masada was taken and that he can therefore be considered the main instigator of the uprising. But if Menahem rather than Eleazar b. Ananias had been the central figure in the first days of the rebellion, Josephus would surely not have hesitated to say so. For a different view, see M. Stern, 'Sicarii and Zealots', in M. Avi-Yonah and Z. Baras, eds., *Society and Religion in the Second Temple Period* (The World History of the Jewish People I. 8) (London, 1977), p. 274.

though it marked the formal declaration of rebellion, is described by Josephus in isolation as an act of motiveless lunacy.

The decisive moment for the ruling class came three months or so earlier, when the rulers of Jerusalem refused to hand over those who had reacted to Florus' partisan behaviour in Caesarea and rapacious attack on the Temple treasury in Jerusalem by insulting the procurator with a public joke. The joke was not a very good one: some of the malcontents carried round a basket asking for small change for the governor as if he were a destitute beggar (*B.J.* 2.295);[20] but its effects were far-reaching.

Florus, says Josephus, was horrified at the insult and marched to Jerusalem (*B.J.* 2.296). On arrival in the city he ordered the chief priests, nobles and most eminent men of the city – that is, the local elite according to the Roman view – to present themselves before his tribunal (301). He then instructed them to hand over the men who had joked at his expense (302).[21] The normal and expected reaction of a provincial upper class to such a request from a Roman governor was to comply without hesitation: their function consisted precisely in thus using their local knowledge and roots in the community to spot trouble-makers and give adequate information to the Roman authorities to deal with them. So the actual reaction of the Jerusalem rulers is extraordinary. In their reply to Florus they refused to identify the delinquents and, instead, implored pardon for them (302–4). Such courting of Florus' displeasure was extremely rash, for Florus' violent reaction, described in 305–8, can hardly have been unexpected given his earlier behaviour and explicit threats (302). There must have been a good reason for their folly.

And yet the reason they professed according to Josephus (303) is feeble in the extreme. They claimed, Josephus says, that 'it was impossible to pick out the delinquents as everyone was now penitent and would, for fear of the consequences, deny what he had done'. A strange excuse which, if regularly advanced, would paralyse the administration of justice altogether. It was not beyond the abilities of these Judaean rulers to discover the perpetrators of so public an act. Nor was it reasonable to expect a Roman governor to accept so blatant an affront to his dignity. The danger to which the Jews

[20] Perhaps Florus felt this was more of an insult than a Jew would have done; see above, pp. 129–30, on attitudes to poverty. For a fuller discussion of this episode, see my article, 'A bad joke in Josephus', *JJS* 36 (1985) 195–9.

[21] That the insult to which Florus refers at *B.J.* 2.302 was the joke and not the rest of the behaviour of the Jerusalem Jews is clear from the use of the word *skoptein* at *B.J.* 2.299.

alluded, that innocent citizens would suffer because of the actions of a few reckless youths (304), was far more probable when the youths were *not* identified and punished than if they had been. The suggestion that a denial of guilt would prevent conviction for a crime (303) was valid neither in Roman nor in Jewish law, for the evidence of the numerous witnesses would suffice.

Florus at any rate was not impressed by such reasoning. He let loose his soldiers against the inhabitants of Jerusalem in general (305) and against the upper class in particular: he tried, scourged and crucified before his tribunal Jews who were Roman citizens of equestrian rank (308), that is, Jews who, because of their wealth, were automatically considered as part of the local elite by Rome.

So a different explanation for the rulers' behaviour is clearly needed. They were evidently concerned to cover up for the perpetrators of the joke. For some reason these young[22] men were too important in the eyes of their elders to be handed over to the procurator for punishment. Only one group of youths sufficiently anti-Roman to insult the procurator but also sufficiently close to the Jerusalem rulers to be protected by them suggests itself.

The leading man of the Jerusalem ruling class was presumably at this date still the ex-High Priest Ananias b. Nedebaeus: his influence had been paramount in A.D. 63 (*A.J.* 20.213) and was to be exceptional later in the summer of A.D. 66, so it is likely that his views carried greatest weight in the decision to defy the procurator. It is reasonable to suggest that the jokers protected by Ananias and his friends included his son Eleazar, who in July or August was to show his contempt for Florus and for Rome by stopping the loyal sacrifices.[23]

If this is correct, it is not surprising that Ananias, who with the rest of his faction was presumably prominent among the Jewish rulers approached by Florus after the perpetration of the joke, was unwilling to hand over his son to an almost certain death at the governor's hands. Nor is it surprising that Josephus chose to remain so reticent about the reasons just outlined for this intransigence, for he is at pains throughout the *B.J.* to suggest as far as he plausibly can that his own class was not responsible for the outbreak of the war. He

[22] Josephus only makes the vague comment that the troublemakers were 'too rash and foolish because of their age' (*B.J.* 2.303), but in comments of this sort folly is more likely to be associated with youth than with any other time of life.
[23] Eleazar is described at *B.J.* 2.409 as a 'most rash young man'; the same description is applied to the (perhaps deliberately unnamed) jokers at *B.J.* 2.303. For this suggestion, see Goodman, 'A bad joke', pp. 196–7.

prefers, therefore, to leave the jokers anonymous and to depict Florus as monstrously unreasonable. Silence and vagueness suited Josephus better than writing the precise details which he surely in fact knew.

For Josephus would also be well aware that this cover-up for a silly joke was a direct cause of the rebellion. Florus assumed that the refusal of the Jewish rulers to hand over the culprits showed that they opposed him, and therefore Rome. In a desperate attempt to reinstate their position as loyal allies of Rome without sacrificing the jokers, some of the upper-class Jews went in a mass to Agrippa; but he only berated them for their folly (*B.J.* 2.336–8), refusing to bring a complaint to Nero against Florus on the grounds that it would be odious (*epiphthonon*) to choose a delegation to carry such a message (343). Successful deputations had been sent to higher Roman authority to denounce previous procurators, so the hesitation on this occasion is most likely to have been caused by the Jews' awareness of their own guilt.

Within days the same upper-class youths had progressed from insulting but mild jokes to deliberate provocation of the Roman troops. When Florus attempted to put on a public demonstration of his control over all the population by telling the Jewish rulers to lead the people out of Jerusalem to greet the cohorts coming from Caesarea, the factious element refused to obey (*B.J.* 2.318,320). Precisely whom this 'factious element' included Josephus does not say, but it included notables who were known to the leading priests by name (322). Those such as Eleazar b. Ananias may have already decided that their political future under Roman governors who despised them was too bleak to consider. They may have put their confidence instead in their popularity with the people outraged by Florus' massacres and looting. If so, they chose their time well: the 'mob inclined towards the bolder men' (320), and Florus was forced out of the city by their mass resistance (328–32). The whole governing class had connived to prevent the suppression of revolt when the governor demanded it. Revolt was only a short time coming.

That it was rebellion that resulted, and not just sporadic disturbances, was largely the result of this participation by the ruling class. There had been much violence in Judaea before A.D. 66 but it rarely constituted serious revolt in the eyes of Rome. During the reign of Tiberius, John the Baptist, Jesus and Barabbas were all arraigned for sedition and there were disturbances about the weight of the tribute in A.D. 17 (Tac. *Ann* 2.42), but Tacitus could still write that 'under Tiberius all was quiet'.[24] Tiberius Julius Alexander, governor A.D. 46–8, executed among others two sons of Judas the Galilean (*A.J.* 20.102); yet Josephus (who, aged ten at the time, should have known but is here perhaps defending the procurator's record) writes that during his rule over Judaea the nation was at peace (*B.J.* 2.220).

Urban rioting against tactless procurators had similarly caused Rome only slight worry. Such disturbances were not uncommon elsewhere among the urban *plebs* of other cities in the empire. The need for occasional suppression of small incidents was taken as a matter of course; so much so that at least one occasion, when Pilate 'mingled the blood of Galileans with their sacrifices' (Luke 13.1), may have escaped the attention both of Josephus and of Tacitus, although the silence of these authors may be better explained by casting justifiable doubt on Luke's accuracy. Even massed civilians could usually be easily controlled by regular Roman troops if they were sufficiently swift and ruthless.[25]

Nor did banditry and attacks on the rich in the countryside cause Rome any greater concern. It was clearly desirable that violent robbery be eliminated but Roman rule itself was not obviously threatened by such acts. When Josephus alleges that the procurators colluded with brigands to the detriment of the rich (e.g. *B.J.* 2.278), he points to a real division of interest: for the local ruling class their property was of prime concern, but the governors preferred to concentrate their energies on protecting the cities.

Nor was the bickering between Jews and gentiles in Caesarea and other mixed cities particularly worrying to the Romans. No such bickering was in itself anti-Roman and it was even plausible for Josephus to suggest that Florus was happy to let the parties fight the matter out (*B.J.* 2.288).

Until A.D. 66, then, the Romans only rarely felt seriously

[24] P. W. Barnett, 'Under Tiberius all was quiet', *NTS* 21 (1975) 564–71. It is not necessary to argue that there was *no* anti-Roman movement before A.D. 44, as does Rhoads, *Israel in Revolution*, pp. 59–68, but such disturbances as there were were evidently not seen by Rome as dangerous.

[25] For urban rioting elsewhere in the empire, see R. A. MacMullen, *Enemies of the Roman Order: treason, unrest and alienation in the Empire* (Cambridge, Mass. and London, 1967), pp. 163–91; for the use of troops against civilians, see Gichon, 'Cestius Gallus' campaign', p. 46. The procurator Sabinus in 4 B.C. had to be rescued by Quinctilius Varus after riots in Jerusalem, but the Jewish rebels then were much strengthened by the bulk of Herod's troops (*B.J.* 2.52), and Varus had other uprisings to deal with in addition (see below, n. 29).

threatened in Judaea. A prophet proclaiming upheaval in society was let off with a flogging in the early sixties A.D. (*B.J.* 6.300–9). Those like the followers of Theudas or another leader known in the sources only as an Egyptian, who looked more dangerous because they collected in small groups inspired by messianic or other religious aspirations, were easily suppressed with bloodshed (above, p. 92).[26]

There were of course serious incidents which sparked off mass indignation. Agitation against the census in A.D. 6 was widespread. Outrage against Caligula's plan to put his statue in the Temple was more or less universal and would surely have exploded spontaneously if the plan had been carried out. The riots sparked off during the governorship of Cumanus by the murder of a Galilean at the hands of Samaritans did not require military intervention by the Syrian legate Quadratus at the time but appeared sufficiently threatening for Claudius to respond soon after by settling veterans in Ptolemais (cf. Pliny, *Nat. Hist.* 5.75) and by paving the legionary road from there to Antioch for the rapid movement of troops in a crisis.[27]

Nonetheless these uprisings fizzled out, and not only because the causes of complaint in some cases dissolved. The crucial, though doubtless by no means the only, reason for this seems to me to be the lack of leadership for such movements. Thus when crowds responded in opposition to Pilate's plans to introduce military standards into Jerusalem (*B.J.* 2.169–74) and in the anti-Samaritan riots in Cumanus' time, the mob was leaderless (cf. *B.J.* 2.234) and unable to protest against Rome except by passive resistance and riots. Suppression was achieved by intimidation, by beating members of the crowd (*B.J.* 2.176–7) and by crucifying prisoners (241). In sum, mass movements against Rome tended to lack leadership, and charismatic leaders such as the pseudo-messiahs lacked followers.

It seems to me that rebellion against Rome was doomed without powerful local leaders. In every other province where revolt is recorded, it was the notables who led. The poor could not harm Rome, as Domitian recognized when, according to Eusebius (*Ecc.Hist.* 3.20), the relatives of Jesus, who had been arrested some time in the eighties or nineties A.D. because they were of the royal family of David, were released on the grounds that they were only working-class folk. True revolt in Judaea was thus only possible

[26] Schürer, *History* I, pp. 456, 464, 467–8.
[27] R. G. Goodchild, 'The coast road of Phoenicia and its Roman milestones', *Berytus* 9 (1948) 91–127.

when the ruling class here too turned against Rome. Despite both provocation and opportunity they long remained loyal, but Florus' severance of the tie which should have bound the wealthy to him finally pushed them into war in A.D. 66.[28]

The new situation was immediately recognized by Cestius Gallus in Syria. Revolt led by the upper class could be suppressed only by massive force. There were precedents for such action. The Syrian legions had marched on Judaea under Varus in 4 B.C. when a variety of leaders, some of them related to the Herodian house, had sought independence from Rome.[29] Similar massive intervention had been used by the Syrian legate C. Cassius Longinus when, as a necessary precaution against revolt by the ruling class in *c.* A.D. 44 after Cuspius Fadus had taken the High Priest's vestments out of Jewish and into Roman custody, he ensured the obedience of the leaders of the people, while they awaited the return of a delegation sent to Rome to protest against this action, both by holding their children hostage for their good behaviour and by stationing a large force in Jerusalem (*A.J.* 20.6–9).

In A.D. 44 such tactics proved successful, but twenty-two years later Cestius Gallus' legions moved too slowly to frighten the Judaean rulers into submission. They were embarked already on the road to independence, and the efforts of the faction leaders now were concentrated on winning power for themselves within the new Jewish state.

[28] On other provincial revolts, see Brunt, 'Did Rome disarm her subjects?', p. 270. The role of the ruling class during the crisis over Caligula's statue in A.D. 40 is obscure (see above, p. 46); it is impossible to tell whether they would have led a rebellion if Caligula had lived. The Romans were well aware of the pivotal role of rebel leaders, as their treatment of the Jews who rioted against the Samaritans in Cumanus' governorship shows: the Jewish mob was leaderless according to *B.J.* 2.234, but the Syrian legate Quadratus accepted the word of the Samaritans that a Jew called Doetus and four companions had led their opponents and had these men executed (*A.J.* 20.130); *some* sort of leaders were reckoned necessary. Some time later Felix captured by a ruse the brigand chief Eleazar b. Deinaeus who had directed the looting by the Jews (*B.J.* 2.235; *A.J.* 20.121); though he was not the instigator of the original uprising, he was not executed on the spot as a bandit but was sent to Rome for trial like an honorary member of the upper class (*A.J.* 20.160–1). But perhaps Eleazar was more than just a bandit: Felix tricked him by promising safe conduct, and it is hard to see why any bandit should wish to negotiate about anything with the Roman governor, even in the belief he was protected by a promise of personal safety. There were clear opportunities for rebellion in A.D. 44 and in A.D. 62 when Agrippa I and Festus respectively died, leaving the country ungoverned. Those opportunities were ignored.
[29] On the 'war of Varus', see Smallwood, *Jews*, p. 113.

CHAPTER 8

THE INDEPENDENT JEWISH STATE
A.D. 67–70

The equilibrium in Judaean politics achieved by the end of A.D. 66 under the leadership of Ananus b. Ananus was not to last. The coalition's prestige was severely shaken by its failure in Galilee: Josephus' efforts to hold the area against Rome on behalf of the Jerusalem government were finished by the summer of A.D. 67, and by the autumn his successor John of Gischala had also given up the struggle.

In Jerusalem Eleazar b. Simon, the powerful priest deposed from office by Ananus after Cestius Gallus' defeat, began, with his associates who sported the name of 'Zealots', to campaign for more effective leadership. At first tolerated by Ananus, he was by the winter penned up with his supporters inside the Temple where he had taken refuge. In the meantime John of Gischala, who had at least seen action against the Romans, became something of a popular hero on his escape from Galilee and his arrival in Jerusalem, and in early spring A.D. 68 he abandoned his alliance with Ananus and joined forces with Eleazar b. Simon.

The fate of Ananus' party was sealed when the leaders of the Idumaeans, who had hitherto remained neutral in the Judaean political struggle, threw in their support for John and Eleazar. On a dramatically stormy night in late spring A.D. 68, they infiltrated into the city, and Ananus and many of his more prominent followers were killed.

From spring A.D. 68 to spring A.D. 69 the coalition of John, Eleazar and the Idumaeans remained in control of Jerusalem. But the alliance was not always a happy one, and in the summer of A.D. 68 some of the Idumaeans deserted to a rising star outside the city, another general who had been deposed after Gallus' retreat, Simon b. Gioras. With their help and that of other refugees from Jerusalem, Simon gained control by the end of the year of all the countryside in Judaea and Idumaea not yet under Roman occupation. He encamped outside the walls of Jerusalem and, in the spring of A.D.

69, was granted access to the city itself by the rest of the Idumaeans, who had also grown tired of John and Eleazar.

Simon b. Gioras thus became the main leader of the nation from spring A.D. 69 to the destruction of the Temple in summer A.D. 70. But his opponents still held out against him within the city – Eleazar b. Simon penned into the inner court of the Temple and John of Gischala confined to the outer Temple precincts and the Lower City. That was the situation when Titus arrived outside Jerusalem in spring A.D. 70 for what was to be the final siege. As Tacitus (*Hist.* 5.12.3–4) remarked, there were three generals and three armies, and between these three there was constant fighting, treachery and arson. Only with the approach of the Romans was concord achieved in order to fight the common enemy.

It would be a mistake bred from hindsight to suppose that the Judaean state over which these Jewish politicians fought so bitterly was obviously doomed to destruction from the beginning. The rebels could recall earlier successes, against the Seleucids when the Maccabees had won through to independence and, more recently, against Cestius Gallus. Rome herself was in disorder both in A.D. 66 following the Pisonian conspiracy and in the civil wars of A.D. 68 and 69 (cf. *B.J.* 1.4). The prestige of the empire had noticeably declined as the Julio-Claudian dynasty approached its end. Nero's one great general, Corbulo, was dead, forced to commit suicide by his master's suspicions. Nero himself was more interested in the pursuit of Greek luxury than the preservation of imperial domination, and the recent revolt of Boudicca in Britain in A.D. 60 had been suppressed only with difficulty.

Furthermore, the Jews had grounds for hoping that the Romans might anyway prefer not to exert themselves against the rebellion to the full. There was a strong possibility that, in revenge for Corbulo's campaigns, the Parthians might seek to take advantage from any drawn-out fighting on this front, and the Romans were well aware after Cestius Gallus' failure that rapid capture of Jerusalem would not be easy. Faced with the danger of a lengthy guerrilla war in the Judaean hill country, the Romans might therefore be expected to prefer to make an agreement with the rebels. An independent Judaea cut off from the Mediterranean would anyway not in itself be a threat to the rest of the empire.

The rebels certainly did not expect to fail. Even in A.D. 70 a successful siege seemed impossible. With vast food supplies if they had been carefully rationed, the population could last out for years. The Romans outside the walls suffered from a lack of water and some of them even deserted to the Jews (Cassius Dio 66.5.2–4). Even less in A.D. 66 could anyone reasonably have expected the vigour and disregard for the lives of his troops with which Titus captured the city by direct assault: in contrast to his father or Cestius Gallus, Titus was spurred on to victory by the sudden need of his family, so unexpectedly raised to the principate, to win a famous triumph to glorify their name (see below, p. 236).

In the meantime the Jewish state functioned as if it was to be permanent. The best evidence for this comes from the rebels' coins, for they survive as testimony independent of Josephus' account of the war. The coins were minted in each of the five years for which the Jewish republic survived. Their quality is impressive: the metal used was pure and nearly constant in composition, and the types were beautifully minted, especially on the silver coins of the second, third and fourth years. The thick shape of flan and the use of an artificial palaeo-Hebrew script proclaimed that this was an independent coinage entirely separate from Rome. The slogans emphasized liberty and the holiness of the city of Jerusalem. The symbols conjured up thoughts of the Temple and the great national festivals. The counting of the years from the declaration of independence demonstrated the arrival of a new era. The coin types changed only slightly from the first issues, which may have been produced by any or all of the factions temporarily in control of Jerusalem in A.D. 66 after the cessation of the loyal sacrifices, to the last types minted in evidently difficult conditions in the early summer of A.D. 70. The aims of all the factions was ultimately the same: a free, independent Jewish state.[1]

Furthermore, this state was of some sophistication. The fine silver coins were no doubt primarily intended for payment of the Temple dues, hence the need to ensure the purity of their metal to avoid a charge of sacrilege, but the government also produced a mass of small change, presumably to aid commerce in the city. Many small bronze coins of the second to fourth years of the rebellion have been found. Those of the fourth year (A.D. 69–70) are exceptionally well minted, perhaps because with the shrinking of the silver supply the

[1] Kadman, *Coins of the Jewish War*, with arguments against the view that the different factions used different coinages on p. 100 n. 95. See also Meshorer, *Ancient Jewish Coinage* II, pp. 96–131; Roth, 'Historical implications', pp. 35, 41–2. On the date when the coins began to be minted, see Smallwood, pp. 300–1, who, with others, argues that minting started in October A.D. 66 and that the authorities used April A.D. 67 to begin the production of second-year coins only because in this month dues had to be paid to the Temple. Contrast Roth, 'Historical implications', who ascribes the first coins to Eleazar b. Ananias in May–June A.D. 66; see above, p. 158 n. 7.

minting of shekels became more difficult. A mass of minute bronze coins of at least 14 different types was also produced and are found widely distributed over the city; some at least probably date from the fourth year also.[2]

The same government maintained even in A.D. 70 a public burial fund for the poor (*B.J.* 5.568). Furthermore, a court of seventy prominent citizens was still convened when necessary to hear criminal charges, probably still acting as the *consilium* of the High Priest: in A.D. 68 the Zealots led by Eleazar b. Simon tried to use such a court to get rid of one of their political opponents on a charge of treason, but this was only after they had first ensured the election of a puppet High Priest (*B.J.* 4.153,155–7), and, even then, due legalities were so effectively observed that the defendant was acquitted, though he was soon assassinated by his opponents nonetheless (*B.J.* 4.334–44). Other political opponents fared better, for Josephus' parents were imprisoned (*B.J.* 5.533,544).

Obviously not all of Josephus' allegations of chaos and misery after A.D. 67 can be discounted, for this was a nation at war and much effort went into military preparations which succeeded in efficiently strengthening the city walls, but it can be seen that much ordinary life continued for many Jerusalemites, little hindered by political developments and infighting.

Above all, the Temple service continued uninterrupted until the very last days of the war. Even when the inner courts served as the headquarters of the Zealots, they allowed all who so wished to enter to worship (*B.J.* 5.15); this liberal attitude was indeed responsible for depriving them of their independence when they tried to break away from their alliance with John of Gischala during A.D. 70 (B.J. 5.99–100). If *arnon* be read at *B.J.* 6.94, it was only in August A.D. 70 that the supply of lambs for the daily sacrifice came to an end, so up to that time the animals had presumably been regularly provided from the countryside and transported through the streets of Jerusalem despite all the faction fighting that marked off spheres of influence within the city for particular groups. All Jews must have cooperated to keep the sacrifices going. Furthermore, pilgrims still flooded into the city at the great festivals, for many of those caught up in the siege in A.D. 70 had, according to Josephus, blithely come to Jerusalem for the Passover and were only unwittingly enveloped in the war (*B.J.* 6.421). They were evidently not even then expecting the sudden demise of the Jewish state.

[2] Kadman, *Coins of the Jewish War*, p. 98; cf. Roth, 'Historical implications', pp. 40,45,46 n. 31; Avigad, *Discovering Jerusalem*, p. 195.

By A.D 70 there were indeed many signs to confirm this belief that Rome was not eager to press the suppression of the revolt with any speed. Cestius Gallus had failed to take the city in A.D. 66 despite his three legions. Vespasian had spent A.D. 67 in the slow reduction of Galilee, although that area was distant from Jerusalem and perhaps irrelevant to the outbreak and course of the revolt. In A.D. 68 the slow Roman conquest of the Judaean countryside again appeared like deliberate avoidance of the central task in crushing the rebellion, the investment of Jerusalem.

When even these operations halted because Vespasian suddenly stopped his campaign on hearing of Nero's death in June of that year, the delusion that Jerusalem was truly impregnable was unassailable. Vespasian, as legate of Nero, was constitutionally correct in suspending the war until his position was reinstated by a new emperor – the Syrian legate Vitellius had similarly given up a Nabataean campaign in A.D. 37 when Tiberius died (*A.J.* 18.124) – but few Judaeans will have understood this Roman constitutional theory.

In A.D. 69 Vespasian seemed even more reluctant to prosecute the war. He took no action until May/June and even then only conquered parts of the countryside, ignoring both the city and the great Herodian fortresses of Masada, Herodium and Machaerus, before his elevation to the principate on the first of July brought another halt to operations against the Jews. No Roman forces reached the walls of Jerusalem between Gallus' defeat in A.D. 66 and Titus' arrival there a few days before the Passover of A.D. 70.

The Jews might be forgiven if they became complacent. Not understanding the niceties of Roman law or the complexities of imperial politics which rendered Vespasian's position simultaneously dangerous and advantageous after Nero's death, they saw only the reluctance of the Romans to commit themselves to the fight. Nor were the Jews the only subjects of the empire to assume that the chaos in Rome, with the election of four emperors in the year A.D. 69, was an opportunity for rebellion. A revolt was led in north-east Anatolia by Anicetus, the ex-commander of the royal fleet of Polemo II of Pontus whose territory had been taken over by Nero about five years previously (Tac. *Hist.* 3.47); in Britain by Venutius in opposition to Cartimandua and her Roman backers (Tac. *Hist.* 3.45); and in Germany where Civilis sought some sort of independence with the Batavi (Tac. *Hist.* 4.12–37, 54–79). The energy and disregard for the unnecessary loss of life among his own soldiers with which Titus prosecuted the siege of Jerusalem in A.D. 70 was entirely due to Vespasian's need to win a famous victory to justify his seizure of power: without that factor Roman hostilities against Judaea might have been as lackadaisical as those against Civilis on the Rhine.

In many ways, then, the Jews were right to be optimistic in A.D. 66. There was precedent for success in the revolt of the Frisii who had maintained their independence from A.D. 28 to 47. The Jews' hopes must have been lifted by the fact that their first military opponent, Gallus, was incompetent, as his placing of his baggage at the rear of his line during his advance on Jerusalem shows: his retreat from the city may have been the result of sheer panic, for Josephus professed himself mystified by it (*B.J.* 2.539–40).[3] Nor were the abilities of Gallus' successor, Vespasian, necessarily much greater, for it was a long time since he had been on active service.

Certainly Vespasian's lack of military practice would be a better explanation for his cautious strategy in the opening stages of the war than other reasons that have been proposed. It is, for instance, possible that he had an enlarged command in the East like that entrusted some years before to Corbulo, in which case his slow approach to the Judaean war could be explained by his interest in dealing with other parts of his province, but there is no direct evidence for this.[4] Similarly, he may have hoped to starve out Jerusalem by the capture of the surrounding countryside, but if so he was too optimistic since only a manned siege wall could have such an effect. It is even possible that his prime interest in attacking Galilee before the capital city was to frighten off Parthian attempts to aid the rebels by attacking from the north, but the Parthians were actually better kept at bay by the threat of a flank attack from the legions stationed at Antioch in Syria.

It is not, however, necessary to postulate either incompetence or any of these strategic reasons to explain the slow advance of the Roman forces, for Josephus' narrative gives another explanation which, though Josephus himself is unwilling to emphasize it for fear of prejudicing the good relations between Jews and Romans which he urges as possible for the future, nonetheless fully accounts for the deliberate delay. Even in spring A.D. 68, when Vespasian's advisers urged an attack on the capital, he *preferred* to wait (*B.J.* 4.366–76).

---

[3] Cf. Gichon, 'Cestius Gallus' campaign', pp. 53–4, on the baggage; cf. Rajak, *Josephus*, p. 74.
[4] The first suggestion was made to me by L. J. F. Keppie in conversation. On Vespasian's possible tenure of an enlarged command in A.D. 67, see J. Nicols, *Vespasian and the Partes Flavianae* (*Historia Einzelschriften* 28) (1978), pp. 114, 119–24.

Whether or not Josephus was correct to claim that Vespasian was simply waiting for civil dissension to ruin the rebels, the Roman commander surely knew that Jerusalem's walls would be exceptionally difficult to breach. Any technique that could avoid a direct assault with the danger of the loss of thousands of soldiers must be avoided. So he, like Cestius Gallus before him, chose a strategy of terror.

Romans had used a technique involving the deliberate massacre, enslavement and destruction of a part of the population at the start of wars in previous campaigns. The aim was to frighten their opponents into surrender. In the Third Macedonian War of 171–168 B.C. the city of Haliartus suffered just such a catastrophe (Livy 42.63.3–12), and as a result fewer Greeks joined Perseus against Rome in the rest of the war than might have been expected.[5] Vespasian's tactics were identical.

Thus, although in A.D. 67 few Galileans joined in the revolt, many were killed. There was great slaughter by the victorious troops at Tarichaeae without discrimination between rebels and others (B.J. 3.500). Of the proven rebels, twelve thousand were massacred in the stadium at Tiberias, while six thousand young men were sent as slaves to work on the canal being built by Nero at the isthmus of Corinth, and thirty thousand four hundred were sold as slaves (*B.J.* 3.539–40). The city of Jotapata was similarly razed and all the men found were killed (*B.J.* 3.336–9). The same technique was used the following year (A.D. 68): when the town of Gerasa, probably in north-east Judaea, was captured, most of the young men were killed, property was plundered and many others who did not escape were enslaved (*B.J.* 4.488–9). Other examples could be quoted.[6] Even when the siege of Jerusalem was under way in A.D. 70, Titus used public torture of Jewish prisoners for the same purpose, to demoralize and frighten the rebels. The steady trickle of deserters to the Roman side even then demonstrates that the strategy was not a failure (cf. *B.J.* 5.420–2, in A.D. 70).

But the long and unplanned delays in A.D. 68 and 69 while Vespasian dabbled in Roman politics will have much lessened the effect of such terror tactics, which need to be applied relentlessly to work well, and for much of the existence of the Jewish state the people of Jerusalem succeeded in ignoring these awful events in the rest of the country. The city's rulers acted as if the external threat of Rome was irrelevant. For them, the prize for political intrigue was now control

[5] De Ste Croix, *Class Struggle*, p. 524.
[6] See the detailed notes in Alon, *Jews, Judaism and the Classical World*, pp. 282–8.

of an independent nation. It is not surprising that the claim to power by the loose coalition led in November A.D. 66 by Ananus b. Ananus was challenged by ambitious politicians both within and outside that coalition.

The immediate danger for Ananus in later A.D. 66 and early A.D. 67 was that squabbles between the factions combined under his leadership would lead to the dissolution of his government. It will be recalled that Ananus' party contained the factions of Eleazar b. Ananias and the ex-High Priest Jesus b. Gamalas as well as his own long-term supporters (above, p. 164). These factions cooperated only uneasily in the prosecution of the war. Their mutual suspicions can be best illustrated from Josephus' account of his own career in early A.D. 67 as the emissary in Galilee of Ananus' provisional government.

Josephus himself was an associate of Jesus b. Gamalas (above, p. 165). In Galilee he found himself constantly dogged by the ambitions of the friends of Eleazar b. Ananias, to whose group he himself clearly had not originally belonged since he had joined Eleazar in the Temple in summer A.D. 66 only after the Antonia fortress had been captured (*Vita* 20; cf. *B.J.* 2.430; see above, p. 159). The two factions of Jesus and Eleazar were for the moment in alliance under Ananus' overall command, and Josephus accordingly delegated power to Eleazar's supporters in Galilee as appropriate. But he did not trust them, and much of his energy was directed to preventing them from supplanting him from his post.

The most prominent member of Eleazar's faction in Galilee was John b. Levi of Gischala, who was later, in A.D. 68, to become master of Jerusalem for a year. John's membership of that group has to be inferred from his other known friendships (see above, p. 164); as a resident of Galilee, he was evidently not much involved in Jerusalem politics before the outbreak of the war. He was a close friend of the leading Pharisee Simon b. Gamaliel (*Vita* 190–2) and thus had reasonable expectations that Ananus might appoint him as commander in Galilee in preference to Josephus: he was to be warmly welcomed into Jerusalem by Ananus' supporters when Galilee finally fell (*B.J.* 4.121), and he had many followers in the ruling coalition even before he began to demonstrate his powers of generalship in the city (*B.J.* 4.213).

It is Simon b. Gamaliel who provides the link to Eleazar's faction, for it was at his behest that a deputation was sent by the Jerusalem government to depose Josephus from the Galilean command and appoint John in his stead, and that deputation contained two close associates of Eleazar, namely Ananias b. Sadok and Judas b. Jonathan (*B.J.* 2.628, cf. 2.451, and above p. 164).

Josephus' attitude towards John and the rest of Eleazar's faction was ambivalent, since they were technically in coalition with his own political associates. He thus rather reluctantly found John a natural ally in organizing the defence of the region (*Vita* 43–5,71–3; *B.J.* 2.575) and, despite John's constant intrigues to win power (*Vita* 70, 122–4,189–98, etc.), forbore to punish him (*Vita* 82). The social relations of the two men remained good despite their rivalry, so that Josephus prepared a lodging for John when he came to Tiberias to use the hot baths for health reasons (*Vita* 85–6).

But this veneer of cooperation disguised the real danger that Eleazar's faction would deprive Josephus of his command. Right at the beginning of his rule the two subordinates sent from Jerusalem to help Josephus to organize Galilee were already prone to prefer John as general. By name Joazar and Judas (*Vita* 29), they were prepared from the start to assign responsibility to John for the defence of Upper Galilee, allowing him to sell the imperial corn stored there to raise funds to restore the walls of Gischala (*Vita* 71–3). According to the *Vita* (cf. 72), Josephus seems to have been unwilling to allow John any role in the war whatsoever; but it is striking that when, at the urging of Joazar and Judas, he did transfer power in the north of Galilee to John, he was able to pretend to the world that this concession had been a voluntary decision justified by the fact that he and John were, technically, in alliance (*B.J.* 2.575).

Giving control of the north to John did not, however, satisfy Eleazar's faction. The two men sent with Josephus to Galilee, Joazar and Judas, returned to Jerusalem as soon as they had conferred with John in Gischala (*Vita* 77). It was probably the latter of these, now described more fully as the priest Joazar (or Joesdrus) b. Nomicos (*Vita* 197 with *B.J.* 2.628), who returned to Galilee in the four-man deputation including Ananias b. Sadok and Judas b. Jonathan (in the *Vita* consistently called simply Jonathan) which was directed by Simon b. Gamaliel to remove Josephus from his post.

Josephus charts in some detail in the *Vita* his intrigues against this deputation. These men were not his enemies as the Romans were: in the end all four emissaries were returned under safe escort to Jerusalem. Josephus even sought to win over one of them, Joazar, to his side by pretending to offer to divide his command with him (*Vita* 324), although Joazar was too suspicious of him to agree even to discuss such a deal (325). The youngest delegate, a certain Simon of high-priestly family (*Vita* 197), was perhaps not as fully committed to Eleazar's faction as the others, for he showed himself prepared to consider an alliance with Josephus (*Vita* 325), and, though Josephus did not trust him (326), he was at least sufficiently friendly to reckon it worthwhile to invite Simon to a pleasant dinner (330), presumably in the hope of winning him over to his own party. The remaining two delegates, however, Ananias b. Sadok and Judas b. Jonathan, were more firmly committed to Eleazar, whom they had supported from the beginning (see above, p. 158). Ananias, in Josephus' eyes, was thus simply wicked and criminal (*Vita* 290). Judas b. Jonathan seems to have been the leading spirit of the opposition (cf. *Vita* 216, 226,246, etc.), at times even more intent on deposing Josephus than was John of Gischala (cf. *Vita* 271).[7]

Despite all the efforts by the deputation and by John, Josephus survived, often through trickery, as commander of Galilee. Jesus b. Gamalas, Josephus' patron, was to increase his power within Ananus' coalition, perhaps as a result. By December A.D. 67 his role was at least as influential as that of the spokesman of Eleazar b. Ananias' friends, Simon b. Gamaliel (*B.J.* 4.159–60).

It can be assumed that this bickering between temporary allies was repeated elsewhere besides Galilee during A.D. 67. Nonetheless, Ananus remained in control of Jerusalem throughout the year until the fall of Galilee undermined his popularity and encouraged the factions excluded from power in November A.D. 66 to seek renewed popular backing.

The first to do so was that led by Eleazar b. Simon.[8] Calling themselves 'Zealots' (*B.J.* 4.161; cf. below, p. 219), Eleazar b. Simon's

[7] On the leadership struggle from October A.D. 66 to mid A.D. 67, see Cohen, *Josephus in Galilee and Rome*, pp. 195–231. It is odd that Judas b. Jonathan is described throughout the *Vita* simply as 'Jonathan the Pharisee'. Given the major role this man played, Josephus can hardly have forgotten his name. Rajak, *Josephus*, p. 165, suggests that Josephus was at the time of writing the *B.J.* embarrassed by his own enmity with a leading Pharisee and therefore omitted Jonathan entirely (in which case Judas was a different man, perhaps his son); but, if so, why did Josephus reinstate Jonathan among his opponents in the *Vita* when he (Josephus) was claiming that he himself was also a Pharisee and admission of Jonathan's past opposition might be even more distressing? Cohen, *Josephus in Galilee and Rome*, p. 224 n. 88, follows Schlatter in amending *B.J.* 2.628. He denies any connection between the delegation to Josephus and Eleazar's faction and claims that the text at *B.J.* 2.628 has been corrupted under the influence of *B.J.* 2.451. But this, though possible, seems a desperate solution to the problem. It is worth noting that the equally odd confusion over the name of Agrippa's lieutenant Noarus or Varus cannot be easily explained by any apologetic intent on Josephus' part.

[8] *B.J.* 4.225. Some manuscripts read 'Eleazar b. Gion', but *B.J.* 5.5 describes the leader of the Zealots as Eleazar b. Simon, making the link with *B.J.* 2.564, where his followers are already called 'Zealots'.

supporters appealed most effectively to the refugees from the countryside who, having seen the effects of the war and appreciated the terror tactics of Vespasian, were particularly keen that opposition to Rome be intensified (*B.J.* 4.138).

The Zealots thus won influence first by imprisoning members of the ruling class who were not part of Ananus' provisional government but who had retained positions of authority from the procuratorial period. Chief among these was Antipas, a relative of the Herodian house who had charge of the public treasury (*B.J.* 4.140). His arrest, along with two other relatives (*B.J.* 4.141), was little more than a symbolic indication that those uncertain about the desirability of an independent Jewish state had no place in it. It is likely that the execution of the same men on a charge of treason had the same intention (*B.J.* 4.145–6).

It is clear that Ananus did not feel able to oppose the Zealots at first. He could hardly protect those who were accused of treachery. Josephus says mysteriously that the Zealots brought the official authorities into collision with each other by clever rumours and tricks, thereby providing an opportunity for an intensification of the internal squabblings (*tais pros allelous ... philoneikiais*) within the coalition (*B.J.* 4.150). At any rate, a brilliant coup by the Zealots was the seizure of the Temple and selection by lot of a puppet High Priest (*B.J.* 4.148–9,153–4). The High Priest thus appointed naturally felt loyalty to his patrons, as Josephus rightly observed, but this was not particularly useful since he was a political nonentity (155). More significant was the fact that this move prevented Ananus and his friends from claiming to be the 'establishment' because the previous High Priest was, tacitly, on their side.

Ananus had to react to preserve control and he thus became openly hostile to the Zealots, seeking in December A.D. 67 to oust them from their growing influence (*B.J.* 4.151,159–62). His position was still far from desperate. The coalition remained intact at the top, with Gorion b. Joseph, Simon (here 'Symeon') b. Gamaliel and Jesus b. Gamalas still allied to him (*B.J.* 4.159–60). He could rely on the support of all the numerous politicians still in Jerusalem descended from or related to, the main high-priestly families, for Eleazar b. Simon had alienated them all by ignoring them in the appointment of the new High Priest (148) and seems never to have received any backing from any of them in the rest of his turbulent career.

Furthermore, Ananus had the support of John of Gischala. John had been received into Jerusalem as a returning general (*B.J.* 4.121–

7), the irregularity of his command being conveniently forgotten; oblivion was doubtless aided by general regret at the traitor Josephus who had been appointed to the post (*B.J.* 3.438–9). John's right to join the controlling group under Ananus was not in doubt – his friend Simon b. Gamaliel could offer him powerful patronage (*B.J.* 4.159) and his military competence, demonstrated in Galilee, brought him a following of his own among the young men (*B.J.* 4.128).

But it was John who was to bring about the destruction of Ananus' coalition which had fostered his own rise to prominence (*B.J.* 4.208–26), and his treachery is best understood in terms of faction politics, despite Josephus' ascription of his behaviour to his evil character (208). John had been accepted into the ruling circle by Ananus. He accompanied Ananus on his rounds of the sentries who blockaded Eleazar b. Simon and the Zealots in the Temple precincts (209), flattering Ananus and the other leaders of his party (210), But, though a man of considerable importance in his own right (213: *ou tōn asēmōn*) and with a growing number of followers among the most influential (213), he knew that he was fated to remain very much a junior member of Ananus' coalition because of the collapse of the rest of the faction that had been led by Eleazar b. Ananias and to which he had originally been committed.

The collapse of Eleazar b. Ananias' faction can admittedly only be surmised, since Josephus is never explicit about its aspirations after the first few days of the rebellion, but it seems to me striking that all those known to have been connected with it disappear from Josephus' record altogether after the fall of Galilee, apart from John himself and Simon b. Gamaliel. Nor perhaps is it accidental that, with John's transfer of allegiance to Eleazar b. Simon, Simon b. Gamaliel too disappears from Josephus' history, either because he also joined John and Eleazar b. Simon, and Josephus (who was inclined to be polite about him (*Vita* 191), probably because of the growing importance of his family, the descendants of Hillel, in the years after A.D. 70 in Palestine) was too embarrassed to admit it, or because his position within Ananus' party was so undermined by the defection of his friend and protégé John that he retired from the fray. If the late and confused rabbinic legend that he was killed by the Romans be reckoned correct, the former alternative must be considered the most likely.[9] In general, then, Eleazar b. Ananias' col-

[9] See Alon, *Jews, Judaism and the Classical World*, pp. 335–8, with further arguments and rabbinic evidence for a connection between Simon b. Gamaliel and the Zealots in A.D. 68.

leagues seem to have disappeared into obscurity, and Jesus b. Gamalas, the leader of the main opposing faction within the coalition, reached the peak of his influence in the coming weeks (*B.J.* 4.238,322).

John decided, therefore, that his future gleamed more brightly away from Ananus' suspicious (211) patronage, and the alliance with Eleazar b. Simon beckoned, not least because Eleazar may well have been rather flush with funds: Josephus claims in *B.J.* 2.565 that Eleazar's later influence was at least partially caused by the financial needs of the people and the fact that he had retained possession of the money taken from Cestius Gallus (564), while John had had no opportunity to take his own wealth with him on the panicky flight from Gischala (*B.J.* 4.106–15) and will have needed money to establish his position among the Jerusalem upper class.

Eleazar b. Simon and his immediate entourage for their part accepted John's leadership probably with some relief. It is likely enough that, without his aid, they would have accepted the treaty offered by Ananus and his party according to *B.J.* 4.215. They had seized the Temple only for protection and on impulse when threatened by Ananus (151), and their loss of the outer court (204) penned them into the area immediately round the sanctuary, from which their egress was barred by sentries; many of Ananus' party were still sufficiently relaxed about the struggle at this stage to pay poorer citizens to undertake the sentry duty on their behalf (207). It was true, as Josephus remarked (162), that it was not easy to dislodge determined defenders of the Temple site, especially given scruples about avoiding shedding blood within the precincts (205); but it was also dispiriting for Eleazar b. Simon's Zealot faction to be reduced to a state of impotence where they were incapable of leaving the Temple site, let alone acting as the legitimate leaders they aimed to be. On the other hand, a treaty with Ananus would mean a total end to their ambitions, as Ananus had already shown by excluding Eleazar from his command in October A.D. 66, and, given that blood had been shed by both sides in the most recent conflict, the Zealots were justified in fearing for their very safety once they were in Ananus' hands – this being the main lever used by John to persuade them to hold out against his former allies (224–6).

John of Gischala and Eleazar b. Simon, then, had need of each other for their separate reasons. Both, however, needed further support if Ananus' party was finally to crumble. Once their coalition was properly established, they might, and did, expect other young members of the ruling class to join them in seizing the power from which they had been excluded (*B.J.* 4.327); Josephus claims that twelve thousand (!) such men refused the invitation despite imprisonment and torture, though he names not one of them (328–33). In the meantime, however, the obvious coalition was with the Idumaean leaders who had been so studiously ignored by Ananus, and two delegates were sent to them, both named Ananias.[10]

A favourable reaction was elicited from the Idumaeans by the not implausible assertion that Ananus was preparing to betray the city to the Romans in order to ensure his continuation in supreme power (226). The accusation was plausible both because some of Ananus' coalition, including Josephus, had taken that route and also because successful treachery at this stage in the rebellion would indeed have confirmed Ananus' ability to control the populace on Rome's behalf, which was just the quality desired by Rome in selecting the provincials through whom she ruled. Just as important for the Idumaeans was the need to find competent generals to replace Ananus' colleagues in the fight against Rome. The problem was urgent for them, for they expected an attack on their own home ground within the next few months, in the spring and summer of A.D. 68.

When John and Eleazar offered them a share in power as partners in their rule (cf. *B.J.* 4.348, rather rhetorically stated), they were thus inclined to accept. When Jesus b. Gamalas on behalf of Ananus by contrast not only assumed their hostility by shutting the city gates against them (236), to their justifiable disgust (270), but insulted them by suggesting that they should either disarm and act as arbitrators between the existing factions (265) or leave the parties to fight it out among themselves (267) – no word about joining the ruling coalition in the struggle against Rome – their minds were made up. And so the Idumaean generals, of whose ambition that of James b. Sosas is later explicitly attested (523), threw in their lot with John and Eleazar and, aided by a storm, entered the walls and rapidly took control of the whole city (286–313). The destruction of Ananus' party began with their murder of the two main leaders, Ananus and Jesus b. Gamalas (316); others simply withdrew from positions of power, leaving Jerusalem to her new masters, and sur-

---

[10] One of the men may have been John's old associate Ananias b. Sadok, who is described at *B.J.* 2.628 as distinguished for his oratorical abilities just as the Ananias here (*B.J.* 4.230) is described as an able speaker. It would be surprising if none of Eleazar b. Ananias' faction was still alive and prepared to seek power in Jerusalem with John just as they had supported him against Josephus in Galilee (see above, p. 164).

vived in obscurity until the gruesome fate of some of them later in the war revived their memory.

The new coalition was to last with little change for a year, from spring A.D. 68 to spring A.D. 69. The state functioned throughout this period quite efficiently, with John providing a single leadership for the whole city. There were sporadic outbreaks of vicious attacks on the remnants of Ananus' supporters. Gorion b. Joseph and Niger the Peraean were both murdered, perhaps to prevent them reviving their old coalition (*B.J.* 4.358–64), and the consolidation of the new oligarchy was a pretext for paying off old scores (364), though only, be it noted, among fellow-members of the ruling class who might be potential rivals (365). Others, who had been more on the fringes of Ananus' group, such as Josephus' own father who, perhaps only through his son, had been a friend of Jesus b. Gamalas (*Vita* 204), were left at liberty despite their eminence: Josephus' father was not imprisoned until the siege was well under way in A.D. 70, and then not by John or Eleazar b. Simon or Idumaeans but by Simon b. Gioras (*B.J.* 5.533). But some of Ananus' supporters must have deserted to the Romans, since this explains the frequency of the accusation against those who remained that they intended to do the same. Others, however, sought, as John of Gischala had done, a new power base for their own careers within the Jewish state.

Their opportunity to find such a new base was not slow to arrive. The coalition of John, Eleazar and the Idumaeans was as vulnerable as Ananus' had proved to be. Some of the Idumaeans, including at least one of their leaders, James b. Sosas, who by August was apparently commanding troops in Idumaea (*B.J.* 4.521–8), broke away from the alliance and returned home, feeling that they were very much the junior partners in the coalition and that the violence involved in the destruction of Ananus' party was distasteful (352); in the process of splitting from their allies they liberated about two thousand citizens from the prisons. These prisoners, according to Josephus, immediately joined up with a rapidly growing group of malcontents excluded by John and Eleazar. This group was centred around Simon b. Gioras out in the Judaean countryside (353), and James b. Sosas himself was soon to join the same rising star (523).

Simon b. Gioras was by August in command of enough citizens of standing (510) to merit a full-scale attack by the forces of John and Eleazar (514). The failure of that attack, unlike the expedition by Ananus' generals nearly two years before, is a tribute to Simon's growing power. So, too, is the fact that James b. Sosas preferred his alliance to John's (523). Where did this support come from?

The prisoners freed by James b. Sosas are only part of the answer, for some of these must have been quite close associates of Ananus for John and Eleazar to have wished to imprison them, and Simon's suspicion of Ananus went, justifiably, so deep that he commenced rebuilding his faction in the Judaean hills only when he knew Ananus was dead and his party crumbling (508). On the other hand, many of Ananus' followers had owed their *primary* allegiances to a variety of leaders, as has been seen, and they might not all be tainted in Simon's eyes. But others, too, might join him. The Idumaeans' split from John and Eleazar had been prompted by one of Eleazar's followers – 'one of the Zealots', as Josephus calls him, coyly failing to identify him by name either because he did not know or out of embarrassment at admitting that someone still alive might have been involved in such revolutionary activities as have just been described (346). Presumably such a man might quite happily transfer himself to Simon, who had after all been Eleazar b. Simon's old comrade at arms in the original battle against Cestius Gallus, however, opposed they might have become now that the supreme control of the city was at stake between them.

John of Gischala, meanwhile, tried to prevent this dangerous flood of refugees to Simon b. Gioras by trying to reassure his old colleagues in Ananus' faction. He made a conscious attempt to keep his distance from Eleazar b. Simon's Zealots (389) and to assert firm control over his own followers (390). He could not in practice afford to break away from his new allies entirely, although friction occasionally broke out in small skirmishes (395–6), but even Josephus does not accuse him of full involvement in the worst excesses of the Zealots and Idumaeans (381–8) and this ostentatious moderation helped to keep him firmly in control of the city until March/April A.D. 69, when it was precisely envy of his power that finally broke his grip (566). Whatever Josephus has to say about John's followers at this time, claiming that with Eleazar's they ransacked houses, murdered and raped while indulging in the most polluting practices as in a brothel (560–3), it remains significant that it was never easier to escape from Jerusalem either to Rome or, from perhaps July A.D. 68, to Simon b. Gioras, than in the period of John's despotism, and yet many of the most 'respectable' citizens, including some of Ananus' old supporters, remained. Those citizens may not have liked the faction that controlled their government, but it was a government nonetheless, and not an anarchy.

John's monopoly of power was broken by those Idumaean leaders who had remained loyal to him throughout A.D. 68 – which may have been up to four of the original generals who had helped him to power, since only James b. Sosas is known to have joined Simon b. Gioras at some time in the summer (523). In March/April A.D. 69, they grew dissatisfied with their minimal influence over their ally (566) and, being militarily better equipped (571), rapidly reduced John and Eleazar b. Simon to the same powerless state of siege in the Temple from which their intervention had originally rescued them (570).

The timing of this coup can be explained only by the growth in the power of Simon b. Gioras outside Jerusalem. Within the city there were no powerful members of the ruling class left to whom the Idumaeans could look for support against John and Eleazar, for the man they chose as a figurehead, Matthias b. Boethus, seems to have been no more than that. A scion of the high-priestly Boethid line, his support for the Idumaeans on this occasion was presumably caused by his natural hostility to Eleazar b. Simon (and John by association with him) for abrogating the right to monopolize the high priest-hood that his family, along with a few others, had claimed for the last half-century and more (*B.J.* 4.148). Other members of his family may have been involved with the earlier government led by Ananus through their connections with Jesus b. Gamalas (see above, p. 144), but, despite his alleged popularity (*B.J.* 5.527), there is no evidence that Matthias himself had any political ambitions before the Idumaeans thrust him into prominence.

However, although Matthias' leadership was irrelevant to the Idumaeans, the powerful presence of Simon b. Gioras outside the walls was not. Exactly when Simon had encamped outside Jerusalem is not clear from Josephus' account, but by the time he had done so he had made clear his reluctance to enter into any sort of alliance with John and Eleazar b. Simon. These latter may, by contrast, have been quite prepared by now to share power with Simon, for they kidnapped his wife in the hope that he would lay down his arms to ransom her and, when he proved immune to blackmail, they returned her to him to placate his fury (*B.J.* 4.538–44). Perhaps Simon was pushed into a firmer stance than theirs by the number of political opponents of John and Eleazar who had fled from Jerusalem into his ranks. He would lose their support by any deal – for example, the Idumaean James b. Sosas might feel unhappy about any proposal to reunite with the men he had deserted.

The Idumaeans with John at any rate had a clear choice between factions as a result of this policy. Simon may already have proved his worth at keeping his promises to his followers, since in August A.D. 70

James b. Sosas was still found in the preeminent position within his party that he had been offered for his defection to Simon's side (*B.J.* 6.92), and this will have encouraged defections to his camp. But the final impetus for the Idumaean leaders was probably again the situation in their home province: Simon was fully in control there, with or without the connivance of the local populace (*B.J.* 4.534,556), and good generalship was urgently needed there in March/April A.D. 69, for the Roman attack was to come hardly more than a month later, in June, with an assault on Caphethra, Capharabis and Hebron (552–4).[11] All the Idumaeans moved over to Simon's side, joining their colleague James b. Sosas and thereby giving Simon control over all Jerusalem apart from the Temple site, where John and Eleazar b. Simon took refuge (577).

The Idumaeans who thus brought Simon b. Gioras to supreme power in March/April A.D. 69 were not to know that for much of the coming year Jerusalem was to be a city free from siege. The threatening manoeuvres of May A.D. 69 by Vespasian and his lieutenants came to an abrupt halt once again, with the proclamation of Vespasian as emperor by the eastern armies (*B.J.* 4.601–4), and Rome was not to resume hostilities between July 69 and spring 70, withdrawing at least some of the legionary force not just to Caesarea but presumably out of the country, since in A.D. 70 some of Titus' legionaries were stationed in Alexandria (658); other soldiers were kept occupied in the construction of a road from Caesarea to Scythopolis.[12]

During this time Simon's government became as firmly established as John's had been the previous year. The details have to be pieced together with care: Josephus was not only not in Jerusalem but had presumably followed Vespasian to Alexandria after receiving his freedom as a reward for his prophecy (cf. 622–9); the details given of Titus' route to Caesarea in early A.D. 70 (659–63) suggest that Josephus accompanied the march. His rhetoric against the men who were to lead the Jewish resistance to the final siege gains in vitriol what it lacks in knowledge. Nonetheless it seems reasonable to assert that Simon won the support of much of the remaining ruling class. The names of few of his close confidants are known – though

[11] For the time of year, see *B.J.* 4.550. Smallwood, *Jews*, p. 317 n. 99, notes that Josephus seems to be unaware that a year has passed between *B.J.* 4.450 and *B.J.* 4.550–5, whence the unchronological order of his narrative. But G. Schmitt, 'Zur Chronologie des jüdischen Krieges', *Theokratia* 3 (1973–5) 224–31, is surely wrong to deduce from Tacitus' failure at *Hist.* 5.10 to mention any campaign in A.D. 69 that these events belong to the year A.D. 68. Cf. Rhoads, *Israel in Revolution*, p. 144.

[12] B. Isaac and I. Roll, 'A milestone of A.D. 69 from Judaea: the elder Trajan and Vespasian', *JRS* 66 (1976) 15–19.

they included his nephew Eleazar (*B.J.* 6.227) – but one may stand for the rest. Ananus b. Bagadatus was one of his bodyguards (*B.J.* 5.531: *doruphoron*), responsible for seeing to the execution of would-be deserters to Rome during the siege. This man's membership of the Judaean ruling class is strongly suggested by the treatment accorded him by Titus when he deserted to the Romans in August A.D. 70, just before the Temple was destroyed (*B.J.* 6.299): although the tardiness of his desertion and his reputation for cruelty made Titus inclined to punish him on the grounds that he had come over from necessity rather than inclination (230), he was nonetheless treated like the wealthy deserters who had been honourably retired to the small town of Gophna a few weeks earlier (231; cf. 114–15).

It is also probable that the late desertion of a large number of junior members of high-priestly families (114–15) was owing to their participation in the revolutionary government until August A.D. 70.[13] For the same reasons as Matthias b. Boethus, they will have preferred to join Simon's faction rather than any other. The same is likely to be true of the sons and brothers of the king of Adiabene, who did not surrender until September (356); one of their countrymen is explicitly attested within Simon's forces earlier in the year (*B.J.* 5.474). The defence of the long circuit of the Jerusalem walls needed far more officers than Simon's 'bodyguards' could provide, even with the help of the Idumaeans, and many of the young members of the upper class took the opportunity for advancement. Thus, for instance, Mannaeus b. Lazarus, who successfully found refuge with Titus in late spring of A.D. 70 with many of the eminent citizens (*B.J.* 5.567–9), had, up to his desertion, been entrusted with command over one of the gates of the city (567).

Simon b. Gioras' control of the city made the alliance between John of Gischala and Eleazar b. Simon – always one of temporary convenience only – no longer useful to the latter. John's support had originally been accepted by Eleazar at a time when he could ensure the backing of the Idumaean leaders. That was no longer the case, and he had become a liability; Eleazar and his Zealots split the coalition and reestablished their independence within the inner court of the Temple (*B.J.* 5.5–7).

[13] It is impossible to do more than speculate on the earlier careers of the politicians mentioned here. The three sons of 'Ishmael who was beheaded in Cyrene' were probably sons of Ishmael b. Phiabi who had been kept hostage in Rome by Nero in the late fifties A.D. (*A.J.* 20.194–5, cf. above, p. 142). But whether and how they had intrigued on their father's behalf is unknown. Ishmael himself was presumably, given his eventual fate, sympathetic to the revolt.

Josephus is not clear about the timing of the split – perhaps he just did not know – saying only that it had occurred before Titus had left Alexandria (*B.J.* 5.2). According to this, the latest date would be the early months of A.D. 70, while the earliest possible time would be the late autumn of A.D. 69. Titus probably accompanied Vespasian in June A.D. 69 first to Beirut (*B.J.* 4.620) and then to Antioch (630). Though it is not clear whether Titus then returned alone to Judaea from August to October, it seems certain that Vespasian and he arrived on the borders of Egypt only in early November and did not *arrive* in Alexandria until the end of the month. The faction split in Jerusalem is thus unlikely to have taken place before December.[14] Eleazar's followers had, therefore, remained in alliance to John for at least six months and probably rather longer, and the fact that their factions are portrayed as divided by Tacitus or his source (Tac. *Hist.* 5.12.3–4) is entirely owing to the (quite significant) ignorance of the Romans about the internal power struggle in Jerusalem until the moment that Titus led his troops up to the walls in March/April A.D. 70, and does not show the division to have been long in operation.

The fact was, however, that Eleazar had in the final analysis little choice but to look for alternative political allies. His own supporters included some impressive men, as Josephus states (*B.J.* 5.6): Judas b. Chelcias may indeed be the son either of the Temple Treasurer of the fifties A.D. or of the friend of Agrippa I (see above, pp. 141, 143), since 'Chelcias' seems to have been a variant spelling of the latter's name (compare *A.J.* 19.355 to 20.140). But, although Eleazar could expect a reasonably sympathetic welcome from Simon b. Gioras himself, he knew that Simon risked alienating all the scions of the high-priestly families by having any truck with someone who had led so drastic an assault on their dignity, and the importance of their support to him has already been seen. Simon, therefore, at first kept aloof from Eleazar, much as John had tried to do, less vigorously, the previous year, and for the summer of A.D. 69 a stalemate resulted, with John and Eleazar shut up and besieged within the Temple precincts (B.J. 4.577–84).

It was probably a shift in Simon's position, probably in late autumn 69, that encouraged Eleazar to break off from John's faction in the hope of an alliance with the much more powerful group attached to Simon. That shift was caused by an increase in John's control of the area outside the Temple. Penned up within the precincts in April A.D. 69 (*B.J.* 4.584), John had won over a part, albeit

[14] For the movements of Titus and Vespasian, see K. Wellesley, *The Long Year A.D. 69* (London, 1975), p. 185.

a small one, of the Lower City by the spring of A.D. 70, for by then Simon is described as occupying only 'a large part' of the Lower City (*B.J.* 5.11). Josephus describes with some vehemence John's depradations from the townsfolk in the search for supplies, which would have been impossible if he had been confined to the Temple (*B.J.* 5.21). John's increasing power perhaps gave a handle to Eleazar to try to extract a political alliance from Simon in return for secession from John (*B.J.* 5.5–7); the possession of the inner court of the Temple where, through paucity of numbers, they could achieve nothing but await deliverance from John by Simon's forces (*B.J.* 5.8), can hardly have been Eleazar's end in itself.

Whether Simon accepted Eleazar's proffered alliance in the new circumstances, on the other hand, is unclear. If he did, that would explain the new viciousness in the assault on John, with Eleazar's control of the inner Temple giving Simon the first opportunity since his arrival in the city the previous year to win total control (*B.J.* 5.21–3). But John preempted the success of any new coalition by regaining the inner Temple by a trick, smuggling in armed men for worship at Passover (98–105), and Eleazar with his supporters accepted their failure resignedly, reuniting with John (104–5) and accepting his leadership against both Rome and Simon for the rest of the war (250).

By this stage, however, the struggle for power suddenly began to appear a foolish diversion from the task of defending the city from the Roman attack. It is worth re-emphasizing that the preeminence of this task was genuinely uncertain until the spring of A.D. 70. As soon as Titus arrived outside the walls of Jerusalem, the factions united against the Roman legionaries (*B.J.* 5.71–3) with considerable success (75–93), despite the fact that in the end Titus succeeded in setting up camp outside the walls (94–7). It may well have been realization of the need for unity that encouraged Eleazar's followers to accept a renewal of their old alliance with John, given the impossibility of joining up with Simon (98–105). All three factions turned their attentions against Rome.

Josephus claims that this first show of unity did not last (255), and that John's followers were inhibited from helping with the defences of the walls and the harassment of Roman preparations for assault by fear of attack by Simon's faction (266). In fact, however, this continuing suspicion – despite the rhetoric of 256–7, no actual interfactional fighting is described – cannot have lasted more than about a fortnight, for as soon as Titus brought the battering rams into action against the outer walls, John accepted Simon's offer of an effective truce to enable his men to participate in the defence of the city (277-9). This final agreement to cooperate was on about 23 Xanthicus, at the start of a siege of fifteen days which ended on 7 Artemisius (302). 23 Xanthicus fell only nine days after the start of the feast of the Passover at which John and Eleazar had reunited, since Passover began on 14 Xanthicus (98), and the original show of unity between all the factions had occurred soon before that (71-97), so the time elapsed between the first and second truces is not likely to have been much more than ten days.

At any rate, the eventual unity of the Jewish forces did not fragment even under the stresses of the siege. Only those who were suspected of going over to the enemy, i.e. Rome, were now at risk. Josephus gives so many names of successful deserters that it seems unreasonable to portray the discipline imposed on unsuccessful ones as a continuation of the faction struggle, much though Josephus would like to suggest that this is the case (cf. *B.J.* 5.527-33): it is significant that, since Titus liberated those prisoners of Simon whom he found in captivity (*B.J.* 6.412), he must have assumed that they had offended the rebel leader by being pro-Roman rather than through political intrigue within the free Jewish state. Commanders of cities under siege cannot afford to be lenient to such men. Even one of Simon's own officers, a certain Judas b. Judas who had command of a tower on the wall, was put to death in full view of the Romans and mutilated for trying to betray the city in June when a successful defence was still not impossible (*B.J.* 5.534-40).

For the last few months before the demise of the state the faction rivalry took on a new aspect. No longer opposed to each other, in the increasingly desperate battles against Titus' forces the Jewish contingents nonetheless retained their separate identities (cf. *B.J.* 6.72), vying against each other in the heroic defence of the nation (*B.J.* 6.92). Doubtless, if the Romans had been beaten back from Jerusalem, John, Simon and Eleazar would all have vaunted their achievements against Rome in their continuing attempts to win supreme control over the populace. But the Roman victory put an end to their ambitions and intrigues.

CHAPTER 9

TRENDS IN FACTION POLITICS
A.D. 50–70

The internal politics of the Jewish state from A.D. 67 to A.D. 70 have proved to be susceptible to the same kind of analysis as was appropriate for the faction struggle before and at the start of the war. Josephus' account is therefore to be dismissed when he marks a distinct break in the nature of the Judaean leadership after the middle of A.D. 67: just as he was misleading when he suggested that all generals appointed by the people before he was elected in A.D. 66 did not hold legitimate authority (above, p. 156), so he was mendacious when he asserted that all who remained on the rebel side after his own defection to the Romans were rabid scoundrels prevented only by their wickedness from realizing the uselessness of revolt.

For his own peace of mind Josephus was bound to condemn in this way his erstwhile colleagues who continued the revolutionary struggle after his capitulation. He even persuaded himself that his knowledge of the impiety of further resistance to the Romans had been vouchsafed to him by a divine vision (*B.J.* 3.352–4). But it is not necessary for modern historians to follow Josephus' prejudices, though surprisingly many of them do.[1]

The whole of Josephus' picture of the last years of the war is coloured by this apologetic for his own career. The condemnation of rebellion from Rome was a central motif of the *B.J.* but it naturally had to be held in check in his description of the period of the war when he himself was one of those who led the Jews. After his defection at Jotapata, however, Josephus had no need for such subtleties, for, ensconced as an honourable prisoner on the Roman side, he could no longer be held responsible for the rebellion by anyone.

The result is a stream of invective poured onto the heads of the remaining Jewish leaders. Precisely because Josephus was not present in Jerusalem during the 'reign of terror' which, so he asserts,

---

[1] Cf., among many, Rajak, *Josephus*, pp. 132–5; Schürer, *History* I, pp. 497–8. Baer, 'Jerusalem in the times of the Great Revolt', is an important exception to the general tendency.

gripped the city during the siege, he could allow full rein to his imagination in describing it. From the point of view of his apologetic the more abuse directed at the Zealots, John of Gischala and Simon b. Gioras the better. It would exculpate the Romans from embarrassing responsibility for the destruction of the Temple and indicate at the same time to the gentile audience how different Josephus and his friends were to the scum who had opposed Titus. Besides, the Jewish readership of the *B.J.* would expect *someone* Jewish to be blamed for the sin that had provoked divine hostility, and Josephus was determined that he would not be a scapegoat.

Josephus therefore indulged himself in vituperation: the rebels now were all brigands who terrorized the populace; the old elite was now the enemy of the revolutionaries; general gloom enveloped the whole city as soon as Galilee had fallen (though John of Gischala was surely right to point out that the capture of Jerusalem was a military operation on quite a different scale from the mopping-up of lukewarm rebels in Galilee). The best abuse is culled from Greek, and specifically Thucydidean, political vocabulary rather than Josephus' own imagination: the *stasis* was caused by revolutionary tyrants whose brutality to their compatriots and self-imposition on an unwilling population are constantly stressed. The leaders were all socially inferior, hence their enmity to the *dunatoi*, the old ruling class. Hence also the consistent portrayal of the Zealots as a group separate from the rest of the populace (precisely who they were being deliberately left vague), and of the Idumaeans as not really Jewish at all, although their rulers had in theoretical Jewish law as much right to leadership in the new Jewish state as did any of the other Jews from Galilee, Peraea or Jerusalem itself (see below, p. 223).

In fact, despite Josephus' rhetoric, there is evidence that many members of the Judaean ruling class of the pre-war period remained actively involved in the revolt right up to the destruction of the city in A.D. 70. Their role in the outbreak of the war has been discussed above (p. 167), but even as the siege of Jerusalem reached its height in A.D. 70 there were still many well-born (*eugeneis*) Jerusalemites within the walls who were moved by Josephus' appeal to them to surrender (*B.J.* 6.113), for it was then that the leading priests Joseph and Jesus, and no less than eight sons of three different High Priests with many other *eugeneis*, took the opportunity of almost certain good treatment by the Romans to escape from the city (*B.J.* 6.114).

Their presence inside the city at such a late stage shows that these men at least connived at, if they did not participate in, rebellion. The 'reign of terror' described by Josephus had been in full operation for almost two years, but these nobles still remained committed to their people and the war.

No other explanation of their decision to stay seems to me satisfactory. There were no physical restraints around Jerusalem to prevent their departure: the rebel leaders were never able to block all exits from the city and were reduced in A.D. 70 to psychological tactics to prevent desertions (cf. *B.J.* 5.454), while the Roman circumvallation was still incomplete throughout A.D. 69 (despite Josephus' rhetorical claim at *B.J.* 4.490). Furthermore, the ruling class could be optimistic about their possible reception by Titus if they chose to desert: not only could they expect a moderately friendly welcome by the Roman side (cf. *B.J.* 6.115–16) but the success of some of their fellows in finding such a haven under Titus' wing (cf. *B.J.* 5.420–2,567) was well publicized to them by the Romans and their Jewish collaborators.[2]

It was, then, presumably out of conviction that the two thousand 'nobles' released by the Idumaeans from the prisons manned by the Zealots in mid A.D. 68 continued to support the free Jewish state. They had every opportunity to desert to Rome, but they positively preferred to join Simon b. Gioras in the countryside or to stay in the city and connive with Simon for the overthrow of the Zealots and John (*B.J.* 4.353). Josephus' own brother and fifty of his friends captured on the fall of the city were sufficiently deeply implicated in revolt to be freed only after Josephus had petitioned Titus on their behalf (*Vita* 419), and, although an attempt was apparently made to ensure that only proven rebels should be condemned to formal execution (*B.J.* 6.417), Josephus writes that three of his close acquaintances suffered crucifixion until rescued by his intervention (*Vita* 420); it is probable that all these men, too, belonged to the ruling class.

Confirmation that the ruling class remained deeply involved to

---

[2] The failure of most of the ruling class to accept the Romans' invitation to desert meant, however, that this welcome was a guarded one. Alon, *Jews, Judaism and the Classical World*, pp. 278–80, 282 n. 37, 290, argues strongly that rich deserters were not received by Titus with quite the warmth that Josephus tries to suggest. According to *B.J.* 6.115, Titus offered even in A.D. 70 to restore rich deserters to their property, but in the meantime he confined them to the small town of Gophna (116). Those quartered in Jamnia in A.D. 68 were also in effect confined to open prisons (*B.J.* 4.444); this place was probably chosen to house them because it was an imperial estate. I assume that such details, which Josephus includes despite his wish that the Romans had behaved otherwise, are more likely to be true than his general statement that in A.D. 70 the majority of deserters were allowed to go wherever they wanted (*B.J.* 5.422). Neither Vespasian nor Titus trusted upper-class deserters to stay loyal to Rome, and their suspicions were reasonable.

the end may be found in Titus' attitude to the Jews after the war. His triumph was held for a victory over *all* Judaea, not just a rebellious section or class of the population. The Judaean ruling class was deprived of its land and power. Many were crucified or enslaved, and all survivors (and all Jews outside Judaea) were subjected to the ignominy of the *fiscus Judaicus*, regardless of their economic or social background (see below, pp. 231–9).

I would argue further that the ruling class did not only connive at the revolt to the very end but that the leaders of the factions in A.D. 70, who suffer from so much vituperation from Josephus, were also wealthy. The impressive origins of Eleazar b. Simon, leader of the Zealots, are admitted even by Josephus, as are those of his closest supporters (*B.J.* 5.6): it is significant that when the Zealots first gained power after the deaths of Ananus and Jesus b. Gamalas, they arrested the young men of good birth in the hope that they would join their faction (*B.J.* 4.327), so Josephus' general picture elsewhere in his history of the Zealots as fanatically opposed to men of distinction (cf. *B.J.* 4.357) cannot be correct.[3] But the origins of John of Gischala and Simon b. Gioras from within the ruling class are often denied and will need demonstrating in rather more detail.

John of Gischala is introduced by Josephus in *B.J.* 2.585–9 as a brigand who mustered four hundred men from the Tyrian countryside to plunder the villages of Galilee, and some have accepted this evaluation without question. The parallel account in the *Vita*, however, suggests that John's position was nothing like so disreputable. In *Vita* 43, John is said to have been opposed to rebellion in the first place and to have become involved only in order to help his fellow-countrymen to defend themselves against attacks from the neighbouring gentile cities (44–5). Such a comment is strange from Josephus, a bitter enemy of John by the end of the war, unless it is true, and it is striking that a number of members of the Judaean ruling class treated John as of equal standing with themselves. Even Josephus cooperated with him for some time (*B.J.* 2.590–2), entrust-

---

[3] Josephus claims, of course, that all these young 'nobles' refused the Zealots' invitation (*B.J.* 4.333); twelve thousand of them preferred death. (This number is one of the least plausible in all Josephus' writings.) The significance of the report is that Josephus should state that such an offer was ever made, since it hardly fits well with the rest of his picture of the Zealots. That picture is taken surprisingly seriously by some modern scholars, e.g. Rajak, *Josephus*, pp. 135–6. Josephus' portrayal of the Zealots in late A.D. 68 or early A.D. 69 running riot in the city, dressing up as women as they murdered and looted, is ancient invective at its most blatant. These are the same men who were later to defend the Temple to the last (cf. *B.J.* 6.148 and *passim*) and who produced in this period some of the best minted coins of the revolt.

ing to him (under pressure, admittedly) control of Upper Galilee, and his friendly relationship with Simon b. Gamaliel and other associates of Eleazar b. Ananias has been described (above, p. 164). He was rich enough to take advantage of a monopoly on selling Jewish olive oil to Jews in Caesarea Philippi or Syria (*B.J.* 2.591–2; *Vita* 74–6). But the main testimony to his upper-class origins is his treatment by Titus. The Romans treated him as a rebellious aristocrat rather than a bandit, being prepared to negotiate with him as commander at Gischala (*B.J.* 4.98–103), and John was thus condemned when the war was over to life imprisonment rather than a criminal's fate of enslavement or crucifixion (*B.J.* 6.434).[4]

Many modern scholars, though not all, have shown themselves ready to doubt the low social origin of John of Gischala. That of Simon b. Gioras by contrast, has never, so far as I know, even been questioned. He is usually taken as a son of a proselyte from the Decapolis city of Gerasa in Northern Transjordan (*B.J.* 4.503). His birth is seen as evidence of low social status and as a cause of his supposed commitment to social and political revolution, for which the evidence is said to lie in his use of freed slaves and the poor among his earliest supporters (*B.J.* 4.508). Josephus' description of him as a bandit in Acrabatene in north-east Judaea, and later at Masada, is usually taken at face value (*B.J.* 2.652–4). Many would add that part of his appeal to his followers lay in the messianic pretensions supposedly demonstrated by his appearance in a white tunic and purple mantle after the Temple was destroyed and his attempt to escape by underground tunnels had failed (*B.J.* 7.29). The case for a socially committed, messianic, proletarian leader, with the motives of a brigand but such charisma that his followers would die for him, is rarely questioned. Since Simon was overwhelmingly the most important Judaean leader by the end of the revolt, this characterization would, if correct, be important for understanding the motivation of the rebels in A.D. 70.[5]

---

[4] The argument against the portrayal of John of Gischala as a bandit leader is quite widely, but by no means universally, accepted, cf. U. Rappaport, 'John of Gischala: from Galilee to Jerusalem', *JJS* 33 (1982) 479–93, with dissentients recorded on p. 479 n. 4. The view upheld here requires the description of John at *B.J.* 2.585–9 to be ignored, but I think that the detail elsewhere in *B.J.* and in the *Vita* suggests that, contrary to this passage, John did not attack his fellow Galileans, cf. Cohen, *Josephus in Galilee and Rome*, pp. 221–7. It is hard to see how a poverty-stricken bandit (cf. *B.J.* 2.585) could have become a close associate of the rich Pharisee from Jerusalem, Simon b. Gamaliel, before the war (cf. *Vita* 190–2). Nor did Josephus have any motive to invent that association, which was embarrassing to him.

[5] See O. Michel, 'Studien zu Josephus: Simon bar Giora', *NTS* 14 (1968) 402–8.

This picture of Simon can, however, be challenged at almost every point. To begin, as with John of Gischala, at the end. Simon was reserved by Titus for the honour of a ceremonial execution in his triumph at Rome (*B.J.* 6.434; 7.153–4). Such a death was, so far as is known, accorded by Romans only to enemy chiefs of high status. When in 71 B.C. M. Crassus celebrated an ovation, much less than a triumph, in honour of his defeat of escaped slaves led by Spartacus, he was reckoned ignoble and mean to rate so highly a servile war (Plut. *Crassus* 11). Titus risked losing the propaganda battle in Rome to portray the Jewish war as a great victory worthy of an emperor if Simon could not be judged by all to have been a worthy opponent. Titus was not forced to choose Simon. There were plenty of other undoubtedly wealthy Jews captured in the sack of Jerusalem who could have graced his triumph (see above, p. 200), and Simon was never the only important general commanding the Jews: neither Romans nor Jews ever named the war after him, as the Jews were to describe the later Bar Kochba rebellion after its leader. It seems inescapable that Simon appeared to Titus to be a worthy enemy and that he therefore cannot have been a poor bandit but rather a respectable member of the ruling class.[6]

The evidence cited for the usual view of Simon is not in fact very compelling. The only reason to believe that his father was a convert to Judaism is his name 'Gioras', which may possibly be related to the Hebrew word *ger* which means proselyte. It is, however, hard to see how a description of Simon as a convert's son would help to identify him: there were many other proselytes' sons in Jerusalem, some of them, like the royal family of Adiabene, very influential, and many will have been called Simon since that was a common name. As a description, 'Gioras' would be useless, and *ger* and its cognates are found in use in this period only as nicknames attached to proper names. It seems to me more likely that 'Gioras' is the proper name of Simon's father, even though it is nowhere else attested, for it is not uncommon in this period to find names unique to one family.[7]

The information that Simon came from Gerasa is given at *B.J.* 4.503. In the immediately preceding passage about events in Judaea (the narrative is briefly interrupted by a section about the death of

---

[6] S. Applebaum, 'The Zealots: the case for revaluation', *JRS* 61 (1971) 166, suggests that Simon b. Gioras' death in Titus' triumph shows his lower-class origins, but he offers no evidence for this assertion. A further reason for Simon's execution may have been his impressive appearance (*B.J.* 4.504). Titus was concerned that only tall, fine-looking captives should be paraded in the triumph (*B.J.* 7.118).

[7] Hachlili, 'Names and nicknames', pp. 188–211, esp. p. 198.

Nero in *B.J.* 4.491–502), Josephus was describing the suppression of a place called Gerasa (487–9). This city was carried by assault, a thousand young men were killed, the women and children were made prisoner and the houses were fired. As a result Jerusalem was cut off (490). This Gerasa cannot possibly be the great city of Jerash in the northern Peraea, if only because most of the population there was gentile and remained firmly on the Roman side.[8] Either a different Gerasa must be postulated or the text at *B.J.* 4.487 must be emended. Since Vespasian was himself occupied in placing garrisons in Jericho to the east and in Adida to the north-west of Jerusalem, his strategy of sending Annius to Gerasa in order to invest Jerusalem on all sides (486) will have been best served if this Gerasa lay in north-east Judaea in the toparchy of Acrabatene; it is true that no remains of such a site have been found in that area and that the place is never heard of before or after this incident, but the same is true of other important sites mentioned by Josephus (cf., for example, Caphartoba, *B.J.* 4.447). In that case it is at least possible that Simon, whose original power base was in Acrabatene (*B.J.* 2.652), came from this Judaean town and not from the city of Jerash.[9]

Josephus describes Simon's proclamation of freedom for slaves and the abolition of debt not as part of a wider social programme but as a tactical move to win supporters for his aspirations to despotic power (*B.J.* 4.508). As soon as he had collected a strong force he was glad to accept many men of standing into his faction (510). His appeal to slaves and to debtors was as cynical a manoeuvre for popular support as the similar appeal by Eleazar b. Ananias' faction earlier in the revolt when the archives were burnt (*B.J.* 2.427). In neither case did such action indicate a policy for social reform or revolution. Simon showed no class solidarity with the peasants when it was to his

[8] Cf. C. H. Kraeling, ed., *Gerasa, city of the Decapolis* (New Haven, 1938). At pp. 45–6 Kraeling assumes that Jerash is the place referred to at *B.J.* 4.487–8, but he is then forced to state that Josephus' account must in that case be 'highly questionable even if not all untrue'.

[9] Gerasa is placed in north-east Judaea on the (somewhat weak) grounds of the survival of a similar name in a modern village by M. Avi-Yonah, *Historical Geography of the Land of Israel*, 2nd edn (Jerusalem, 1951), p. 122 (Heb.), cited with other views by A. Schalit, *Namenwörterbuch zu Flavius Josephus* (Leiden, 1968), p. 34. Schalit accepts Avi-Yonah's identification and takes this Judaean Gerasa as Simon's birthplace; F.-M. Abel, *Géographie de la Palestine*, 3rd edn, 2 vols. (Paris, 1967) II, p. 332, remains agnostic. Professor Isaac has made to me the ingenious suggestion that in place of Gerasa should be read Gezara, that is, Gezer, for which there is some support in the earliest edition of Rufinus' Latin translation. I hesitate to accept this plausible hypothesis only because the site of Gezer seems to have declined considerably from its earlier importance by the first century A.D.

advantage to instil terror into his opponents: he was quite prepared to kill any labourers whom he caught going out of Jerusalem once he began to invest the city (*B.J.* 4.557), and the victims of his rage when his wife was kidnapped by the Zealots were those unarmed and elderly poor who ventured outside the gates to gather herbs or fuel; they were either killed or maimed (*B.J.* 4.541–3).

The arguments for Simon's messianic pretensions are no more convincing. It is clear that he liked to appear impressive to his followers and to act in a regal fashion (cf. *B.J.* 4.510), but his white tunics and purple cloak were put on not to win their support but to scare Roman soldiers (*B.J.* 7.29). The significance of the white clothes is anyway ambiguous: he may have wanted to stress his coming martyrdom rather than his messianic power.

Finally, it is dubious whether Simon was ever a brigand. Josephus at *B.J.* 2.652 describes him as attacking the houses and persons of the rich in Acrabatene in late A.D. 66 or early A.D. 67. But if, as I have argued, he had been the official governor of the area earlier in A.D. 66 (above, p. 163), this charge must be read in the context of Simon's role in the faction struggle of the time. He had been deposed by Ananus b. Ananus, and when he refused to relinquish his command it was Ananus who sent an army to oust him (*B.J.* 2.653). Their mutual antagonism was such that Simon did not try to restore his fortunes until Ananus was dead (*B.J.* 2.653; 4.508). The rich men he attacked were therefore probably the supporters of the rival faction led by Ananus, in which case this was no random brigandage. The hypothesis that the imitation *pruta* coins of the second and third years of the war which are found outside Jerusalem were minted by Simon as part of his bid to present himself as the legitimate revolutionary government is very plausible.[10]

Similarly, Simon's connections with the sicarii at Masada after his ejection from Acrabatene have often been held against him as evidence that his prime concern was the acquisition of plunder (*B.J.* 2.653–4), but his relations with these brigands, as described at *B.J.* 4.505–7, show precisely that he was not their natural ally. With his unbrigand-like following of women, he remained separate from the sicarii, being at first allowed access only to the lower part of the fortress (505; it is not clear to which part of Masada Josephus refers). The sicarii regarded him with suspicion. Only later was he allowed to accompany them on their raids. And when he tried to tempt them

[10] Kadman, *Coins of the Jewish War*, pp. 112–13. On the symbolism of Simon's clothes, see Rhoads, *Israel in Revolution*, p. 147.

to support his more ambitious designs in the wider sphere of Judaean politics, they proved unwilling to follow him.

In sum, Josephus' vituperation against Simon b. Gioras may be caused by their political opposition in A.D. 66–7, when Josephus supported Simon's enemy Ananus, and by Josephus' desire to exculpate his own class from responsibility for the revolt by imputing lower-class origins to the rebel leaders in the final years of the war. Despite Josephus' slanders, it is probable that Simon was a member of the same class to which Josephus himself belonged, and that it was as an already leading figure that he was granted a command in the summer of A.D. 66. That Simon held such a command then seems almost certain (see above, p. 163), and his eclipse after Gallus' defeat at the hands of Ananus was to last less than two years. By A.D. 70 he was to rule supreme in Jerusalem. In many ways the internal political history of the Jewish state is the history of his rise to success.

It seems likely that, if Simon can be added to their number, it can safely be asserted that *all* the prominent figures who proposed themselves as national leaders between A.D. 50 and A.D. 70 were derived from the old ruling class. If this is correct, it becomes all the more difficult to discern good reasons for the continual conflict between them which culminated in the bloody war of the final years of the independent Judaean state.

Surprisingly little attempt to discover reasons for this conflict has been made by historians interested in Judaea in this period. The causes of the faction struggle within the ruling class *before* A.D. 66 have been almost entirely ignored.[11] As for the cause of the continued dissension *during* the war, it is usually asserted to be disagreement over the best way to fight or to come to a satisfactory accommodation with Rome. But, though this might just explain the political struggle in A.D. 66, it hardly provides a satisfactory model for the hostility of the three groups left mutually opposed in A.D. 70: the Zealots, John of Gischala and Simon b. Gioras all fought Rome with vigour, so this was not the ground for their disputes.

Historians have therefore tended to have recourse to vague and unsubstantial assertions to explain the continued existence of these mutually opposed factions. Regional differences between the groups, the hostility of the town to the countryside, variant religious practices, alternative social programmes and other causes have been

---

[11] The struggle is merely described and deplored by, for example, Smallwood, pp. 280–1. Horsley, 'High priests', pp. 44–8, argues cogently against Smallwood that the desirability or otherwise of opposition to Rome was not an issue for such politicians before the traumatic events of A.D. 66.

blamed. Josephus noticeably fails to make these factors clear, though it is hard to see why he should obfuscate if they were genuinely responsible for the divisions he deplores, but his silence is discounted. It is seen as chance that social and class divisions are not explicitly mentioned by him as the causes of the civil strife which he sees as the Jews' main sin.[12]

This is not very satisfactory. I have argued above (p. 168) that as early as November A.D. 66 the war against Rome was not an issue still in dispute: all leaders who remained in Jerusalem by definition accepted the need to fight. Regional differences did not dictate attitudes: John of Gischala's Galileans won popularity in Jerusalem (*B.J.* 4.121–8). Josephus nowhere states that townspeople fought those from the countryside; on the contrary, he stresses that the violent from each sphere joined forces (*B.J.* 4.138). The divisions between the factions are never ascribed to the teaching of the established Jewish religious sects and no group is said specifically to have subscribed to the so-called Fourth Philosophy (above, pp. 93–6). Finally, although all the factions except Josephus' allies are accused by him of looting the houses of the rich, none seems to have proposed a social revolution (see above, p. 204, on Simon b. Gioras).

It seems to me preferable therefore to accept instead the motivation which is consistently ascribed by Josephus to all the Judaean leaders both before and during the revolt. The aim of those in power was more power. In Josephus' terminology, they were bent on tyranny (cf. *B.J.* 7.261), that is, sole control unchecked by others.[13]

Tyranny, says Josephus (*B.J.* 2.275–6), was the aim of the politicians who caused chaos by their faction fighting when Albinus was procurator; from his parallel account at *A.J.* 20.205–10,213–14, it becomes clear that these 'tyrants' were Ananias b. Nedebaeus and his opponents, and that their struggle was simply for power (see above, pp. 138–9). Tyranny was also the motivation of the leaders throughout the war, as Josephus could hardly have made clearer in his estimation of John, Simon b. Gioras and Eleazar b. Simon: they are described as tyrants no less than five times in the prologue to *B.J.* (*B.J.* 1.10,11,24,27,28). The nation had throughout the war been

---

[12] Rajak, *Josephus*, p. 94, cf. pp. 91–6. For a list of possible causes, see Rhoads, *Israel in Revolution*, p. 148.

[13] Rhoads, *Israel in Revolution*, pp. 162–3, 182, provides a brief discussion of the term 'tyrants' in Josephus, but I think that he misses the point. Tyrants were not just those who seized and misused power (p. 163), for Simon b. Gioras had been granted his position by many of the citizens of their own volition, as Josephus stresses (*B.J.* 7.265). Tyrants are those who monopolize power.

full of the quarrelsome strife of tyrants, according to the speech attributed to Titus by Josephus (*B.J.* 6.343); Eleazar b. Simon, disposed to tyranny himself even in A.D. 66 (*B.J.* 2.564), could not brook a tyrant younger than himself and therefore broke away with his Zealot following from John (*B.J.* 5.5); Simon b. Gioras had also been bent on tyranny in A.D. 66 (*B.J.* 2.652) and it was this desire which impelled him to collect a force to attack John and the Zealots (*B.J.* 4.508); the same motivation had impelled John to power (B.J. 4.208), and, once achieved (cf. *B.J.* 4.389), it was his tyrannical monopoly of power which persuaded his Idumaean allies to desert him in A.D. 68 (*B.J.* 4.566). Josephus uses the language of tyranny consistently to describe the Zealots (*B.J.* 4.151,158,347). This is the main term used of John and Simon throughout the narrative of the end of the revolt (cf. *B.J.* 4.564; 5.439; 6.286,323,325, etc.).

To some extent this language of tyranny may be employed by Josephus because it was apparently in current use during the war in abusing political opponents. Ananus, addressing the people, called the Zealots 'tyrants' (*B.J.* 4.166,178), as did Jesus b. Gamalas speaking to the Idumaeans (*B.J.* 4.258). In return, the Idumaean leader described Ananus' coalition as a tyranny (*B.J.* 4.278). Josephus himself was accused of the same crime, being denounced by his enemies not only for wanting to rule in Galilee as a despot (*Vita* 260,302) but even for grander designs on a monopoly of power in Jerusalem (*B.J.* 2.626). Clearly the wide currency of such charges does not in itself prove their truth, but it must be stressed both that there is no evidence to postulate any basis for the violent faction struggle of the last years of the war other than this one, and that the fact that it is both explicit and implicit in Josephus' narrative makes it less likely to be simply the product of the historian's polemical invention than his other attacks upon his political opponents.

Naturally the causes of conflict between the factions *may* have been quite different from those put forward by Josephus, but in that case we have no idea what they were. It seems to me preferable to accept Josephus' account rather than invent explanations for which no evidence exists. The value of holding power in the independent state in Jerusalem from A.D. 67 to 70 is even more clear than that of the influence won by victory in the faction struggle before A.D. 66 (see above, p. 138). I take the great increase in the level of violence used by the factions after A.D. 66 (see below, p. 221) as confirmation that the rewards for which they fought were perceived as greater, and I can think of no reward other than power in itself for which independence from Rome would make this the case.

The factors which encouraged politicians to club together in their search for such power may now be discerned rather more clearly. So far as is known, policy was not important except perhaps when each man had to take the critical decision in A.D. 66 whether to support the factions pressing for revolt or to seek a compromise with Rome. Otherwise all members of the upper class who remained active in Judaea wanted the same sort of society centred on the Temple and its scrupulously observed cult.

Similarly irrelevant to faction membership was, probably, adherence to any particular sect. In Acts 23.6–10 it appears as if the Pharisees and Sadducees could be guaranteed to oppose each other, but, if this is indeed an historically accurate account, Paul ensured their hostility to each other in this particular case by pretending that his trial was on a rather thorny religious issue, the resurrection of the dead. In matters of public policy there was no reason for members of these sects to differ; perhaps only when there was discussion about prayers and sacrifices, concerning which they were particularly influential (*A.J.* 18.15), would Pharisees tend to stick together (*B.J.* 2.411–13). Thus Ananus b. Ananus was a Sadducee (*A.J.* 20.199), but his coalition after Cestius Gallus' defeat included a number of Pharisees, of whom Simon b. Gamaliel is only the best known, though it is worth noting that the relationship between Ananus and Simon, though friendly, does not seem to have been close (cf. *Vita* 191). Pharisees were evidently sometimes recognizable as such (cf. *B.J.* 2.411; *Vita* 21), perhaps because they wore ostentatiously pious clothes (Matt. 23.5), but there is no reason to suppose that they naturally cooperated with one another politically except in so far as the scrupulous observance of purity and tithing laws by such of them as were ḥaverim (see above, p. 82) encouraged them to consort with each other at meal times (see above, p. 83) and thereby also fostered social ties.[14]

[14] The extent to which the Pharisees remained an identifiable single political grouping after the Hasmonaean period has been hotly debated. There is very little evidence in Josephus that they did, which for some, e.g. J. Neusner, *From Politics to Piety: the emergence of Pharisaic Judaism* (Englewood Cliffs, N.J., 1973), pp. 45–66, is the end of the matter. But Schwartz, 'Josephus and Nicolaus', presents a strong case for attributing this silence to Josephus' deliberate suppression of incidents which might have implicated in revolt the sect to which he himself adhered. On the other hand, L. I. Levine, 'On the political involvement of the Pharisees under Herod and the procurators', *Cathedra* 8 (July 1978), pp. 16–20 (Heb.), points out quite rightly that the admission of political activity by some Pharisees in the first century A.D. need not imply that they acted *qua* Pharisees. Alon, *Jews, Judaism and the Classical World*, pp. 18–47, demonstrates that the view that Pharisees were ideologically opposed to political action in this period has no foundation and suggests that they

The main element in the formation of factions was not membership of a sect or party but the tendency of families to stick together, and this tendency has indeed been assumed in the detailed reconstruction of faction politics presented above (e.g. pp. 143, 146). It can most easily be demonstrated from the alliances of members of the high-priestly families. In A.D. 70 three of the sons of Matthias b. Boethus were executed with him for alleged treachery (*B.J.* 5.530). Soon afterwards, the three sons of the High Priest Ishmael went together to escape to the Romans, as did four sons of another Matthias (*B.J.* 6.114). It was assumed by the opponents of Ananias b. Nedebaeus in A.D. 63 that he would intervene to help his son Eleazar (*A.J.* 20.208–9). The generalized use of the term 'high priests' both by Josephus and by the New Testament writers suggests that members of such families often acted in concert (cf. *B.J.* 2.322,342; 5.36; 6.422; Matt. 27.41; Acts 4.23, etc.)[15]

Furthermore, political friendships could perhaps be inherited, for the High Priest Jesus b. Gamalas, who helped Josephus in A.D. 67, was also in touch with Josephus' father (*Vita* 204). The solidarity of the immediate family in political intrigue thus made marriage

were (therefore?) deeply involved in such behaviour. His argument that there existed two separate coherent Pharisaic philosophies which diverged on the issue of the correct attitude to take to Roman rule is much amplified by Ben-Shalom, 'The Shammai school'. This very plausible hypothesis has the attractive characteristic that it explains the appearance of Pharisees, even when they are described as such, on opposing sides in the revolt. I am perhaps too cynical in my belief that, since Pharisees were able to justify theologically both participation and non-participation in the revolt, it is most likely that their political alliances were in fact taken up without regard to their religious affiliations and that the divergent religious attitudes of the two schools were used by Pharisee politicians on both sides to justify policies which were in fact adopted for political reasons.

[15] I think that this is the only useful deduction about the distribution of power in Judaea that can be made from the use of this term. Schürer, *History* II, pp. 212–13, argues that the high priests were the 'real leading personalities' in the ruling class. The evidence for this assertion is that (a) the high priests are usually mentioned in the Gospels before other categories of rulers, and that (b) Josephus never uses the term *archontes* ('rulers') in conjunction with the term for high priests, which might suggest that he took the two terms to refer to the same group of men. Neither argument is strong. The precedence of the high priests in references to groups of influential men may reflect constitutional theory rather than the actual distribution of power (cf. *A.J.* 20.251), and the appearance of *archiereis* together with *archontes* at Luke 23.13 and 24.20 shows that not all authors reckoned the terms to be equivalents (though Luke may of course simply be confused). Even Josephus distinguishes on occasions between high priests and the powerful (*B.J.* 2.301), and between the high priests and the leading men (*Vita* 9). Perhaps the high priests are so often distinguished as a category of men who participate in government not because they were exceptionally powerful but because they can be easily identified as a group by their birth.

alliances a useful means to extend influence. Herod had used political marriages to excellent effect in the disposal of the surviving
female members of the Hasmonaean house, who were married off to
his own brother (*B.J.* 1.483) and son (*A.J.* 17.92). The great high-
priestly families followed his example, as is evident from the report in
John 18.13,24, which there is no reason to doubt, of the close cooperation of the elder Ananus (High Priest from A.D. 6) with his son-
in-law Caiaphas.

But Josephus insists that, under the pressure of impending war,
traditional political friendships crumbled, and, though the passage
in which he laments the splitting up of families and the opposition of
the young men to their elders (*B.J.* 4.132–3) is much influenced by
Thucydides' description of a similar situation (Thuc. 3.81–4), his
analysis can on this occasion be documented from his detailed narrative. Eleazar b. Ananias turned against his father, uncle and brother
at the beginning of the war (*A.J.* 2.418, 426). Josephus abandoned
his family when he capitulated to Rome (*B.J.* 5.419) and, at least in
public, his mother did not forgive him (*B.J.* 5.544–5).

Doubtless other families were divided by another general
phenomenon, of which these two are only examples, namely, the
tendency of the younger members of the ruling class to seek new
political alliances as greater opportunities for power arose with the
establishment of a Jewish state. Thus, Eleazar b. Ananias was probably not much more than thirty in A.D. 66 since his father was still
very active; at *B.J.* 2.409 he is described as a youth. Josephus was
aged twenty-nine in that year. John of Gischala was also probably
young; he was at any rate considerably junior to Eleazar b. Simon
(*B.J.* 5.5). Simon b. Gioras is also explicitly described as a youth
(*B.J.* 4.503). In the analysis of the rash men most keen on insulting
Florus and provoking a final break with Rome (above, p. 170), those
responsible proved to be young (cf. *B.J.* 2.303); I have suggested
grounds to suppose that they were the sons of the older faction
leaders (above, p. 171).

It is not surprising that men of this new generation were prone to
be particularly hostile to Rome. They had grown up in the immediate aftermath of the crisis caused by Gaius' attempt to place his
statue in the Temple. That episode had taken on legendary propor-
tions: Josephus' account is in many respects fantastic when compared to the contemporary narrative of Philo; Josephus clearly did
not know the details of events which had occurred in A.D. 40 when he
had been three years old, though the importance of the crisis was
manifest to him. He and his generation had been small boys when

Agrippa I's glorious reign briefly flourished and Jerusalem's splendour was raised to its greatest height under a popular Jewish king. Again, Josephus' narrative of Agrippa's rule is surprisingly vague compared to his detailed narrative of the king's early life; the years A.D. 41–4 had also apparently taken on the aspect of myth.[16] Furthermore, the continual troubles of the past twenty years and the success of faction leaders such as Ananias in winning political influence through violence may have suggested the viability of such means to gain power. If, as seems likely, these young men were more influenced by the events of their own lifetimes than by consideration of the centuries of Jewish history and long-past incidents in the relation of Rome to the Jews, it is natural that they should have been more keen on rebellion than their elders.[17]

At any rate, in the faction struggle during the war such men often proved prepared to abandon allies, including relatives, and to seek others when greater opportunities for power beckoned. John of Gischala was the supreme exponent of such cynicism (cf. *B.J.* 4.208–16), but he too was abandoned both by the Zealot leaders when they saw their own power threatened by him (*B.J.* 4.393–4) and by his Idumaean allies for the same reason (*B.J.* 4.566). As Josephus lamented, there were no principles or parties at stake, only the lust for power.

Up to A.D. 66 the means by which such power could be won were limited. Power derived essentially from the procurator and his support was essential to overcome rivals (above, p. 147). Popularity with the people was doubtless gratifying but it was effective only in so far as it encouraged the Roman governor to trust the politician in question because he might prove efficient at preserving good order in the province (see above, p. 150). The faction struggle therefore took place on a less public plane. The High Priest might sometimes try to use his court to silence rivals by semi-legal means, as Ananus perhaps did in A.D. 62 (*B.J.* 20.200), but not all incumbent High Priests were ambitious faction leaders – neither of the last two holders of the office had any known political role at all – and, so far as is known, no other politician could manipulate the Jerusalem court. For lack of any other weapons, ambitious men thus had recourse to violence to intimidate rivals and force them out of public life.

[16] On Josephus' ignorance about the former episode and reticence about the latter, see Smallwood, *Jews*, pp. 174, 187.

[17] This is brought out excellently by L. I. Levine in A. Kasher, ed., *The Great Jewish Revolt: factors and circumstances leading to its outbreak* (Jerusalem, 1983), p. 375 (Heb.), and by U. Rappaport, *ibid.* p. 417. Rappaport adds some interesting speculation about the behaviour of the youths in terms of 'psychohistory' and aggression.

Josephus naturally reserves most indignation for the occasions when such violence led to death. The murder of Jonathan b. Ananus early in Felix's rule led, he writes, to an atmosphere of intense suspicion: politicians watched their enemies warily and did not trust even their friends (*B.J.* 2.257). Political murder certainly became more common from that time: more than forty supporters of (probably) Ananias b. Nedebaeus are said to have tried to kill Paul in the heart of Jerusalem even when he was in the custody of a Roman tribune (Acts 23); when that failed they tried to engineer an ambush on the road from Caesarea to Jerusalem (Acts 25.1–3).

However, such extremes were clearly not normal. The violence of which Ananias, Costobar and Saul, and the others are accused in *A.J.* 20.213–14 is comparatively trifling. They beat up their opponents, exchanging insults and hurling stones, but their greatest crime was only the plunder of other people's property (cf. also *B.J.* 2.275–6) and they apparently treated human life as, in general, sacrosanct. Similarly, when a group of sicarii kidnapped the secretary of Eleazar b. Ananias and then other members of Ananias' household, they assumed, rightly, that Ananias would succumb to such blackmail by bribing Albinus to release other sicarii from prison (*A.J.* 20.208–10). At least before A.D. 66, the political struggle was not considered by its leading participants worth the risk to life.

Even this undramatic violence, however, needed manpower. Politicians had to raise troops for their urban gangs from somewhere.

Few if any of the Judaean upper class were able to rely on the support of the tenants of their estates since the relationship of tenants to landlords was contractual rather than customary and no system of local patronage seems to have developed (above, p. 67).[18]

Ananias b. Nedebaeus used members of his household (*A.J.* 20.206), but ownership of so many slaves was probably unusual, for Ananias was exceptionally rich.

Other politicians, such as Jesus b. Damnaeus, Jesus b. Gamalas, Costobar and Saul, 'collected' gangs of reckless villains (*A.J.* 20.213–14), presumably by promising financial rewards in the form of pay or booty. That plenty of desperate men were available for such dirty work was of course a direct result of the social and economic factors which left young males unemployed and rootless on the streets of Jerusalem (see above, pp. 60–6). Their motive for serving

---

[18] Against this view could be cited the fact that upper-class Judaeans were sometimes identified by their place of origin, cf. Hachlili, 'Names and nicknames', p. 199, which might suggest that such men had ancestral estates in those areas, cf. Joseph of Arimathaea etc.

such masters may thus have been entirely mercenary. There is no good reason to suppose that members of these gangs joined up in defence of any particular principle or class interest. It seems to me more likely that they were hired hands.

The role of the sicarii before A.D. 66 can profitably be seen in this light. Their behaviour is much easier to understand if they were bought men of violence than if, as is often suggested, they were principled anti-Roman terrorists (see above, p. 95).

The latter view is essentially based on Josephus' implication at *B.J.* 7.253–5 that all the sicarii subscribed to the Fourth Philosophy, but I have already expressed some doubt about this relationship on the basis of Josephus' own narrative (above, p. 96). In the historian's description of the last stand at Masada, the long speech advocating suicide put into the mouth of Eleazar, the leader of the defenders (*B.J.* 7.340–88), again gives the impression that the sicarii were devoted to freedom from Rome, but it has been plausibly argued that the sole function of this speech was to act as a literary balance to Josephus' own oration at *B.J.* 3.362–82, which advocates a precisely opposite attitude to self-inflicted death;[19] in any case the suicide of the defenders may be better explained by justified fear of the consequences of capture than by a devotion to the cause of liberty. Josephus' own suggestion at *A.J.* 20.162–3 that the procurator Felix hired some of the sicarii to assassinate the High Priest Jonathan would have been very odd if they were known to be totally committed to the fight against Rome.

I suggest, therefore, that what was frightening about these assassins was not their fanaticism or their ideology but the characteristic first singled out by Josephus, namely their method of concealing their daggers under their clothes and mingling in the festival crowds until they could attack their victims without detection (*B.J.* 2.256–7; see above, p. 145). Josephus is quite explicit that they killed not only their own enemies but also for money (*A.J.* 20.165), though the nature of their work made it impossible to tell who had hired them on any particular occasion: thus Josephus claims at *A.J.* 20.163 that the murder of Jonathan b. Ananus was arranged by one of Jonathan's friends, Doras, in return for a bribe from Felix, but in *B.J.* 2.256 he is not so sure.

---

[19] P. Vidal-Naquet, 'Flavius Josèphe et Masada', *Revue historique* 260 (1978) 3–21; D. J. Ladouceur, 'Masada: a consideration of the literary evidence', *GRBS* 21 (1980) 245–60. There is a useful and balanced reconsideration of the Masada story in S. J. D. Cohen, 'Masada: literary tradition, archaeological remains and the credibility of Josephus', *JJS* 33 (1982) 385–405.

Thus, the fact that, when one of Ananias' many enemies had put up some sicarii to kidnap his son's secretary and then some of Ananias' own staff (*A.J.* 20.208–10), the procurator acceded to his request to free further sicarii in order to ensure the release of these menials, suggests strongly that the crime of the imprisoned sicarii had in this case at least been simply that of acting as tools in the faction struggle. The whole curious custom of Roman governors setting free prisoners who (only after release?) took to brigandage (*A.J.* 20.215) seems most comprehensible if the prisoners concerned were only involved not in anti-Roman violence but either in pure banditry or in such civil strife; it seems to me to stretch credulity too far to believe that any procurator would deliberately set free committed rebels to create further trouble for himself and his successors. (The fact that the release of such men is said to have pleased the native population (*A.J.* 20.215) may have a social rather than political explanation: according to *B.J.* 2.273, these prisoners were ransomed by their relatives (see above, p. 63, on 'social banditry').) When Josephus described the faction leaders in *c.* A.D. 63 acting like brigand-chiefs employing their bodyguards to plunder peaceable citizens (*B.J.* 2.275), he may have written with total accuracy.

The methods of winning power underwent a gradual change in A.D. 66 as popular support became more crucial. It could be assumed that the populace was in general in favour of independence from Rome. Their fury against Florus after the massacres he perpetrated had been sufficient to prevent his troops marching through the city (*B.J.* 2.329; cf. above, p. 153) and they gave mass support to the rebel factions at the start of the revolt. Nor should Josephus be believed when he tries to claim that this enthusiasm had altogether waned by A.D. 70, for his aim in proposing such apologetic was to put all blame for the continuation of the war on the 'tyrants' Simon, John and Eleazar (cf. *B.J.* 1.10, etc.).

It is true that Titus apparently recognized that some of those who remained in Jerusalem up to the end had been less enthusiastic than others, and that these were spared when the city was almost captured (*B.J.* 6.386). Degrees of zeal in rebellion are hardly surprising. But when Josephus implies that the people of Jerusalem were less keen than the refugees who came to the city from outside (*B.J.* 4.135–6; cf. Tac. *Hist.* 5.12.2) he cannot be taken to exculpate all the local inhabitants, for elsewhere he claims the opposite, that it was non-citizens who were unwittingly caught up in the fighting when they had come to celebrate the Passover festival in all innocence (*B.J.* 6.421).

Independent testimony suggests that even in A.D. 70 the majority of the Jews in Jerusalem supported the Jewish state, for Tacitus commented on the final siege: 'There were arms for all who could use them, and the number ready to fight was larger than could have been anticipated from the total population' (*Hist.* 5.13.3).[20]

Nor is this continued popular support for the war hard to explain. Those who came from outside Jerusalem had been confirmed in their anti-Roman sentiments by their own sufferings, whether at the hands of their gentile neighbours whose outrages were left unchecked by the Romans (cf. *B.J.* 2.457–86) or at the hands of the Romans themselves (see above, p. 182). As for the city's inhabitants, there was every reason for them to accept the slogans meted out to them by the politicians eager for their support: they positively wanted to believe that they were fighting with God's help (cf. *B.J.* 5.459) in defence of the Law and the Temple, and, as the coins proclaim, for the holy city itself. It was hard to argue against anyone who might insist that all good Jews should fight on behalf of their brethren. Josephus' assertion that bearing arms against fellow Jews contravened the Law (*Vita* 26) will have met with instinctive assent. Freedom, which the coins stress, was seen as a self-evident good even by Agrippa II as portrayed by Josephus (*B.J.* 2.356–7), and it was for liberty that the Idumaean troops claimed that they finally joined the revolt (*B.J.* 4.272–82). All Jews would be attracted by such battle-cries.

Anyway, once their initial hostility to Florus had, under the leadership of ambitious politicians, brought them into revolt, the people would for practical reasons need to justify their own actions. Unlike the rich, the poor who fought against Rome could expect no mercy from Titus (cf. *B.J.* 5.447). They were bound to pay heed to

[20] There is no reason to believe that the people were in general unwilling to provide supplies to the factions, despite Josephus' invective against the troops' attempts to forage. In A.D. 69 and 70 most of the inhabitants will have been supplying Simon b. Gioras' men, since John had control of only a small area outside the Temple and Eleazar's men had use of the stores in the Temple (*B.J.* 5.21), and the loyalty of the masses to Simon is probable (cf. *B.J.* 4.574; 5.528). The supplies destroyed by one faction in order to deprive the other (cf. Tac. *Hist.* 5.12.3) will all have lain in the small area of the Lower City between the palace of Queen Helena of Adiabene and the border of the Ophel district. According to *B.J.* 5.254, cf. 5.24–6, all these supplies must have been contained in the area between John's forces and Simon's. This excluded most of the city, which was *firmly* under the control of one or other of them (*B.J.* 5.11,252–4). Few of the citizens will thus have seen their food stocks destroyed by their commanders, despite Josephus' general tirades about this calamity. There is no reason to believe that this area, on the eastern edge of the Lower City and south of the Temple, was particularly used as a general repository for supplies.

any slogans, prophecies or interpretations of portents that might make sense of their predicament (*B.J.* 6.286–315). It is possible that, eventually, their credulity reached such a peak that even the final disaster was interpreted by some as the woes of the end-time that would precede the messianic age, hence the smiling faces with which, according to *B.J.* 6.364, they watched the city burn. The ability of the desperate to delude themselves is considerable.

Their leaders were not slow to provide the people with the words to encourage such delusions for, lacking any natural authority in their own persons or from the offices that they held, they relied primarily on popularity with the masses to win power. The Jewish state was a genuine democracy in A.D. 66, for acclamation in the mass assembly gave authority to the faction in control (cf. *B.J.* 4.255) in conformity with ancient Jewish custom (see above, p. 110).

It was thus in an assembly that Agrippa appealed to the Jews not to revolt (*B.J.* 2.344) and that Ananias b. Nedebaeus tried to counter the effect of his son's cessation of the loyal sacrifices (*B.J.* 2.411). A similar meeting in the Temple was responsible for appointing Ananus b. Ananus and Joseph b. Gorion to the supreme command after Cestius Gallus' defeat (*B.J.* 2.563); according to Josephus, the generals elected there (*Vita* 341) could not be deposed without the consent of the popular assembly (*Vita* 309), which would not be forthcoming so long as they remained in the people's favour (*Vita* 194,237). In a later assembly, Ananus and his friends tried to organize opposition to the Zealots (*B.J.* 4.159,162), and it was probably by decision of the people (*demos*) that Simon b. Gioras was eventually invited into the city to oppose John of Gischala in A.D. 69 (*B.J.* 5.528; but 4.574 mentions only 'some of the natives of Jerusalem'). Finally, it was precisely because of the power of such mass meetings that, once the siege was under way in A.D. 70, Simon forbade public assemblies of all kinds 'for fear of treason' (*B.J.* 5.533): a mass meeting might depose him as easily as it had appointed him.

Popularity with such assemblies was achieved by a well-developed use of propaganda, as Josephus attests. Most blatantly, all politicians portrayed themselves as democrats. This was the height of praise for Josephus' ally Ananus in the eulogy pronounced on him by the historian in recounting his death. Ananus, despite his high-priestly birth, delighted to treat the very humblest as his equal, loving liberty, democracy and the public welfare. He excelled in rhetorical appeals to the people; he was a true leader of the *demos* (*B.J.* 4.319–21; cf. 4.210). Gorion b. Joseph is also described as a person of exalted rank and birth who was nonetheless a democrat (*B.J.*

4.358). Every faction tried to portray itself as the genuine representative of the people opposed to self-seeking tyrants.

But other methods too could be exploited to win over the people. Eleazar b. Ananias appealed to debtors (*B.J.* 2.427), as perhaps did Simon b. Gioras: the slaves to whom he offered liberty were expected to join the fight against Rome and are therefore likely to have been Jews who had presumably fallen into bondage through debt (*B.J.* 4.508). Eleazar b. Simon made capital from the poverty of some of the citizens by using public money and loot taken from Cestius Gallus to win popularity; presumably Josephus means to insinuate that he won influence by bribery (*B.J.* 2.564–5). In general, however, slogans of social or economic reform seem to have been used less than might be expected. No faction, for instance, is said to have advocated redistribution of land, though Josephus would not have been slow to condemn such a programme if any of his opponents could have been accused of contemplating it.

Instead, the slogans used by ambitious politicians were, characteristically for Jewish society, religious. Their content can be derived from Josephus' attempts to counter them: his polemic in the *B.J.* and *Vita* against his rivals takes up their avowed purposes and systematically claims that by their actions they defeated their own intentions (cf. *B.J.* 6.99–102).[21]

Each faction claimed that it was best able to defend the Law, the city and the Temple by preserving the purity and piety of the cult. The people accepted such claims with enthusiasm in the hope that in return for their piety God would be their ally and save them from the fearful punishment that they rightly expected from Rome. It was only sensible to follow the leaders most ostentatiously acceptable to God, just as it was only sensible to win divine approval by such acts of vandalism as the destruction of Agrippa's palace at Tiberias, which was ordered by the Jerusalem assembly because of the representations of animals it contained (*Vita* 65).

Unfortunately, as has been demonstrated above (p. 76), there was no agreement in first-century Palestine about what constituted pious behaviour; in itself, the fact that Josephus can produce his reverse polemic is testimony to this. Thus, when John of Gischala claimed to be protecting the Temple for God by fighting from within its precincts, Josephus retorted that such fighting was itself a pollution and that the proper performance of the sacrifices would be better ensured

[21] See the discussion of Josephus' techniques in Rhoads, *Israel in Revolution*, pp. 166–73.

by capitulation to Rome (*B.J.* 6.99–102). These were arguments about the nature of piety as much as about tactics in confronting Rome.

Despite these limitations politicians throughout the war claimed divine sanction for their action. The opponents of Eleazar b. Ananias, for instance, even claimed that stopping the loyal sacrifices was an affront to God (*B.J.* 2.412–14). It may be for this reason that faction leaders are sometimes explicitly described by Josephus as Pharisees: when, as on the occasion when the loyal sacrifices ceased, the issue under dispute was a religious one susceptible to scholarly interpretation in accordance with the oral law which they accepted, Pharisees might be expected to emphasize to the people their sectarian qualifications (*B.J.* 2.411) since they could usually guarantee to sway the people in regard to prayers and sacrifices (*A.J.* 18.15).

But the most powerful religious slogan used to commend their faction was that used of themselves by the associates of Eleazar b. Simon, the Zealots (cf. *B.J.* 4.161). This faction prided itself on being zealous for all that is good (*B.J.* 4.161; 7.270); the magnificent vagueness of their adopted name was probably a cause of its appeal. Being keen for God was obviously a desirable attribute, as the author of Acts 22.3 assumed when he wrote that St Paul used the term 'zealot' of himself in the fifties A.D. in referring to his time spent learning at the feet of Gamaliel. Some contemporaries may even have associated the slogan with the biblical account of the priest Phinehas who had discouraged Jews from intermarrying with gentiles in a particularly gruesome way according to Num. 25.6–15, for this Phinehas is described as a 'zealot' in the Septuagint Greek translation of the Old Testament and Josephus, in writing the *Antiquities*, seems to have been rather embarrassed by the Septuagint application of the same term to God Himself. However, there is no explicit ancient evidence that these biblical connotations of righteous priestly anger were ascribed to Eleazar b. Simon's followers, and although two of the Zealot leaders were certainly priests (*B.J.* 4.225), there is no good reason to assert priestly descent for other important figures in the faction, such as Judas b. Chelcias, Simon b. Esron or Ezechias b. Chobari (*B.J.* 5.6).

All that can be asserted for certain about the Zealots is that they portrayed themselves as keen to promote the preservation of a pure cult in the Temple and that they believed this could best be achieved by vehement opposition to Rome. Their leaders perhaps believed their own slogans: whereas John of Gischala and Simon b. Gioras both survived to be captured by Rome, the Zealots seem without exception to have died in the fighting (cf. *B.J.* 7.214–15, on the Judas b. Ari mentioned as a Zealot leader at 6.92). Such dedication appeared in marked contrast to the feeble conduct of the war by the friends of Ananus b. Ananus, and this fact alone provides a sufficient explanation for the people with justification finding the Zealots attractive in late A.D. 67. There is no reason to believe that the Zealots promoted any new political or religious ideology rather than a more active pursuit of war aims already accepted by their compatriots.[22]

Appeals to the people were thus important in the shifting balance of power between factions, but, as the war progressed, they gradually became less and less crucial. In A.D. 66 the Jerusalem crowd had been able to crush the sicarii led by Menahem b. Judas (*B.J.* 2.445–9), but when Ananus b. Ananus and his associates led a great mass of citizens a year later to crush the Zealots in the Temple (*B.J.* 4.159–207), their deficiency in arms and training (197) meant that, despite their numbers, they could achieve no more than occupation of the outer court (204); and when the Idumaean contingents later gained access to the city the crowd gave way to them altogether (307–9). As a military force the mob thus became irrelevant by early A.D. 68, and at the same time the faction struggle moved onto a new plane of greater violence more akin to civil war.

This increase in the level of violence was not immediate in A.D. 66. I have already suggested that the revolt had been precipitated by the reluctance of Ananias b. Nedebaeus to hand over to Florus for punishment, after their joke against the procurator had misfired, his young opponents, and that these opponents of Ananias probably included his own son Eleazar (above, p. 171). When the same Eleazar brought the loyal sacrifices to a halt a few months later, he demonstrated his opposition to his father's faction by setting fire to his father's house (*B.J.* 2.426). This violent action would hardly hurt Ananias disastrously since he was notoriously rich (*A.J.* 20.205,213);

---

[22] On the origins of the name, see H. P. Kingdon, 'The origins of the Zealots', *NTS* 19 (1972–3) 74–81; on its currency in the first century A.D., see M. Borg, 'The currency of the term "Zealot"', *JTS* 22 (1971) 504–12; on the alleged priestly origin of the Zealots, see Stern, 'Sicarii and Zealots', p. 297; against contemporary awareness of the Phinehas parallels, see Rajak, *Josephus*, p. 87 n. 17. On Zealots preferring to die rather than be captured, cf. M. Stern in Kasher, ed., *The Great Jewish Revolt*, p. 183. On the Zealots as a historiographical problem cf. L. I. Levine, *ibid.* pp. 367–76. R. A. Horsley, 'The Zealots. Their origin, relationships and importance in the Jewish Revolt', *Novum Testamentum* 28 (1986) 159–92, restates in greater detail the arguments put forward in the important article by M. Smith, 'Zealots and sicarii'.

its effect was intended to be symbolic. But when the sicarii who had attached themselves to his faction took violence further and killed Eleazar's father and uncle (*B.J.* 2.441), Eleazar was appalled and turned against them (*B.J.* 2.443). What this seems to show is that, as in the years before A.D. 66, human life still remained sacrosanct within the faction struggle even as full rebellion loomed.

To some extent this attitude remained normal right to the last days of the Judaean state. When Ananus b. Jonathan tried to win Roman gratitude (and preeminence in Judaea) by betraying Jerusalem to Cestius Gallus, he was not killed by the revolutionaries (as one might expect for such treachery) but simply hauled down from the walls where he was signalling his intentions and driven, with showers of stones, into his house (*B.J.* 2.533–4). Josephus' struggle against his rivals in Galilee in A.D. 67 similarly eschewed personal violence most of the time: he sat down to dinner with one of his opponents to console him for losing (*Vita* 330) and sent back unharmed the whole deputation which had come from Jerusalem to depose him (*Vita* 332). When an attempt was made by John and the Zealots in A.D. 68 or early A.D. 69 to blackmail Simon b. Gioras by kidnapping his wife with her attendants (*B.J.* 4.538–9), in the same way as pressure had been put on Ananias b. Nedebaeus in *c.* A.D. 63, it was assumed that he would capitulate, as Ananias had done, to protect the kidnap victim, though in fact he refused to bow to blackmail and went berserk until she was released unharmed without concessions (*B.J.* 4.544).

In general, those involved in the faction struggle were not usually attacked without due process of law. Even when describing the regime of John of Gischala and the Zealots, Josephus assumes that the rich (unlike the poor) sometimes had the benefit of a trial before sentence, although he mocks such trials as unjust (cf. *B.J.* 4.327,334–44). Political opponents were often imprisoned rather than killed (*B.J.* 5.533), even when the city was under siege in A.D. 70 (*B.J.* 6.380). Josephus narrates as a sign of the cruelty of John and Simon that even after the Temple had been destroyed they kept their enemies imprisoned (*B.J.* 6.432), but it is even more remarkable that those enemies were allowed to remain alive.

Nonetheless, inter-factional violence did increase after A.D. 67 and death became more common as the fate of the losers. Thus, whereas the deputation sent to remove Josephus from Galilee had quite a large force at its disposal (*Vita* 200; *B.J.* 2.628), they strikingly failed to use it against him, whereas in the battle between the Zealots and Ananus b. Ananus' followers in A.D. 68 stone-throwing was accompanied by use of javelins and swords (*B.J.* 4.200). Even then, however, the Zealots were left in peace when they took refuge in the inner court of the Temple; Ananus just posted guards to prevent their egress (*B.J.* 4.204–7) and did not attempt to evict them.

Josephus attributes Ananus' tactics on this occasion to his piety in not wishing to send unpurified soldiers into the sanctuary, but it should also be noted that he lacked the equipment to assault the Zealots where they were. This would explain why, according to Josephus, the quite gentle nature of the faction struggle was dramatically altered in spring A.D. 68 by the eruption of the Idumaean forces into the city at the request of the Zealots (*B.J.* 4.305–14). It has been noted that much of Josephus' account of the events of this year is tendentious (above, p. 198), but it is probable that he is right that the Idumaeans' intervention led to the first use of genuinely military tactics in the civil strife.

In Josephus' summary of the men responsible for barbarities in Jerusalem the crimes of the Idumaeans are given special mention (*B.J.* 7.267), and he accuses them of being particularly savage and murderous by nature (*B.J.* 4.310). More to the point, however, may have been their good organization and equipment and the fact that, unlike the Judaean Jews, they were used to a military role (cf. *B.J.* 4.231,234,243–4,571). Most of the Jewish troops used by the Herodian kings were probably recruited from Idumaea, which was the original Herodian homeland, and it is quite possible that the Idumaeans still kept weapons as a matter of course (cf. *B.J.* 4.234), perhaps (though there is little evidence for this) to defend their homes against desert raiders, and that the contingents they sent in A.D. 68 under four generals were more than just scratch troops raised to deal with the crisis of the revolt.[23] At any rate their military power was reckoned by all the participants in the internal Jerusalem struggle to be on a quite different level from theirs, and they were feared and courted accordingly.

It may seem strange that the leaders of such troops never sought power in their own right. Between A.D. 68 and A.D. 70 the Idumaean generals held the balance of power in Jerusalem. They supported first the Zealots and John of Gischala and later Simon b. Gioras, but they never tried to lead the nation on their own behalf despite their military ability. The reason for this reticence does not seem to have

---

[23] For the Idumaeans as a rural frontier militia, see Gichon, 'Idumea and the Herodian limes', pp. 27–42. I do not think that it is necessary to imply, as Gichon does, that the Romans had control over such a militia in peace-time; a local police force under local direction would be neither surprising nor unique, cf. A. H. M. Jones, *The Greek City from Alexander to Justinian* (Oxford, 1940), pp. 211–13.

been lack of ambition, for one of their number, James b. Sosas, joined Simon b. Gioras precisely because the latter offered him a position of influence (*B.J.* 4.523). Rather, the Idumaeans knew that they could never be wholly acceptable leaders to the Jerusalem populace and that without popularity it would be impossible to hold power. This disability emerges from the curious way that Josephus asserts that Idumaeans were only half-Jews (*A.J.* 14.403). This last assertion was technically quite incorrect, but such a slur was no less damaging for being untrue. The Idumaeans had been forcibly converted by the Hasmonaean rulers of Judaea as long ago as the 120s B.C., and in other contexts their full Jewishness is entirely assumed (e.g. *B.J.* 4.244,272–82,311). Since Titus also treated the Idumaean generals as important leaders of the revolt and therefore of the ruling class (cf. *B.J.* 6.378–80), they would have been well placed to take a full part in Judaean politics if they wished to do so, but only if the Judaean prejudice against them had not been so strong.

As it was, their violence was at the service of others. By spring A.D. 69 the factions were thus using towers, missiles, catapults and *ballistae* against each other (*B.J.* 4.577–84), and this level of conflict was to continue until they united against the Romans after Passover A.D. 70.

Both in the stone-throwing of the early stages of the revolt and in the more intense later fighting, these politicians must have relied on loyal troops in their search for power, and the question arises why such troops should support self-seeking ambitious members of the ruling class such as I have described. Enthusiasm for the war against Rome would not suffice to induce the followers of the faction leaders to risk death for the latter's ambitions, for all the factions claimed to be equally committed to the fight and accepted, however keen they might be to see some accommodation with the Romans, that to betray the city to the enemy would be evil (*B.J.* 4.249–58): even Josephus, who after his own defection ought surely to have approved of such treachery, vehemently denies that a rich man such as the Herodian Antipas would seek to hand over Jerusalem to Rome (*B.J.* 4.146). Some other factor must therefore be postulated for the loyalty of the soldiers to their factions. For their loyalty and numbers are remarkable: by A.D. 70 Simon b. Gioras was leading ten thousand men, the Idumaeans had five thousand, John had six thousand, and the Zealots had two thousand four hundred (*B.J.* 5.248–50).

There is no reason to suppose that these soldiers supported one faction rather than another in pursuit of any ideology, for the leaders seem to have offered similar political and social programmes. Nor was any one of them a religiously inspiring figure, though John and Simon were both personally charismatic. Other motives for loyalty must be sought.

Some of those who came from outside Jerusalem attached themselves to patrons from their home areas. Thus John of Gischala could command such great loyalty in his native town in Upper Galilee that Josephus was sometimes afraid to go there (*Vita* 235), and this loyalty, derived at least partly from John's successful depredations on behalf of the local population against their enemies in Gadara and the territory of Tyre (*Vita* 44–5, unemended), was reinforced for those Galileans who followed John to Jerusalem by the knowledge that he would reward them for their services more richly because he had come to power through their efforts (*B.J.* 4.558–9). Simon b. Gioras may also have relied on local support at the start of his career if his home town of Gerasa lay in Acrabatene where he had his original power base (*B.J.* 2.652; see above, p. 204). As for the Idumaean soldiers, they seem to have followed Idumaean generals only and to have always retained their identification with their area of origin.

Such support based on regional considerations will, however, only partially explain the disposition of forces. At least one Galilean preferred to fight for Simon b. Gioras rather than John (cf. *B.J.* 5.474), and the Judaean upper class, which included the Zealot leaders, lived in peace-time in Jerusalem and could not rely on the political support of any of the Judaean peasants, including even their own tenants (see above, p. 67). If they could nonetheless rely on plentiful support it was because now, as before A.D. 66 (see above, p. 213), they had available to them the forces of the bandits and brigands who so infested the country and who, for the sake of booty, could be easily induced to support a politician's ambition.

Perhaps the best evidence that these upper-class politicians still relied on bandit troops comes from the career of Josephus himself in Galilee. His own troops there included brigands, to whom he persuaded the Galileans to give regular pay in order to prevent them ravaging their territory (*Vita* 77–8), but bandits were also hired to oppose him: eight hundred men or so, followers of a brigand chief called Jesus, were bought for a large sum by the people of Sepphoris to prevent Josephus taking control of Galilee against the Romans (*Vita* 105–6). Josephus contrived to defeat this brigand by trickery and induced him to bring over his men to his side (*Vita* 107–11).

Presumably, however, the pay Josephus offered was too low, for his political rivals in the deputation sent from Jerusalem (above, p. 184) persuaded a brigand Jesus, who is probably the same man, to follow them in return for three months' pay (*Vita* 200), and, since this Jesus controlled a particularly impressive robbers' lair, his aid was of considerable assistance to them (*Vita* 246). It seems that Josephus was unreasonably mean when he tried to bribe such bandits to help him: he offered them no more than their pay (*Vita* 77–8) and gave the spoils he took, presumably with their help, from the Syrian inhabitants of the areas around Galilee not to them but to his relatives in Jerusalem (*Vita* 81).

It should be noted that Jesus, the brigand leader, was already in Jerusalem when he was contracted to join the deputation against Josephus (*Vita* 200), although, since the defeat of Cestius Gallus had occurred some months previously and the capital was no longer under threat, this cannot have been in opposition to Rome. Jesus, like other brigands, had apparently gone to the city to look for employment with one of the sides in the faction struggle. Menahem b. Judas, who had added his sicarii to the forces of Eleazar b. Ananias at the very start of the revolt (above, p. 153), had showed how powerful brigands could become in such service, and how they could become rich by looting (*B.J.* 2.440,442). Menahem's fate was also a dreadful warning to other bandit leaders to be satisfied with their role as allies of those who hired them and not to seek power for themselves (*B.J.* 2.442–8); the populace would not stand for them if they tried to make a political career for themselves.

As the Roman advance into Galilee and the Judaean countryside deprived such bandits of their lairs, more and more of them sought opportunities as followers of the Jerusalem factions. The Zealots in late A.D. 67 made use of the brigand bands newly arrived from Judaea (*B.J.* 4.135,138–9): the Zealot faction was thus comprised not of bandits alone, as is sometimes claimed, but of bandits led by priests and others of distinguished birth (cf. *B.J.* 5.5–6). Simon b. Gioras tried to use the sicarii on Masada for similar purposes but found them impossible to lure into his service (*B.J.* 4.507). Perhaps, after the fate of Menahem b. Judas they had become wary of intriguers from the ruling class who could turn so easily against their supporters. In gathering the force with which he was eventually to subdue Jerusalem, Simon nonetheless used many of the methods favoured by brigands in peace-time to ensure secrecy for their operations (see above, p. 63), withdrawing to the hills with his supporters

(*B.J.* 4.508) and in the lowlands making use of caves as hiding-
places for stores and for quartering troops (512–13).[24]

The bandits who thus provided much of the manpower for the
civil war seem to have chosen the faction they joined for reasons
common to all mercenaries, the prospect of pay and booty and the
likelihood of success. This latter calculation was essential, for failure
might mean death. Peasant soldiers, including even the highly competent Idumaeans, were apparently at a loss without firm leadership
(cf. *B.J.* 6.381). Furthermore even bandits had only paltry weapons
except for those provided by their commanders, though perhaps
only the civilian townsfolk were usually reduced to fighting with
improvised stones and slings (*B.J.* 2.423; 4.197,200). Such success as
Eleazar b. Ananias achieved after the start of the revolt may have
come from the weapons presumably captured by his faction from the
Roman garrison in the Antonia fortress (*B.J.* 2.430) and in Herod's
palace (*B.J.* 2.450), though by A.D. 70 the artillery taken from the
Antonia was in the hands of Simon b. Gioras (*B.J.* 5.267). The
Zealots may also have had arms taken from Cestius Gallus with the
rest of the spoils by Eleazar b. Simon (*B.J.* 2.564); at any rate, the
weapons they gave to their bandit supporters were very effective
against the mob attack led against them by Ananus b. Ananus (*B.J.*
4.197). Simon b. Gioras had possession by A.D. 70 of Gallus' artillery
(*B.J.* 5.267), though presumably in A.D. 66 his own raid on Gallus'
lines will have netted him only lighter arms (cf. *B.J.* 5.267). Above
all, as mercenaries the bandits preferred to follow commanders with
some evident competence at warfare. Even the best weapons were
useless in the wrong hands, as was shown by the inability of Simon's
men to use the captured Roman artillery until instructed by
deserters (*B.J.* 5.268).

I hope that this analysis may explain both Josephus' rhetoric
about the factions which opposed him and his failure to give any
deeper reason for the bitterness of their civil strife than lust for
tyranny and greed. The leaders indeed sought power, as he claimed,
and their followers sought booty. Lacking any more authority over
his troops than that of a paymaster to mercenaries, each faction
leader was bound to let his soldiers seek what remuneration they

---

[24] On the underground hiding-places found in many parts of Judaea, see Kloner,
'Underground hiding complexes'; cf. above, p. 60. Since many of these caves apparently contained coins of the revolt of A.D. 66–73, it does not seem to me necessary to
follow Kloner in insisting that they were all constructed for the Bar Kochba rebellion, though doubtless some were. It seems likely that in peace-time they were used
by bandits (see above, p. 63).

could from the rich civilians of Jerusalem (cf. *B.J.* 4.559). If the houses of the wealthy were sacked with particular enthusiasm (*B.J.* 4.560), that may be because the same pressures which had made these soldiers take up banditry in the first place had also engendered intense class hostility (see above, pp. 60–6). As so often, the civil war in which these peasant soldiers exulted and in which many of them died was not ultimately to the benefit of any of them. They fought against each other as the tools of the rich ruling class of Judaea, who exploited them politically in the free Jewish state just as they had exploited them economically while Roman power remained intact.

In A.D. 70 Titus' forces brought an end to the whole struggle for power. For the nation as a whole the final blow to the hopes of the faction leaders was a matter of little concern as all Jews in Judaea came to terms with the total collapse of their society and of the expectations of divine aid which had inspired all the rebels, of whatever class, during the war against Rome (see above, p. 216). In the aftermath of the destruction of the Temple the civil war that had racked the independent Jewish state faded into insignificance alongside the grimness of defeat in the larger conflict; it may be indeed that this is one cause of the obscurity of the evidence in later Jewish writings about the civil strife discussed in this chapter. Not only did the power of the ruling class of Judaea abruptly fade but so too did memories of their hopes and aspirations in the heady years before 70.

PART III

THE AFTERMATH OF THE REVOLT

PART TWO

DEVELOPMENTS OF THE THEORY

CHAPTER 10

THE ROMAN REACTION

The ambitions and divisions of the Judaean ruling class thus brought war onto their country.[1] Shunned by the Roman procurator after a series of mishaps, of which the most serious was the cover-up for the perpetrators of the joke which had hurt the governor's dignity, the rulers of Judaea clung onto power by courting popularity through the advocacy of rebellion. Their leadership turned popular discontent into full-scale revolt against Rome, and the Romans recognized this both by the power and ferocity of their response to the ruling class in A.D. 66 and by the exceptional violence with which the province was treated after its defeat.

The Judaean ruling class was consigned to oblivion and the worship of God in the Jerusalem Temple was brought to an end. Many rich landowners were imprisoned, enslaved or executed. Priests who surrendered when the Temple was already on fire were put to death on the grounds that, as Titus said, it behoved them to perish with the sanctuary (*B.J.* 6.322). His attitude to the rest of the rebels was as rigorous: many of Josephus' friends and acquaintances, including his brother, were rescued from punishment only by the historian's intervention with Titus (*Vita* 419), and three other acquaintances were saved by him only after they had already been crucified with many other prisoners; two of these had already suffered too much to survive (*Vita* 420–1). Most of those who escaped without physical punishment lost their land, which was confiscated by Vespasian and sold up to the highest bidder (*B.J.* 7.216),[2] and the rich were subjected

---

[1] To some extent Josephus is therefore justified in blaming the disaster on their *stasis* (see above, p. 19). In military terms, however, the effects of civil strife were negligible. It is hard to see how a united leadership could have opposed the Romans any more effectively than in fact was done. The strategic strength of the rebels lay in the supposed impregnability of Jerusalem.

[2] For this interpretation of this passage, which is often mistranslated, see B. Isaac, 'Judaea after A.D. 70', *JJS* 35 (1984) 44–50, especially p. 46. Josephus was exceptional in being permitted to keep his estates, cf. *Vita* 422.

along with other Jews to a much resented poll-tax of two drachmas, to be paid annually to Capitoline Jupiter just as it had formerly been contributed to the Temple in Jerusalem (*B.J.* 7.218).

This tax, the *fiscus Judaicus*, symbolized the deliberate destruction not just of the free Jewish state but of the religion and society of Judaea before A.D. 66. No thought of repairing the Temple was to be entertained and it is highly unlikely (though not impossible) that any sort of sacrificial cult was revived on the ruined site. No new High Priest was to be appointed to mediate between people and governor as the old ruling class had been intended to do, not because of a change in Jewish religious attitudes – both Josephus (*c.Ap.* 2.193–8) and Clement of Rome (*Epistle to the Corinthians* 40.4–5; 41.2) wrote about the Temple sacrifices as an essential element in Jewish worship even twenty or more years after the destruction of the sanctuary – but because of the new attitude of Rome and King Agrippa. Agrippa seems to have avoided all contact with the province after A.D. 70, and 'Vespasian, apparently having decided both that the cult was pernicious and that the local rich Jews were simply not trustworthy as local rulers, determined to do without both of them altogether.

According to Josephus, this Roman decision, which he much regretted, must have been reached after the war was over. The historian insists that throughout the revolt Titus intended the restoration to power of the most loyal members of the ruling class and a return to Roman rule through them. Even in A.D. 70 Titus, he wrote, was promising rich deserters that he would restore every man's property so soon as he had leisure after the war (*B.J.* 6.115). Josephus is at pains to record the way deserters were welcomed to the Roman side (*B.J.* 6.116).

However, Josephus may be misleading himself, or his readers, or both. Immediate tactical reasons for Titus' generosity during the war can be surmised. Deserters brought useful information to the enemy: Josephus himself may have both provided such intelligence and interpreted that of other deserters for the Roman high command (cf. *c.Ap.* 1.49). If Vespasian and his son had genuinely expected their upper-class Jewish prisoners to form the nucleus of the ruling administration after the war, they would not have found it necessary to compel such men to settle away from their estates, in Jamnia (*B.J.* 4.444) or, at least temporarily, in Gophna (*B.J.* 6.115). The imposition of restrictions on the movement of these men suggests that they were not trusted to remain loyal to Rome.[3] It is

---

[3] For these arguments, see Alon, *Jews, Judaism and the Classical World*, pp. 277–80.

thus probable that from some time before the war ended the Romans had already decided not to reinstate Jewish rulers in the country.

At any rate the Judaean ruling class did disappear. The installation of a garrison at Jerusalem (*Vita* 422) under highly competent legates of praetorian rank was intended to solve all problems of disorder. The mopping-up of pockets of resistance, including that of the sicarii on Masada, was the first task for the new governors, and the massive siegeworks erected against Masada show how seriously they took the task of eradicating the brigandage which had been endemic in Judaea long before the revolt.

The economic effects of the presence of such a garrison are unclear. Josephus states, rather surprisingly, that Titus gave him a new estate in the Judaean plain because his fields near Jerusalem would be rendered unprofitable by the presence of this garrison (*Vita* 422), although the availability of Roman soldiers with money to spend to buy his surplus might have been thought a bonus for a landowner in the area of the capital. Perhaps the tenth legion was itself granted some land to ensure its supplies, just as eight hundred veterans were given farms to settle at Emmaus, thirty stades from Jerusalem (*B.J.* 7.217), but there is no explicit evidence for this. Certainly no Jew is attested as possessing a large estate close to the city after A.D. 70, though the paucity of sources for Judaean history after Josephus' narrative ends makes any argument from silence only tentative.

Order was at any rate to be preserved by a much larger Roman military presence. The other function of the old ruling class, the collection of taxes, was presumably entrusted to the local gentiles who had so long been the Jews' rivals in Palestine. Josephus was correct when he wrote that Vespasian founded no cities on the land of the Jews (*B.J.* 7.217), but he did found a new city, Flavia Neapolis, in southern Samaria and he may have re-founded Emmaus in Western Judaea with the new name Nicopolis, although the testimony of Sozomen (*Hist. Eccl.* 5.21.5) to this effect is contradicted by Eusebius and others, and the coin evidence, which is in Sozomen's favour, is not conclusive. Caesarea was promoted to colonial status and probably engulfed the area of Narbatene, within which many Jews had lived in A.D. 66, into its jurisdiction. It is highly unlikely that the ruling elite of any of these cities will have included more than the very occasional Jew; it is exceptional that in Joppa, whose acquisition of the title Flavia between A.D. 70 and A.D. 96 suggests a mainly gentile population when the city was refounded after its destruction by Vespasian during the revolt (*B.J.* 3.427), an *agoranomos* in the reign of Trajan was named Ioudas and was therefore probably Jewish.[4]

The destruction of the power of the High Priest and the rest of the ruling class was not in fact of as much concern for the surviving Jews in Judaea as their grief for their own physical and economic sufferings and the destruction of the Temple and its worship. The ruling class had, after all, never been seen by the rest of the population as a natural elite. On the local level, civil disputes and religious problems could still be decided by legal experts just as effectively after the demise of the state as before, and in practice the Pharisaic tradition of legal interpretation, as advanced by the rabbinic schools at Jamnia and Lydda and from the mid second century in Galilee, gradually won dominance over rival methods of expounding the law, though it was probably to take many years before this dominance was achieved.

In the absence of the Temple, there were thus few functions of the old rulers of the country which were essential to Jewish society. An exception may be the fixing of the calendar which had been the prerogative of the High Priest before A.D. 70: it was clearly important for all pious Jews to know that they had celebrated, for example, the Day of Atonement on the right day, since it would be a heinous sin to err. It may well be, indeed, that the rabbinic leaders eventually won authority over the Jewish population precisely by the way they gave definitive guidance about the calendar. In A.D. 70, however, such overriding authority was far from theirs, and there is no evidence worth taking seriously that the Romans viewed them as in any respect the new Jewish rulers for mediating between them and the local population. It is indeed likely that the rabbis never achieved such standing in Roman eyes until the fourth century A.D. Not only had some leading Pharisees, including Simon b. Gamaliel, played a leading part in the war, but few if any of the leading personalities in the rabbinic schools after A.D. 70, apart from the descendants of Gamaliel, seem to have been men rich enough to warrant Rome's confidence. The rabbinical schools in Jamnia and Lydda quietly

---

[4] J. Kaplan, 'Evidence of the Trajan period at Jaffa', *EI* 15 (1981) 412–16 (Heb.), with remarks in *SEG* XXXI 1410. On the cities after A.D. 70, see in general Smallwood, pp. 342–3. The evidence for the cities and for the colony comes primarily from coins, but that for the extent of these cities' territories comes from Eusebius, *Onomasticon*, and other later writers. The methods used by M. Avi-Yonah (*A Map of Roman Palestine*, 2nd edn (Oxford, 1940); *idem*, *The Holy Land, a historical geography* (Grand Rapids, Mich., 1977)) to establish answers to these questions are cogently criticized by B. Isaac and I. Roll, *Roman Roads in Judaea* (Oxford, 1982) I, pp. 11–12.

evolved their new theology as their influence as interpreters of the Law burgeoned, but the Romans simply ignored them.[5]

It is, then, inescapable that the Romans ended all further co-operation with any Jewish ruling class in Judaea. The defeated status of the province was emphasized by the minting of coins with Greek legends about the capture of Judaea and depictions of captives in dejection which were struck in Palestine during Titus' reign (*BMC, Palestine*, 276–9). Such types, usually issued by Rome only to commemorate victory over foreign enemies such as Armenia – the suppression of Boudicca in Britain in A.D. 60, for example, went unrecorded on the coins – proclaimed that the Jews were a hostile people subjected by the might of Rome.

It should be realized that this Roman attitude is most unusual in the context of the normal suppression of revolts in the first-century empire. When rebellions were put down in Gaul, Pannonia, Dalmatia, Britain and among the Batavi, the Roman reaction was to destroy the troublemakers and restore the rest of the ruling class to their earlier prominence, hoping, usually justifiably, that peace would encourage an upsurge of pro-Roman sentiment.[6] Furthermore, the cults of defeated enemies were usually either wooed to Rome during the war to aid the Romans, or were worshipped at Rome in syncretistic guise within the cult of a Roman divinity, or, perhaps most common of all, were carried to Rome as one of the prizes of conquest.

Josephus at least expected the last of these to be the Roman treatment of the Jewish cult, since he claimed that in effect God had crossed over to Rome from Jerusalem and had taken up residence on the Capitol (cf. *B.J.* 3.354; 6.300).[7] He was bitterly disappointed, for the settlement of Judaea was, as has been seen, in stark contrast to normal Roman practice.

Special reasons for this harsh Roman attitude can be postulated.

---

[5] For these arguments, see Goodman, *State and Society*, pp. 93–118,175–81.

[6] See Dyson, 'Native revolts in the Roman empire'. Note however that Tiberius sold men of military age in Pannonia in 12 B.C. into slavery, cf. Brunt, 'Did imperial Rome disarm her subjects?', p. 261. S. S. Frere, *Britannia*, rev. edn (London, 1978), p. 176, mentions a coin of Antoninus Pius minted in A.D. 154–5 with a reverse type of Britannia and suggests that this commemorates the suppression of a revolt in the province.

[7] The attitude that the gods of a defeated nation should be destroyed is not unnatural in semitic societies, but among Indo-Europeans, including the Romans of the early Republic, the more common attitude was that of *evocatio*, the luring of an enemy's divinity to the other camp (cf. J. Bayet, *Histoire politique et psychologique de la religion romaine* (Paris, 1957), p. 122).

The Flavian dynasty needed a great victory to give it the prestige which, as a scion of a quite insignificant family, the new emperor Vespasian urgently needed. Hence the series of coin issues which proclaimed to Romans *Judaea Capta* and portrayed a Jewish woman in a state of defeated submission or a Jew with his hands tied as a captive (*BMCRE* II, 115–18 and *passim*). Hence, too, Vespasian and Titus celebrated a great triumph for their victory (*B.J.* 7.116–57), an occasion later commemorated by Titus with the still extant posthumous triumphal arch on the Via Sacra (*ILS* 265) and another, which no longer survives but which was erected in A.D. 80, in the Circus Maximus (*ILS* 264).

The Flavians emphasized their achievement further by building a temple to Pax, the goddess of Peace, and depositing in it the vessels of gold from the Jewish Temple, with the clear intimation that the Roman world had been saved from war only by the suppression of the Jews (*B.J.* 7.158–62). Untrue though this was, the claim was psychologically effective since Vespasian's seizure of power had indeed ended extremely bloody warfare but, since that warfare was of the civil variety and Vespasian's role in it had been as self-seekingly ambitious as that of the other contenders for the imperial throne, it was not possible to boast publicly about his achievement in bringing it to an end. This technique of tacit celebration of the cessation of civil war by openly marking a foreign victory had been used by Augustus in the erection of the Ara Pacis, and Vespasian's temple to the same divinity was probably built in direct imitation of the first emperor.[8]

But it is not obvious that all this exultation at Rome required the destruction which occurred of the Jewish cult and the ruling class in Judaea. It has therefore seemed reasonable to some to suggest that a cause for this violence might be that the Romans were already particularly prejudiced against Jews and Judaism as such before the war. The evidence for such prejudice is not, however, strong: in all the surviving Latin literature written before A.D. 70 only Cicero in the context of a speech for the defence in the law-courts (*Pro Flacco* 28.67) and Pompeius Trogus relying on Greek ethnographic sources are strongly disparaging rather than amused or contemptuous about Jewish religious practices.

---

[8] On the civil war, see K. Wellesley, *The Long Year* A.D. *69* (London, 1975). On the Ara Pacis, see *Res Gestae Divi Augusti* 12. The revolt of Saturninus in A.D. 89 is described on inscriptions as a *bellum germanicum* (*ILS* 1006), probably for similar reasons.

On the contrary, there had been many signs before A.D. 66 of Roman approval of the Jerusalem cult (see above, p. 15). There is no reason to take the evidence for occasional Roman exasperation with the Jews in the cities of Rome and Alexandria as suggestive of a deeper antisemitism. Jews were expelled from Rome in 139 B.C., in A.D. 19 and possibly in A.D. 49, but all three incidents were probably related to the need to keep order in the city rather than to any revulsion against Judaism. This is indicated perhaps most clearly by the way the expulsion of Jews was linked in A.D. 19 to the eviction of worshippers of Isis (*A.J.* 18.65–80; Tac. *Ann.* 2.85; Suet. *Tib.* 36). The only threat to Roman society was apparently seen in the spread of Judaism from the decidedly lower-class Jews of Rome to upper-class Romans like the high-ranking proselyte Fulvia (cf. Cassius Dio 57.18.5a; *A.J.* 18.82), and that this problem arose at all is evidence that Judaism was not abhorrent to Roman sensibilities but was, on the contrary, more congenial than a conservative emperor like Tiberius was prepared to countenance.[9] As for the continual struggles between Jews and Greeks in Alexandria which led Claudius to exclaim in exasperation that the Jews had fomented a common plague on the whole world (*CPJ* II, no. 153, lines 99–100), there is extensive evidence from both Philo and Josephus that this never had, nor was perceived to have, any religious dimension, and that the quarrel was purely over political rights and power.[10]

The hostility to Judaism which flooded the Roman upper class after A.D. 70 was therefore a result of the revolt itself. Flavianic propaganda now emphasized the restoration of the *Pax Deorum* by the victory over the impious Jews. Such a claim presumed that the rest of the divine pantheon had been disturbed by the existence of the Jerusalem Temple and rejoiced in its destruction.[11] The claims of antisemitic Egyptian writers such as Apion were taken up and further disseminated by Roman authors such as Tacitus (*Hist.* 5.2–4). Romans began to take it for granted that Judaism should be considered as a negation of religion since Jews worshipped no visible god. Against Jews no action could be impious (*B.J.* 3.536) since their cult was no more than a barbarous superstition (cf. Tac. *Hist.* 13.1, with the contrast between *superstitio* and *religio*). Not only was the Jerusalem Temple destroyed, probably deliberately despite

[9] See in general Smallwood, *Jews*, pp. 130–1, 202–19; M. Stern, 'The expulsion of Jews from Rome in antiquity', in *Yitzhak F. Baer Memorial Volume* (*Zion* 44) (Jerusalem, 1980), pp. 1–27 (Heb.).

[10] Smallwood, *Jews*, pp. 220–55.

[11] P. Fornaro, *Flavio Giuseppe, Tacito e l'Impero* (Turin, 1980), pp. 71–2.

Josephus' attempt to shift the blame from his patron Titus,[12] but the temple at Leontopolis in Egypt, which had not been the centre of any disturbances, was closed down (*B.J.* 7.420–36).

To some extent this new hostility may have been just a natural corollary of four years of fierce fighting. Roman soldiers during the war mocked their Jewish captives by trying to compel them to blaspheme or eat forbidden food and, when some refused, tortured them, occasionally to death (*B.J.* 2.152–3). When the Temple was captured the victorious troops offered sacrifice to their standards in the outer court (*B.J.* 6.316); it was perhaps a deliberate symbol of its desecration.

But it would still have been possible to incorporate the Jewish God in the Roman pantheon if Vespasian had so desired once victory was assured. The peculiar dietary and other habits of the Jews would not have proved a stumbling block, for, ever since the admission of the rites of Cybele to Rome during the Hannibalic war (Livy 29.10.4–8), Romans had grown used to housing cults whose more devoted adherents conformed to habits that the Romans found objectionable for themselves. The Romans fixed their own criteria for the worship of new deities brought to Rome: the cults of Cybele, Bacchus and Isis all looked rather different in their official Roman setting from the original religions from which they were derived. Adaptations of foreign religions by the Roman state became less common after the end of the Republic. But they were not unknown. In A.D. 218 it proved possible to enshrine the worship of the sacred black stone of Elagabal on the Capitol (Cassius Dio, *Epit.* 80.11.1), with violent senatorial opposition being evoked only because the young emperor wanted to make this imported cult the main rather than a minor part of the public worship of the Romans. In the same way the Jerusalem cult could have been brought to Rome in Roman guise if Vespasian had so wished.[13]

But Vespasian did not so wish. Evidently he and Titus, and per-

[12] Rajak, *Josephus*, pp. 206–11, argues strongly for the truth of Josephus' defence of Titus. Against its truth, see Alon, *Jews, Judaism and the Classical World*, pp. 252–68; M. Stern, *Greek and Latin Authors on Jews and Judaism*, 3 vols. (Jerusalem, 1974–84) II, pp. 64–7, with bibliography.

[13] On Roman methods of incorporating foreign cults, see J.A. North, 'Conservatism and change in Roman religion', *PBSR* 44 (1976) 1–12; Wardman, *Religion and Statecraft*. Romans found the lack of a cult statue in Jerusalem odd, and this might have proved a practical problem for *evocatio*, but a romanized cult could have portrayed the Jewish god in human form. Both Greeks and Romans did just this in the iconography of Isis and Byzantine Christian depictions of the divinity show that such representation was not impossible.

haps all their fellow Romans, had become deeply convinced that Judaism was a pernicious religion. It was to be tolerated in the private lives of diaspora Jews only because its suppression throughout the Mediterranean would be too vast an undertaking. Public sacrifices to the Jewish God and the conversion of non-Jews to Jewish practices were sternly forbidden, and the rooting out of proselytes and sympathizers with Judaism who had adopted Jewish customs reached something of a climax in Domitian's reign when, as Suetonius recorded (*Dom.* 12), even an old man of ninety might be hauled in front of a large bench of assessors to see whether he had undergone the operation of circumcision.[14]

And yet dislike of the Jewish religion did not extend to any racial hostility against Jews themselves, since Titus himself, who was the man primarily responsible with his father for this new Roman attitude of hostility to the cult, remained friendly to Agrippa II, who had once been custodian of the Jewish Temple, and happily spent the winter after the destruction of Jerusalem with Agrippa in Caesarea Philippi (*B.J.* 7.23); and Agrippa's sister, Berenice, was Titus' lover (Suet. *Div. Tit.* 7).

I wish therefore to argue that the extraordinary hostility of the Roman state towards Judaism as a cult after A.D. 70, which must have been caused by the Jews' behaviour during the war since it had not apparently existed widely before, derived from the Romans' fury at precisely the participation in the revolt of the Judaean ruling class which this book has documented. From the point of view of the Romans, that ruling class had been favoured as a provincial administration as much as that in any other province. They had repaid trust and favour with ingratitude and violent revolt. Their actions were therefore inexplicable except as the mad barbarity of adherents of a religion committed to oppose the civilized world. Therefore both the religion and the ruling class were to be altogether expunged for the sake of the empire's security. Jews evidently could not live in the Roman world in peace.

This political explanation of Roman antagonism to Jewish worship may be strengthened by consideration of the only other established religion in the world conquered by Rome which is known to have suffered from similar persecution. The successful suppression of the

[14] On Domitian's attitude and on the less rigorous policy of Nerva advertised by the coin legend *fisci Iudaici calumnia sublata*, see E. M. Smallwood, 'Domitian's attitude towards the Jews and Judaism', *CPh* 51 (1956) 1–13; L. W. Barnard, 'Clement of Rome and the persecution of Domitian', *NTS* 10 (1963) 259–60 n. 4.

druids of Gaul and Britain in precisely the period when the Jewish revolt was fomenting and crushed was, I believe, due to a parallel failure of Roman provincial administration to understand a social system so different from their own. Just as in Judaea, Roman ignorance about the subject nation's culture and Roman governors' attempts to impose their own values on the province led to unrest and, eventually, to revolt. Just as in Judaea, the suppression of rebellion was followed by an attack on the native religion which the Romans believed responsible for the revolt. Just as in Judaea, the Romans were right in their ascription of responsibility to the extent that native religious ideals made Roman assumptions about the relationship of authority to wealth unpalatable, even though they were wrong in the cruder conclusions that druidic religion, any more than Judaism, necessarily fomented anti-Roman nationalist aspirations among the druids' followers. In essence, when faced by societies in Judaea, Gaul and Britain where high status was accorded to many who were not rich, the Romans could explain such societies to themselves only by assuming that their 'unnatural' attitudes were the result of religious fanaticism.

That it was not druidic practices but the druids' authority with the Celtic population which shocked Romans is suggested by the very gradual way in which the persecution of the druids was imposed. Caesar, although he knew about druids (cf. *B.G.* 6.13), in effect ignored them in the conquest of Gaul, unless the reestablishment of druidic rites after 49 B.C., recorded with dubious accuracy over a century later by Lucan (1.450–1), reflects a temporary ban during his presence in the province. Augustus took the mild action of prohibiting any Gaul who had received Roman citizenship from participating in druidic activities (Suet. *Div. Claud.* 25). Then Tiberius had a decree of the senate passed which forbade druidism altogether (Pliny, *Nat. Hist.* 30.4 ff.) with the result that by the time that Pomponius Mela mentioned them, in *c.* A.D. 43, druids were reduced to hiding in caves and woods. A further attempt to finish off the suppression was carried out by Claudius (Suet. *Div. Claud.* 25). In A.D. 60 the campaign of Suetonius Paulinus against Anglesey may have had as its prime intention the destruction of the British centre for druidic operations (Tac. *Ann.* 14.30), although Tacitus states only that druids were among those who defended this stronghold and other reasons for Paulinus' campaign can be surmised.

The reasons for this savage attack have long been debated. As in their assault on the Jewish cult, the Romans consistently justified their opposition to druids on the grounds of the nature of their religion. Druids were accused of carrying out human sacrifice, and even cannibalism, along with other unspeakable rites, and the Romans claimed to be protecting civilization by imposing their ban (cf. Suet. *Div. Claud.* 25). Such charges of immorality were almost certainly false: human sacrifices had indeed once existed among the Gauls, but by the early Empire other symbolic rituals had taken their place. If druidic practices had really been so horrendous, it would be most odd if it took more than seventy years after Caesar's conquest of Gaul until a Roman emperor, Tiberius, took action to suppress them.[15]

The causes of Roman hostility must, then, lie rather deeper. The obvious alternative explanation, at which, indeed, the Roman sources themselves hint, is that the druids were implacably nationalist and opposed to Roman rule.[16] In favour of this view may be the name of one of the leaders of the revolt of A.D. 21, Sacrovir, which may suggest that he held some religious function, and the possibility that the Aeduan rebels seized the young nobles who were being educated at Augustodunum, the new Roman university which had been set up in direct competition with the old Aeduan capital and druidic centre Bibracte, in order to win these young men and their relations back to the Gallic way of life.[17] It has also been suggested that the religious inspiration which lay behind the uprising of a certain Mariccus, who led eight thousand of the Boian plebs in A.D. 69 against the Aedui and Vitellius (Tac. *Hist.* 2.61), was druidic in origin,[18] and Tacitus explicitly records the role of the druids in encouraging the Gauls to revolt on the death of Vitellius in A.D. 69 (Tac. *Hist.* 4.54).

On the other hand, simple nationalism cannot be the whole explanation. When classical texts of the first century A.D. attest extreme druidic hostility to Rome, that may reflect a reaction to, rather than cause of, Roman suppression. The druids had played no

---

[15] H. Last, 'Rome and the druids: a note', *JRS* 39 (1949) 1–5, argued that the Roman explanation should be accepted and that the druids were really so savage in the name of their religion that the Romans were genuinely disgusted; but see, against this view, D. Nash, 'Reconstructing Poseidonios' Celtic ethnography: some considerations', *Britannia* 7 (1976) 125. Note Dio's accusations of cannibalism against the followers of Boudicca (62.7), against Jews in Cyrene under Trajan (68.32.1), and against Egyptian rebels in A.D. 171 (74.4.1); such atrocity stories are perhaps not surprising.

[16] J. Vendryes, *La religion des Celtes* (Paris, 1948), p. 294.

[17] N. K. Chadwick, *The Druids* (Cardiff, 1966), p. 72.

[18] S. Lewuillon, 'Histoire, société et lutte des classes en Gaule: une féodalité à la fin de la république et au début de l'empire', *ANRW* II. 4 (1975) 530.

attested role in the Gallic opposition to Caesar, nor in the minor agitations which affected the country between 49 and 10 B.C.[19] Rebellions on every recorded occasion were actually led by war-leaders who are explicitly distinguished by Caesar from the druids as a separate status group (*B.G.* 6.13).

Thus, like the opponents of Caesar, the leaders of the rebellion of A.D. 21 were all war chiefs who sought power through independence (cf. Tac. *Ann.* 3.40–2,45). If druids were involved in instigating this revolt, they remained always as shadowy figures gesticulating in the background of the historical picture. And yet it seems to me certain that it was for those gesticulations that the druids were so severely punished, for it would be stretching coincidence too far not to connect Tiberius' institution of a total ban on druidism with this serious revolt early in his reign.

So what did Tiberius believe connected the druids to the revolt? Tempting though it is to assume that some particular aspect of their lore or teaching was held responsible for Gallic antagonism to Rome, there is no evidence for it. Druids were teachers and interpreters of Celtic law and experts in a form of philosophy and astronomy which, though doubtless misreported by classical authors who interpreted them in the light of their own traditions, may quite plausibly be supposed similar to Greek scientific speculation.[20] There is no reason to believe that any of this knowledge was subversive for Roman rule. If it had been, Augustus too would have had to forbid it to all Gauls and not just to those who were Roman citizens.

Roman hostility may, then, be most plausibly ascribed to the single aspect of druidism which simply could not be incorporated into a Romanized province. Druids enjoyed extremely high status among the Gallic and British populations even though many of them were not rich.

Druidic status was achieved by learning alone. As far as is known, no birth qualification was required, nor was a druid expected to own any particular amount of property. On the contrary, druids could be itinerant scholars, possessing no land and handing on their wisdom by word of mouth. They needed no great buildings, only the open glades of the woods. That such men should

---

[19] For opposition to Caesar, see N. J. De Witt, 'The druids and romanization', *TAPA* 69 (1938) 319–32; for troubles after Caesar, especially in 27 and 19 B.C., see Lewuillon, 'Histoire, société et lutte', pp. 486–511. These problems were probably caused by the census and taxation.

[20] Most of the evidence is found in Strabo and Diodorus, who got it from Posidonius' ethnography; cf. Chadwick, *Druids*, pp. 16–30.

be accorded high status was, to the Romans, not only uncivilized but extraordinary.[21]

Druids certainly did achieve such status. According to Caesar (*B.G.* 6.14), they had the right to stand somewhat aloof from the politics of the war-leaders, with freedom in an independent Gaul from the payment of tribute and the performance of military service. They were the main teachers of wisdom and the judges responsible for legal interpretation and arbitration on civil matters such as inheritance as well as for the excommunication of criminals from the sacrificial cult. According to Caesar (*B.G.* 6.13), they decided nearly all cases concerning property and boundaries. Their prestige may have been even further enhanced by a general belief that their wisdom gave them insight into the future, though it is possible that such powers were ascribed in Celtic society not to druids but to a separate college of seers.[22]

In fact, the functions and status of druids in Celtic society were precisely parallel to those of the expert interpreters of the Torah in contemporary Judaea. But the influence of the druids was even greater than that of their Jewish counterparts because, so far as is known, they all agreed on the way in which the ancestral laws should be applied and they stood together as representatives of ancient tradition.

There is every reason to suppose that these men retained their authority in Gaul in the first century A.D. Roman conquest had,

[21] A. N. Sherwin-White, *Racial Prejudice in Imperial Rome* (Cambridge, 1967), pp. 10–11. E. M. Wightman, 'Peasants and potentates', *AJAH* 3 (1978) 103 n. 35, and *Gallia Belgica* (London, 1985), p. 22, surprisingly assumed that druids were drawn from the 'noble aristocracy', i.e. presumably the war-leaders. This may have occurred on occasions: Cicero's acquaintance Divitiacus was doubtless an aristocrat (cf. Cic. *De Div.* 1.41.90) and Pomponius Mela, *De Situ Orbis* 3.2.18–19, wrote that the druids numbered Gallic nobles among their pupils. But there is no evidence that such birth was a necessary condition for druidic status. Caesar quite clearly considered the druids as a source of power separate from the war-leaders (*B.G.* 6.13–14), and his testimony should be taken seriously, cf. Nash, 'Poseidonios' Celtic ethnography', pp. 121–4. If the evidence of Mela and Caesar that a full druidical training could take up to twenty years is to be believed, this fact alone would prevent most young Gallic war-leaders learning more than a part of druidic lore unless they underwent the training after retirement from an active military life. Wightman, *Gallia Belgica*, p. 71, tried to avoid this problem by claiming that druids were those youths of the families of war-leaders who preferred learning to fighting, but neither Caesar nor any other source states that they derived from those families. Dio Chrysostom (*Or.* 49) wrote with insight about the conflict of authority between the rich Gallic 'Kings' (i.e. the war-leaders) and the druids who advised them.

[22] Cf. S. Piggott, *The Druids* (London, 1968), p. 97 and generally, on the functions of druids as Celtic holy men. For the other functions of the druids, see Chadwick, *Druids*, pp. 51–68; Nash, 'Poseidonios' Celtic ethnography', pp. 124–6.

after all, been over the war-leaders, not them, and it is a mistake to assume that Roman culture was so obviously superior to Celtic that the latter would naturally wither away. Even the most 'primitive' societies may combine savage religious practices and a preference for oral over written education while nonetheless achieving great sophistication in other spheres. Indeed, continued druidic power is proved by the Roman actions taken against them. If they had really lost all importance, there would have been no need for Rome to court opposition in the provinces by putting druids outside Roman law in Gaul and perhaps deliberately seeking them out for destruction in Britain.

In Gaul as in Judaea, then, the Romans tried to impose their own assumptions about acceptable criteria for status onto an alien society, and when their efforts did not succeed they attributed their failure to the stubborn and vicious religious instincts of the inhabitants.

But there the parallel between the druids and Judaea ends, for in Judaea the legal experts survived unharmed to teach their lore to future generations, whereas in Gaul the druids were so effectively suppressed that they were reduced to the magical practices that are so often the mark of the pursuit of power outside social institutions. Roman Gaul became a monument to the success of romanization and the druids became a picturesque folk memory.[23]

Gaul was easier for the Romans to deal with than Judaea because alongside the druids there had existed from long before Caesar's conquest a separate Gallic aristocracy whose basis for status and power was far more congenial to Rome. The Gallic war-leaders boasted in many respects the same justification for their power as their Roman counterparts. From well before the mid first century B.C. they had been the established leaders of well-administered states with central political institutions, coinage and so on. Their methods of political struggle were thoroughly familiar to a Roman aristocrat. Clientage had long been well established, with the massive use of wealth to bribe both other leaders and the plebs and to hire mercenary armies to win power.

These men, with their masses of clients and love of warfare and ostentatious expenditure, spoke the same political language as Caesar, who called them the Gallic 'knights' (*B.G.* 6.13). It was against this war aristocracy that Caesar had negotiated and fought, and it was they whom he finally brought into submissive alliance.

[23] On druids as magicians, see Chadwick, *Druids*, pp. 31–3. On Ausonius' circle with its sentimental claims of druidic descent, see Wightman, 'Peasants and potentates', p. 115.

From the Gallic point of view this was hardly surprising: warfare was the task of such leaders, and other leading personalities in their society, including the druids, had no part to play in the military struggle against Rome.

Caesar showed himself inclined immediately after the conquest of Gaul to treat these war-leaders as the *sole* aristocracy of the province. Many of the younger men were granted Roman citizenship and used as cavalry commanders in the civil war against Pompey.[24] If they were not already rich landowners they rapidly became such. Aristocrats whose wealth lay in cattle and whose political support consisted in the clients who herded those cattle on common land probably found that under the Roman tax system their pasturage land was treated as their private property and their clients were treated as tenants.[25] Some were doubtless granted land directly by Caesar as a reward for services in the civil war,[26] and, although the opportunities to rise high in the Roman army were rather more limited after 31 B.C., when, with the end of Octavian's fight against Antony, the need for a large supply of energetic military men was much lessened, there were still many Gallic war-leaders in command of Roman auxiliaries in A.D. 21 when the Aedui rose in revolt. Indeed both the leaders of this rebellion, Florus and Sacrovir, and their opponents such as Julius Indus (Tac. *Ann.* 3.42), had been granted or inherited Roman citizenship in return for their military services. The Romans treated them as a natural elite on the model of their own and assumed their absolute reliability as local rulers.

It must then have been a considerable shock to Rome when some of that apparent elite chose to rebel in A.D. 21, seventy-two years after their predecessors had been granted power in their land under Roman hegemony. Florus and Sacrovir were not crazy mavericks despite their eventual defeat, for Sacrovir in seizing Augustodunum hoped to blackmail others of the ruling class to join him by holding their children hostage (Tac. *Ann.* 3.43). He could therefore at least hope for the participation of such men, even though in the event he was disappointed. In setting up the Gallic ruling class the Romans

---

[24] Drinkwater, 'The Gallic Iulii'.

[25] This suggestion is made by Wightman, 'Peasants and potentates', pp. 97, 102. It would usefully explain popular resentment at the three censuses held in Gaul under Augustus. But the way that the Celtic system of landownership was integrated into the Roman system is still much debated, cf. Lewuillon, 'Histoire, société et lutte', pp. 564–9. E. M. Wightman, 'The pattern of rural settlement in Roman Gaul', *ANRW* ii. 4 (1975) 619, assumes, in contrast to Lewuillon, that much land was in private ownership before Caesar.

[26] Drinkwater, 'The Gallic Iulii', p. 828.

had, as in Judaea, miscalculated. I suggest that the element they had failed to take into account was, as the ensuing persecution showed, the influence of the druids.

For Caesar, and even more Augustus, had tried to hand over to the war-leaders the functions within Gallic society which had traditionally been reserved to the druids. In Roman eyes it was necessary that an aristocracy should not only be rich and lead in battle but that it should also control the administration of justice and the organization of religion (see above, p. 35). The Gallic war-leaders thus became, as magistrates of the new towns, judges of legal cases heard in the urban courts, and their decisions rather than those of druids were upheld by the Roman authorities. They became the priests of new urban cults in which Celtic gods were worshipped in the Roman fashion. The privileged among them were given the control of the worship of Rome and Augustus which was set up at Lyons in 12 B.C. under Roman instruction and with intensive propaganda disseminated on coins.[27] They boasted excellence in a system of knowledge different from that of the druids, for their enthusiasm for Latin wisdom was sufficient by A.D. 48 for Claudius to treat them as culturally Roman and urge their admission to the Roman senate (Tac. *Ann.* 11.23–4; *CIL* XIII 1668).

In the process of usurping the druids' role as cultural, religious and legal experts, the Gallic war-leaders must have realized the danger that they, like the Judaean upper class, would lose the authority they needed to control the populace on behalf of Rome. Their clients had followed them while Gaul was free, and indeed during their adventures in the Roman civil wars, because of their qualities as warriors – but now there were no more wars to fight. In the eyes of the Gauls they had never had any right whatsoever to decide on law or set themselves up as priests.[28] Particularly when Roman censuses seemed increasingly to favour the material prosperity of the upper class in which they were included to the detriment of the poor, they must have become aware of the possibility of popular disaffection.

One obvious way to preserve their status in local eyes was for

[27] D. Fishwick, 'The Temple of the Three Gauls', *JRS* 62 (1972) 46–52; Wightman, *Gallia Belgica*, pp. 72,177–87. On the new towns, see J. F. Drinkwater, *Roman Gaul: the three provinces, 58 B.C.–A.D. 260* (Beckenham, 1983), pp. 141–60; cf. also pp. 103–10 on their administration, pp. 144,147, on the urban cults.
[28] There is no reason to doubt that all Gallic courts normally took account of Celtic customary law in civil cases, since few of the litigants will have been Roman citizens in this period, but only legal experts, i.e. druids, will have been trusted by ordinary Gauls to interpret the law correctly.

themselves to seek druidical wisdom, which was not in itself incompatible with the lifestyle either of a war-leader or of a Roman citizen as the career of Divitiacus had shown (above, n. 21). It is clear that some sought this route to strengthen their authority: Augustus' prohibition on Roman citizens indulging in druidic practices must have been directed at them, for only war-leaders in Gaul had been honoured by Roman citizenship at this early date. Augustus presumably hoped to prevent the war-leaders becoming druids on the grounds that if they admitted their need for druidical wisdom other druids, including poor ones, could claim an equal right to status among the Gauls.

Augustus' attempt did not succeed entirely, for Pomponius Mela, writing under Tiberius and Claudius, records that the nobles of Gaul still went to the druids for instruction (*De Situ Orbis* 3.2.19), but it may have been sufficiently effective to push some of the war-leaders into drastic measures to preserve their local power base. At any rate, they reverted to their old role. Presenting themselves as warriors and appealing to freedom and national solidarity and the self-interest of debtors, they led their people into revolt.

This rebellion in A.D. 21 was successfully crushed and the elimination of the druids soon followed. With their suppression the Gauls lost any hope of a source of authority or wisdom alternative to that of the remaining descendants of the war-leaders. This upper class could thus now afford to content itself with the rich prizes offered by Rome. They ceased to worry about their status in local eyes now that the druids were no longer in evidence to shake confidence in their authority.[29]

The upper class in Judaea had been more deeply implicated in revolt than that in Gaul, and, unlike the Gauls, they were not given a second chance. The Jewish rulers lost all power after A.D. 70 and were never given an opportunity to regain it. The problems of both Gaul and Judaea, however, equally reflect the same deep flaw in the nature of Roman provincial administration which arose from Rome's failure to understand the population she ruled.

The Roman government was culpably ignorant about the social structures of the subject peoples of the empire. This ignorance was deep and ingrained in the whole Roman mental framework through which they understood other nations. Despite the sterling efforts of

[29] On the prosperous and peaceful development of Gaul under the High Empire, see Drinkwater, *Roman Gaul*, pp. 186–211.

Greeks like Polybius and Posidonius in the collection of ethnographic details, it did not occur to any Roman to use that information to try to understand the anthropology of the peoples concerned. The details amused them as they noted the strange differences revealed between foreign behaviour and Roman. Similarities, like the 'Stoic' philosophy of the druids, were assumed to show how everyone, in essence, thought the same way because that was the natural way to think. When native writers like Josephus tried to put the record straight about their own peoples, their writings were ignored by the aristocratic Romans at whom they were aimed.[30]

In other systems of imperial government such ignorance might not matter, but for the Romans it was potentially disastrous. Roman rule was almost always activated by pressure from below. Provincials requested and thanked, blamed and praised, and emperors reacted accordingly. It was rare that emperors or even governors initiated any action at all, except in regard to special projects that were expected to bring fame and glory.[31]

This passive system worked excellently in provinces where an elite trusted by the populace was also treated by the Romans as representatives of that populace. Thus it operated well in Greece and Asia Minor; indeed, most of the evidence for the system is found in the plentiful inscriptions from those areas. It may well have been successful in other provinces from which there is less evidence: the silence of the sources elsewhere may sometimes have occurred only through chance, and it is possible that a ruling class that did not bother the imperial government kept quiet because the people were contented rather than out of a refusal to cooperate with Rome.

But the crucial moment when the success or failure of Roman administration in any province was decided was the one time when the Roman government did have to make a positive, active decision. That moment came at the very beginning of direct Roman rule over a new province, when some Roman official, perhaps usually the emperor, had to decide which group of provincials would constitute the ruling class to which Rome would entrust local authority and whose representations alone would be accepted as the genuine voice of the people. It was this crucial decision, I have argued, which went wrong in Gaul and in Judaea, with disastrous results.

[30] A. D. Momigliano, *Alien Wisdom: the limits of hellenization* (Cambridge, 1975), pp. 91–3.
[31] Much evidence that this was the normal system of Roman government can be found in Millar, *Emperor in the Roman World*; cf. esp. *ibid.* pp. 363–456, on the provinces.

The importance of this decision has been overlooked in modern studies of Roman provincial administration. Modern scholars' lack of concern reflects the attitude of the Roman sources. Romans believed that they knew an aristocrat when they saw him, that there could be no dispute over what sort of person should rule a province, and that, naturally, the body of men to whom they had entrusted power consisted entirely and only of such suitably qualified men.

The rulers so chosen were not likely to blow the gaff on the system when it went wrong, for by doing so they would lose, in the eyes of Rome, their own credentials for power. Since almost all surviving Greek and Latin literature of the early imperial period emanates from this ruling class or from those writing under their patronage, there is in many provinces no way of knowing whether or not the Roman assumption that landed wealth deserved political power was generally accepted by the population. The revolt in Judaea, in contrast, shows clearly, both because of the abundance of evidence not from the ruling class and because of the inside information of Josephus, what could go wrong when the Roman choice went awry.

For sixty years Roman procurators tried with increasingly bad temper to govern through local rulers who should never have been granted power in the first place. The requests and embassies flooded in to the governor and the emperor in the normal way; the Roman administration reacted more or less in the approved fashion; and the whole system nonetheless collapsed because the Judaean rulers were not equipped with the local prestige that would enable them to do their allotted task. In desperation at their invidious position, they rebelled.

The same Roman ignorance about Jewish society and culture which had led Augustus to trust an incompetent upper class as rulers of the province just because they were rich misled Vespasian and Titus into believing that the failure of that upper class, and its resulting disloyalty to Rome, had been wilful. Deliberate refusal by Judaea's rulers to accept the hand of friendship proffered to them seemed to Romans so extraordinary that it could be explained only by the promptings of a mysterious and vicious religion. Both the Temple with all its cult and the rulers of the city were therefore swept into oblivion. Jerusalem was so thoroughly destroyed that those who had visited it could not believe it had ever been inhabited (*B.J.* 7.3).

But this solution for the government of Judaea was no more satisfactory than Augustus' had been. Titus won the lasting enmity of the Jews against Rome by destroying the Temple, for all Jews, including

Josephus (cf. *c.Ap.* 2.193–8), still assumed that the sacrificial cult was an essential element in worship: priests were still entitled to receive their due tithes (*m.Shek.* 8.8), presumably in the vain expectation that they might once again preside over sacrifices. Nor did the hostility felt by the Judaean peasants lessen as the years went by.

The emperors seem to have calculated that such hostility could simply be ignored. Titus and Vespasian knew that, without a Jewish ruling class bribed by Rome like that before A.D. 66 to suppress open manifestations of the disappointment and hatred felt by the ordinary people, violent antagonism would often break out in the countryside, but since Jews no longer controlled any urban centre in the empire larger than the small towns of Tiberias and Sepphoris in Galilee, the emperors evidently reckoned that the enmity of those peasants, impoverished by the war and the loss of their great market in Jerusalem, would prove easy for Roman legionaries to control.

For sixty years this calculation proved correct for, despite social, economic and religious turmoil, Judaea probably remained at peace even through the upheaval of a Jewish revolt in the diaspora from A.D. 115 to A.D. 117; at any rate if there were disturbances at this time they were tardy and short-lived.[32] In A.D. 132, however, an administrative initiative by the emperor Hadrian – probably a ban on circumcision intended as a measure against what the Romans viewed as barbaric mutilation, whether it was practised by Jews or by others[33] – sparked off a further revolt in Judaea.[34]

A vicious war lasting over three years was led by a certain Bar Kosiba, better known from the rabbinic texts as Bar Kochba. Nothing of value can be gleaned from surviving sources about his origins and only this about his character, that he was a fierce and disciplined military leader.[35] But the documents found in the Judaean desert in the 1960s reveal a striking fact about his sup-

[32] Any reconstruction of the history of Judaea after A.D. 70 is necessarily tentative. No further narrative survives from Josephus, and the rabbinic sources of the second century A.D. are more concerned with religious than with economic, social or political affairs. For a brief sketch, see Schürer, *History*, pp. 514–57, cf. 529–34 on the revolt under Trajan. See also Alon, *The Jews in their Land*.

[33] Schürer, *History* I, pp. 537–40. The causes of the Bar Kochba war are as hotly debated as those of the first revolt, but with less evidence and little consensus. See the summary of the state of modern scholarship by B. Isaac and A. Oppenheimer, 'The revolt of Bar Kokhba: ideology and modern scholarship', *JJS* 36 (1985) 44–9.

[34] The geographical extent of the revolt is debated, cf. Isaac and Oppenheimer, 'The revolt of Bar Kochba', pp. 53–5. But no one denies that the rebellion's centre lay in the hills of Judaea.

[35] See P. Schäfer, *Der Bar Kokhba-Aufstand: Studien zum zweiten jüdischen Krieg gegen Rom* (Tübingen, 1981), pp. 51–77.

porters. Some of those who fought with the revolutionaries to the bitter end were rich.[36] Their pathetic bundles of documents, and in some cases their bones found where they died in the desert solitude, attest the ferocity and dedication of their fight. Before A.D. 66 such Jews would have seen a natural escape for themselves in surrender to the Romans and a promise to uphold Roman rule among their compatriots in the future, but after A.D. 70 Titus had made it clear that Rome would no longer trust wealthy Jews who made such avowals of loyalty.

Rich Jews, like their poorer brothers, thus had no option in A.D. 132 but to fight to the end. Even without the help of a stronghold such as Jerusalem had been in the earlier conflict, the rebels contrived to occupy the best efforts of huge numbers of Roman troops for three and a half years. Pockets of resistance had to be destroyed one by one. At the end the whole of Judaea was practically a desert and Roman losses were so great that Hadrian, in his letter to the senate about the campaign, left out the usual opening formula that he and the army were well (Cassius Dio 69.14.3). The Jews of Judaea without the control of a native ruling class had proved even more difficult to suppress than they had when the ruling class had turned against Rome.

Hadrian's solution to the intractable problem was awesomely simple and in its crude efficiency unique in the Roman treatment of revolts. The rebellious nation was deported from its homeland. No Jew was ever again to enter the territory of Jerusalem, on pain of death (Justin Martyr, *I Apol.* 47.6). In their treatment of Judaea the Romans had made a desert and called it peace (Tac. *Agric.* 30).

---

[36] P. Benoit, J. T. Milik and R. de Vaux, *Les Grottes de Murabba'at* (*Discoveries in the Judaean Desert* II) (Oxford, 1960); for a description of the unpublished archive of Babatha, see N. Avigad *et al.* 'The expedition to the Judaean desert, 1961', *IEJ* 12 (1962) 235–62.

Abel, F. M. *Géographie de la Palestine*, 3rd edn, Paris, 1967

Alon, G. *Jews, Judaism and the Classical World*, E. T., Jerusalem, 1977

—*The Jews in their Land in the Talmudic Age (70–640 C.E.)*, 2 vols., Jerusalem, 1980–4

Applebaum, S. 'The Zealots: the case for revaluation', *JRS* 61 (1971) 156–70

—'The struggle for the soil and the revolt of 66–73 C.E.', *EI* 12 (1975) 125–8 (Heb.)

Avigad, N. *Discovering Jerusalem*, Oxford, 1984

Avigad, N. *et al.* 'The expedition to the Judaean desert, 1961', *IEJ* 12 (1962) 167–262

Bar-Adon, P. 'Another settlement of the Judaean desert sect at 'En el-Ghuweir on the shores of the Dead Sea', *BASOR* 277 (1977) 1–25

Baer, Y. 'Jerusalem in the times of the Great Revolt', *Zion* 36 (1971) 127–90; 37 (1972) 120 (Heb.)

Bar-Kochva, B. 'Seron and Cestius at Beith Horon', *PEQ* 108 (1976) 13–21

Barnett, P. W. 'Under Tiberius all was quiet', *NTS* 21 (1975) 564–71

Benoit, P., Milik, J. T. and de Vaux, R. *Les Grottes de Murabba'at (Discoveries in the Judaean Desert* II), Oxford, 1960

Ben-Shalom, I. 'The Shammai school and its place in the political and social history of Eretz Israel in the first century A.D.', Ph.D. thesis, Tel Aviv, 1980 (Heb.)

Bilde, P. 'The causes of the Jewish War according to Josephus', *JSJ* 10 (1979) 179–202

Blenkinsopp, J. 'Prophecy and priesthood in Josephus', *JJS* 25 (1974) 239–62

Brandon, S. G. F. *Jesus and the Zealots*, Manchester, 1967

Broshi, M. 'The credibility of Josephus', *JJS* 33 (1982) 379–84

Brunt, P. A. 'Charges of provincial maladministration under the early principate', *Historia* 10 (1961) 189–227

—'Did imperial Rome disarm her subjects?', *Phoenix* 29 (1975) 260–70

—'The romanization of the local ruling classes in the Roman empire', in D. M. Pippidi, ed., *Assimilation et résistance à la culture gréco-romaine dans le monde ancien (Congrès, Madrid 1974)* (Paris and Bucharest, 1976), pp. 161–73

—'Josephus on social conflicts in Roman Judaea', *Klio* 59 (1977) 149–53

Chadwick, N. K. *The Druids*, Cardiff, 1966

Cohen, S. J. D. *Josephus in Galilee and Rome; his Vita and development as a historian*, Leiden, 1979

Davies, P. S. 'The meaning of Philo's text about the gilded shields', *JTS* n.s. 37 (1986) 109–14

De Lange, N. R. M. 'Jewish attitudes to the Roman Empire', in P. D. A. Garnsey and C. R. Whittaker, eds., *Imperialism in the Ancient World* (Cambridge, 1978), pp. 255–81

De Ste Croix, G. E. M. *The Class Struggle in the Ancient Greek World*, London, 1981

De Vaux, R. *Archaeology and the Dead Sea Scrolls*, London, 1973

Douglas, M. *Natural Symbols: explorations in cosmology*, London, 1970

Drinkwater, J. F. 'The rise and fall of the Gallic Iulii', *Latomus* 37 (1978) 817–50

Dupont-Sommer, A. 'Exorcismes et guérisons dans les récits de Qoumrân', *Vetus Testamentum Supplement* 7 (1960) 246–61

Dyson, S. L. 'Native revolts in the Roman empire', *Historia* 20 (1971) 239–74

—'Native revolt patterns in the Roman Empire', *ANRW* II. 3 (1975) 138–75

Eddy, S. K. *The King is Dead: studies in the Near Eastern resistance to Hellenism*, Lincoln, Neb., 1961

Farmer, W. R. *Maccabees, Zealots and Josephus, an inquiry into Jewish nationalism in the Greco-Roman period*, New York, 1956

Feldman, E. 'The rabbinic lament', *JQR* 63 (1972) 51–75

Fornaro, P. *Flavio Giuseppe, Tacito et l'Impero*, Turin, 1980

Freyne, S. *Galilee from Alexander the Great to Hadrian, 323 B.C.E. to 135 C.E*, Notre Dame, 1980

Fuks, G. 'Again on the episode of the gilded Roman shields at Jerusalem', *HTR* 75 (1982) 503–7

Gichon, M. 'Idumea and the Herodian limes', *IEJ* 17 (1967) 27–45

—'Cestius Gallus' campaign in Judaea', *PEQ* 113 (1981) 39–62

Goodman, M. D. 'The First Jewish Revolt: social conflict and the problem of debt', *JJS* 33 (1982) 417–27

—*State and Society in Roman Galilee, A.D. 132–212*, Totowa, 1983

—'A bad joke in Josephus', *JJS* 36 (1985) 195–9

Hachlili, R. 'Names and nicknames of Jews in Second Temple times', *EI* 17 (1984) 188–211 (Heb.)

Hachlili, R. and Killebrew, A. 'Jewish funerary customs during the Second Temple period, in the light of the excavations at the Jericho necropolis', *PEQ* 115 (1983) 109–39

Hengel, M. *Judaism and Hellenism: studies in their encounter in Palestine during the early Hellenistic period*, 2 vols., E. T., London, 1974

—*Property and Riches in the Early Church*, E.T., London, 1974
—*Die Zeloten*, 2nd edn, Leiden, 1976
Holladay, A. J. and Goodman, M. D. 'Religious scruples in ancient warfare', *CQ* 36 (1986) 151–71
Horsley, R. A. 'Josephus and the bandits', *JSJ* 10 (1979) 37–63
—'The sicarii: ancient Jewish "terrorists"', *The Journal of Religion* 52 (1979) 435–58
—'Ancient Jewish banditry and the revolt against Rome, A.D. 66–70', *CBQ* 43 (1981) 409–32
—'Menahem in Jerusalem: a brief messianic episode among the sicarii – not "Zealot Messianism"', *Novum Testamentum* 27 (1985) 334–48
—'The Zealots: their origin, relationships and importance in the Jewish Revolt', *Novum Testamentum* 28 (1986) 159–92
—'High priests and the politics of Roman Palestine. A contextual analysis of the evidence in Josephus', *JSJ* 17 (1986) 23–55
—'Popular prophetic movements at the time of Jesus', *Journal for the Study of the New Testament* 26 (1986) 3–27
Isaac, B. 'Judaea after A.D. 70', *JJS* 35 (1984) 44–50
—'Bandits in Judaea and Arabia', *HSCP* 88 (1984) 171–203
Jeremias, J. *Jerusalem in the Time of Jesus*, E.T. London, 1969
Juster, J. *Les Juifs dans l'empire romain*, 2 vols., Paris, 1914
Kadman, L. *The Coins of the Jewish War of 66–73 C.E.*, Tel Aviv, 1960
Kasher, A., ed. *The Great Jewish Revolt: factors and circumstances leading to its outbreak*, Jerusalem, 1983 (Heb.)
Kingdon, H. P. 'The origins of the Zealots', *NTS* 19 (1972–3) 74–81
Klausner, J. *The Messianic Idea in Israel*, E.T., London, 1956
Kloner, A. 'Underground hiding complexes from the Bar Kochba war in the Judaean Shephelah', *Biblical Archaeologist* 46.4 (December 1983) 210–21
Kochavi, M., ed. *Judaea, Samaria and the Golan: archaeological survey 1967–1968*, Jerusalem, 1972 (Heb.)
Kraabel, A. T. 'The Roman diaspora: six questionable assumptions', *JJS* 33 (1982) 445–64
Kraft, R. A. 'The multiform Jewish heritage of early Christianity', in J. Neusner, ed., *Christianity, Judaism and Other Greco-Roman Cults*, Leiden, 1975, part 3, pp. 174–99
Kreissig, H. 'Die landwirtschaftliche Situation in Palästina vor dem Judäischen Krieg', *Acta Antiqua* 17 (1969) 223–54
—*Die sozialen Zusammenhänge des judäischen Krieges: Klassen und Klassenkampf im Palästina des I. Jahrhunderts v.u. Z*, Berlin, 1970
McEleney, N.J. 'Orthodoxy in Judaism of the first Christian century', *JSJ* 9 (1978) 83–8
MacMullen, R. *Roman Social Relations 50 B.C. to A.D. 284*, New Haven, 1974
Mendelsohn, I. *Slavery in the Ancient Near East*, New York, 1949
Meshorer, Y. *Ancient Jewish Coinage*, 2 vols., New York, 1982
Michel, O. 'Studien zu Josephus: Simon bar Giora', *NTS* 14 (1968) 402–8

Millar, F. G. B. *The Emperor in the Roman World (31 B.C.–A.D. 337)*, London, 1977
—'The background to the Maccabean revolution', *JJS* 29 (1978) 1–21
Momigliano, A. D. *Ricerche sull'organizzazione della Giudea sotto il dominio romano, 63a.C.–70d.C.*, Bologna, 1934
—*Alien Wisdom: the limits of hellenization*, Cambridge, 1975
Nash, D. 'Reconstructing Poseidonios' Celtic ethnography: some considerations', *Britannia* 7 (1976) 111–26
Netzer, E. *'Miqvaot* (ritual baths) of the Second Temple period at Jericho', *Qadmoniot* 11(1978) 54–9 (Heb.)
Neusner, J. *The Rabbinic Traditions about the Pharisees before 70*, 3 parts, Leiden, 1971
Nickelsburg, G. W. E. *Resurrection, Immortality and Eternal Life in Intertestamental Judaism*, Cambridge, Mass., 1972
Oppenheimer, A. *The 'Am Ha-aretz: a study in the social history of the Jewish people in the Hellenistic-Roman period*, Leiden, 1977
Rahmani, L. Y. 'Ancient Jerusalem's funerary customs and the tombs: part three', *Biblical Archaeologist* 45.1 (Winter 1982) 43–53
—'Some remarks on R. Hachlili's and A. Killebrew's "Jewish funerary customs"', *PEQ* 118 (1986) 96–100
Rajak, T. *Josephus: the historian and his society*, London, 1983
Rappaport, U. 'The relations between Jews and non-Jews and the Great War against Rome', *Tarbiz* 47 (1978) 1–14 (Heb.)
—'Jewish–pagan relations and the revolt against Rome in 66–70 C.E.', *The Jerusalem Cathedra* 1 (1981) 81–95
—'John of Gischala: from Galilee to Jerusalem', *JJS* 33 (1982) 479–93
Rhoads, D. M. *Israel in Revolution: 6–74 C.E.: a political history based on the writings of Josephus*, Philadelphia, 1976
Roth, C. 'The historical implications of the Jewish coinage of the First Revolt', *IEJ* 12 (1962) 33–46
—'The constitution of the Jewish republic of 66–70', *JSS* 9 (1964) 304–19
Safrai, S. and Stern, M., eds. *The Jewish People in the First Century (Compendia Rerum Iudaicarum ad Novum Testamentum*, Sect. 1), 2 vols., Assen, 1974–6
Sanders, E. P. *Jesus and Judaism*, London, 1985
Schalit, A. *Namenwörterbuch zu Flavius Josephus*, Leiden, 1968
—*König Herodes: Der Mann und sein Werk*, Berlin, 1969
Schürer, E. *The History of the Jewish People in the Age of Jesus Christ*, rev. G. Vermes, F. Millar, M. Black and M. Goodman, 3 vols., Edinburgh, 1973–87
Schwartz, D. R. 'Josephus and Nicolaus on the Pharisees', *JSJ* 14 (1983) 157–71
—'Ishmael ben Phiabi and the chronology of Provincia Judaea', *Tarbiz* 52 (1983) 177–200 (Heb.)
Segal, A. F. *Two Powers in Heaven*, Leiden, 1977

Sherwin-White, A. N. *Roman Society and Roman Law in the New Testament*, Oxford, 1963

Smallwood, E. M. 'High priests and politics in Roman Palestine', *JTS* n.s. 13 (1962) 14–34

—*The Jews under Roman Rule*, Leiden, 1976

Smith, M. 'Zealots and sicarii: their origins and relations', *HTR* 64 (1971) 1–19

Speidel, M. P. 'The Roman army in Judaea under the procurators', *Ancient Society* 13/14 (1982/3) 233–40

Stern, M. 'Herod's policy and Jewish society at the end of the Second Temple period', *Tarbiz* 35 (1966) 235–53 (Heb.)

—'The status of Provincia Judaea and its governors in the Roman Empire under the Julio-Claudian dynasty', *EI* 10 (1971) 274–82 (Heb.)

—*Greek and Latin Authors on Jews and Judaism*, 3 vols., Jerusalem, 1974–84

—'Aspects of Jewish society: the priesthood and other classes', in S. Safrai and M. Stern, eds., *The Jewish People in the First Century*, 2 vols. (Assen, 1974–6), II, pp. 561–630

—'Sicarii and Zealots', in M. Avi-Yonah and Z. Baras, eds., *Society and Religion in the Second Temple Period* (The World History of the Jewish People I. 8) (London, 1977), pp. 263–301

—'The expulsion of Jews from Rome in antiquity', in *Yitzhak F. Baer Memorial Volume* (*Zion* 44) (Jerusalem, 1980), pp. 1–27 (Heb.)

—'Social and political realignments in Herodian Judaea', *The Jerusalem Cathedra* 2 (1982) 40–62

—'The suicide of Eleazar ben Jair and his men at Masada, and the "Fourth Philosophy"', *Zion* 47 (1982) 367–98 (Heb.)

Stone, M. E. *Scriptures, Sects and Visions: a profile of Judaism from Ezra to the Jewish revolt*, Oxford, 1982

Theissen, G. *The First Followers of Jesus: a sociological analysis of the earliest Christianity*, E.T., London, 1978

Vermes, G. *Jesus the Jew*, London, 1973

Veyne, P. *Le pain et le cirque: sociologie historique d'un pluralisme politique*, Paris, 1976

Vidal-Naquet, P. 'Du bon usage de la trahison', in Josephus, *De Bello Judaico*, translated by P. Savinel, Paris, 1977

Wardman, A. *Religion and Statecraft among the Romans*, London, 1982

Wilkinson, J. 'Ancient Jerusalem: its water supply and population', *PEQ* 106 (1974) 33–51

Winter, P. *On the Trial of Jesus*, revised by T. A. Burkill and G. Vermes, 2nd edn, Berlin and New York, 1974

Yadin, Y., ed. *Jerusalem Revealed: archaeology in the holy city 1968–1974*, Jerusalem, 1975

Zertal, A. 'The Roman siege system at Khirbet el-Hammam (Narbata) in Samaria', *Qadmoniot* 14 (1981) 112–18 (Heb.)

INDEX

abortion, 61
Acrabatene, 163, 164, 202, 204–5, 224
Adiabene, royal family of, 54, 127, 162, 168, 194, 203
agricultural production, 51–2, 56, 62
Agrippa I: appointed as king, 2, 15; clients of, 43 n. 24, 44, 140; popularity of, 122, 212
Agrippa II: after A.D. 70, 232; army of, 47, 146, 159–60, 161; attempts to overlook Temple, 142–3; control of Temple by, 112, 149; friendly with Titus, 239; in A.D. 66, 18, 147, 152, 155, 163, 172, 217; popularity of, 123
Albinus: accepts bribes, 149, 213; later career of, 14
Alexander Jannaeus, 31, 121, 122
Alexandra Jannaea, 31
Alexandria in Egypt: High Priests from, 41, 60; Jewish community in, 18, 98 n. 22, 237
Alexas, friend of Herod, 42, 43 n. 24, 141
allegorists, 102 n. 26
Ananias b. Nedebaeus: bribery by, 127 n. 22, 149; high priesthood of, 142 n. 5; intrigues of, before A.D. 66, 145–7; opposes son, 154–5, 158–60, 217; power of, 150; ransoms son's secretary, 210, 215; refuses to punish jokers, 171; sent to Rome in chains, 49; violence used by, 139, 213
Ananias b. Sadok, 158, 164, 184–5, 189 n. 10
Ananus b. Ananias, 49, 146
Ananus b. Ananus: described by Josephus, 156; faction dissolves, 183–5; faction leader, 163–7, 217; family origins, 143, 168; opposes Simon b. Gioras, 205–6; political intrigues before A.D. 66, 144–7, 151, 212; power destroyed in A.D. 68, 176, 186–90, 220, 221, 222; Sadducee, 209
Ananus b. Bagadatus, 194

Ananus b. Jonathan, 147, 155, 163, 168, 221
Ananus b. Sethi, 44, 141, 143, 144, 211
ancestry, importance of, 117–23
angels, belief in, 78
Antigonus, 112 n. 2; supporters of, 38, 114
Antiochus IV Epiphanes, attacks Temple, 11, 30
Antipas, son of Herod, 40, 78 n. 5, 131
Antipas, *floruit c.* A.D. 60, 147, 149, 162, 186, 223
Antipater, 32, 38 n. 14, 48
antisemitism, 8, 236–9; not universal in Rome, 15, 236
Antonia, fortress, *see* garrison massacred
aqueducts, 54, 149
archaeological evidence, use of, 24, 55
Archelaus, 139, 140; appointed ethnarch, 1, 42, 131; deposed, 1, 33, 38–9, 59, 109; problems in 4 B.C., 131, 139–40, *see also* Herod, uprisings at death of
Aristobulus III, 41, 110, 121
asceticism, 79–80, 130
assembly, 110–11, 112, 158, 217–18
Athronges, 92
attitudes to the body: Greek, 100–1; Jewish, 99–106
authority, attitudes to, 77–8, 81

Babatha, 68
Babylonian Jews, 41, 42 n. 21, 48, 60, 121
banditry: endemic after A.D. 50, 2, 60; not dangerous to Rome, 173, 215, 233; origin of, 60–1, 63
bandits: factions described as, 138, 163, 202, 203, 205; fight for factions, 224–7; not instigators of revolt, 168–9; rebels described as, 20, 51, 69; relations of with population, 63–4
Bannus, 78 n. 5, 79
Barabbas, 63, 172
Bar Kochba, 41, 203, 250–1
Baruch, Second book of, 85 n. 9

257

Index

Index

James, brother of Jesus, 145
James b. Sosas, 189, 190–1, 192–3, 223
Jamnia, 59, 200 n. 2, 232, 234
Jerusalem: economic role of, 51; *polis* status of, 46
Jesus: attitude of, to poverty, 130; career ignored by Tacitus, 172–3; charismatic, 78; Josephus on, 145 n. 8; problems in reconstructing life of, 22–3; trial of, 113, 115
Jesus, brigand, 63, 224–5
Jesus b. Ananias, 90, 174
Jesus b. Damnaeus, 139, 144, 145, 146, 165, 213
Jesus b. Gamalas, 139, 144, 165, 185, 186, 188, 189, 213; friendly with Josephus, 165, 183, 185, 210
Joazar b. Boethus, 42, 43–4, 139–40, 144
John of Caesarea, 131, 149
John of Gischala: aims of, 208, 212, 218; career of, A.D. 67–70, 186–7, 188–93, 194–7; member of ruling class, 201–2; opposed to Josephus, 183–5; treatment of by Romans, 80, 219; young, 211
John the Baptist, 78 n. 5, 79, 81 n. 7, 85, 172
John the Essene, 165
joke, at outbreak of revolt, 170–2, 211, 220, 231
Jonathan b. Ananus, 49, 143, 145, 148, 213, 214
Joseph b. Ellem, 41–2
Joseph b. Gorion, 164 n. 11, 217
Joseph Cabi b. Simon, 143, 165 n. 15
Josephus: ancestry, 38; brother, 200, 231; career, 6, 148 (after A.D. 70) 60, (in Galilee) 21, 156, 176, 183–5, 221, 224–5, (political allies in) 165, 210, (in religious sphere) 74, 79, 82, 130, (at start of revolt) 159, (with Titus' forces) 193, 232, 233; father, 165, 190, 210; mother, 211; writings, usefulness as evidence: (*A.J.* differs from *B.J.*) 139 n. 3, 145 n. 8, (biased by apologetic for own career) 21, 156, 167, 198–9, 201 n. 3, (on causes of war) 5–7, 24–5, (on events A.D. 6–50) 43 n. 23, 140, (on Fourth Philosophy) 94 (on Jesus and James) 145 n. 8, (on Pharisees) 74, (trustworthiness of narrative of events) 20–1, (use of reverse polemic) 218
Jotapata, 182, 198
Jubilee, 126
Judaism after A.D. 70, 4, 231, 234–5
Judas b. Chelcias, 195, 219

Judas b. Jonathan, 158, 164, 184–5
Judas the Galilean, 43, 93–6; Menahem b. Judas related to, 169; sons executed, 173
Julius Archelaus, 141, 143

kidnap as weapon in faction struggle, 192, 215, 221
kosher food, 97, 101, 102, 106, 238

lambs for Temple sacrifice, 179
Leontopolis temple, 238
levites, 5, 123
life after death, 87–9
loans, 56–8, 62
local rulers in other provinces: role, 33–6; selection, 35
Lydda, 157, 234

Maccabees, 9, 11, 12, 30, 177
Mannaeus b. Lazarus, 194
Mariamme, 33, 122
marriage alliances, 210–11
matrilineal descent, 117
Matthias b. Boethus, 192, 194, 210
medicine: Greek, 101; Jewish, 105–6
Menahem b. Judas: ambitions of, 169; leads sicarii, 147, 153; sophist, 93; violence used by, 159–60
mercenaries: bandits act as, in faction struggle, 224–7; gentiles, in Hasmonaean armies, 38; Jews, in hellenistic armies, 47
merkabah mysticism, 86
messianic beliefs: political effects of, 90–1, 92–3, 121, 174, 217; prevalence of, 11–12, 89–90
military service, Jewish attitude to, 47–8, 160, 162, 222, 226
mob power, 154, 215, 220, 226
monarchy, Jewish attitude to, 111, 120–3; Davidic, 90, 120–1, 174; Hasmonaean, 121–2; Herodian, 122–3, 147
motivation of faction leaders, 138, 207–8
mourning customs, 87
mysticism, 85–6

Narbata, 157
nationalism in Judaism, 11–12, 16, 17 n. 30
Nero: apparent weakness of, 11, 177; favours gentiles in Caesarea, 14
Niger the Peraean, 160–1, 162, 165, 166, 190

old age, attitudes to, 73, 123
olive oil, 103, 202

Index

Index

Zacchaeus, 131, 132 n. 26

Zealots: aims of, 206, 219–20; elect High Priest, 179; Fourth Philosophy and, 95 n. 19, 96; Josephus abuses, 199, 201; leaders belong to ruling class, 201; role in faction struggle, 176, 185–97; supporters of, 223, 225–6